STATE, NATION, RELIGION

Politics and the Public Sphere in Modern India

Edited by

Ishita Banerjee-Dube
Avishek Ray

Orient BlackSwan

STATE, NATION, RELIGION: POLITICS AND THE PUBLIC SPHERE IN MODERN INDIA

ORIENT BLACKSWAN PRIVATE LIMITED

Registered Office
3-6-752 Himayatnagar, Hyderabad 500 029, Telangana, India
Email: centraloffice@orientblackswan.com

Other Offices
Bengaluru, Chennai, Guwahati, Hyderabad, Kolkata,
Mumbai, New Delhi, Noida, Patna

First published by Orient Blackswan Private Limited 2026

ISBN 978 93 5442 592 9

Typeset in Minion Pro BT 11/13 *by*
K. Divya, Hyderabad 500 060

042536

Printed at
Ashwin Printing Agency

Published by
Orient Blackswan Private Limited
3-6-752 Himayatnagar,
Hyderabad 500 029, Telangana, India
Email: info@orientblackswan.com

Contents

Acknowledgements

This is a revised and enlarged edition of *Nation, Nationalism, and the Public Sphere: Religious Politics in India* published by SAGE in 2020. Working on this volume has been an enriching and pleasurable experience. We have learnt a lot from the detailed and insightful analyses on a variety of themes provided in the chapters, the new contributions in particular, that comment on some critical themes related to questions of citizenship, democracy, law and religion in the India of today. We also appreciate the effort made by earlier contributors to rework and update their chapters. Our thanks extend to all the contributors for making this teamwork possible, pleasurable, and worthwhile. We express our gratitude to SAGE for returning the copyright of the earlier edition, enabling the publication of this revised volume.

Our gratitude also extends to the Orient Blackswan editorial and production team for their competent and professional support through this project. We thank Sreenath Sreedharan of Orient Blackswan, and Aditi Jha in particular, for guiding us through.

This book has immensely benefited from the invaluable technical and research support rendered by Luis Gamaliel Quiñones Martínez, Agnidh Baruah and Diyali Bhattacharya; and the incisive feedback and suggestions from Saurabh Dube, Suhash Bhattacharjee and Neha Gupta.

We also thank the anonymous reviewers whose well-considered reports have substantially enhanced the quality of this volume.

Ishita Banerjee-Dube
Avishek Ray

Notes on Contributors

Maribel Elliet Alvarado Becerril, from Mexico City, has a Bachelor's Degree in International Relations from Universidad Nacional Autónoma de México. She also has a Master's in Asian and African Studies with a specialisation in South Asia from El Colegio de México. Her Master's Thesis, 'Media and Nationalism in India: NDTV, Times Now, and Republic TV', is a study about how television has been an active element in the material and symbolic reproduction of 'nation', 'nationalism' and 'patriotism'. Her thesis also explores how these concepts have been recurrent topics in debates broadcasted by news channels. She did an internship at the Mexican Embassy in India under the supervision of Ambassador Melba Pría Olavarrieta. She was affiliated as a research worker in Centre for Historical Studies/School of Social Sciences of Jawaharlal Nehru University guided by Sucheta Mahajan. She is currently working as a public servant at the Secretaría de Bienestar.

Ishita Banerjee-Dube is Professor-Researcher (Distinguished category) at the Centre for Asian and African Studies, El Colegio de México, Mexico City and a member of the National System of Researchers, CONAHCYT-Mexico at the highest level. A historian by training, her research combines ethnographic history, and postcolonial, gender and subaltern studies to address themes of empire, nation, gender, citizenship in India and Mexico, religion, law and power, caste and politics, food and emotion, time and temporality, and democracy and social justice in India over the nineteenth to the twenty-first centuries. Banerjee-Dube has authored six books including *A History of Modern India* (2015), *Religion, Law, and Power* (2007), and *Divine Affairs* (2001); edited and co-edited over a dozen volumes and has published articles in a wide range of acclaimed English and Spanish journals.

Anuradha Bhasin is Managing Editor, *Kashmir Times*, one of the oldest English news outlets in Jammu and Kashmir, India. A journalist since 1989, she was among the first journalists to have done an in-depth investigation into the impact of landmines on the lives of the people living on the borders and the psychological impact of the Kashmir conflict. She is the author of *A Dismantled State: The Untold Story of Kashmir after Article 370* (2022), and has contributed to several anthologies and monographs, besides Indian and international publications. Under her leadership, the newspaper has continued to maintain an independent voice despite many threats and intimidations from state and non-state actors amidst an ongoing violent conflict. When the government of India blocked internet and phone service in the region in 2019, Bhasin launched a court challenge while leading her newsroom to find ways to keep publishing despite the blackout. She has been a Commonwealth Fellow 2016, John S. Knight Fellow 2023 and a Senior JSK Journalism Fellow at Stanford 2024.

Manjima Chatterjee is a drama explorer, teacher, and arts advocate. Her training is in sociology and arts in education and her primary explorations seek to understand how art may influence human interactions in the digital era. She is on the Editorial Board of *Arts Praxis*, the Arts in Education journal of NYU Steinhardt, and has contributed to newspapers such as *The Hindu, The Hindu Business Line, Education World, Mint* and *Hindustan Times.* She was shortlisted for the BBC's International Radio Playwriting Competition and she won *The Hindu Metro Plus* Playwright Award in 2013. Her book, *Two Plays on Hunger*, was published in 2018, and her play, *Mountain of Bones*, was published as a part of *Creating a Profession: Disparate Voices of Indian Women Playwrights*, edited by Shirley Huston-Findley. Other plays have also been performed and published in anthologies in India and abroad.

Swati Dyahadroy is Assistant Professor in the Department of Women and Gender Studies at Savitribai Phule Pune University. Her research interests include gender, nation and nationalism, gender and development, women's studies in India, and inequalities in higher education. She focuses on developing women's studies as a critical field of inquiry, emphasising caste, gender, and community politics. She has been involved in curriculum building and setting up institutional practices at the department and in a wider dialogue with the different worlds of Women's Studies for more than two decades.

Sayori Ghoshal is a postdoctoral fellow at Moturi Satyanarayana Centre for Advanced Study in the Humanities and Social Sciences, Krea University, India. Prior to this, she was a postdoctoral fellow at the Institute for the History & Philosophy of Science & Technology (IHPST), University of Toronto. She completed her PhD from Columbia University, New York and is currently working on her first monograph, *A Sense for Statistics: Constructing Religious Minority in Modern India*, which focuses on the historical development of statistical sciences, including race science, demography, and applied statistics, and their impact on community identity formation, in colonial and postcolonial India. Her articles have been published and are forthcoming in *Isis*, *History Compass*, *British Journal for the History of Science Themes*, and the *Economic and Political Weekly*.

Anne Hartig is the chief curator of the South and Southeast Asia department at the Museum Fünf Kontinente in Munich. Her research focuses on the relationship between visual culture, religion, and politics. As a lecturer, she taught at the Institute for Asian and Islamic Art History (AIK) at the University of Bonn and at the Center for Religious Studies (CERES) at the Ruhr University Bochum.

Mark Juergensmeyer is Distinguished Professor Emeritus in Sociology and Global Studies, and Founding Director of the Orfalea Center for Global and International Studies at the University of California, Santa Barbara. He has also taught at UC-Berkeley and Punjab University, Chandigarh. He is author or editor of over thirty books including *Global Rebellion: Religious Nationalism Confronts the Secular State* (2008).

Himani Kapoor is Assistant Professor at the Department of English and Cultural Studies at Christ University, Delhi NCR. She holds a PhD from the Department of English, University of Delhi. Her PhD research focuses on anglophone gurus in India in the context of consumer-culture, modernity and the desire for happiness and wellbeing. She has published in the areas of translation studies, religion, and disability studies.

Esha Meher is a lawyer with a Constitutional law practice before the High Courts of Calcutta and Delhi and the Supreme Court of India. She is currently a doctoral candidate at Yale University.

Sanghamitra Misra is Professor of Modern Indian History at the University of Delhi. She researches the intersecting dimensions of economic and legal history in the context of conquest, colonisation, 'primitivism' and resistance. She has been a Commonwealth Scholar and a British Academy-AHRC-ESRC Visiting Fellow at the SOAS, London, and a Fellow at the Nehru Memorial Museum and Library, New Delhi. Her work has been published in academic journals including the *Indian Economic and Social History Review*, *Studies in History*, the *Economic and Political Weekly* and the *Modern Asian Studies* and in anthologies. She is the author of *Becoming a Borderland: The Politics of Space and Identity in Colonial Northeastern India* (2011) and *The Long Conquest: Territorialisation, Rebellion and the 'Tribe' in Eastern India, circa 1760 to 1900* (2024).

Sreya Mitra is Associate Professor at the Department of Media Communication, American University of Sharjah, UAE. Her research focuses on popular Hindi cinema, television and new media discourses, stardom and celebrity culture, fandom studies, gender, globalisation, and culture industries. She has presented her research at various international conferences and her work has been published in the edited collections *Reorienting Global Communication* (2010) and *Transnational Stardom* (2013); and in the peer-reviewed journals, *South Asian History and Culture* (2012), *Celebrity Studies* (2018, 2020, 2021), *South Asian Popular*

Culture (2020), *Transformative Works and Cultures* (2020) and *Middle East Journal of Culture and Communication* (2021).

Shobna Nijhawan, Associate Professor at York University (Toronto), is a scholar of South Asian Studies as well as Gender, Feminist and Women's Studies with focus on Hindi literature of the early twentieth century. She is the author of *Hindi Publishing in Colonial Lucknow. Gender, Genre and Visuality in the Creation of a Literary 'Canon'* (2018), *Women and Girls in the Hindi Public Sphere. Periodical Literature in Colonial North India* (2012), co-editor of *Literary Sentiments in the Vernacular. Gender and Genre in Modern South Asia* (2022) and editor of *Nationalism in the Vernacular: Hindi, Urdu and the Literature of Indian Freedom* (2010). Apart from her Area Studies research, she has published on South Asian Studies classroom and digital pedagogies including heritage language and second-language acquisition, pedagogies for less-commonly taught languages, decolonising pedagogies and pedagogies of care.

Avishek Ray teaches at the National Institute of Technology Silchar. He is the author of *The Vagabond in the South Asian Imagination: Representation, Agency & Resilience* (2021) and co-author of *Digital Expressions of the Self(ie): The Social Life of Selfies in India* (2024). His research appears in reputed journals like *South Asia: Journal of South Asian Studies, Contemporary South Asia, Inter-Asia Cultural Studies, Continuum: Journal of Media & Cultural Studies, Tourism, Culture & Communication*; and he has held research fellowships at the University of Edinburgh, Purdue University Library, Centre for Advanced Study Sofia, Mahidol University, IFK International Research Center for Cultural Studies (Vienna), Pavia University and University of Minnesota, among others. In 2021, his academic excellence was recognised with the Fulbright-Nehru Academic and Professional Excellence Fellowship.

Roluahpuia is Assistant Professor, Sociology at the Department of Humanities and Social Sciences, Indian Institute of Technology Roorkee (IITR). He was the former Raghunathan Family Fellow

(2018–19) at the Lakshmi Mittal and Family South Asia Institute, Harvard University and also a former fellow at the Centre for the Study of Developing Societies (CSDS), New Delhi. He works on issues concerning ethnic and nationalism studies, indigenous and borderland studies. His recent monograph titled *Nationalism in the Vernacular: States, Tribes, and the Politics of Peace in Northeast India* was published in 2023.

Ridhima Sharma is a PhD candidate at the Department for the Study of Religion, University of Toronto. Her dissertation is an anthropological study of the intersections of Hindu nationalism with claims of work, service, and entrepreneurship. Her research is supported by the Wenner-Gren Doctoral Dissertation Grant, Ontario Graduate Scholarship, Connaught Scholarship, and others.

Figures and Photographs

Introduction

Nation, State, Religion, Public Sphere: Critical Considerations

Ishita Banerjee-Dube and Avishek Ray

On the eve of the 2024 general elections in India, Prime Minister Narendra Modi proclaimed in the course of an interview on News18 that he was not 'born biologically' and that God had sent him as an instrument of divine intervention. Modi was also going to meditate at the sanctified Vivekananda Rock Memorial – where the celebrated saint Swami Vivekananda is believed to have attained enlightenment – after he was done with the election campaign. Such bold proclamations capped the numerous populist metaphors Modi had been using in his speeches and interviews to connect with his audience, and this one in particular was meme-fied in the wake of the elections. By referring to himself as 'God-sent', Modi implied that his political ascent had divine validation. Such an assertion sought to cement his political narrative of several 'guarantees' and false promises with divine sanction to set the seal on his success through a combination of democratic processes and divine intervention.

Modi's declaration was a follow-up on the dramatic construction of a massive Ram Temple at the site of the destroyed Babri Masjid – the spectacular ploy of the Bharatiya Janata Party to retain and gain more support in the politically significant state of Uttar Pradesh and in other parts of northern and western India. On 22 January 2024, Narendra Modi had consecrated an unfinished Ram temple in Ayodhya constructed where the Babri Masjid was. The ceremony was boycotted by the *shankarancharyas* – the heads of the monasteries (*mathas*) of the Advaita Vedanta order of Hinduism – on grounds that the consecration of an unfinished temple violated the conventions of Vedic-Hindu orthodoxy and the Constitution. A day before the *rashtra-nayak* (hero/leader of the state-nation) was to sanctify the temple, Professor Gautam Bhadra had commented in an interview published in the Bangla daily *Ei Samay* (The Time Now) that in a situation where a state-dominated, state-centric present was busy composing the *Purana* (legend/mythic history) of today's India, it was futile to search for multiple and different pasts. This was so because *bhakti* (devotion) had come under the complete control of the *rashtra*.

The Hindi word *rashtra*, it bears mention, although used to signify the nation, has close affinity with the *rajya* (terrain/territory) of a ruler, a sovereign, and tends to give priority to the state over the nation. In the context of an all-powerful state-nation driven by the presentism and uncontrolled materialisation of intent of the *rashtra-nayak* and his acolytes to leave their impress upon history, notions of faith, devotion, nation and 'religion' have become critical and contingent. The ten years of single-party majority rule under Modi and the BJP has made visible the irrepressible march of the Hindu state-nation to make 'culture and political authority congruent' with the 'national model of space' (Duara 2010, 964). This has found reflection in the swift and significant reconfiguration of the 'religious'-cultural-political terrain of the nation. The abrogation of the special status of Jammu and Kashmir afforded by Article 370 of the Indian Constitution, the move to change the nature and scope of Indian citizenship through the National Register of Citizens and the Citizenship Amendment Act, the laying out of roads and railway tracks to connect refurbished Hindu sites of pilgrimage together with the open violence against minority communities and prejudice against Dalits and Adivasis, have served to underscore the chest-thumping Hindu-first narrative of the BJP.

The results of the 2024 general elections, however, have demonstrated that the promises of establishing the global glory of a particular kind of strident Hinduism and its invented past by a divinely ordained leader have not paid off. The inverse relation between figures of unemployment, hunger, farmer unrest and proclaimed economic growth, the contradictory consequences of dominant caste-centred politics, and the blatant authoritarianism of an unabashed vainglorious national hero that stimulated the coalition of an important Opposition, made a large section of the electorate turn against the BJP and Modi. After ten years, BJP has failed to secure single-party majority in the Lok Sabha, the lower house of the Indian Parliament, and Modi has been forced to fall back upon allies of different hues to form a coalition government to conserve his premiership for the third term. It remains to be seen whether his self-projection as divinely ordained would continue to hold sway in the political–spiritual language of the public sphere. Modi's prior success and his declarations, nonetheless, exemplify how political 'speech acts' in contemporary India blur the lines between religion and the state, and underscore the mutual imbrications of 'religion' and politics in the Indian public sphere.

At a significant juncture when a 'religion-centric' state-nation domination is being reconstituted, this volume reconsiders the varied dimensions and everyday lives of the concept-categories of nation-state, nationalism, religion and politics by means of a close attention to their quotidian grounding, articulations and apprehensions in the public sphere. Public sphere here is used both in the sense of a realm of social life where public opinion can be formed by citizens coming together in an unrestricted fashion to confer on issues of general interest and on matters related to the activity of the state (Habermas 1964, 49), as well as a public domain affected by state actions and proclamations of public morality that have serious impact on citizen politics. This volume interrogates the religious and the secular as purportedly tidy, self-evident, universal categories and probes the validity of the clear separation of the religious and the political by showing their mutating yet constant mutual imbrication.

It is perhaps redundant to affirm that 'religion', in its constructed and essentialised as well as empirical and experiential dimensions, has turned the table upside down on initial and enthusiastic expectations of the secular-modern by stubbornly refusing to disappear from the public arena (and private domain). Years ago, Peter van der Veer had made a very incisive suggestion.

Instead of getting caught in the tentacles of debates and theories of modernisation and secularisation, he had argued, it was much more important and productive to examine the crucial relationship between state, nation and religion (van der Veer 1999, 17–40) in order to unpack the implications of the hyphenated phenomenon of the modern nation-state. Such an examination reveals that religion has played a vital role in sustaining the modern nation-state form by undergirding the production of the modern subject (in Europe), a fact eloquently elaborated in Max Weber's *The Protestant Ethic and the Spirit of Capitalism* (1930). Religion, moreover, has also been crucial in the construction of the modern public that emerged in consonance with the modern subject. It was critical both in shaping 'individual conscience' and 'civilised conduct', and for grounding the public sphere in morality. Van der Veer alluded to the close connection between the emergence and spread of the nation-state and the nationalisation of Protestantism together with the inclusion of Catholicism in the national public in nineteenth-century England, of Hinduism in the renascent public sphere of colonised India, and of Islam in different parts of the world. This suggestive affirmation queried the idea of the 'modern' permeated by human reason, science and technology as essentially opposed to 'religion' by underscoring the co-constitution and mutual dependence of the nation-state and religion (conscience/morality). The use of 'modern' in this volume's subtitle alludes both to the modern nature of the nation-state, its constitutive tensions, and its interface with citizens and the modern public sphere.

Aamir Mufti viewed the conjoint processes of secular nation-building and the creation of a unified (moral) national culture in Europe as generative of 'minority' and 'marginal' religious and ethnic communities (Mufti 2007) that fitted awkwardly with the construct of a homogenous national culture. Such an idea transported to India by the British had resulted in the invention of the existence of religion as a coherent, unified category as well as the creation of the idea of Muslims as a minority. Mark Juergensmeyer's chapter extends Mufti's insights in his analysis of the variety of terms with wide connotations that signified 'different aspects of religiosity' drawn from more than one faith or one way of life in the Punjab and elsewhere in India till the 1970s. A heterogeneity that made it difficult for his 'scheduled caste' subjects of study to answer his query about their 'religion'. This lack of a sense of a unified religion is reflected in the absence of a single term for it in different Indian languages, which fits in perfectly with the absence of a singular notion of the secular or secularism. Juergensmeyer traces the foundations of 'religious politics' in India to the British colonial state's attempts to classify, identify and ascribe a particular religion to particular groups of Indians. The idea of an integrated national culture as a key element of the nation was taken over by Indian nationalist leaders to construe a coherent 'Hinduism' as the binding moral element of national culture and community. This produced a variety of 'minority communities' as a 'problem' to be dealt with. The militant, political Hinduism of today's India exemplifies a virulent manifestation of this construction in the public sphere.

If we keep the above insights in view, it becomes easier to understand the close, crisscrossing, conjoint and disparate interaction of the influential and changing categories of the nation-state and religion over time. It also explains why nationalism in India, despite India's secular constitutionalism – defined from the beginning as neutral and equal distance of the state from all religions rather than a facile separation of religion and politics – often takes recourse to the ideals of a majoritarian Hindu faith as its normative basis constructed in discrete ways at different moments.

State, Nationalism, Religion

The convoluted trajectory of the interpretation and implementation of secularism in India by the state, and its appropriation by citizens, has provoked rich academic debates as well as bitter political feuds over a proper balance between religious freedom and state intervention (Bhargava ed. 1998, for instance). This volume inserts itself in this ongoing discussion by exploring distinct facets of the long and enduring interface of the state, nationalism and 'religion' from the early twentieth century to the present. Treating nation and nationalism as 'social artefacts and historical processes' (Dube 2023, 37), it offers vistas of divergent configurations of an emergent nation as 'Hindu' in colonial India, and the changing processes of democratic politics and state action that made religion acquire supreme significance as a part of nationalist sentiments. *State, Nation, Religion* distinguishes itself in its modes of study and analysis: instead of focusing on discursive constructions and categories, it pays close attention to spaces, subjects, temples, deities, ways of life along with policies and politics of the colonial and post-colonial Indian state, implications of significant Supreme Court judgements, and changing articulations of citizen politics to make palpable the multiple meanings and conjoint quotidian articulations of religion, nation-state, and politics. Examinations of diverse spaces, ideas and ideals, and peoples and practices from different perspectives underscore the superfluity of tracing a linear progression of Hindu religious nationalism from its inception in late-nineteenth-century India to its aggressive articulation in the present. At the same time, it also emphasises the interdependence of the nation-state, public morality, majoritarian ideas and nationalism in the triumphant march of the political, authoritarian Hindu *rashtra* of today.

The humanist poet-philosopher Rabindranath Tagore, a stern critic of nationalism, had indicated the distance of 'nationalism' from the ethos of India by highlighting that there was no single word/term in any of the several Indian languages that could translate directly as nationalism. 'India', he had asserted, only followed 'the West in its acceptance of the organised selfishness of Nationalism' (Tagore 2002, 21); without ever having 'a *real* sense of nationalism' (ibid., 115; italics ours). It is true that different terms used in Indian languages – *deshabhiman, swadeshprem, deshbhakt* – signify love and devotion for one's land (country), and a sense of its glory, which might loosely relate to patriotism. Nationalism translates as *rashtrabad* in Hindi and *jatiyatabad* in Bangla, one giving precedence to *rashtra* and the other to the plurivalent term *jati*. Pained and frustrated by the aggressive nationalism of European countries and Japan on the eve of World War I, the humanist poet had foreseen the violence and exclusion that underlie nationalism. The career of the Indian nation-state and others across the globe has displayed to great effect both the continued relevance of nationalism as a sentiment of belonging and the constant exclusion and othering it involves.

It is perhaps clear that this volume does not treat concept-categories such as 'religion', politics, nation-state, nationalism, majority, minority, and their underlying assumptions of totalising power relations as given, static, or self-evident. It recognises power as 'formative facts of social worlds' (Dube 2003, 37), and attends to their varied constructions and changing interrelations. Our effort is to shed light on the transforming salience, conceptual charge and empirical concretisation of state, religion, nationalism, politics in accordance with time, space, political regimes, and historically contingent processes. We also want to understand how rituals of political identity and of expressive (religious) nationalism cross paths in India at a time when cultural histories get woven through authoritarian political partisanship amid struggles over the meaning of nationhood and citizenship.

In using expressive nationalism, we display our agreement with understandings of the nation as pedagogy and performance (Bhabha 1990; Dube 2023) and as scandals of the state that implicate citizens (Sunder Rajan 2003). We are also in accord with Michael Billig's (1995) provocative positing of the everyday, banal recreation of the nation (and nation state) that sustains a sense of national identity and makes nationalism 'endemic'. Indeed, the banality of a particular variety of a militant, statist nationalism and its pedagogy and performance have been so blatant in India over the past decade that it becomes almost redundant to state it. The Indian state enacts the nation on an everyday basis by demanding of its citizens a flagrant, ritual display of their national allegiance. The banging of utensils during the pandemic lockdown purportedly to rid India off the virus, the hoisting of the *tiranga* (the Indian tricolour flag) and taking selfies with it on Independence day, or the lighting of *diya* (oil lamps) and the broadcast of Ram bhajans through public microphones to celebrate the Ayodhya temple inauguration, provide only a few of the countless instances.

Even though dictated from the top, the quotidian enunciation and enactment of the nation-state create and perpetrate a(n) (im) permissible display of nationalism, which then helps different groups of citizens to reimagine, recreate, reconfigure, and reinforce their belonging to the imagined 'national community' (Anderson 2006), and by extension, naturalise their relationship with themselves and the Other. Such rites and rituals of expressive–performative nationalism have far-reaching consequences for the shaping of cultural–historical–social–political memories through the optics of 'religious' identification. In the process, the nation-state gradually gets elevated to the domain of pre-eminent religious significance – and the *rashtra-nayak* to that of a 'saviour', a phenomenon that has been termed 'Vaticanisation' in the popular media.

The resurgence of 'religion' in the political domain across the globe in recent times, scholars have noted, has been consequent upon a gradual erosion of the bourgeois public sphere, the emergence of the Right-wing to political predominance, and the increasing credibility of authoritarian states that make use of cultural nationalism to 'reify' history and 'aestheticize politics' in the name of 'authenticity' and 'culture' (Bannerji 2000, 1). In such projections, '...culture is collapsed into "civilization" and "civilization" into religion as a kind of patrimony' (Ahmad 2000, 16). These processes have meant that debates and reflections on the many meanings of the religious and the secular, their variable and fortuitous constellations, their application as universal categories by the colonising West, and their discrete and diverse apprehensions in social worlds have remained a lively part of academic culture. Here, we will briefly touch upon some important arguments of the debate, in order to see their intersections and disjunctions with India.

The Religious and the Secular

Talal Asad's important formulation on the 'construction of religion as an anthropological category' had insisted on the need to excavate the genealogy of 'religion'. Such an examination laid bare its gradual construction as an essentialist, trans-historical phenomenon beginning with the separation of religion and politics (the church and the state) in a few societies of western Europe at a particular historical juncture that was later sustained and bolstered by influential definitions in disciplines such as anthropology (Asad 1993, 27–54). The separation of the religious and the political in turn, had generated careful delineations of the secular as 'a central, modern, epistemic category', secularism as a worldview, and secularisation as 'an analytical conceptualization of modern world-historical processes' (Casanova 2009, 1049). While Talal Asad and Jose Casanova, two leading scholars who have critically analysed the secular, coincide in accepting the secular as an epistemic category, Casanova views secularism as a worldview and Asad sees it as a political doctrine of Euro-America with far greater force than a worldview. It is an ideology that 'presupposes' new concepts of religion, ethics and politics and the imperatives such concepts entail (Asad 2003, 1–2). And it is precisely the divergent perceptions and apprehensions of the implicit imperatives of the secular that have produced a variety of responses to secularism including its rejection as a 'western' doctrine in some societies of the Middle East and elsewhere and an assertion by the advocates of secularism that despite its parochial roots the doctrine has universal applicability (ibid., 2).[1]

These debates, that arose in the wake of actual historical and sociopolitical occurrences in various societies, reaffirmed the significance of religion in the public, political sphere. The analytical distinction made by scholars between the three jumbled

[1] Asad is referring to the work of Charles Taylor (1999). A more detailed and intricate argument of Taylor is contained in Taylor (2008). Indeed, the literature is copious. For a productive understanding, see the many writings of and debates between Asad (1993; 2003) and Casanova (2009).

empirical entities of the secular, secularism and secularisation allows an understanding of the conditions that made possible the emergence of the secular as an episteme, and indicates the happenings and aspirations that occasioned the consolidation of secularism as a redemptive worldview/ideology. By formally separating the spheres of the religious (the church, and the ecclesiastical) from the 'secular' (the state, economy, science and art) in the 'early-modern' period, secularism as an ideology/worldview – accompanied by secularisation as a plural process – is taken to have slowly transformed the dominance and influence of the religious/ecclesiastical in politics and public life into an autonomy of the secular, signalling thereby a break with the 'medieval' or the pre-modern and the onset of the 'modern'. It is in this sense that secularism has been widely acknowledged as a liberating force that made possible the transition to modern contemporary societies by breaking loose the grasp of 'religion' (Casanova 2009, 1050). These analyses, apart from questioning the universality of the 'universal' categories of the 'religious' and the 'secular', underscore the necessity of attending to empirical contexts that disclose diverse perceptions and experiences that stimulate disparate processes of secularisation. This results in distinct configurations of 'secular' democracies with varied manifestations of religion in the public sphere. If we link these arguments with van der Veer's emphasis on the significance of public morality and conscience in the modern public sphere, the assumptions that accept pre-constructed understandings of the secular and its prevalence in 'modern' democracies as axiomatic appear thoroughly problematic.

The 'liberation', inaugurated by secularism, moreover, has come at a cost particularly in societies without a clearly identifiable church and with intricate mingling of the religious and the secular (Bhargava ed. 1998, for instance). For Ashis Nandy (1997), a tireless critic of the 'modern', secularism has been a pretext for de-indigenisation and deculturation.These distinct orientations enable an understanding of how a critique of thc 'pseudo-secularism' practised by the Congress regime allegedly apparent in its policy of 'appeasing (religious) minorities' in India helped the Hindu-Right gain popularity among large sections of urban and semi-urban citizens grappling with processes of rapid, unplanned urbanisation and liberalisation.

Attention to concrete conditions show that it was possibly the Iranian Revolution - often termed the 'Islamic Revolution' of 1978–79 - that occasioned a serious rethinking of the widely acknowledged separation of the religious and the secular in state policies and public politics. This revolution brought monarchy to an end through a coming together of clerics, leftist forces and popular upheaval. Mohammad Reza Shah (Pahlavi) of Iran had sought to legitimise his regime on a programme of 'modernisation' and appeals to patriotism poised on the strategic support of Western allies, particularly the United States, and propped up by state repression. If the predominant US presence occasioned a 'conservative' backlash that spoke in the name of saving Shi'i Islam, the Shah's repressive policies and economic turmoil brought students and workers with disparate but broad leftist ideologies together with the clerics. A collective belief in a 'primordial' Iran as a twenty-five-hundred year-old 'nation' with several shared elements made this curious and unusual combination possible (Aghaie 2014, 187–188).[2] As a consequence, an 'Islamic Republic' was proclaimed at the end of the 'Revolution'. A 'religious' republic that was primarily Iranian: an anachronistic combination that disrupted the tidy separation of the religious and the political as well as their categorisation as 'non-modern' and 'modern'.

Nation, Culture, Belonging

Significantly, the Islamic Revolution ceased to be an 'anomaly' and soon became a major theme in international politics as peoples in different countries began to express a longing for 'indigenous' alternatives to 'secular' Western politics that had

---

[2] We thank Kamal Soleimani for referring us to this and other publications on Iran and the Islamic Revolution.

religion and culture as key components (Juergensmeyer 1993).[3] The upsurge of 'ethnic' and other cultural 'nationalisms' that led to the disintegration of powerful, multi-nation-states such as the Soviet Union, Yugoslavia (and Czechoslovakia) in the early 1990s, urged a close scrutiny of the relation between the state and its institutionalised nationalism with other loyalties and modes of identification among different sections of a heterogeneous population that contravened the 'nationality' policies and politics of these states (Ludden 1996, 2). Nation and nationalism (and the nation-state) came under close scholarly examination; influential theories emphasised how they were imagined and constructed on the basis of some common markers that generated a sense of belonging and sharing (Gellner 1983; Anderson 2006; Chatterjee 1986, 1993, for instance), often defined by the territorial sovereignty of the state. Formidable formulations of the intimate links between nation, nationalism and racism in configurations of belonging underscored the contradictions that lie at the very core of the nation with its diverse history, and revealed how racism often shored up ideologies of nationalism to uphold and legitimise the 'integrity of the nation' internally and externally (Balibar 1988). Roluahpuia's chapter in this volume probes the construction and impact of racialised citizenship for 'tribal' and minority communities of northeastern India.

It is interesting to note in this connection that even though India has been conspicuous for the absence of a centralised state for a long time, indications of territorial integrity marked by natural boundaries found expression in crisscrossing pilgrim and trade networks that spawned the four *dhams* (abodes) of Lord Vishnu located in Badrinath, Kanyakumari, Puri and Dwaraka, roughly four extreme geographical limits in the north, south, east and west India since 'pre-modern' times

[3] Instead of taking issues with 'religious nationalism' as something that pertains to the Islamic, Hindu, Buddhist, and Zionist worlds, Juergensmeyer looks at 'religious nationalism' from the perspective of its proponents to examine the problems of secular nationalism.

(Bandyopadhyay 2006; Eck 2013; Mohapatra 1996). They were bolstered by the *satipeethas*, the sites for Kumbh *mela* and the four *mathas* founded by Sankaracharya,[4] as well as the pilgrim network of Gaudiya Vaishnavism that connected Nabadwip in Bengal to Puri, Mathura and Brindaban in current Uttar Pradesh. While such pre-modern configurations of 'sacred geography' illustrate the inefficacy of the modular approach or the modern(ity)/tradition dyad as analytics in understanding notions of belonging, they also indicate the lack of a homogenous sense of Indian-ness.[5] The recent reconfiguration of sacred geography aims at erasing this heterogeneity in order to uphold a singular nationalism that fosters a singular sense of belonging.

It is time to briefly comment on Anthony D. Smith's (2000, 792) important formulation that the nation is a 'sacred communion of citizens', a 'felt and willed communion' of peoples who 'assert a particular moral faith and feel a common ancestral affinity'. Devotion to the cult of authenticity, and the ideals of national unity and identity in a historic homeland (Smith 2003, 254) confers cohesiveness on the nation and shores-up its self-confidence and exclusivity, a fact that has important implications for the global inter-state order of 'national-states'. Affirming that most national identities are 'suffused and underpinned' by a belief in the sacred that often results in a politicisation of religion and a 'messianisation' of the people (Smith 2000, 795), Smith delineated the markers that contribute to the constitution of the nation as

4 *Satipeethas* are religious shrines erected on the sites where, according to 'Indian' mythology, parts of goddess Sati's corpse had fallen. Kumbh *melas* are quasi-religious fairs organised since antiquity, rotationally in different 'Indian' cities based on the celestial configuration and 'Indian' calendrical systems. The *mathas* refer to the four monasteries – located at Joshimath (in north India), Puri (in the east), Shringeri (in the south) and Dwarka (in the west of 'India' – founded by Shankaracharya roughly between mid-eighth and early-ninth centuries.

5 India's Sanskritic past, Spivak (1990, 39) contends, is too Indic. The name 'India' was mistakenly given by Alexander, Hindustan by Islamic conquerors, and Bharat is reminiscent of a mythic king.

'sacred communion' of an imagined community of the dead, the living, and the to-be-born in an upward linear trajectory of time (ibid., 800–810).

The relevance of these statements finds lucid illustration in the Hindu-Right's insistence that only the pure, authentic, autochthonous Indians who feel a strong sense of belonging to the sacred and sovereign territory of the fatherland (*pitrubhumi*) and the *rashtra* are the true citizens of Hindu-India, an insistence that has been accompanied by confident measures to reconfigure citizenship and belonging by a state intent on erasing and rewriting the past and has won the support of a considerable part of citizens.

The powerful critique by feminist and gender studies scholars of the masculine and masculinist language and idiom of theories and analyses of nation and nationalism as well as of their applications by nation-states (Yuval-Davis 1993, for instance), have been accompanied by newer explorations of how nations are fashioned and sustained materially, and the vital 'social force' nationalism and religion accord to the nation to uphold and sustain these 'cultural constructs' in everyday lives (van der Veer and Lehman 1999, 3). These studies have underscored the inadequacy of the 'conventional dichotomies' of social theory poised on an 'ideological a priori distinction' between national imagination and religious imagination, and indicated how national and religious loyalties, instead of being rivals and mutually exclusive, can and do blend to shore up loyalty to the imagined community (van der Veer and Lehman 1999; van der Veer 1994; Aghaie 2014).

Marxist scholars in turn, have combined a reading of the evolution and interaction of nationalism and capitalism to offer a distinct and important analysis of the materiality of nations by analysing their 'class character' (Desai 2008; Patnaik 2016). Disagreeing with assessments that nation-states have become less relevant under regimes of neoliberalism and globalisation in the last quarter of the twentieth century and the first quarter of the twenty-first, they argue that 'developmental nationalisms' of the third-quarter of the twentieth century have got transformed into 'cultural nationalisms' that are flagrantly neoliberal, and frame their cultural politics in terms of religion, ethnicity, and culture, where culture is taken to be 'pre-given, static and original' (Desai 2008, 648; Patnaik 2016).Together, these readings of the recent growth of cultural (religious) nationalisms the world over, have demonstrated the hollowness of the binaries of religion and politics, the religious and the secular and of the assumed secular nature of modern democratic nations, urging a serious probe of our own orientations and approaches to social worlds and politics.

National Culture and Public Culture

India offers an illuminating example of how the social force of a religious–cultural–political imagination blends easily with imaginings of a territorially sovereign, powerful nation-state in the persuasive projection of an intimate association between national pride and the so-called authentic, pure, roots in *pitrubhumi* and Hindu-ness bolstered by the discursive practice of Hindutva. This imposing combination of the religious–cultural–political with the national–territorial has conferred a unique significance and authority on parties of the Hindu-Right in the public sphere over the past three decades (Hansen 1999), and continues to uphold the rule of the Hindu state-nation and its national leader.

In his important and sensitive study published in the wake of the first success of the Hindu-Right to form a government at the Centre, Thomas Blom Hansen (1999, 5) had commented on the 'relative ease' with which the Hindu nationalist discourse had fitted in with the most authorised discourses on India and the authorised discourses on politics and culture in the postcolonial world. This was because Hindu nationalism in India owed its shaping to 'public culture', the 'public space' in which a society and the individuals and communities it is composed of, 'imagine, represent, and recognize through political discourse, commercial and cultural expressions, and representations of state and civic organizations' (ibid., 4).

Two and a half decades later, the Hindu-Right reigns in near totalitarian glory. The Hindu nationalist aspiration to transform

Indian public culture into a disciplined Hindu national culture premised on a supposedly superior Hindu/Indic past, and the zeal to avenge and correct Hindu-India's humiliation at the hands of inferior (Muslim) aggressors appears to have gained great legitimacy. Public avowals of faith in a strong Hindu *rashtra* have been complemented by *bhakti* (devotion) and loyalty of citizens ready to offer *seva* (service) to this *rashtra*. The return to power for a third term by a government at the Centre under Narendra Modi – a Rashtriya Swayam Sevak (RSS) *pracharak* who rose to political prominence in Gujarat – on the basis of the trust he acquired as the man of the hour and subsequently as a national hero, tends to vindicate the Indian population's belief in and support for a strong, unified, intolerant nation-state as India's way forward in the international order in a world increasingly dominated by neoliberal economies, multinational corporations and populist, authoritarian leaders.

A convoluted yet successful amalgamation of nation and culture shored up by an increasing assertion of the demographic dominance of the Hindus has resulted in a majoritarianism that openly and confidently rejects consensus based on a recognition of and respect for plurality and acceptance of dissent. Flagrant Hindutva, which is meant to inhere in all true Hindus – autochthonous residents of a 'sacred' fatherland – has gained wide acceptance among considerable sections of the vast urban and rural middle and lower classes that believe in an avowal of Hindu cultural pride as the way to India's national and international glory. To them, the veritable problems of a huge and diverse democratic nation appear to have been occasioned by a negligence of Hindu cultural roots.

The gradual transformation of the idea of the majority in Indian democracy from one being based on 'consensus' to one based on numbers, in particular of members of 'religious' communities, has been evident in an unstated yet tangible accord among political parties on the 'Hindu vote' from the turn of the twenty-first century. This problematic consensus together with a shift towards a 'religious Right' has fostered a re-configuration of the Hindu majority as 'democracy', and of Hinduism as the most tolerant of religions, turning the 'secular' into a false, anti-Hindu construct (Vanaik 2017, 246). Never before in the history of independent India has structural 'racism' in the sense of racial segregation and marginalisation of minorities, the Muslim minority in particular (and the 'tribals' of the Northeast) – comparable to the social-political dynamics of racial marginalisation of the 'Blacks' in the Jim-Crow-era of the United States (Varshney and Staggs 2024) – and the resultant intolerance and violence been flaunted in the name of 'national integrity' with greater confidence. This volume carefully considers the varied processes, visions, actions and imaginings that have been conducive to this state of affairs.

Nation, Imaginings, State, Religion

State, Nation, Religion traverses the early-twentieth century to the present in order to trace the distinct and overlapping elements, sentiments, politics and actions that went into the making of the 'national' and the national state and continue to sustain them in distinct ways. It offers insights into the material and the symbolic, the ideological, the 'sacred' and the political components of nation, nationalism, the nation-state and their ramifications in the public sphere through analyses that straddle the historical, ethnographic, literary, legal, political, audio-visual and spatial.

In the first chapter, Mark Jurgensmeyer points to the colonial roots of 'religious nationalism' in India by highlighting the enduring impact of colonial demarcation of 'religion', caste and other categories, their application in colonial policies and their internalisation by elite reformers, political leaders and different groups of Indian subjects (and citizens). He highlights the consequences of the paradoxical co-existence of the absence of a common perception of what constitutes the 'religious' and/or a 'national community' among several marginal groups of late-twentieth century India with the acceptance by Indian elites and political leaders of a clear separation of the 'religious' and the 'secular-political' as an integral part of democracy in independent India. A combination of the problematic ideal of a singular national culture that lies at the core of the modern nation-state with the imagined difference between the religious and secular spheres of culture generates conditions in which 'extreme religion' and 'extreme secular' vie with each other. The recent and rapid success of 'extreme religion' in India represents the rise of global religious politics at a moment of late modernity.

Sanghamitra Misra's examination of the Northeast highlights the profound effect of colonial categories. Situating the categories of 'customary law', 'traditional/indigenous authority', the 'hill tribe' and the 'primitive' within the processes of state ethnogenesis under colonialism, she underlines the intimate links between imperial conquest and imperial knowledge that included anthropology. Misra urges us to examine the perpetration of such categories in the 'recognition of the traditional authority' and 'custom' of communities of 'tribes' in the Sixth Schedule of the Indian Constitution and their apprehension, essentialisation and fetishisation in the contemporary politics of indigeneity in northeastern India. A politics that constructs and projects 'authentic', archaic, homogeneous, and timeless communities.

The third and fourth chapters track the emergence and consolidation of nationalist imageries often conceived as Hindu through the invocation of a sense of belonging to and serving the cause of a nation. Shobna Nijhawan's careful reading of the new genre of travel writings in Hindi published in a well-known journal in the first half of the twentieth century unpacks the dual purpose they served: that of establishing a standardised Hindi as a language of literary expression and of evoking an inchoate yet palpable sense of the territorial expanse and the grandeur of the 'nation'. Sayori Ghoshal, on the other hand, focuses on the consciously majoritarian concerns of sections of the Hindu elite to show how, by the beginning of the twentieth century, colonial policies of classification and enumeration had consolidated and made them acceptable terms of public, political discourse. A combination of race, religion and numbers had come to uphold the notion of the Hindus as a superior race and authentic inhabitants of India, whose dwindling numbers was causing great concern.

Esha Meher's incisive intervention in the fifth chapter throws light on a crucial yet relatively unexplored element of public culture, namely the structured hierarchy embedded in the presence of Hindu deities and religious institutions of other communities in public spaces. Her close reading of the undue advantage afforded to Hindu deities by colonial and post-colonial law through the conferral of *legal personality*/personhood underscores how such personhood puts the Hindu deities at par with human beings and enables human litigants to make claim on public property on their behalf. Such privilege is not accorded to institutions of other religious communities. The skewed ramifications of the divergent application of 'public' law and legal personhood to the political–religious landscape of India got exemplified in the significant 2019 verdict of the Supreme Court on the Ramjanmabhoomi–Babri-Masjid dispute. Ram Lalla triumphed over the Muslim waqf board.

In the sixth chapter, Roluahpuia complements Misra's analysis of the impress of colonial categories in postcolonial India by focusing on the racialised constructions of citizenship of 'tribal' communities of the Northeast by the Indian state. Looked upon with suspicion as peoples who inhabit a 'troubled' frontier zone – the 'Mongolian frontier' of colonial times – the dubiously loyal 'tribal' citizens of the Northeast are subjected to a double othering on account of their Mongoloid physical traits and their strange eating habits.

The seventh chapter by Anuradha Bhasin takes up the abrogation of Article 370 of the Indian Constitution that deprived Kashmir of its special status and converted Jammu and Kashmir into union territories under the Indian state. Bhasin examines the legal–constitutional, civil–political, economic–ecological and cultural implications and effects of this bold move to conclude that it constitutes a tactical but unconstitutional strategy of the Modi government to erase Kashmir – the only erstwhile Muslim-majority state in India.

Maribel Elliet Alvarado-Becerril focuses on contemporary televisual debates in top news channels to analyse the significant role they played in the spread of the Hindu-Right rhetoric of a singular nationalism. In constantly telecasting debates around the issues of the nation, the national and what/who constitutes the 'true national', they simultaneously constructed such notions and offered a wide range of viewers and participants a sense of active participation in the creation of public opinion and a feel of 'deliberative' democracy.

The ninth chapter offers an incisive ethnography of a *gaushala* (cow-shelter). Ridhima Sharma unpacks the existence of gendered hierarchies and discriminatory practices in the valourised Hindu nationalist cause of the protection and conservation of the cow as the nation's mother. Swati Dyahadroy's study of Jnana Prabodhini, a Pune-based educational organisation in the tenth chapter, lays bare the strategic deployement of the discourse of *seva* by a Hindu-nationalist organisation to mobilise ordinary middle-class women, and the distinct adaptation and interpellation of conservative notions of femininity by women members of the organisation. The eleventh and twelfth chapters focus on the cult of the hero. While Manjima Chatterjee tries to understand the electoral success of the Hindu-Right (and cultural nationalism) by focusing on the charisma of Prime Minister Narendra Modi as the 'national hero', Sreya Mitra reads the words and world of Bollywood superhero, Shah-Rukh Khan. Chatterjee sees in Modi a cult figure and an alpha male whose populism inspires devotion among his *bhakt*s (devotees), women in particular,who seek to become 'true' Indians and serve the cause of the nation by expressing devotion to Modi. Mitra culls out the multiple and contingent meanings of Khan identifying himself as a 'cosmopolitan' citizen of a 'minority' community and traces the tensions that underlie his nuanced portrayal of minority characters in films that depict ways of belonging to the nation.

Anne Hartig's sensitive analysis of the Lakshminarayan Birla temple in Delhi opens a vista to a different aspect of Hindu religious presence in the public sphere. Built under the aegis of G.D. Birla – a close associate of Mahatma Gandhi – and inaugurated in 1939, the temple contributed significantly to the political project of nation-building, steeped in 'Hindu' religious ethos. While the unorthodox, eclectic design of the temple embodied a 'modern' architectural style, its plaques emphasised India's Hindu past. In the final chapter, Himani Kapoor studies a 'cosmopolitan' Guru-led faith movement, the Art of Living Foundation, to argue that despite its global outreach, the foundation's activities within India invoke and give expression to a primordial Hindu-Vedic community that sustains cultural nationalism.

Taken together, these fourteen chapters, diverse in approach and focus, illuminate the complex and often contradictory ways in which the 'nation' and the 'national' are constituted, contested, and experienced. They reveal how religious, secular, cultural, and political forces intersect, shaping both state actions and citizen politics in ways that simultaneously reinforce and disrupt established boundaries of belonging. By examining the entanglements of religious nationalism, spatialised nationhood, and the territorialisation of religion, this volume offers critical insights into the shifting dynamics of tradition, identity, and political ethos. Ultimately, it underscores the fluidity of nationalism, showing how it is continually reimagined through intersecting identities and conflicted passions that challenge fixed categories and destabilise conventional narratives.

References

Aghaie, Kamran Scot. 2014. "Islamic-Iranian Nationalism and its Implications for the Study of Political Islam and Religious Nationalism." In *Rethinking Iranian Nationalism and Modernity*, edited by Kamran Scot Aghaie and Afshin Marashi. Austin: University of Texas Press.

Ahmad, Aijaz. 2000. "Nationalism and Globalisation." *Occasional Papers Series*: 4. Department of Sociology, University of Pune.

Anderson, Benedict. (1983) 2006. *Imagined Communities: Reflections on the Origin and Spread of Nationalism*. London and New York: Verso.

Asad, Talal. 1993. *Genealogies of Religion: Discipline and Reasons of Power in Christianity and Islam*. Baltimore: Johns Hopkins University.

———. 2003. *Formations of the Secular: Christianity, Islam, Modernity*. Stanford: Stanford University Press.

Balibar, Etienne, and Peter van der Veer. 1988. "Racismo y nacionalismo." In *Raza, Nación y Clase*, edited by Etienne Balibar and Immanuel Wallerstein. Madrid: IEPALA.

Bandyopadhyay, D. "The Pre-colonial Imagined Boundaries." Adhir Chakroborty Memorial Lecture, delivered at the Centre for Archaeological Training and Research, Govt. of West Bengal, India on 8 December 2006.

Bannerji, Himani. 2000. *The Dark Side of the Nation: Essays on Multiculturalism, Nationalism and Gender*. Toronto: Canadian Scholars' Press Inc.

Bhabha, Homi K. 1990. *Nation and Narration*, London: Routledge.

Bhadra, Gautam. "Rashtrer kabale Bhakti, ateet ghente labh ki." Interviewed by Simool Sen. *Ei Samay*, 21 January 2024.

Bhargava, Rajeev, ed. 1998. *Secularism and its Critics*. New Delhi: Oxford University Press.

Billig, Michael. 1995. *Banal Nationalism*. London: Sage Publications.

Casanova, Jose. 2009. "The Secular and Secularisms." *Social Research* (special issue, *The Religious-Secular Divide: The U.S. Case*) 76, no. 4: 1049–66.

Chatterjee, Partha. 1986. *Nationalist Thought and the Colonial World: A Derivative Discourse?* London: Zed Books.

———. 1993. *The Nation and Its Fragments: Colonial and Postcolonial Histories*. Delhi: Oxford University Press.

Desai, Radhika. 2008. "Conclusion: From Developmental Culture to Nationalisms." *Third World Quarterly* 29, no. 3: 647–70.

Dube, Saurabh. 2023. *Disciplines of Modernity: Archives, Histories, Anthropologies*. London, New York: Routledge.

Eck, Diana L. 2013. *India: A Sacred Geography*. New York: Harmony.

Gellner, Ernest. 1983. *Nations and Nationalism*. Oxford: Oxford University Press.

Habermas, Jürgen. 1964. "The Public Sphere: An Encyclopaedia Article." Translated by Sara Lennox and Frank Lennox. Originally published in *Fischer Lexikon, Staat und Politik* (Fischer Taschenbuch Verlag).

Hansen, Thomas Blom. 1999. *The Saffron Wave: Democracy and Hindu Nationalism in Modern India*. Princeton Princeton University Press.

Juergensmeyer, Mark. 1993. *The New Cold-War? Religious Nationalism Confronts the Secular State*. Berkeley and Los Angeles: University of California Press.

Ludden, David. 1996. "Introduction." In *Making India Hindu: Religion, Community, and the Politics of Democracy in India*, edited by David Ludden. New Delhi: Oxford University Press.

Mohapatra, Bishnu. 1996. "Ways of Belonging: The Kanchi-Kaveri Legend and the Construction of Oriya Identity." *Studies in History* 12, no. 2: 203–21.

Mufti, Aamir. 2007. *Enlightenment in the Colony: The Jewish Question and the Crisis of Postcolonial Culture*. Princeton: Princeton University Press.

Nandy, Ashis. 1997. "The Twilight of Certitudes: Secularism, Hindu Nationalism and Other Masks of Deculturation." *Alternatives: Global, Local, Political* 22, no. 2: 157–76.

Patnaik, Prabhat. 2016. "Nationalism, Hindutva, and the Assault on Thought." *Marxist* XXXII, no. 1. https://cpim.org/content/nationalism-hindutva-and-assault-thought. Accessed on 05 May 2025.

Smith, Anthony D. 2000. "The Sacred Dimension of Nationalism." *Millennium: Journal of International Studies* 29, no. 3: 791–814.

———. (1998) 2003. *Nationalism and Modernism*. New York: Taylor and Francis.

Spivak, Gayatri C. 1990. *The Post-Colonial Critic: Interviews*. New York: Routledge.

Tagore, R. (1917) 2002. *Nationalism*. Madras: Macmillan India.

Taylor, Charles. 1999. "Modes of Secularism." In *Secularism and its Critics*, edited by R. Bhargava. Delhi and New York: Oxford University Press.

———. 2008. *A Secular Age*. Cambridge, MA: Harvard University Press.

Vanaik, Achin. 2017. *The Rise of Hindu Authoritarianism: Secular Claims, Communal Realities*. London: Verso.

van der Veer, Peter. 1994. *Religious Nationalism. Hindus and Muslims in India*. Berkeley and Los Angeles: University of California Press.

———. 1999. "The Moral State." In *Nation and Religion: Perspectives on Europe and Asia*, edited by van der Veer and Lehman, 17–40. Princeton: Princeton University Press.

van der Veer, Peter, and Harmut Lehman. 1999. "Introduction.". In *Nation and Religion: Perspectives on Europe and Asia*, edited by van der Veer and Lehman, 3–14. Princeton: Princeton University Press.

Varshney, Ashutosh, and Connor Staggs. 2024. "Hindu Nationalism and the New Jim Crow." *Journal of Democracy* 35, no. 1: 5–18.

Yuval-Davis, Nira. 1993. *Gender and Nation*. London: Sage Publications.

ONE

The Clash of Religious Politics in India

MARK JUERGENSMEYER

Years ago when I was a young graduate student in political science attempting to do research in rural Punjab, I had prepared a thirty-page questionnaire for an extensive survey on religious and political attitudes. My targets were members of Scheduled Caste communities from several villages in Punjab. But when I actually got around to asking the questions the whole project ran into trouble with the first question. When I got to the second question it all fell apart.

The first question was, 'What is your name?' The problem with this was that Schedule Caste people often had different names for different contexts – did I want a religious name, a caste name, a village name, or a name associated with their work? Just what kind of name did I want?

The problem with the second question was even more difficult. I wanted to know their religion. 'What do you mean by that exactly?', my Punjabi tutors asked. They were trying to help me translate, and since I had used the term *dharm* in my questionnaire to indicate religion, as many Christian missionaries had done earlier, I assumed that that was the acceptable term in India for what we in the West meant by the word – the combination of ideological beliefs and communal loyalties in a definable single religious package.

'You know, religion', I replied. They stared back at me blankly.

What they told me was that there did not exist a single term for this idea, at least not traditionally, in any Indian language. Instead, there were many terms that described different aspects of religiosity – *qaum*, a word that means 'nation' or 'community'; *mazhab*, which means 'beliefs'; *dharm*, the term often used by missionaries, which means ethical law or moral order; and *panth*, which means a fellowship of faithful believers. Someone who wore the *qaumik* turban of Sikhs could ascribe to traditional Hindu dharmic values and follow a Muslim pir as part of a local *panth*. Religion could mean many things. What was it, asked my Punjabi tutors and Schedule Caste respondents again, that I wanted to know?

I wanted to know what 'religion' meant in the rural Punjabi context, and in the befuddled answers to my questions I learned quite a bit. What I discovered was that the English word 'religion' is not easily translated, and by implication the absence of religion – secularism – has a different meaning in the Indic context as well. This is what makes thinking about religion and politics in India so interesting, and at the same time so vexing.

The European Origins of India's Religious Politics

In an interesting book, *Enlightenment in the Colony*, a UCLA scholar of Comparative Literature, Aamir Mufti (2007) argues that the British helped to invent not only the idea of religion in India but also the concept of religious minorities. Mufti points out that although Muslims in South Asia were in the numerical minority over the centuries ever since Mughal rule brought Islam to the subcontinent, they did not think of themselves as minorities. Nor were they treated as such within a society that was unselfconsciously pluralistic. Traditional Indian society encompassed a variety of religious communities, and the tradition that we know as 'Hinduism' has been a congeries of different sects and lineages of teachers and teachings that vary widely from one another. Muslims, Sikhs, Christians, Jains and other religious communities fit easily into this pattern of religious diversity, as did Brahmanical, epic, bhakti and panthic forms of what we call Hinduism.

According to Mufti, the process of secular nation-building in Europe has gone hand in hand with the conceptualisation of a national culture that marginalises some religious and ethnic communities in the process of creating the idea of a unified national culture. In doing so, the byproduct of this nationalist paradigm is the invention of the notion of 'minorities' as a problem. The paradigmatic case in Europe is the 'Jewish question', in which Jews do not fit into the idea of cultural consensus in emerging modern national communities. Adolf Hitler's infamous 'final solution' to the Jewish problem was an attempt at cultural and physical extermination. Alternatively, the British solution at the end of World War II was to help create the modern state of Israel as one that would serve as a national homeland for the Jews.

Mufti argues that this idea was transported to South Asia where both British and Indian nationalist leaders identified the national culture with Hinduism. They imagined that, as with European nations, the national culture of India was part of one homogeneous religious entity. This way of thinking results in establishing Muslims as a minority and, like the Jews in Europe, these minorities create a problem for the building of a modern national community. In Mufti's examination of the literature in Britain as well as the literature produced by Indian writers in English, Hindi and Urdu, he finds that this notion of Muslim minority identity as a problem creeps into writing about nation-building in the subcontinent in the nineteenth and twentieth centuries. No surprise, then, that Jinnah – the urbane, London-trained leader of the Muslims – as well as the cosmopolitan Nehru, would think of nation-building in modern terms. This meant thinking of a homogeneous cultural unity that would be problematic for minorities. Nehru's 1946 book, *The Discovery of India*, chronicles his own self-discovery of the unity of India's past, implicitly a cultural as well as political unity. No wonder then that Jinnah thought that Muslims would be uncomfortable in such a nation, and no wonder, also, that the British Viceroy Lord Mountbatten would instinctively understand the logic of having a separate nation for a nation-sized minority. The formation of Pakistan became for South Asian Muslims what the creation of Israel had been for European Jews.

The idea of the modern nation-state is a part of the world's inheritance from the European Enlightenment, during which religion played a somewhat paradoxical role. While Enlightenment thinkers such as John Locke regarded political institutions as secular – free from the taint of religious influence – they thought of the culture of a national community as unified, a unity that often involved common religious beliefs. According to the Berkeley sociologist John Lie in an arresting book titled *Modern Peoplehood* (2004), the concept of a national community or 'peoplehood', is one of the major constructs of the Enlightenment's understanding of modernity. The modern nation is inconceivable, Lie argues, without it.

According to Lie, the whole notion of a modern nation rests on the idea that there is such a thing as naturally occurring, geographically configured communities of people united by common cultures. The agreement at the Peace of Westphalia in 1648 indicated that a nation's religion should be in conformity with the state, and since then there has been a tacit assumption that culture – including matters of ethnicity, language and religion – is a criterion for a homogeneous national community. Lie says that this concept is problematic even in European and other Western countries where increasingly large immigrant communities from other parts of the world are changing the character of national societies. But it is even more problematic in non-Western areas of the world – including South Asia – where cultural variation and even deep divisions have existed among the ethnic and religious communities of regions that come to be defined as nations. Often, in fact, the boundaries of these new nation-states were drawn hastily by retreating European colonial powers without much attention to the ethnic makeup within them. The subsequent attempts to create homogeneous national communities in regions of Africa, South and Southeast Asia, and the Middle East, argues Lie, have sometimes led to ethnic cleansing, the disenfranchisement of minorities, and in extreme cases, genocide.

But at the same time that the very notion of a national community needed the glue of culture, including religion, to hold it together, the Enlightenment concept of the political apparatus of the modern state was supposed to be free from religion. The state was supposed to be secular. This dichotomy between religion and secularism as two separate spheres of social reality was something that emerged as a part of the Enlightenment thinkers' views of the world. It made it possible to think of religion as something that could be encapsulated into a limited area of social and cultural influence, leaving the public sphere of governance free from religious influences. In his monumental work, *A Secular Age*, the Canadian philosopher Charles Taylor (2007) shows how the secular idea has taken on various dimensions – from a simple division between the authority of church and state to a whole new way of thinking about human relationships to the cosmos. Secularism, according to Taylor, has its own ideological character.

It is this ideological character of secularism that is the concern of Talal Asad (2003) in his challenging book, *Formations of the Secular: Christianity, Islam, Modernity*. Asad argues that secularism is an ideology that creates its own notion of 'religion' as something that can be encompassed in a limited arena within the public sphere. It is a notion that does not apply easily to many parts of the world, including the Islamic world, and one might argue that it does not work well in South Asia either.

My own contribution to this discussion is found in my co-authored introduction and an essay in the book *Rethinking Secularism* (Calhoun et al. 2011), which is the product of a multi-year series of workshops on the topic involving Taylor, Asad and several other scholars, including Rajeev Bhargava, Jose Casanova, Saba Mahmood, Craig Calhoun and myself. My argument is that the imagined difference between secular and religious spheres of culture has created the conditions in which extreme religion and extreme secularism vie against one another. France, for example, can proclaim its national culture free from the taint of religiosity while Iran and Israel revel in their Muslim and Jewish national identities. Many of the movements that are thought of as terrorists in the twenty-first century, from the Muslim Islamic State to the Christian Militia and the Buddhist militants of Southeast Asia, are propelled by the desire to surmount the secular nationalism of their regions with religious nationalist visions of their own. The very idea that there are differences between secular and religious notions of society has created political tensions.

Nehru's Vision of a Secular and Socialist Society

Even though it may not have been part of the lexicon of South-Asian thinking traditionally, the idea of secularism arrived in South Asia along with European concepts of nationalism and democratic politics as a part of the accompanied baggage of British colonial rule. Both Jinnah and Nehru bought into the European idea that national communities were formed with a homogeneous culture. They also accepted the Enlightenment notion that national governments should be secular – free from the influence of sectarian bias or religious authority. To Jinnah, this meant that South-Asian Muslims constituted a distinct nation within the subcontinent, and this warranted their being granted a semi-autonomous region, or failing that, their own separate nation-state of Pakistan. But the dapper Jinnah, ever dressed in a European-style business suit, was insistent that the government of the new Pakistan would be similar to European states, that is, secular.

Nehru also accepted the European notion of a culturally homogeneous nation with a secular government, but he interpreted both of those concepts somewhat differently than Jinnah had. Nehru's description of India's cultural unity in *The Discovery of India* seemed to many Muslims to be very Hindu, but Nehru thought of it as Indic not narrowly Hindu but a part of a united cultural tradition. He did not think that it privileged Hindu or any other set of religious beliefs. In his mind, Indian culture embraced Islam as well as Hinduism. His notion of secularism, therefore, was not just a matter of keeping religious influences out of government but about treating all religious communities equally and fairly. It was precisely for this reason that Nehru thought that the Muslims should be a part of India and not separate from it.

In fact, neither Jinnah nor Nehru's European notions of national culture and secular government had much connection to traditional ways of thinking about religion and politics in India's history. The concept of a national community is non-existent in India's early history, as it was in most societies, including European ones, before the eighteenth century. There were caliphs and kings, princes and emperors who ruled on the basis of power, not the consent of the governed. Even so, they were expected to uphold certain moral standards in their conduct of governing. In traditional India, there is the notion that kings are expected to be from military castes that have their own ethical codes of conduct. Moreover, the king of a realm is expected to rule on behalf of dharma, the moral order that undergirds all of society. The image that is presented in ancient scriptures is that of a king upholding the 'white umbrella' of moral righteousness over the people. But these rulers are not in any sense religious.

The same can be said of the Mughal rulers, a lineage of Muslim emperors who reigned over much of the subcontinent from roughly the sixteenth through the middle of the nineteenth centuries. Though a quarter of the Indian population converted to Islam during this period, and Muslim holy sites were often privileged over Hindu ones, the imperial rule was hardly a theocratic state. One of the greatest Mughal rulers, Akbar, in the latter half of the sixteenth century, created his own court religion that was dismissive of orthodox Islam and meant to be compatible with all faiths. Famously, Akbar is said to have welcomed theologians and thinkers from all religious persuasions to enter into philosophic discussions in his chambers.

British colonial rule was secular, of course, but the colonial government maintained an ambivalent relationship with the hordes of Christian missionaries who had the run of India during its rule. Many of the British officers regarded them as a nuisance. But others regarded them as an extension of the civilising influence of the British rule. Christian hospitals and educational institutions were especially welcomed as efforts to serve Indian society and bring the benefits of Western civilisation to South Asian shores.

Hence, the inheritors of British rule in South Asia – Nehru and Jinnah – carried on this tradition of secular government with a benign, but wary, attitude towards religious authorities and organisations. Each regarded religious extremists and true believers as potentially dangerous. But each also regarded religion as an essential ingredient of the cultural homogeneity that made India and Pakistan distinctive national communities.

Hindu and Muslim Nationalism in Independent India

The trajectory of religious politics in India and Pakistan after Independence is different than what either Nehru or Jinnah expected. In both cases, religion burst out of the confines of an imagined homogenous national culture into direct participation in politics.

In Pakistan, successive political leaders increasingly found religion to be a useful rallying point for national unity. This also provided a built-in network of support from Muslim religious authorities and activists. Perhaps no political leader in Pakistan did more to pander to conservative Muslim support than Muhammad Zia-ul-Haq, who led the country from 1977 to 1988 after instituting a coup against his mentor, Zulfikar Ali Bhutto. Zia established shari'ah law, outlawed marginal and heretical religious movements, and subsidised the Mujahideen movement against a Soviet-backed government in neighbouring Afghanistan. Though the number of votes gained by Muslim religious parties in Pakistan have consistently been very small, since the time of Zia their influence in the government has been disproportionately large.

One legacy of the Zia regime has been the covert Pakistani support for extremist Muslim political movements in Afghanistan. First the Mujahideen and subsequently the Taliban movements have been secretly supported by elements of the Pakistan military and intelligence services. The ideas of the Taliban are related to the Deoband Muslim reform movement in South Asia that attempted to purify and standardise the teachings and practices of Islam. This was interpreted by groups such as the Taliban in a rigid and uncompromising way. The movement was not only an agent of religious standardisation, but it also became the political wing of the Pashtun tribal community, large numbers of which were within Pakistan's own western borders. Mollifying the Taliban, then, was a way of currying favour with the critical Pashtun community.

At the same time that Pakistan was developing a more strident Muslim political posture, religious nationalism was also surfacing within India. In some ways, the emergence of the Bharatiya Janata Party (BJP) was the re-emergence of a religious strand of Indian nationalism that extended back to the early part of the twentieth century. One of the early voices for Indian independence came from Vinayak Damodar Savarkar, who founded the Hindu Mahasabha and advocated a concept of Hindu culture which he called Hindutva as being the basis of Indian national identity. He once entered into a debate with Mohandas Gandhi over the efficacy of using violence in the struggle for India's freedom.[1] Despite Savarkar's efforts, Hindu nationalism was not a major element in India's nationalist movement. After Independence, several political parties took up the banner of support for Hindu causes, notably the Jan Sangh, but it was not until the 1990s that a new movement of religious consciousness led to spectacular political successes for the BJP.

The BJP was officially launched in 1980 out of the remnants of previous Hindu-oriented political parties (Graham 2007). It did not gain strength, however, until the 1990s with the events that led to the attack on the old Babri mosque said to be located on the site of the birthplace of the Hindu god, Ram, in the town of Ayodhya. Religious activists associated with sectarian Hindu organisations, the Vishwa Hindu Parishad and the Rashtriya Swayamsevak Sangh, championed the destruction of the mosque in order to liberate the grounds on which the ancient Hindu temple was said to have been located. Though archaeologists questioned the authenticity of the assertion, and many questioned whether

[1] The debate between Gandhi and Sarvarkar directly preceded the writing of Gandhi's book, *Hind Swaraj, or Indian Home Rule,* which was undoubtedly influenced by the debate. See my discussion of the incident in my article (Juergensmeyer 2007).

a spiritual entity such as a god actually had a birthplace, the site became a matter of religious contention, fuelled by political rhetoric. It was the secular Congress Party, after all, that allowed the mosque to continue to exist on that site. Though the Indian government said that it was protecting the site in the name of secularism – which in India meant the equal protection of all religious communities – the BJP's political response was that the Congress's position was 'pseudo-secularism' that in fact masked the privileging of minority communities such as Muslims over the interests of Hindus. It is notable that even after the creation of Pakistan, the number of Muslims remaining in India was 15 per cent of the population, enough to constitute a significant electoral base of votes, and a reason for politicians to curry the Muslims' favour.

In 1992, a mob of over 100,000 angry Hindus convened in Ayodhya, attacked the mosque with improvised tools, and rendered it to dust. The BJP capitalised on this sentiment of Hindu nationalism, and employing Savarkar's concept of Hindutva as the bedrock of Hindu nationalist culture, launched a series of political campaigns. The elections brought the BJP into positions of power in the legislatures of several states, and from 1998 to 2004 they were the dominant party in a national coalition that ruled India; in fact, the BJP leader Atal Bihari Vajpayee became India's Prime Minister. The 2014 elections brought the BJP back into power, and the former Chief Minister of Gujarat, Narendra Modi, was installed as the Prime Minister of the country, who was resoundingly re-elected in 2019 and subsequently in 2024 as well. If one considers the BJP to be a movement of religious nationalism, it quite likely has had the largest following of any such movement in world history – it has claimed a membership as large as 110 million. It has also been one of the most politically successful.

January 2024 ushered in a new chapter of Hindu nationalism in India. An enormous temple was established on the site of the demolished Babri mosque in Ayodhya, to be consecrated by no less a figure than Modi himself, who had gone through eleven days of purification in order to qualify for this priestly act. The construction of the edifice was not quite completed, but there were other compelling reasons for an early consecration – the national elections that would be conducted a few months later.

As Ram's idol was lifted into place on the altar and Modi waved the ritual wands to certify the consecration, the crowd of some 300,000 people who had gathered outside began to roar. Helicopters commandeered from the Indian Air Force flew overhead dropping thousands of red flower petals. For Modi, electoral success was virtually assured. The pro-BJP press throughout India proclaimed that something even more significant had occurred, a new day for nationalism in India, one free from the colonial constraints of secularism. A group of Indian human rights organisations issued a different statement, regretting what they called 'a political stunt' that would further India's decline from the principles of secularism and minority rights.

The Sikh Attempt to Create a Religious State

The rise of the BJP has not been India's only recent attempt at religious nationalism. In the 1980s, a sizable number of young Sikhs in the rural areas of the northwest Indian state of Punjab became embroiled in a violent confrontation with the Indian government. Some demanded a separate Sikh state. My own interest in this troubling situation was both intellectual and personal, since for some years I had studied the interrelation between religion and politics in South Asia, and at the same time had a special interest in the Punjab. I had lived and taught in this area for several years and knew the Sikhs to be a generous and tolerant community. The explosion of religious politics in Punjab, thus, was for me something that was not just intellectually interesting but also personally disturbing. I returned to the region to try to understand why this spiral of violence had emerged, and what religion had to do with it.

What I expected to find is what journalists and political observers often tell us they find in such situations, that these are cases where religion has been politicised by wily politicians. However, when I returned to Punjab and listened to recordings of the sermons of the Sikh leader, Sant Jarnail Singh Bhindranwale, and talked with his supporters, I realised that things weren't as simple.[2] Bhindranwale was a rural preacher who spoke with the conviction of someone who knew the details of his religious heritage. He said that the great battles of Sikh history were being repeated in the present day; the present confrontation was 'a struggle … for our faith, for the Sikh nation, for the oppressed' (Bhindranwale 1983, 2). The enemy that concerned Bhindranwale, however, was not a force from legendary history, but something much closer at hand: the secular government of the then Prime Minister Indira Gandhi. She so infuriated Bhindranwale that he did not even use her name. 'That woman born into a house of Brahmins', he would sputter; she was responsible for the sorry state of affairs in which the Sikh community found itself.

Rather than politicising religion, Bhindranwale was religionising politics. He was bringing a contemporary political conflict into the high proscenium of religious drama. The confrontation between his group of angry Sikhs and the Indian government was not just a clash of political views – it was war. And more than war, it was a cosmic confrontation – the battle of good versus evil, right against wrong, religion against anti-religion. Bhindranwale would recount the great battles of Sikh tradition, the heroic sacrifice and martyrdom of early Sikh leaders when confronted with the military force of the Mughal Empire, and by implication suggest that those legendary times were alive once more. He and his followers saw their own struggle in grand historical terms; it was a transhistorical conflict of order versus chaos. They saw themselves engaged in not just a political conflict but also a defence of the entire Sikh culture and civilisation. For these reasons they were willing to kill to defend their position. And they were willing to die for it.

The Sikh uprising in the 1980s, though violent and dramatic, was not the only time that Sikhs had been politically active in the Punjab. In the 1960s, for instance, another Sikh leader, Sant Fateh

[2] A discussion of the Sikh movement based on my interviews with Sikh activists may be found in my book (Juergensmeyer 2003, 85–102).

Singh, threatened to immolate himself in a vat of boiling oil on the roof of the Akal Takht, one of the main buildings in the precincts of the Harmandir Sahib, also known as the Golden Temple, which is the Sikhs' central shrine, located in Amritsar. Sant Fateh Singh never carried out his threat, but the demands of the moment were met. The Indian state of Punjab was carved into three states, so that in the smaller state of Punjab that remained, Sikhs were in the majority. It was a concession by the central government that was intended to solve the Sikh problem once and for all.

This turned out not to be the case. The Sikh militancy in the 1980s was in some ways a repeat of the early movement, but it was also significantly different, in at least two ways. It was more strident, more violent, and its vehemence was aimed against the secular state. The aim was not just to secure more political power for the Sikh community but to reject the secular authority of the Indian government. Hinduism as a religion was not the target, even though some Hindu leaders were seen as sympathising with the state's position, and therefore worthy of attack in the eyes of the Sikh militants. The explicit goal was to reject the legitimacy of the secular state. Though there was controversy within the movement as to what should replace it, many Sikhs who supported the movement thought that its success would lead to the creation of a new religious nation. The proposed new Sikh state was dubbed Khalistan – the land of the Sikh community, the Khalsa. Bhindranwale, the most prominent spokesperson for the movement, said that he was neither for nor against the idea of Khalistan. But he and his followers clearly wanted a new political order, one that would be based on religion.

It may seem preposterous that a religious community could claim the status of nationhood. Where could the Sikhs have gotten such a remarkable idea? The European Enlightenment model of the nation-state presumes a stance of secular detachment from religion. And yet, for the Sikhs, examples of religious nationalism were close at hand. They needed to look no further than the rise of Hindu nationalism in India and Muslim nationalism in the country that formed the western borders of Punjab – Pakistan.

The Invention of a Modern Muslim Nation

Perhaps the most momentous political event in South Asia in the twentieth century was not Independence and the withdrawal of British rule, but the political partition of the subcontinent into two rival states: India and Pakistan. Perhaps even more striking was the fact that the retreating colonial rule of Great Britain consciously participated in the creation of this new national entity based on religion, a Pakistan based on Muslim identity. This event has done more to spur the notion of religious politics – and the possibility of a religious state for Sikhs, Hindus and Buddhists in the subcontinent – than anything else in recent history. But how could the secular government of Britain have allowed such a thing?

It is not clear that partition had to happen. There had not previously been a strong groundswell of support for a Muslim-dominated state, though there were some lone voices calling for an independent Muslim state earlier in the twentieth century, notably by the poet, Muhammad Iqbal, which he expressed in the 1930 meeting of the Muslim League. But most leaders in the League desired a semi-autonomous region in a united India, and according to one historian, Ayesha Jalal (1994), Jinnah raised the issue of an independent Pakistan largely as a threat, a kind of bargaining chip to gain what he really wanted, a semi-autonomous state.[3] Jinnah's rival Muslim organisation, the Unionist Party in the Punjab, was adamantly opposed to secession. Interestingly, the most articulate voices from the religious right were also opposed to the idea of a separate Muslim state. Maulana Abul Ala Maududi, the best-known Muslim political thinker in the region, adopted a position much like that of Said Qutb in Egypt. Maududi regarded the Western concept of the nation-state to be non-Islamic and feared that a secular state, even one comprised largely of Muslims, would be antithetical to the religious community of devout Muslims. Eventually, Maududi joined Pakistan after it

[3] See also Wolpert (2006). As the title of Wolpert's book implies, Wolpert places much of the blame for the partition, and the careless drawing of boundaries between the two states on Lord Mountbatten.

was created, and helped to form a new Muslim political party, the Jamaat-e Islami, which continues today to be a voice for Muslim interests in Pakistan.

So if there was no huge demand for a separate Muslim Pakistan in the subcontinent, where did the idea come from? One might argue that it came from the Muslim political tradition over the centuries, but that is not quite true either. Although Muslim history is full of strong political leaders and caliphs who led armies and empires, there is not really a precedent for the modern idea of a religious nation-state. In fact, the idea of the nation-state – the notion that there is such a thing as a natural national community in a geographical region that supports a state apparatus which is responsible for it – is a foreign idea. Specifically, it is a European idea, and as I mentioned earlier it was the European idea of national community – and the role of religious affiliation within it – that was exported by the British to the emerging Pakistan and India and, for that matter, to much of the rest of the world.

India's Religious Politics in the Global Era

By the third decade of the twentieth century, most forms of religious politics in India were still alive. The BJP had retained its dominance in national elections and remained strong in pockets of support throughout the country. The Khalistan movement in the Punjab had been crushed, but Sikh political influence continued to dominate the electoral politics of the state. Perhaps more importantly, the rise of religious politics in India found parallels in similar movements throughout the South and Southeast Asia regions.

In recent times, Muslim political parties in Pakistan and Bangladesh have become more entrenched, and in some regions of Pakistan the extremism of Muslim political groups has led to violent confrontations and acts of terrorism. Some of these acts have also affected India. The Taliban rebounded from its defeat in the invasion of the United States coalition forces in 2001 and asserted a major role in Afghan politics. The Taliban and its affiliates, such as the extremist Haqqani network, have controlled much of the Pashtun and other tribal regions of western Pakistan.

Elsewhere in South Asia, religious politics have also emerged at the turn of the twenty-first century, often in surprising places. Though one does not often think of Buddhism as a religious culture that supports political activism and violence, strong movements of religious politics have surfaced in several of South Asia's Buddhist nations. In Sri Lanka, Buddhist monks supported movements resisting the government's concessions to Tamil Hindus and Christians in the northern portion of the country, claiming that Sri Lanka should be a Sinhalese Buddhist state. Prime Minister Bandranaike was assassinated by a Buddhist monk. After the failure of the Tamil succession movement, the ideology of Buddhist purity in Sri Lanka was behind attacks on Muslims, leading to major riots in 2014 and 2018. These attacks were led by monks associated with a Buddhist extremist group, the Bodu Bala Sena, though many Buddhist monks also denounced the assaults on Muslims and protected them and their mosques in Sri Lanka.

In the tiny Himalayan kingdom of Bhutan, the longing for a Buddhist state was realised. An almost theocratic alliance among the monarchial, monastic and elected branches of power in Bhutan led to an enormous amount of government support for Buddhist institutions and sites, and established a rigid code of behaviour that mandated that all citizens wear traditional clothing and maintain their homes in traditional styles. Non-Buddhist Nepalese Hindus were forcibly removed from Bhutan, an act of ethnic cleansing that expelled fifteen per cent of Bhutan's population. Many of these exiled ethnic Nepalese were driven into refugee camps in India and Nepal.

In other parts of South Asia, Buddhism has been an instrument of protest and revolt. In the country of Myanmar, formerly known as Burma, Buddhist monks were at the forefront of protests against the autocratic military rule. Even though the military junta was officially dissolved in 2011, the country continues to be racked with anti-Muslim violence, directed especially at the Rohingya minority who live near the border of Bangladesh. A fiery Buddhist monk, Ashin Wirathu, has been blamed for fanning the flames of ethnic hatred. He is the most well-known spokesman for the '969 Movement' – named after the nine special attributes of the Buddha, the six distinctive features of his teachings, and the nine characteristics of monks – which was formed to defend the purity of Burmese Buddhist culture against its alleged adulteration from outside influences, primarily Muslim. Hence, it is widely regarded as an anti-Islamic hate movement. The violence against the Rohingya minority, however, has been supported by the government, with some of the most vicious attacks conducted by military raids on Rohingya villages.

In Tibet, monks protesting the loss of cultural autonomy and the steady increase of Han Chinese presence in the region clashed with Chinese military. Often, despite the Dalai Lama's admonition to adopt only non-violent tactics, Tibetan Buddhist monks have been aggressors in the conflict. From the Chinese perspective, the Tibetans challenged the notion of China's sovereignty. From the Tibetan perspective, China was attempting to undercut the national cultural integrity of Tibet. A similar dynamic has been unfolding in the Xinjiang region of western China where the ethnic group of Uyghurs feel that their traditional culture and Muslim faith is under attack by the increasing attempts of the Chinese government to unify their region both culturally and economically with the rest of China. The old issue of the role of religion in defining a national community has continued to be the central issue in both of these cases.

The reason why it is valuable to look at religious politics in India within the wider context in South and Southeast Asia and around the world is to acknowledge that the Indian developments are part of a global phenomenon; they are not alone. These movements of religious politics persist, somewhat paradoxically, in the global era of the twenty-first century. It is a period in world history in which transnational forces challenge national institutions and communities, and in which the very notion of the nation-state as the prime unit of world political order is being reassessed. A critical aspect of contemporary globalisation is the de-nationalisation of demographic communities. Today everyone can live everywhere, and they often do. It is a phenomenon that affects the established societies of Europe as well as emerging nations of South Asia. For instance, in a time when a large percentage of the French population consists of non-Christians born in the Middle East and elsewhere, and an equally large number of French live abroad, the notion of a French national community has become a subject of grave concern. Everywhere the question is debated about what can be a distinctive national community in an era of globalisation.

Religion is often part of these political discussions. And it can also be a factor in the immigrant communities' responses to their situations. Often their defensiveness is expressed in a heightened sense of their own cultural awareness. In some cases the sense of alienation that immigrants experience is overcome by identifying with a struggle for a religious or ethnic nationalism back home. Paradoxically, the support for such movements can be even stronger in the diaspora than in the homeland. This was often the case with the Sikh Khalistan movement, which was monetarily supported by Sikh communities in the US and the UK, where the symbols of the movement were created. The first currency printed in the name of Khalistan, for instance, was minted in England. The BJP also received widespread support from Hindus living abroad, and I was told by Lal Krishna Advani, one of the BJP leaders, that he relied on sources of funding from expatriate Indian Hindus living in such places as Houston, Los Angeles and Washington DC. Both sides of the struggle in Sri Lanka were supported by Sri Lankans living abroad, especially in the UK, where Sinhalese Buddhists supported one side and Sri Lankan Tamils supported the other.

The global diaspora of ethnic and religious communities has also created something of a global backlash. New right-wing movements of angry Christians in the United States and Europe have targeted the Middle East Muslim community in the US and asserted the importance of a homogeneous ethnicity and religious culture in affirming their European and American national communities. In Hungary, Sweden and the Netherlands, political movements have attempted to marginalise immigrant communities and assert the primacy of traditional notions of ethnic nationalism. In some cases, this hostility has been aimed not only at the immigrant communities but also at secular governments that protect them. The European and American religious nationalists blame their own secular governments for their indifference to matters of religion, and also for their active toleration of an ideology of multiculturalism that welcomes and supports the ethnic and religious diversity of a society impacted by new immigrant communities.

Often the voices of support for such right-wing protests are strident; occasionally their political strength is substantial, and on some tragic occasions the rhetoric moves some desperate extremists to violent actions, even terrorism. In a sad case in Christchurch, New Zealand in 2019, Brenton Tarrant, an angry young Australian, attacked two mosques during Friday prayers, killing fifty-one and wounding a similar number. His manifesto indicated his admiration for Andres Breivik, the Norwegian who attacked the summer camp of a political party pledged to multiculturalism. Like Breivik, Tarrant thought that his efforts would keep European ethnic culture from Muslim control. A similar attack in the United States in 2012 was aimed at a Sikh gurdwara in the suburbs of Milwaukee, where a member of a racist anti-Christian sub-culture killed seven, including himself. The killer, Wade Michael Page, thought he was preserving a pure American culture in the face of multicultural globalism. Ironically it was Sikhs – who in the 1980s were attacking the secular state of India to create their own religiously pure homeland – who were the targets of this Christian terrorist in America who saw them as a problem in his notion of national purity.

It is understandable that religion plays a role in responding to the challenges of the global era, not only because it provides a form of symbolic empowerment to people who feel marginalised by the great impersonal transnational forces of social change, but also because it responds in very basic ways to the insecurities of the era.[4] Globalisation raises three fundamental questions: the question of *identity*, who are we as a people in the public order; the question of *accountability*, who is in charge and who can we trust; and the question of *security*, how can we be safe?

Traditional religion provides answers to all three of those questions. It provides a sense of religious identity that is often combined with national identity to shore up the notion of a national culture. It gives a sense of accountability and authority through traditional religious law and leadership that project an aura of unassailable certainty, and it offers a secure haven of religious community and divine protection that comforts in times of social and political peril. All of these factors are elements in the rise of religious politics in India, as they are elsewhere in the world.

Thus the Indian experience with religious politics – interesting in its own right – also is instructive about the rise of religious politics globally in recent decades. Secularism as an ideology has not been seen as a neutral actor, it seems, neither in South Asia nor in other parts of the world where religious politics have often emerged as a response to what is perceived to be attempts to remove traditional aspects of religious culture from the public sphere. Hence, the rise of religious politics in India tells us much about this particular moment of late modernity, where it may well be not so much a passing fancy as a bellwether of new postmodern and postsecular identities and new forms of imagined transnational publics in a shifting global order.

References

Asad, Talal. 2003. *Formations of the Secular: Christianity, Islam, Modernity*. Stanford: Stanford University Press.

Bhindranwale, Jarnail Singh. 1983. "Two Lectures on July 19, 1983 and September 20, 1983." Translated by Ranbir Singh Sandhu. Dublin; Ohio: Distributed by the Sikh Religious and Educational Trust.

Calhoun, Craig et al., eds.. 2011. *Rethinking Secularism*. Oxford: Oxford University Press.

---

[4] I explore these issues further in my book (Jurgensmeyer 2008).

Graham, Bruce Desmond. 2007. *Hindu Nationalism and Indian Politics: The Origins and Development of the Bharatiya Jana Sangh*. Cambridge: Cambridge University Press.

Jalal, Ayesha. 1994. *The Sole Spokesman: Jinnah, the Muslim League and the Demand for Pakistan*. Cambridge: Cambridge University Press.

Juergensmeyer, Mark. 2004. *Terror in the Mind of God: The Global Rise of Religious Violence*. California: University of California Press.

———. 2007. "Gandhi vs. Terrorism." *Daedalus* 136, no. 1: 30–39. https://doi.org/10.1162/daed.2007.136.1.30. Accessed on 07 April 2025.

———. 2008. *Global Rebellion: Religious Challenges to the Secular State, from Christian Militias to al Qaeda*. California: University of California Press.

Lie, John. 2004. *Modern Peoplehood*. Harvard: Harvard University Press.

Mufti, Aamir R. 2009. *Enlightenment in the Colony: The Jewish Question and the Crisis of Postcolonial Culture*. Princeton: Princeton University Press.

Taylor, Charles. 2007. *A Secular Age*. Harvard: Harvard University Press.

Wolpert, Stanley. 2006. *Shameful Flight: The Last Years of the British Empire in India*. Oxford: Oxford University Press.

TWO

Historicising Indigeneity in Northeastern India

SANGHAMITRA MISRA

The chapter argues that the politics of indigeneity in contemporary northeastern India that spawns from an essentialisation of culture and a fetishisation of communities as authentic and timeless, does so by imposing a moratorium on the historicisation of custom under colonialism. By encouraging communities to be amnesic about the effects of British imperialism in the region, the concept of indigeneity isolates them within typological silos, silencing their long histories of connections with contiguous non-indigenous people. Countering this, the chapter seeks to historicise the categories of customary law, traditional/indigenous authority and the hill tribe as dimensions of the processes of state ethnogenesis under colonialism. It will contextualise the discourse on the tribe and indigeneity within the history of imperial conquest and discern the intractable foundations of these concepts in the structure and processes of colonial political economy.

In a wide swathe of scholarship that includes anthropologists, sociologists and historians (De Maaker 2022; Karlsson 2011; Wouters 2022), the discourse around indigeneity, customary rights of possession and (emerging) claims to political autonomy in northeastern India has been traced to the postcolonial protectionist legislation for tribes. The historicising of custom in this scholarship has, therefore, meant a fixing of the originary moment of the codification of customary law in the Constitution-making process of the postcolonial state. As the politics of ethnic homelands emerges as the new 'political' in northeastern India, consolidating ideals of ethnic purity (Pachuau 2014) as well of ethnic majoritarianism as ethnocracies (Haokip 2022), these ideas too have sought legitimacy in the provisions of the Indian Constitution. Thus, ethnopolitics, embedded in a reification of majoritarian culture now tends to mediate issues not only of citizenship and political rights in the region but of the politics of separatism and secession as well.

The point here is not to erode the significance of the Constitutional moment but to foreground the very significant erasure of the processes of codification of custom among various communities under the colonial state in extant scholarship on the politics of ethnicity and indigeneity. By laying limits on the historicity of custom and the determining role of the colonial state, this selective historical amnesia of scholars has obfuscated more than two centuries of colonial violence and exceptional laws which invented and reinvented custom and customary authority in the interests of profit maximisation for the British Empire. These laws included various Acts passed under the late colonial state, but most specifically the Government of India Act, 1935.[1] Under Chapter V of the Act, certain tracts with predominantly tribal populations were categorised as Excluded and Partially Excluded areas; these areas were to be under the direct rule of the Governor General in Council, or the Governor of a Province (usually a British ICS officer). Under Section 92 of the Act it was decreed that no Act of the federal or the provincial legislature applied to the excluded or to a partially excluded area unless notified by the Governor. This manner of preserving the autonomy of tribes in turn has acquired a long postcolonial afterlife in the form of the Sixth Schedule of the Indian Constitution. Much like the structure of authority in the 1935 Act, the Sixth Schedule recognises the 'traditional authority' of communities (the position and authority

[1] These laws would include the Scheduled Districts Act of 1874 and the Criminal Tribes Acts of 1876, 1911, and 1924 (Chandra 2013). For historical work on these laws and their constitutive role in defining the 'tribe' in India, see Prasad (2011); Singha (1998) and Radhakrishna (2001).

of the village headman, the village council, and the district and regional council) only to limit them through the powers vested in the figure of the Union government-appointed Governor[2] or the government of the state concerned. As scholars have pointed out, this provision effectively negated the Schedule's recognition of rights of the community over land and jurisdiction as traditional and ancient.[3]

Reiterating colonial continuities, the protective Schedules of the Indian Constitution in northeastern India assumed a new dimension such that the Sixth Schedule was initially limited to the hilly areas alone (Baruah 2008, 15–19). This was because the colonial legal history of segregation of the hills and the plain which regularly trotted out exceptional laws such as the Inner Line (Kar 2009; Ludden 2019) to mark a difference between the wider territorial possessions of the British state and the actual jurisdictional limits, had constituted the surrounding hills into a zone of separate political control. The representation of communities classified as 'hill tribes' as people with little or no racial, linguistic, or historical affinity with the inhabitants of the plains thus segued into a legal distinction between communities marked by customary law and those in the plains that were seen as being governed by regular law.

As will be elaborated in the second section of the chapter, this history of colonial laws of exception and classificatory regimes remained deeply imbricated in the history of the military violence of the colonial state. Throughout the period of colonisation from the last quarter of the eighteenth century until the closing decades of the nineteenth century (and particularly in the region of the

---

[2] The decision to include, exclude any area from the provisions of the Schedule or create, increase, diminish and alter the name or boundaries of an autonomous district within the Excluded or Partially Excluded Areas Act was that of the Governor's prerogative. (Sixth Schedule [Articles 244(2) and 275(1)]: https://www.mea.gov.in/Images/pdf1/S6.pdf. Accessed on 27 April 2025)

[3] See Barbora (2002, 1285–1292) for an illustration of the same in the context of land rights and administration of justice in the North Cachar Hills of Assam.

Garo Hills) the colonial legal and fiscal order continued to be driven by the force of military law, manifested in the innumerable instances of burning of villages, standing crops, trade blockades and other brutalities. The project of colonial knowledge, including that of Anthropology, remained welded to imperial ambition as a strategy of conquest throughout the history of colonisation, illustrative of which are the several moments when colonial officials set aside time from military expeditions for revenue extraction and to compose their ethnological treatises on the colonised.[4] While there is incontestable and compelling evidence from various parts of northeastern India throughout the history of colonisation, the chapter will draw upon the specific history of the Garo Hills to uncover the ways in which the colonial state's creation of a body of anthropological knowledge about a hill tribe came to be enmeshed with its history of military conquest and resource extraction, from its first recorded moment in 1794 (Eliot 1794) to subsequent imprints in the mid- and late-nineteenth century (Dalton 1872; Hunter 1879; Mackenzie 1884; Carey 1910; Playfair 1909).

The erasure by recent scholarship on 'custom', of this history of military conquest, exceptional laws, primitivisation and ethnogenesis engendered by British paramountcy (De Maaker 2023; Debbarma 2023) or their dismissive sequestering to a brief preview in the postcolonial history of ethnic politics as constructionist theories (Wouters 2022) must therefore be critically interrogated. For, the amnesia in this scholarship about British economic imperialism and its postcolonial footprints in northeast India's identitarian movements has produced decidedly ahistorical understandings of custom that decouple it from the material conditions of its production, reifying it thereby and endorsing the rhetorical use of 'culture' as 'race' by identitarian movements. Equally importantly, such an expungement extends

[4] See for example, among many other, the careers of Captain Reynolds, Edward Tuite Dalton, W.W. Hunter, Alexander Mackenzie and H. Godwin Austen as learned ethnologists and successful military officers of the East India Company and the Crown.

to that of the protracted resistance to colonialism by communities primitivised under colonial modernity; it is an expungement too of the forging of ethnic identities on the anvil of such resistance. What is presented in this scholarship instead is an anachronistic fusing together of the colonial and precolonial period into a timeless block of 'tribal pasts', transmitted through orality: 'Historically, customary law has in a non-codified form been orally conveyed within given ethnic communities. Whenever conflicts arose that needed to be resolved, people who claimed authority, often elderly men, would state the principles or rules which, according to them, would apply in the given situation' (De Maaker 2023, 104). And since indigeneity perforce must be encased within genealogies of cultural representations that eschew 'economistic' readings, its proponents have produced distorted pictures of the colonial past of communities, truncating the narrative of their economic ties with, and political control over, the plains. Precedence has been given instead to cultural affinities with communities far apart in time and space that are also Western archetypes of the indigenous, such as the Native Americans. For the historian of the British Empire in India on the other hand, such apparent similitudes are reminiscent of the continuity of powerful colonial stereotypes and typologies. This chapter pursues these arguments and counters the constituted difference between the idea of the tribe and indigeneity in recent scholarship, demonstrating instead that the rhetoric of the quintessential primitive (tribe) of classical anthropological and colonial discourse is in fact deeply embedded within the discourse on indigeneity in contemporary northeastern India. This it establishes by identifying some key moments in state ethnogenesis recovered from a reading of the eighteenth and nineteenth century archive on the British conquest of the Garo Hills.

The Politics of Custom and Legal Primitivism

To understand the constitution of the ideas of legal primitivism – requisite for the invention of custom (and later, indigeneity) in the hilly parts of northeastern India – it is necessary to explore the relationship between law, colonial rule as military force, and the rule of property. The Garo Hills between circa 1770 and 1830 provide among the earliest examples in colonial India of the imbrications of the invention of customary law and traditional authority in the Company's revenue demands, shielded and secured by the deployment of military power across the hills. This historical moment was anchored in the beginnings of the East India Company's conquest of the Garo Hills, in the appropriation of the land and revenue of the Garos, and in the ethnogenesis of the 'hill' Garo. Over the course of the nineteenth century, the strategies of imperial control introduced in the region were reproduced across the rest of northeastern India, underscoring the significance of the Garo Hills as the first laboratory of colonial rule in the region as well as sharpening our understanding of the character of the early colonial state.[5]

As extant scholarship illustrates the creation of a new spatial order by the East India Company over the course of the nineteenth century, that classified communities as either of the hills or the plains and fixed them thus in their 'natural' habitats, it did so by interrupting, reorienting and frequently obliterating precolonial connected histories of trade and cultural flows between the plains of Bengal and Assam, the hills above, but also with southeast Asia, Bhutan, Nepal, and these regions (van Schendel and Abraham 2005; Misra 2011; Kar 2009; Ludden 2017, 75–100). The Garos, an agriculturist and trading people with a long history of growing and trading in cotton in eastern India, had political claims over the territory and resources of parts of the Assam and Bengal plains in the pre- and early-colonial period. They are identified by East India Company officials in the post-Buxar years as amongst the earliest groups of people; the 'first among the Assam tribes' that

[5] For the ease of reading, the chapter will assume the sensitivity of its readers and not use quotes to emphasise the constructed nature of the category of the tribe after this first use.

they encountered.[6] In the early decades of the nineteenth century, the Company's aggressive monopolisation of the cotton trade had irrevocably transformed the precolonial connected histories of political economy in this part of eastern India and etched lines of political difference that separated the inhabitants of the hills from those of the plains. From the settled agrarian that were the plough-cultivating plains of Mymensingh and Assam was drawn a line – temporal, civilisational, jurisdictional and economic – beyond which and upwards, the hills receded into zones of primitivity and resistance against British rule (Misra 2021).

The reinvention of custom within a discourse of paternalism was a significant element in the scheme of conquest of this newly constructed community of primitivised 'hill Garos', fixed now in an altered political ecology. Seeking typologies of rule that would allow for similar modes of administration across conquered territories in the subcontinent, officials found affinities between the geography of the hills of Bhagalpur and those inhabited by the Garos. In Bhagalpur, Augustus Cleveland's plan of raising military hill corps succeeded in enforcing the Company's conquest of the Paharias (and the Mundas, Santhals, Bhumij and Kols) by strategically sequestering these recalcitrant communities from the 'civilisation' of the plains below. The new systems of military patronage that it introduced employed recalcitrant chiefs of these communities as recruiting agents for the Company, segregated a precolonial-connected political economy of the hills and plains, and erased all extant spheres of indigenous jurisdiction (Alavi 1995, 154–193).

When Cleveland's ideas (or the Bhagalpur Plan as we will term it for the purposes of this chapter) made its appearance in the Garo Hills in 1788, it represented itself as a policy of conquest and civilisation through a preservation of the legal primitivism of the Garo people. In the journals, reports and correspondence of John Elliot, the first official of the East India Company to visit

---

6 For a discussion of Garo sovereignty pivoted around a political economy of hill cotton, see Misra (2018).

the Garo Hills where the Bhagalpur plan first appears, the hills are circumscribed as zones of relative isolation with archaic practices preserved in time. Casting the Garos within the larger typology of the primitive hill tribe, Eliot is effusive about invoking the Cleveland plan as the veritable trope of conquest (Eliot 1794, 383). Eliot's ideas were part of widely circulating conventions in the late eighteenth century – ways of communicating, directly, of the enduring links between landscapes and law: Bhagalpur and the Garo Hills, but also Bhagalpur and the Khasi Hills, and Bhagalpur and the Chittagong Hills. Towards the south of the Garo Hills in eastern India, where the Khasi Hills met the plains of Sylhet, the earliest rules under the colonial state for fixing ethnic groups in their 'natural habitats' had already been laid out by Lord Cornwallis for the rebellious Khasi inhabitants of the hills (Ludden 2003).

That Cleveland's plan would prove to be an imperfect analogy for the Garo Hills was however immediately evident to colonial officials: Cleveland had centred the regulatory powers of his plan around the erstwhile *majhis* of the Bhagalpur Hills. The Garos, officials would soon discover, did not have leaders who held such positions of command through laws of primogeniture. In the first official report on the Garos in which David Scott[7] introduces them as an 'independent nation of agriculturists', the community fits the description of Sahlin's original affluent societies (Sahlins 1972): 'a general diffusion of wealth amongst this people greatly exceeding what is to be found amongst our own subjects and which seems to evince that imperfect as the political and juridical institutions of the Garrows may be, they appear to be capable of affording no inconsiderable degree of practical security both to persons and to property'.[8] As a community long sedentarised, they are described as a people who produced surplus and traded in a wide range of much-desired products with the lowlands. Despite

---

[7] David Scott was the Judge and Magistrate of the District of Rungpore in 1812 and was appointed the first Commissioner of Assam (of which the Garo Hills formed a part of during this period) in 1822.

[8] Extract Bengal Judicial Consultations: 27th September 1816, Board's Collection 1818–1820/APAC.

the evident prosperity of the community and its accompanying stratification, the condition for the accumulation of wealth by chiefs and hence of despotism were offset, according to Scott, by a specific law of inheritance that allowed 'the daughters to inherit the whole of her parent's property'.[9] To this law Scott attributed the democratic principles of governance extant in Garo society, for it 'had the effect of greatly weakening the personal influence of the chiefs of clans and had greatly counteracted the natural tendency of the government in such a society to assume first the patriarchal and finally the despotic form'.[10] Scott then comments at length on the absence of any structured polity among the Garos and of acknowledged chiefs as well as the strident independence of the clan members.

These egalitarian norms were visible too in the institution of the Council or the Assembly, the *Jingma Chongga*.[11] Their practical ways of assembling together in a manner that reflected ideas of community and group sovereignty had been the subject of study in colonial official and ethnographic writings from the years of initial contact. In these writings, the Garos appear as a people organised around notions of group sovereignty, which while being inscribed in territory were not always territorially fixed. They appear as a people with a place of politics, a demonstrated will to assemble, conferring upon themselves the authority to rule upon what is just and what is unjust (Detienne and Lloyd 2007, 110). Acephalous societies, such as that of the Garos, appear to have practised a fairly egalitarian distribution of wealth, of land, income and booty; a mutual recognition of forms of sameness contributed to the creation of the idea of a community. 'Among such "similars" there emerges some kind of sovereignty that is held by an assembly committed to egalitarianism' (ibid., 118). There is an analogous recognition of 'sameness' and equality among the

[9] Ibid.

[10] Ibid.

[11] The Buchanan Hamilton Manuscripts, Appendix concerning the nations bordering in the Rongopur District, Mss Eur D 76, APAC.

Garos that is apparent in the distribution of land and food, in their mode of settling payments, and in their judicial deliberations.

Every head of family had an equal right to sit in the assemblies which included the women of the village. The council deliberated together to seek reconciliation, and in rare cases, death. Buchanan Hamilton's notes of a few decades later tell us that this council or assembly followed a calendar, was held at regular intervals, and had a fixed venue at the village centre or in the marketplace. The representation of space was a reflection of political thought and a deliberate marking such as this of a place and time is important for it acknowledges the place of politics in a community's life. An impressive oath-taking ceremony acknowledged the gods present, as also the collective solidarity of the Garo people and pledged the community to action – a declaration of war, an imposition of a fine, or death for the crime of adultery, murder and robbery. Such a society refuses authoritarian powers and their interventions, as the Garos clearly did when they refused Eliot's persuasions to change their mode of punishment (Eliot 1794, 393). Augmenting this portrait of a primitive sovereignty were several official observations about the legal primitivism of the Garos: the presence of democratic principles and the absence of evident privilege or extraordinary concentrations of political power in either the chief or the Lushker. Garo assemblies proclaimed this sameness and equality while exhibiting a singular lack of any centralised power in its exercise of justice, all the while preserving the individuality of each member with his clan.[12]

The subsequent colonial invention of chiefs was therefore closely anchored in the ideas of legal primitivism and their 'preservation' of the polities of 'hill Garos'. A set of regulations introduced in 1819 had officially sequestered the Garos in the Garo Hills and identified them as hill tribes;[13] as if to confirm

---

[12] A careful analogy can be drawn here with the Bhils in the eighteenth century. See Skaria (1997).

[13] Letter from Hastings, I Adams, John Findall, to the Honourable Court of Directors for the Affairs of the East India Company, 8th February 1822, BC/APAC 1825–1826.

the place of this the Garos within the new typology of hill tribes, the phrase 'Garos and other hill tribes' occurs with remarkable frequency across the document.[14] The newness of this category is tangible in several other documents from the archive as well, all of which confirm the idea that in multilingual areas such as these, ethnic identities would otherwise have been more of a political choice than a genealogical given. Legal primitivism was the ideological cloak that transformed these undependable categories into impervious, ahistorical ones within colonial discourse. David Scott's tour in the Garo Hills during the winter months of 1817 left the imperious imprint of colonialism behind in a new classificatory order for the Garos.[15] The tour report makes visible the affinities between forms of imperial knowledge – which in this case were geographic and ethnographic – and the politics of colonial law.[16]

If their production and trade in cotton rendered the Garos legible in imperial eyes as non-primitives, the permeable character of their identities could appear pernicious to a state which was seeking to regulate this profitable cotton trade spread across northeastern India and Bengal. Under Company rule the trail of ethnogenesis, therefore, radiates in different directions in the hills, bringing within its panopticon the Koches, the Meches and the Rabha communities, inhabiting and cultivating the hills east of the Brahmaputra to the same tribunal as the Garos. In each of these instances, the specificities of cultural and economic practices were reconfigured as primordial differences between the civilised, Hindu plains and the primitive, animistic hills.[17] Legal primitivism, therefore, has to be seen for the ideological shimmer that it was; for the 'tribes as state effect' phenomenon that it enabled.[18] The

14 The Resolutions of the Governor General in Council, 1819, BC/APAC (henceforth Resolutions 1819 BC/APAC)

15 Scott's Report of 1816, BC/APAC.

16 Ibid.

17 Ibid.

18 For works which critique the category of the 'hill tribe'/tribe and show it as state effect through rich historical and anthropological research on their economic systems, see Leach (1954), George (1991), Junker (1999), and Rosaldo (1980).

land between the lowlands, traversed easily in times of trade, was now represented as furrowed through with ethnic and temporal divides that were impossible to overcome.

The search for a legal system suitable for the hills was paired with critiques of the elaborate legal structures of the Bengal plains. Primitivism, emphasising the cultural and legal backwardness of the inhabitants of the Garo Hills and their difficulty in accessing justice, (following here Bentham's ideal that no inhabitant should be farther from the court than a day's return journey on foot) (Stokes 1959, 71) underpinned such divides. The proposition for suspension of the laws of the plains was accompanied by that for a separate legal idiom for the Garo Hills, to be designed to subdue a recalcitrant hill population. The legal system proposed in place of the 'alien' laws of the Bengal Presidency was to have its origins in 'local' ideas of hierarchy and justice to ensure its accessibility as well as an immediate dispensation of justice.[19] Among the early instructions to Scott from the Governor General's office are those that dwell on an 'endeavour to establish a personal intercourse with individuals who are understood to possess particular insight to influence in their respective tribes, to cultivate their confidence and to induce them to discuss without reserve their wishes or alleged grievances'.[20] These individuals were meant to constitute that necessary discernible authority which paternalists argued would protect locals from central power while submitting them to a single, undivided source of power in the form of a British officer.[21]

The figure of the designated 'chief' with its many nomenclatures of the *nokma/lushker/sirdar/subarkar* makes its appearance in this context. Contrary to these claims of the colonial state, the invented chief of the Garos was not a residue of the precolonial

[19] David Scott to W.B. Bayly, the Chief Secretary to the Government, enclosing the Report on the Garo Hills of 27 September 1819, IOR / F/ 4/ 819/ 21861, Asia, Pacific and Africa Collection (APAC), British Library, London.

[20] W.B. Bayly, Acting Secretary to the Government, to Maxwell, Joint Magistrate, Rungpore, 25th April, 1815, Bengal Judicial Criminal, APAC.

[21] Extra Judicial Letter to Bengal, dated 13 October 1820, IOR/ F/ 4/ 819/ 21861, APAC.

Garo political order, and was certainly not the holdover it was being represented as in the official archive. The invention of 'chiefs' in fact represented a formalisation of the strategies of tribute collection across the lands of the 'tributary' Garos.[22] All persons of significance in the community were subsumed within the apparatus of the revenue-collecting state as tribute collectors.[23] The manner of appointing the chief, with the 'general consent of the community and hereditary' did not confirm their precolonial antecedents. Instead, as appointed salaried officials of the Company, chiefs were dispossessed of any claims to traditional legitimacy that they might have otherwise had.

The affinities between this newly constructed figure of the chief and the codification of a similarly invented customary law through a manipulation of indigenous institutions and traditions in the interests of the state is of course as old as the idea of colonialism itself (Colson 1971). Of the indigenous institutions of the Garos, the assembly as jury was among the first to be impaired in this process of codification. Obliterating its democratic essence, a fixed number of Garo *sirdar*s were now appointed by the East India Company on the basis of their 'character, general behaviour and local influence'[24] to act as assessors or jury for civil and minor criminal offences.[25] The seasonal *haat*s, the erstwhile sites of a thriving commerce but also of the authority and patrimony of regional powers such as the Garos and the lowland zamindars, were now spaces for the administration of revenue for the colonial state. Reinvented assemblies of Garo *sirdar*s convened twice a year at all *haat*s of significance across the hill passes enforced the revenue claims of the state from land and the cotton trade, and recommended penal action against tributary Garos for the non-payment of their arrears of revenue/*nuzrenah*. As in other parts of the colonised

22 For a counter perspective that sees the introduction of non-regulated administration and customary rights by the colonial state as a response to tribal resistance and a protection of their autonomy, see Damodaran (2006).

23 Resolutions 1819 BC/APAC.

24 Letter from the Secretary to David Scott, the Joint Magistrate of Rungpore, dated 9th September, 1817, Board's Collection 1818-1820, APAC.

25 Scott's Report of 1818, BC/APAC.

world, reinvention was nested in a semiotic apparatus in which gifts of dresses were now markers of subjecthood, rewarded by the Commissioner for 'obedience to the orders of the state' including the orderly and timely payment of revenue at annual assemblies, and budgeted under heads of state expenditure.[26]

As state-appointed customary authorities, colonial chiefs in the Garo Hills represented a transient and fragile consolidation of judicial and executive authority, pegged onto the larger order of European political domination. Theirs was a tenuous consolidation of power, their authority a mere phantasm of the figure of the Commissioner which combined within itself the authorities of Judge and Revenue Collector, in direct opposition to the regulations of the Permanent Settlement in the Bengal plains below.[27] Scaffolded onto the Cleveland model, British officials in the Garo Hills presumed that these consolidated authoritarian powers of the chief would enable them to control the territories of the tributary Garos as well as secure the conquest of the Bengal lowlands; what was achieved was an irreversible spatial and temporal divide between the plains and the hills that wrenched the Garo Hills from its precolonial connections with the plains around, in the process savaging the Bemulwa Garos as 'primitive raiders' of civilisation.

Historians of colonial law have read in processes such as the above, situations of 'layered sovereignty' in the hills under imperial rule and a recognition of the legal autonomy of semi-sovereign hill polities on the part of the Company (Benton 2009). Such

---

[26] Copy of a letter from David Scott, the Magistrate of Rangpur to W.B. Bayly, the Chief Secretary to the Government, 20 January 1821, IOR/ F/ 4/ 819/ 21861, APAC.

[27] According to Rule 5 of the Regulations of 1819, the Commissioner was also the collector of land revenue from the 'hill tribes' and of *sair* duties 'at the markets frequented by the Garos' (Resolutions 1819 BC/APAC). The stripping of the Collector of his judicial power and the abolishing of the revenue courts previously under his authority, was Cornwallis' acknowledgement of the need to situate the rule of property within the rule of law.

readings obscure the transfiguration and eventual annihilation by the colonial state of all traces of group sovereignty that the precolonial tribunals such as those of the Garos preserved. In the case of the Garos, this process was reflected in the subjugation of their now reinvented assembly to the British Commissioner, a position that combined within itself the powers of judicature, police and revenue,[28] mirroring the paternalists' commitment to the undivided, authoritarian, personalised rule of a despot (Hussain 2003, 58). The 1819 Regulations made the decisions of the *sirdar*s/*lushker*s in the jury on civil disputes conditional to approval from the Commissioner.[29] All acts designated as 'heinous crimes' by the colonial state, that involved an usurpation of the sovereign's right to life and property, were to be adjudicated by him[30] with the aid of a few Garo *sirdar*s appointed by him to the newly fabricated 'traditional' assemblies.[31]

Custom, therefore, was determined by the state, and this conformed to conceptions of state law and custom in eighteenth-century English jurisprudence and practice. 'In fact according to eighteenth-century jurisprudence, custom itself had to be reasonable, that is 'of artificial and legal reason, warranted by the authority of law…(i)t is within this orientation that customs of the subcontinent were treated; they were legitimized only by competent authority; an authority ultimately derived from the King' (Govind 2017, 4). And hence the repeated prohibition, from the first oaths at Tikri Duar, of the custom of keeping skulls or of wearing brass girdles ('permitted to such persons only as have killed a man') both signs of sovereign powers over life and death, which the King or the Company as his delegated authority alone could possess.[32] As with the sword, another symbol of the right to

---

28 Resolutions 1819 BC/APAC.

29 Clause 11 of the Resolutions of the Governor General in Council 1819 (Resolutions 1819 BC/APAC).

30 Resolutions 1819 BC/APAC

31 Scott's Report of 1818, BC/APAC

32 See Scott's Report of 1816, BC/APAC.

take life, which they had to relinquish before entering the *haats*,[33] brass plates upon girdles and enemy skulls hung outside houses were but empty signs of sovereignty of a conquered people, by the mere possession of which by tributary and independent Garos committed a transgression of the King's sovereignty. By placing prohibitions on their custom of keeping skulls, the Company had subjected them to an all-expansive juridical notion of sovereignty that would 'compel' them to relinquish their right to make war or award death as (now erstwhile) sovereigns. Conquest as a recognised source of political authority would lean on the regulation of custom.[34]

A clause appended to the Regulation X of 1822 invoked the threat of military violence to end the custom of keeping human skulls and its associative practice of raiding among all Garos;[35] as the following years would prove, at no point in the elaborate discourse on legal primitivism did Scott or his contemporaries preclude the possibility of violently conquering the Tributary and the Independent Garos. The principles of paternalism, instead, would segue quite neatly into those of despotism and military rule[36] in the Garo Hills over the succeeding decades.

On Conquest and Anthropological Knowledge

Throughout this history of the colonisation of this part of eastern/northeastern India, the discourse of Anthropology remained integrated into the assemblage of imperial conquest, firmly

---

[33] Agreement executed by the Garo Chiefs/Sirdars of Tikriduar on 5 March 1817 in the presence of David Scott, Joint Magistrate, Rungpore, Bengal Judicial Criminal, 28 December 1821, No. 88, APAC.

[34] Letter from David Scott, Joint Magistrate, Rungpore, to H.J. Princep, Officiating Secretary to the Government of India, Fort William, 23 October 1822, Extract: Bengal Judicial Consultations: 26 February 1822.

[35] Ibid.

[36] 'The paternalists' insistence on the applicability of despotism to the Indian social environment meant that such nostalgia could be expressed in a principled form…through the call for and promulgation of emergency regulations' (Hussain 1999, 61).

establishing associations between the 'wildness' of the 'primitive hill Garo' and his violent resistance to the colonial state. Obliterating the figure of the Garo peasant and trader in the colonial archive and substituting it with the figure of an isolated, 'savage' hill tribe, John Eliot's academic essays inaugurated processes of state ethnogenesis and the emergence of the 'tribe' as a legal category in the Garo Hills, and by extension, in the rest of colonial northeastern India. After Eliot, colonial official ethnographers such as Edward Dalton, W.W. Hunter, Alexander Mackenzie, Godwin-Austen and A.J. Playfair propounded a spatial ideology that fixed ethnicity to territorial spaces, distinguishing between valleys as civilisational spaces and hills as the 'natural habitats' of the primitive or as backward tracts. The ethnic stereotypes that they created distinguished too between 'pure and impure types': to account for those that strayed away from the assigned physical spaces, that is living in the hills instead of the plains or vice versa, or living in the 'wrong' hills.

The Garo Hills of the late eighteenth and early nineteenth centuries appear in these writings as a politically obscure, unfamiliar space, large parts of it belonging to an indiscernible order of Garo tribes, other parts under the uncertain control of token-tribute paying 'frontier' zamindars. Such a reconstruction insists that most of this space is uncultivated, or at best infrequently cultivated. The dense subtropical forests, deep gorges, crevices and waterfalls of the Garo Hills constitute a wild, dark and unexplored landscape, a terrain that finds an appropriate mimetic world in its inhabitants – in the unpredictable but certain prevalence of brutish political force, in the gloominess of tropical forest groves, and in the frequent allusions to dangers of association with the hidden people – the as-yet-unconquered, fierce tribe of independent Garos (Godwin-Austen 1873, 22). Here 'hordes of savages' sweep down from the surrounding hills in violent raids onto the peaceable communities of the plains to carry away heads and poultry in plunder. The violence of the Garo is represented as an endemic one in the mid- and late-nineteenth-century colonial archive, marked as it is by an insistence that the Garo is one whose primitive being is determined by war. In the hazy multitude of eager officious voices from the period, the incessant raids of the Garos on the plains of Bengal and Assam are seen as confirming the natural inclination of these societies towards violence.

Anthropology inaugurates thus an intellectual genealogy of the primitivisation of the Garos that will persist into modern historiography. Modern histories of the Garos, invoking the same colonial archive as authority, alternate between finding an intelligible form of indigenous rationality in headhunting and relegating it to the realm of a ritualised practice that perpetuated more ritual violence in the form of endless feuds between clans (Bhattacharjee 1978, 6); with a few exceptions, these histories continue to reproduce colonial inventories of raids as 'primitive violence'.[37] In a significant section of this historiography the nearly century-long extraordinary resistance of the Garos to the loss of their sovereignty under colonial rule (Misra 2021) has been reduced to 'desultory feuds with the English', their politics of deliberate violence diminished to 'retaliatory raids' (Bhattacharjee 1978, 89). While the Khasis bear the epithet of a proud, freedom-loving people, their resistance accorded the stature of 'wars' and battles, the Garos have been unable to seize such sobriquets from history.

Culture was never seen as discrete from the habitat it was found in, in these writings; it was inevitable then that references to the Garo Hills served as easily transferred tropes for a discourse that associated hilly areas with primitive violence and primitive sovereignty. In his text *The Garos*, A.J. Playfair 'fixes' his subject of study in the hills, setting it apart as a discrete category from the civilisational space of the valleys below.[38] The Garos in his

---

[37] 'The whole brunt of tribal ferocity fell upon the inhabitants of the tracts lying between the foot of the hills and the extremities of the plains' (Bhuyan 1949, 33).

[38] 'They are a people who are little known to the outside world, and, though living in the midst of a civilized province, have remained free from foreign influence in a remarkable degree. This is due partly to the supposed unhealthiness and inaccessibility of their hills, and partly to their natural conservatism' (Playfair 1909, Preface). Playfair's observations on Garo society

text are divided into the categories of the Plains Garos and the Hill Garos (Playfair 1909, 4), a difference that the more illustrious contemporaries of Playfair such as Endle, Dalton and Sachse will echo. Between them, they mark out the Garo as an isolated people, conjuring up a primitiveness so extreme that it becomes a prelude to a narrative about their autochthonous existence in the hills. In the policies of the colonial state, there were other, more concrete mirrorings of this embedding of ethnicity in nature. A proposal to hold an Ethnological Congress in Calcutta in 1869–1870 – eventually abandoned because of the Commissioner of Assam's apprehensions of 'political complications' in the event of the death of some of the specimen hill tribes – had the following entry from Edward Dalton on the Garos carefully distinguishing between the 'pure, hill Garo', and the 'impure types': 'It is the uncivilized, uncoverted Garo that I wish to describe, not the Hinduized animal of the name, and they merit a careful notice, as they are the primitive type of the great Mech Kachari or Bodo nation and have a variety of customs that are singular and interesting' (Dalton 1872, 58).

The propensity for violence is attributed partially to the presumed ancient practices of the community, the most striking among which was headhunting, inspiring many dark passages on the texture of Garo violence. The Garos were possibly among the earliest communities in India who received the appellation of 'headhunters' from the British, there being references to the practice from the second decade of the nineteenth century onwards.[39] Ethnography, doubling up as official chronicle, displayed its quotidian ways of anthropologising the Garos: cultural categories and practices of Garo society, including raiding and headhunting, surface in Dalton and Hunter as predetermined

continue to be summoned uncritically by anthropologists/ethnographers and historians and is received as historical evidence that determine lines of enquiry in contemporary historical research.

39 Magistrate of Mymensingh, W.W. Massie, to G. Dowdeswell, Secretary to the Government in the Judicial Department, Fort William, 29 April 1811, BJC/APAC.

and ahistorical, existing within a structurally reproducing cultural order. Texts teem with references to headhunting and human sacrifices among the Garos, returning a timeless Garo to nature; the introduction to Endle's *Kacharis* mention the Garos only in the context of their apparent 'addiction' to the practice of headhunting. Analogies with the practices of American Indians with whom the Garos were compared only reiterated typologies of the wild and primitive and a proclivity for violence shared with the first primitive (Watson 1832, 48).

Hypnotised by the grotesque, British officials were inclined to fetishise headhunting as a product of primitive thought and depravity, negating possibilities of recognising the social and political dimensions of ritual violence. The recounting of tales of raiding from the early years of British rule lend a certain spatial coherence to the newly conquered territories of the Garo Hills. The spatial order of the Garos now emerges as one that is seen only from Sylhet in the south, Rangpur in the west, Goalpara in the northwest, and Mymensingh in the south. With Bengal, its people and its river valleys as the steady 'other' of the Garos, defining and accentuating the primitiveness of their being, the political and social order of the Garo Hills comes to be constituted by the plains around the hills. Echoing mid- and late-nineteenth-century ethnographies in other parts of India, several anachronistic retellings and recoveries of Garo 'origin myths' in these colonial ethnographies accentuated the primitiveness of the 'hill Garo' and explained their contemporary wildness. These recovered myths recast the Garos as a 'hill tribe', often through the construction of fictive genealogies of Garo chiefs and clans, while their layered qualities were consciously calibrated to generate an image of the hapless hill tribe pursued by superior plainsmen (Hunter 1879, 173). The incessant generation of colonial myths with their ahistorical image of the Garo in flight from the Brahmaputra and Bengal plains occluded the story of the very real subjugation and exploitation of the Garos by their European masters, seeking to veil the true imperial intent of these myths.

By primitivising the Garos thus, anthropology completed the process of their isolation as an Other, and justified their final violent conquest and formal annexation into the British Empire in 1869. By the middle of the nineteenth century, the image of the recalcitrant, valley-raiding, hill Garo is dyed into colonial knowledge and official policy, and is the redoubtable rationale for colonial intervention. The narrative of the incessant raids of a wild hill tribe with a propensity for conflict now comes to rest at the site of immanent conquest: the representation of the Garo raids discussed above becomes analogous with the question of the conquest of the Garo Hills, the legitimacy for which was to be found in the frequent references to the attacks on British subjects (Playfair 1909, 77). With the formation of the Garo Hills into a separate district in 1869 (by the Act of XXII which repealed Regulation X of 1822), the policies of legal exceptionalism effected the administrative separation of the 'hill Garos' from the 'plains Garos' and from the river valleys that they had controlled, traversed and inhabited since the precolonial period. The 'wild frontier' now gradually closes as the official discourse hinges on the necessary conquest of the strategic corridor of the Garo Hills in the interest of British paramountcy in Manipur and Burma. Firmly cast already within a universal taxonomy of 'other primitives' of the subcontinent – the Bhils, the Konds, the Bhagalpur tribes – the history of the Garos in the Garo Hills, imperial discourse directed, would henceforth survive as a mere fragment of analogy.[40] As ethnographic literature travelogues and missionary accounts merged with the official archive to isolate and savage the 'hill Garo', readying him for their civilising mission, we are confronted

40 'We allude not solely to the Bheels of Candesh, the Mhairs of Ajmere and the not very distant tribes of Bhagulpore Hills, but to the still mote striking case of the Khonds on the South Western frontier. These encouraging examples should be never absent from the minds of our officers who are brought into contact with savage tribes. We recommend the adoption of the same course towards the inhabitants of the Garrow Hills which has been so fruitful of benefit in every analogous case to which it has been applied'. IOR/E/4/821 Political Department, 10 August 1853, APAC.

thus with the modernity of the notion of the 'tribe' or the 'hill tribe', or in Morton Fried's now classic formulation, 'of 'tribes' as a secondary sociopolitical phenomenon, brought about by the intercession of more complexly ordered societies, states in particular. 'The "pristine tribe", Fried had observed, 'is a creation of myth and legend, pertaining either to the golden ages of the noble savage or romantic barbarian, or to the twisted map of hell that is a projection of our own war-riven world' (Fried 1975, 114).

Conclusion

To loop around to the beginning of the chapter, much like the structure of authority in the 1935 Act, the Sixth Schedule of the Constitution recognised the colonially invented 'traditional authority' of communities (the position and authority of the village headman, the village council and the district and regional council) only to limit them through the powers vested in the figure of the Union government-appointed Governor[41] or the government of the state concerned. This provision effectively negated the Schedule's recognition of rights of the community over land and jurisdiction as traditional and ancient.[42] In contemporary times, this resultant political ambivalence has spawned conflict between states and communities in northeastern India over the latter's assertion of their rights of indigeneity based on land use customs, made sharper in recent times on account of their growing marginalisation through capital accumulation by the state and multinational corporations.[43] As an anthropologist debating closely with his

[41] The decision to include, exclude any area from the provisions of the Schedule or create, increase, diminish, and alter the name or boundaries of an autonomous district within the Excluded or Partially Excluded Areas Act was that of the Governor's prerogative (Sixth Schedule [Articles 244(2) and 275(1)]: https://www.mea.gov.in/Images/pdf1/S6.pdf. Accessed on 27 September 2025).

[42] See Barbora (2002, 1285–92) for an illustration of the same in the context of land rights and administration of justice in the North Cachar Hills of Assam.

[43] See Karlsson (2011) for a postcolonial history of the relationship between community ownership, the state and multinational capital in Meghalaya.

counterparts on the concatenation of colonialism, modern capital, and the 'traditional' rights of communities claiming indigenous status in another continent, says[44]:

> 'There are also frequent disputes about who should be chief, and land claims regularly pit native against native, chief against chief (and anthropologist against anthropologist). Precisely because myths function as charters, there are inevitably competing stories, and disputes often rage over who owns a particular story and who has the right to use it to back up claims to resources.' (Kuper 2003, 391)

Conflicts over land are of course only symptomatic of a deeper predicament emerging from the project of imperial knowledge and classification. The proposition that the 'indigenous' as the 'original settlers' of a land should have the first and exclusive claims to it at once categorises the 'non-indigenous' as 'immigrants' or 'foreigners', with apposite rights. Such a proposition necessarily rests on a discourse of 'culture' which presents it as archaic and changeless, the inner spirit of the community which must be protected from the perpetual threat of ambush and assault from the materiality of modern civilisation; the 'loss' of culture, in the form of language and other affective dimensions, is represented then as the loss of the community's identity itself. The category of the 'indigenous' therefore carries within it the residues of racial ideologies in the form of arguments about descent.[45] This chapter was a historical exposition of the political stakes involved in the reinvention of such cultural pasts and identities and its implications for communities with fraught and contested narratives of genealogy and place in contemporary northeastern India.

References

Alavi, Seema. 1995. *The Sepoys and the Company: Tradition and Transition in. Northern India, 1770–1830.* Delhi: Oxford University Press.

44 Countered here is the academic characterisation (see Wouters 2022, 41) of Kuper's deeply political critique of indigeneity as apolitical.

45 See Kuper (1988) for an intellectual history of the idea of the 'primitive'.

Barbora, Sanjay. 2002. "Ethnic Politics and Land Use." *Economic and Political Weekly* 37, no. 13 (March–April): 1285–92.

Baruah, Sanjib. 2008. "Territoriality, Indigeneity and Rights in the North-east India." *Economic and Political Weekly* 43, nos. 12–13: 15–19.

Benton, Lauren. 2009. *The Search for Sovereignty: Law and Geography in European Empires, 1400–1900.* Cambridge: Cambridge University Press.

Bhattacharjee, Jayanta Bhushan. 1978. *The Garos and the English.* Delhi: Radiant Publishers.

Bhuyan, S.K. 1949. *Anglo-Assamese Relations.* Guwahati: Department of Historical and Antiquarian Studies.

Chandra, Uday. 2013. "Liberalism and Its Other: The Politics of Primitivism in Colonial and Postcolonial Indian Law." *Law & Society Review* 47, no. 1.

Colson, Elizabeth. 1971. "The Impact of the Colonial Period on the Definition of Land Rights." In *Colonialism in Africa*, edited by Victor Turner. Cambridge: Cambridge University Press.

Dalton, Edward Tuite. 1872. *Ethnology of Bengal.* Calcutta: Printed for the Government of Bengal, under the direction of the Council of the Asiatic Society of Bengal.

Damodaran, Vinita. 2006. "The Colonial Construction of Tribe in India: The Case of Chotanagpur." In *Europe and the World in European Historiography.* Edited by Csaba Lévai. Pisa: Pisa University Press.

De Maaker, Erik. 2022. *Reworking Culture: Relatedness, Rites and Resources in the Garo Hills, North-East India.* New Delhi: Oxford University Press.

———. 2023. "Customary Law." In *Routledge Companion to North East India*, edited by Jelle P. Wouters and Tanka B. Subba. Oxon and New York: Routledge.

Debbarma, R.K. 2023. "Indigeneity." *Routledge Companion to North East India*, edited by Jelle P. Wouters and Tanka B. Subba. Oxon and New York: Routledge.

Detienne, Marcel, and Janet Lloyd. 2007. *The Greeks and Us: A Comparative Anthropology of Ancient Greece.* Cambridge: Polity Press.

Eliot, John. 1794. "Observations on the Inhabitants of the Garrow Hills, Made during a Public Deputation in the Years 1788 and 1789." *Asiatick Researches* 3, nos. 21–45.

Fried, Morton. 1975. *The Notion of Tribe.* Mento Park: Cummings Publishing Company.

George, Kenneth. 1991. "Headhunting, History, and Exchange in Upland Sulawesi." *The Journal of Asian Studies* 50, no. 3: 536–64.

Godwin-Austen, H.H. 1873. "On the Gāro Hills." *Journal of the Royal Geographical Society of London* 43: 1–46.

Govind, Rahul. 2017. "The King's Plunder, the King's Justice: Sovereignty in British India, 1756–76." *Studies in History* 33, no. 2: 151–86.

Haokip, T. 2022. "Ethnocracy in Deeply Divided Societies." *Vernacular Politics in Northeast India: Democracy, Ethnicity, and Indigeneity*, edited by Jelle P. Wouters. Delhi: Oxford University Press.

Hunter, W.W. 1886. *The Imperial Gazetteer of India 1840–1900*. London: Trubner and Co.

———. 1879. *A Statistical Account of Assam*, Vols. I and II. London: Trubner and Co.

Hussain, 2003. *The Jurisprudence of Emergency: Colonialism and the Rule of Law*. Michigan: University of Michigan Press.

Junker, Laura Lee. 1999. *Raiding, Trading, and Feasting: The Political Economy of Philippine Chiefdoms*. Hawaii: University of Hawaii Press.

Kar, Bodhisattva. 2009. "When Was the Postcolonial? A History of Policing Impossible Lines." In *Beyond Counterinsurgency: Breaking the Impasse in Northeast India*, edited by Sanjib Baruah. Delhi: Oxford University Press.

Karlsson, Bengt G. 2011. *Unruly Hills: A Political Ecology of India's Northeast*. New York: Bergahan Books.

Kuper, Adam. 1988. *The Invention of Primitive Society: Transformations of an Illusion*. New York: Routledge.

———. 2003. "The Return of the Native." *Current Anthropology* 44, no. 3: 389–402.

Leach, Edmund. 1954. *Political Systems of Highland Burma*. London: Berg Publishers.

Ludden, David. 2003. "The First Boundary of Bangladesh on Sylhet's Northern Frontiers." *Journal of the Asiatic Society of Bangladesh* 48, no. 1: 1–49.

———. 2017. "Cowry Country: Where Zomia Meet the Sea." In *Asia Inside Out*, Vol. 3, edited by Peter C. Perdue & Eric Tagliacozza. Cambridge, Massachusetts: Harvard University Press.

———. 2019. "India's Spatial History in the Brahmaputra-Meghna Basin." In *Landscape, Culture and Belonging: Wiring the History of Northeast India*, edited by Neeladri Bhattacharya and Joy L.K. Pachuau. Delhi: Cambridge University Press.

Mackenzie, Alexander. 1884. *History of the Relations of the Government with the Hill Tribes of the North East Frontier of Bengal*. Calcutta: The Home Department Press.

Misra, Sanghamitra. 2011. *Becoming a Borderland: The Politics of Space and Identity in Colonial Northeastern India*. Delhi and London: Routledge.

———. 2018. "The Sovereignty of Political Economy: The Garos in a Pre-conquest and Early Conquest Era." *Indian Economic and Social History Review* 55, no. 3: 345–87.

———. 2021. "Peasants, Colonialism and Sovereignty: The Garo Rebellions in Eastern India." *Modern Asian Studies* 55, no. 5.

Pachuau, Joy. 2014. *Being Mizo: Identity and belonging in Northeast India*. Delhi: Oxford University Press.

Playfair, A. J. 1909. *The Garos*. London: D. Nutt.

Prasad, Archana. 2011. *Against Ecological Romanticism: Verrier Elwin and the Making of an Anti-Modern Tribal Identity*. Delhi: Three Essays Collective.

Radhakrishna, Meena. 2001. *Dishonoured by History? Criminal Tribes and British Colonial Policy*. New Delhi: Orient Longman.

Rosaldo, Renato. 1980. *Ilongot Headhunting 1883–1974: A Study in Society and History*. Stanford: Stanford University Press.

Sahlins, Marshall. 1972. *Stone Age Economics*. Chicago: Aldine Atherton, Inc.

Singha, Radhika. 1998. *A Despotism of Law: Crime and Justice in Early Colonial India*. Delhi: Oxford University Press.

Skaria, Ajay. 1997. "Writing, Power and Orality in the Dangs." In *Subaltern Studies: Writings on South Asian History and Society*, Vol. 3, edited by Shahid Amin and Dipesh Chakrabarty. Delhi: Oxford University Press.

Stokes, Eric. 1959. *The English Utilitarians and India*. Oxford: The Clarendon Press.

van Schendel, Willem and Itty Abraham. 2011. *Illicit Flows and Criminal Things: States, Borders, and the Other Side of Globalization*. Bloomington and Indianapolis: Indiana University Press.

van Schendel, Willem. 2011. "The Dangers of Belonging: Tribes, Indigenous Peoples and Homelands in South Asia." In *The Politics of Belonging in India Becoming Adivasi*, edited by Daniel J. Rycroft and Sangeeta Dasgupta. Delhi and London: Routledge.

Watson, Archibald. 1832. *A Memoir of the Late David Scott*. Calcutta: Baptist Mission Press.

Wouters, Jelle J. P. 2022. *Vernacular Politics in Northeast India: Democracy, Ethnicity, and Indigeneity*. Delhi: Oxford University Press.

THREE

Journeying in the Vernacular: Hindi Travelogues and the Discovery of the Nation

SHOBNA NIJHAWAN

The expansion of the colonial Indian railway network from the mid-nineteenth century onward, alongside other public infrastructure, engendered new forms of social mobility for a diversity of South Asian populations. By the 1930s, the travel infrastructure in British India – set up initially for the purposes of the British colonial apparatus and Anglo-Indian travels – had become accessible to upper-middle-class Indians. It is in this context that a specific literary and ethnographic print genre emerged in South Asian vernacular languages and developed into what came to be known as the travelogue.[1] The vernacular print medium proved particularly suitable for writers to promote their travels and communicate their experiences to emerging middle-class readers and potential travellers.

Travel narratives may be read as reflections of the impact of colonial modernity on the lives and tastes of travellers. In their claim to provide factual, 'true' and honest observations, travel writers contemplated national places and religious spaces while offering critical assessments of colonial society. They embedded social reformist discourse of the time in their travel narratives and

[1] In North American academia, travelogues are often subcategorised as travel memoirs, travel diaries, travel essays, travel guides and more recently travel blogs, amongst others. As the travelogues discussed in this chapter have fluid boundaries, I use these terms freely and distinguish between travel memoir, travel essay and travel manual whenever accurate to do so.

with the airs and authority of the urban, educated, high-caste and upper-class traveller, did not shy away from voicing dismay over the deplorable living, housing and working conditions of a people (most commonly the labourer), the stench of run-down localities, and overcrowded bazaars encountered on their travels. They did so as visitors of their own country (*deś bhramaṇ*), away from home while simultaneously at home in the nation. This chapter engages with the form and content of travel writing of the late 1920s to the early 1940s in light of nation-building and identity formation with the objective of analysing (1) how Hindi writers mapped Hindu national space and sought to impact the lives and imagined travels of their readers, and (2) how they embedded their socio-literary project in service to literature (*sāhitya sevā*) by writing in the projected national language and idiom of the nation-to-be. As will be shown through select travel essays gathered from Hindi periodicals, in the process of imagining the nation for their readers and for themselves, new centres were created alongside old ones and common pilgrimage sites were appropriated into the Hindu nationalist project while others were excluded from it.

(Im)printing the Nation: Travelogues at the Intersection of Tourism and Pilgrimage

Travel writing in various South Asian vernacular languages can be situated on a sacred–secular scale ranging from pilgrimage to tourism. Correspondingly, professional and lay travel writers may be described as religious tourists and secular pilgrims depending on how they weighed their objectives for travel. The South Asian historian and scholar of literary studies, Vasudha Dalmia, has described vernacular travel writing of the nineteenth century as an exercise of mapping a place, during which the traveller 'took experiential and cultural possession of it. It meant a new awareness of cultural identity, in togetherness and separateness. In writing of it, the traveller shared this experience with his readers' (Dalmia 1997, 322). Referring to the literary legacy of the Hindi writer and editor Bharatendu Harishchandra (1850–1885), also a traveller and pilgrim, Dalmia traces the first travel writings in Hindi back to late nineteenth-century periodicals, in which he published his own travel narratives as well as the travel letters of his contemporaries (Dalmia 1997, 322–328). Such travel writing predates the Hindi travelogue that is generally attributed to Sachchidananda Hirananda Vatsyayan 'Agyeya' (1911–1987) and Rahul Sankrityayan (1893–1963), the latter of who is said to have established the literary genre in post-Independence India (Machwe 1998).[2]

Within a few decades after Bharatendu Harishchandra's publications, travel writing found recognition in the larger literary project of *sāhitya sevā* and became a regular feature in Hindi socio-literary periodicals such as *Sarasvatī* (1900–1975, ed. Mahavir Prasad Dwivedi et al.), *Mādhurī* (1922–1950, ed. Dularelal Bhargava et al.), *Chāṁd* (1922–1940s, ed. Ramrakh Singh Sahgal et al.) and *Sudhā* (1927–1940s, ed. Dularelal Bhargava et al.). Travel essays in periodicals were indexed as *bhramaṇ* (touring) and *yātrā sambandhī* (related to travel). They were written in Khari Boli Hindi prose – the standardised, but by no means inflexible, language of prose writing promoted in socio-literary periodicals of the time – and carefully edited. Longer essays were serialised over a number of issues. Despite claiming to be involved with the creation of a Hindi literary canon, the choice of lexis depended on individual authors, who chose a more or less Sanskritised Khari Boli Hindi variation with a low to moderate number of Urdu words.

In line with early travel writing of the late nineteenth century, Hindi travel writers mapped the nation by cultivating a sense of Hindu identity and belonging that was at once modern and secular as well as religious and pious. Characteristic of travel writings published in Hindi periodicals was the autobiographical

2 Two national awards on Hindi travel writing conferred by the Government of India are named after Rahul Sankrityayan, commonly described as the father of the Hindi travelogue.

and authoritative voice of the author who vowed for the accuracy of the provided travel information.[3] While the travelogues I have consulted in this chapter were written by and for the male reader, the assumption was that he would facilitate travels for the entire family.[4] The personalised travel accounts provided first-hand insights into travel destinations, logistics and other useful information on the geography, climate, geology, botany and demographics of a specific place and region. The information on the logistics of travel that commonly happened via rail was detailed and included hints on reaching and navigating places and sites of interest or attractions, lodging and boarding recommendations as well as comments on hygiene and safety. All writing was accompanied by photographs of people, places, sites, and, very often, the author himself. Curiously, maps were absent from the accounts, even though their geographical detail would have enhanced the visual imagination of the nation (Ludden 2003) and supported the project of nation building (Mukhopadhyay 2018, 165).

North Indian Hindu pilgrimage sites (*tīrth sthān*) featured prominently in Hindi travelogues. Situated within hill stations set up by colonial rulers as an escape from the heat of the northern Indian plains in the summer months, Shimla, Solan Hills, Mussoorie, Srinagar, Dehradun, and the immensely popular Nainital became popular travel destinations for travel writers who visited the mountain range for pleasure and purpose as nature

---

[3] I use the male gender as the writings consulted for this chapter are written by men. Female Hindi travel writers include Rameshwari Nehru who published her travels to Burma in the late 1910s in *Strī Darpaṇ* and Krishna Nehru, who published in the same women's periodical. Kumari Kaushalyadevi Gorovala and Prabhavati Devi were regular contributors of travel accounts to the socio-literary periodical *Sudhā*.

[4] There was no scarcity of women travelers on the British Indian railways, which led to public debates on their accommodation in women-reserved zenana carriers (Prasad 2012). For Urdu travel narratives by Muslim women, see Daniel Majchrowicz (2020). Bengali female travel writers are covered by J. Gupta (2020).

lovers, tourists, pilgrims, and a combination thereof.[5] Other travel destinations were Delhi and Wardah, the former being the seat of the colonial government and the latter the abode of the nationalist politician and freedom fighter Mohandas Karamchand Gandhi (1869–1948).[6] This chapter focusses on travel destinations in north India, being cognizant of the fact that travel writing published in Hindi periodicals not only regularly included places in central India and the Deccan, but also stretched beyond the Indian subcontinent. Travel to European cities in Austria (Vienna), England (London), France (Paris), Italy (Genoa, Naples, Rome), Scotland (Edinburgh) and Switzerland (Geneva, Lugano, Zürich) was covered in socio-literary as well as women's and children's periodicals,[7] as were travels to North America and Asia (Japan, Persia, Russia). Such writings by women, political activists, religious authorities, and students offer a plethora of gazes onto the world by Indian natives and warrant a comprehensive study of their own.[8]

Travel writing in the Hindi periodical did not emerge out of a vacuum. Pilgrimages such as the *tīrth yātrā* for Hindus, the *hajj* for Muslims, and annual or intentional visits to significant shrines and temples formed long-established pre-colonial modes

---

[5] See, for example, Dhaniram 'Premi' (*Sudhā*, December 1929), Shivnarayan Tandan 'Premi' (*Sudhā*, May 1928), Gurunarayan Sukul (*Sudhā*, June 1932), Prithvipal Sinha (*Sudhā*, August 1929), Dharmadev Shastri (*Sudhā*, August 1940), Lakshminarayan Tandan 'Premi' (1940) and Bhyohar Rajendrasinha (1939).

[6] See Kaushalya Devi 'Gorovala' (*Sudhā*, September 1928) and Lakshminarayan Tandan 'Premi' (1941d).

[7] For children's periodicals, see Chandra (2007); for women's periodicals, see Nijhawan (2012) and Majchrowicz (2020). For socio-literary periodicals, see Krishna Nehru (*Sudhā*, December 1928), Kripanath Mishra (*Sudhā*, February 1929, September 1929, June 1930), Dhirendra Varma (*Sudhā*, November 1936, March 1937, August 1938), Suryanarayan Vyas (*Sudhā*, August 1938, June 1940) and Dhaniram 'Prem' (*Sudhā*, February 1930). Shukdevbihari Mishra wrote a travel report covering his trip to Europe, serialised in *Sudhā* (1931).

[8] See, for example, the acclaimed travel writings on Europe and the United States by Swami Satyadev 'Parivrajak' (C. Gupta 2020).

of travel. There existed a thriving market of readily accessible and affordable pilgrimage manuals published from smaller and larger presses and publishing houses often conveniently located in pilgrimage towns (Orsini 2015). Consequently, apart from providing personalised accounts of their travels, travel writers gathered their information from multilingual sources that included travel guidebooks, pilgrimage manuals in Hindi and other vernacular languages, essays in periodicals, colonial surveys, and other publication formats. English-language railway guidebooks on Indian travel destinations initially prepared for Anglo-Indian travellers, also became guides for the vernacular writer and traveller (Mukhopadhyay 2014) despite his pretensions of providing a more refined type of travel writing for the modern Hindi reader and potential traveller. Furthermore, travel writing was not solely intended to promote travel and tourism; some travel writers composed travel memoirs and other forms of self-writing that intersected with autobiographical and auto-ethnographical literary genres.

Siting the Sacred and the Secular: Travelling the Himalayas

Travel narratives from the 1920s to the early 1940s were reflections of what the writers literally saw on their travels (mostly out of trains and while on foot) through the lenses of caste, class and privilege. Appreciation for the British Indian railway system that had made remote places accessible to the upper-middle-classes prompted writers to frequently comment on railway stations, coaches, engines, tracks, speed and infrastructure. This was particularly true for travel to the hill stations, which was challenging and not always comfortable.[9] Travelogues offered plenty of information that broached the utilitarian-nationalist project of (re)discovering

[9] See Vishveshvarnath Reu (*Sudhā*, August 1939), Lakshminarayan Tandan 'Premi' (1940, 1941a, 1941b, 1941c, 1941d), 'Premi' (*Sudhā*, December 1940, May 1941, July 1941) and Siyaramsharan Gupta (1939).

and claiming supposed heritage sites on the subcontinent. In the process, 'sacred' places with historical significance were marked as sites of national importance in texts and images of travelogues.

In their analysis of new imaginings of nation-spaces in Bengali travelogues of the late nineteenth and early twentieth centuries, Sandeep Banerjee and Subho Basu (2015, 610) point out that while writers such as Devendranath Tagore had identified the Himalayas as a Hindu-religious site, towards the end of the nineteenth century, a new generation of travel writers infused 'the sacred Himalayan geography with a secular politics'. Shalini Singh has written about British travellers to the Himalayan mountain range that they 'introduced a novel interpretation in their appreciation of the Himalayan mountains – that of comfort and temporary settlement', concluding that 'it is pertinent to note that this altitudinal belt, which at one time constituted the buffer around the pilgrim zones, was gradually transformed into "romantic zones" of greenery, nostalgia and gaiety' (Singh 2005, 220). As the following section shows, Hindi travel writers sited similar national spaces.

Objectives for travelling into the Inner Himalayan region, as listed by Rameshwar Dayal Dube (1940, 391), were to escape the heat, get medical treatment, visit religious sites or, in his case, 'for travelling, just for travelling' (*ghūmne, keval ghūmne ke liye*). This is not to suggest that his travels had turned into tourism exclusively. The sacred history and spiritual gratification of these sites was as thoroughly described in his account as their supposedly secular side. Like other travel writers, Dube linguistically and politically projected himself as a modern, secular Hindu traveller who performed *darśan* (viewing and being viewed) at a Hindu temple while seeing (*dekhnā*) or strolling (*ghumnā*) Buddhist and Jain places of worship and revelling in the beauty nature offered while on a hike. The pronouncedly fluid boundaries of pilgrimage and tourism were also reflected in the linguistic choices of Hindu travel writers, who described temples as tourist attractions, ashrams as hotels, and immersions in holy waters as plunges or refreshing baths. In the context of projecting historical and archaeological sites as markers of national and religious heritage, Buddhist and Jain sites of history and worship (most notably Sarnath, Rajgrih, Nalanda and Ayodhya/Saket) were readily appropriated into the narrative. Contrarily, Muslim, Sufi and Sikh pilgrimage sites or places of cultural and religious interest were denied national space and at the most became geographical markers in Hindi travelogues written for the by-default Hindu reader.

Dube's travel narrative of an extended family vacation in the Himalayas titled "In(side) the Himalayas", would today be described as backpacking tourism or trekking. A well-recognised Hindi writer and literature graduate, Dube had made preparations for the 24-day stay in and around Srinagar based on different guidebooks, including the Kashmir guide of the Indian Railways (Dube 1940, 391). He was travelling with a group of people 'aged between eight and eighty' that included female travellers, whom he explicitly praised for their stamina and endurance as they hiked on trying terrain (391). Relinquishing hotel or ashram accommodation, his group had hauled a lorry and was travelling with 'tents, mats, tables and chairs, leather socks, woollen clothes, some medicine and own food' (392). Dube spent the first evening in awe: 'Upon lying down it occurred to me how far away I was from home in this corner of the Kashmir Valley, lying somehow on the veranda of this post-office. What a big country, so many high mountains, how far away and I (a man) how small and insignificant.'[10] Dube's humility and fascination for Kashmir's overwhelming beauty was part of his secular-spiritual experience that was repeatedly triggered by nature experiences. While heavy rain made the hike cumbersome on the next day, the beauty of the lush valley encouraged the group to continue with fervour.[11] Dube's

---

[10] '*Leṭne par khayāl āyā, ghar se dūr, kitnī dūr, kaśmīr-ghāṭī ke is kone meṁ, is coṭe-se ḍāk-bāṅgle ke barāmade meṁ, kahaṁ leṭā hūā hūṁ | Kitnā baṛā deś, kitne ūṁce pahāḍ, kitnī dūr aur maiṁ (ek manuśya) kitnā laghu, kitnā kṣudra*' (Dube 1940, 392).

[11] Siyaramsharan Gupta in his account, on the other hand, deplores that he didn't get to leave his hotel room in Nainital due to the bad weather and consequently never got to see a glimpse of the Himalayas (1939, 349–355).

writing displays an awareness that Banerjee and Basu (2015, 614) have attributed to an upper-middle-class urban writing style that focusses on the spiritual and the secular more than on the sacred and religious. At the end of this travel, Dube seems gratified. The accompanying photograph shows him and his friend getting their grown beards shaved after their return.

Shimla's Stain: The Subaltern Other

Despite being one of the most popular travel destinations, the hill station Shimla reveals its 'dark' side in the travel narrative by Bhyohar Rajendrasinha. Titled 'Shimla's Stain', it begins in typical travelogue fashion with a description of the journey to Shimla. Rajendrasinha, an employee with the Imperial Council of Agricultural Research, had been summoned to a board meeting in Shimla and decided to extend his stay there for one week before continuing his travels to Kashmir for his summer vacation. He briefly lays out the travel route from Hardwar via Rishikesh to Kalka, from where he embarks on the small and adventurous Kalka-Shimla Railway, in an ordinary third-class carriage of the train.[12] He describes the scenery as it passes: fields and mountains, mountain-dwellers and tourists and the change in temperature as the train reaches higher altitudes (Rajendrasinha 1939, 67). He also notes that the population size increased from 60,000–70,000 to 80,000–90,000 inhabitants in the summer months, which led to overcrowding of Shimla. Furthermore, the failure of local politicians to invest in sanitation infrastructure and canalisation was causing mosquito-borne diseases. The climax of Rajendrasinha's account concerns the deplorable condition of temporary migrant workers,

[12] Traveling in third-class carriers seems to have been trendy for authentic travel experiences. Siyaramsharan Gupta (1939, 349) did the same on his trip from Lucknow to Kathgodam via Nainital. According to colonial records, about 460 of the 520 million travelers on Indian railways travelled in third-class carriers (*Statistical abstract relating to British India from 1910–11 to 1919–20*, 1922). Today, the Kalka–Shimla Railway (completed in 1903) alongside the Darjeeling Himalaya Railway (completed in 1881), are recognised as UNESCO World Heritage Sites.

whose exploitative working conditions put a stain on Shimla's scenery: 'All the days that I stayed in Shimla, this load kept occupying my mind and this is why I could not cherish Shimla's natural beauty. [...] The figure of the *kulī* [labourer] is attached on to the heavenly beauty of Shimla like a stain and painted on to it like a chronic disease.'[13] He admonishes a fundraising event organised by the Young Women's Christian Association (YWCA) in support of Jewish refugees, wondering whether 'those women' will ever 'direct their attention towards reforming the condition of the inhabitants of their own Bharat' (68). The remainder of Rajendrasinha's essay is ethnographic in nature and provides detailed information on the labourers' ethnic, religious, linguistic and cultural backgrounds, their working and living conditions, food consumption and clothing.

Like Rajendrasinha, Dube described the subaltern 'other' in ethnic, linguistic, economic, and – arguably – casteist terms as he voiced compassion for the plight of labourers. He describes the carriers of his luggage with appreciation and pity. They were ill-paid and exploited, wore torn clothes, and had emaciated bodies – nevertheless, they were essential for a successful vacation. They knew the terrain, provided reliable weather forecasts and skilfully navigated muddy mountain paths and dangerous slopes with the heavy loads they carried (Dube 1940, 393–94). Siyaramsharan Gupta's experience with labourers at the train station was described less favourably: in his travel account titled 'A Glimpse of the Himalayas', he describes how he and other travellers were harrassed by the carriers who vied for their luggage (Gupta 1939, 351). He describes their torn clothes with disdain: 'just as we can call an old person a child, we could call these rags clothes'.[14]

---

[13] '*Jitne dinoṁ śimle meṁ rahā, yahī bhar citt ko dabāe rahā, aur isī kāraṇ śimle ke prākṛtik saundarya kā pūrā ānand nahīṁ uṭhā sakā | [...] Yah kulī-mūrtī śimle ke svargīya saundarya-pat par kalaṅk kī tarah dṛḍh tathā sthir rogoṁ meṁ citrit hai*' (Rajendrasinha 1939, 68).

[14] '*Kisī vṛddh ko bālak kah sake to un cithṛoṁ ko bhī ham kapṛe kah sakte haiṁ*' (Gupta 1939, 351).

Religion, Nature, and Nationalism: The Travel Writings of Lakshminarayan Tandan 'Premi'

A prolific member of the Hindi intelligentsia, Lakshminarayan Tandan 'Premi' seamlessly straddled the 'sacred' and 'secular' in his travel writing as a pilgrim, tourist and Hindu nationalist. His travelogues, written in highly Sanskritised Khari Boli Hindi, were serialised over a span of two years (1940–1941) in *Sudhā*. They covered his north Indian travels to Nainital, Mussoorie, Dehradun, Sarnath, Nalanda, Rajgriha, Haridwar, Vindhyachal and Tanda Falls, amongst other places, as well as a trip to Aurangabad in Maharashtra where he visited the Ellora Caves. Couched in the genre of the travelogue was also a travel to Wardah and Sevagram, where 'Premi' interviewed Mohandas Karamchand Gandhi, provided a detailed description of Sevagram Ashram, and visited places of economic and nationalist interest in Wardha. The M.A. graduate 'Premi' travelled frequently: sometimes he was on his own, at other times with Rashtriya Swayamsevak Sangh (RSS) compatriots and friends, and then also with his extended family. As he marked sites of national, historical and religious interest for his readers, he gave advice to potential travellers and complemented his accounts with photographs of the places he had visited.

In 'My Travels to Nainital', 'Premi' dwells at length on a hike to China Peak. Revelling in the beauty of the flora and fauna, he comments, 'man forgets all about his domestic duties (*ghar-gṛhastī*) and worldly troubles, his eyes directed at the beauty of the nature, his soul satisfied, he forgets about his own vanity' (Tandan 1940, 492). Sights of local temples made his heart pound and awakened his spiritual and religious pride in Hindutva [sic].[15] Amongst the 33 places worth visiting in and around Nainital, his

[15] '*Hindutva kā bhāv ek bār hṛday meṁ hiloreṁ mārne lagtā hai*' (Tandan 1940, 490).

account enlists places of Hindu worship alongside missionary schools and colleges, government buildings, a cinema hall, a skating rink, the mansions of Nainital and the commanding Secretariat-Bhavan. The latter buildings are described as spectacular when illuminated in the dark. Unlike Rajendrasinha and Dube, 'Premi' is not moved by the condition of the labourers. He does, however, admonish the poverty, filth, congestion and overpopulation of areas in and surrounding Nainital, where drinking water was contaminated, government employees were stressed, and the infrastructure was lacking. He concludes with a call to protect the pristine nature and its ecosystem.

Premi's account of Haridwar, a travel destination located north-west of Nainital, may be described as pilgrimage tourism of the prototypical early twentieth century modern Indian (Hindu) traveller who delights in spirituality, good food and comfortable travel. 'My Travels to Hardwar' begins with a description of the author's arrival by train, his check-in at the *dharmśālā* and his immersion in the holy, albeit freezing cold, waters of '*gaṅgājī*', the river Ganges. He takes the reader along as he strolls the ghats and bazaars, visits numerous temples on the way, and undertakes spiritually rewarding hikes in the mountains. He even books a sightseeing flight over Haridwar and its surroundings. 'Premi' describes the holy city also known as Gangadwara, Hardwar (in Shaivaite terminology) or Haridwar (in Vaishnaite terminology), as one of the seven most sacred and mythologically significant places for Hindus to visit. He concludes with a description of the Kumbh Mela.

'Premi' situates the nation at the intersection of the worldly and the spiritual as captured in the description of a day trip that included an arduous mountain hike. The spiritual reward experienced by the breathtaking scenery, was augmented upon entering the local temple for *darśan*. He visits Haridwar's famous educational institutions, strolls the riverbanks with his friends, and discovers Aminabad bazaar, a place of bustling energy:

> There were speeches, there was storytelling, there was bell ringing, there were religious services, there was a crowd of saints and devotees

> as well as worldly women and men' [...] This place offers so much happiness, peace, and satisfaction to the soul. [...] It is a unique sight – thousands of men and women are bathing, thousands are looking at the beauty of *gaṅgājī*, thousands are praying. (Tandan 1941c, 428)

Apart from writing as a Hindu pilgrim and tourist, 'Premi' was also an ethnographer who observed saints, tourists, other pilgrims and women. As he participates in religious rituals as a pilgrim and enjoys himself with his friends as a tourist, he also observes other travellers: Punjabis in the bazaar and the ghats of Haridwar arouse his indignation. He disapproves of the customary naked bathing of Punjabi women and condemns unsanitary food stores and restaurants run by Punjabis in the bazaar. It is only after the author and his co-travellers chance upon 'a Pandey from Mathura' who also happens to be a pilgrim guide and offers them advice on where to find a clean and tasty meal, that they find comfort. 'Premi' is aware that some Brahman Pandey guides try to exploit pilgrims, but he credits most of them as being 'trustworthy' and of good service to the pilgrim-travellers.[16]

In "My Travels to Rajgrih", 'Premi' visits Buddhist and Jain places of worship in Bihar as an educated citizen-traveller with a genuine interest in the nation's religious and ethnic diversity. His accounts of travels to Nalanda, Bihar Sharif and Rajgriha are short, prosaic, and not interspersed with spiritual exuberance. He frequently uses the presumptive and subjunctive mood, suggesting that the historical and archaeological information he is providing relies on secondary sources. He appreciates Buddhist and Jain sites, while also denying them entry into the specific Hindu nationalist narrative by making it a point to inform Hindu readers how to locate Hindu sites of interest: 'Naland is not the *tīrth* of Hindus, but there is another site not far away in a village for Hindus to visit' (Tandan 1941b, 142). Inadvertently, 'Premi' advises potential travellers to make alternative boarding and lodging arrangements as Rajgriha's Buddhist ashram houses exclusively Buddhists

16 For the role of Pandit guides in institutionalising pilgrimage travel, see Singh (2005).

(unlike Wardha, where Sevagram *dharmśālā* accepts Hindus and Muslims, which he points out in another account). He explains that 'a mosque next to a bridge', and a Japanese temple are not accessible to non-believers and that Burmese and Jain temples are 'just to see' and 'not to worship'. Also part of the narrative is a description of an adventurous hike in the region.

The author's travel to Sarnath falls into the same framework of nation discovery. Inscribed as 'sweet reminiscences', this travel essay reveals his dilemma of visiting a major pilgrimage site for Buddhists. For the title to his account, 'Premi' deliberately chooses the Sanskrit word *smṛti*, commonly used to designate a genre of Hindu scriptures, and not the more common Urdu word *yād* (memory). 'Premi' does not reference larger movements of the archaeological rediscovery and religious revival of Buddhism (including Dalit [neo-]Buddhism and Tibetan Buddhism) and Buddhist sites of pilgrimage. He also does not claim these spaces as sacred, even though Sarnath is located just 'four miles north of Kashi' (Tandan 1941a, 677), as the first sentence of the narrative holds. Instead, he travels as a citizen-tourist discovering his nation and taking his readers along. He visits the museum, Buddhist temples and stupas and takes photographs together with his travel group. He describes Sarnath as a peaceful and extraordinarily clean place (678). In the course of the travel essay it turns out that the 'sweet reminiscences' insinuated in the title are not those of (Buddhist) religious-historical sites, but of a village that is described as emblematic of the nation. As he is searching for drinking water, 'Premi' makes acquaintance with a 14-year old girl whose health, beauty and rural simplicity impress him. The girl, in turn, is also curious about the visitors from the city. It is during this encounter that 'Premi' reallocates his gaze from Sarnath, a Buddhist pilgrimage site, to the Indian village: 'It is in our villages', he exclaims, 'that our true Indianness manifests'.[17]

The excitement arising out of the 'discovery of the nation' recurs during his travels to an event of the RSS in Nagpur and

---

[17] '*Hamāre gāṁvoṁ meṁ ab bhī saccī bhāratīyatā ke darśan ho sakte haiṁ*' (Tandan 1941a, 677).

on his subsequent way to Wardah (by train) and Sevagram (by horse carriage), where he receives an audience by Mohandas Karamchand Gandhi (1869–1948). 'A few hours in Sevagram' was longer and more descriptive than his other travel accounts. As a citizen-traveller with ethnographic curiosity and openness, 'Premi' describes the places he had visited on his way and the chats he had had with a Punjabi from Sialkot and other 'pilgrims' who had come for *darśan* of the Mahatma. In this account, he situates the nation's citizens at the intersection of the worldly and the spiritual. Sevagram, where Gandhi had set up his residence and built a model village, is described as a secular pilgrimage centre for Indian citizens with a guest house adjacent to the ashram that accepts people of all creeds – 'a model for simplicity, frugality, love, self-sufficiency, high thoughts and dutiful devotion' (Tandan 1941d, 44). 'Premi' highlights that he had been instructed by Gandhi's secretary that his account on Gandhi's daily routine and life in the ashram was not to carry any errors or misconceptions so that the public would not be misled.[18] His account retains the main elements of a travel narrative, despite avoiding usage of the word *yātrā* (religious travel) in the title. This notwithstanding, Sevagram ashram and Wardha are also framed as Hindu nationalist sites with Gandhi as an icon of the Hindu nationalist struggle. Premi's audience with Gandhi is described as *darśan* and the accompanying images of Gandhi deify him as (1) 'Sevagram's saint', (2) 'reverential father' (*pūjya bāpū*), (3) *bāpū* spinning cotton, and (4) the travelling Mahatma Gandhi.

Conclusion

Travel was not a new phenomenon of the early twentieth century; disseminating travelogues through the by-then well established Hindi print networks, however, made it possible to share experiences through text and image with a steadily increasing number of Hindi readers. While travel writers got to know their

18 '*Kahīṁ koī galat bāt dhoke se nā chap jāy, iskā dhyān rakhiegā jismeṁ pablik ko galatfahmī nā ho jāe*' (Tandan 1941d, 49).

country and its people through first-hand experiences, travel writing developed through the interplay of travel writers, publishers and an emerging Hindi-reading public that was provided with information in the vernacular on how to imagine the nation from their own locality and possibly also on where and how to travel.

Travel writing was also conceptualised as a distinct, albeit fluid genre that offered the possibility for literary expression and social critique in Khari Boli Hindi for the education and entertainment of the Hindi reader. In the early twentieth century, the periodical became an important place for the travel essay to be conceptualised as an exercise in literary writing of the nation and *sāhitya sevā*, thus also furthering the linguistic and literary project of creating a standardised language and canon that spoke to women, men and children. The travel writings by Rameshwardayal Dube, Siyaramsharan Gupta, Bhyohar Rajendrasinha and Lakshminarayan Tandan 'Premi' offer insights into the literary imaginings and constructions of sites of archaeological, religious and national significance from the vernacular. As they traversed possible boundaries of tourism and pilgrimage travel, they maintained their specific Hindu, high-caste and upper-class gaze. It is this triangulation of Hindu/pilgrim, traveller/tourist and Indian/secular citizen that enabled an idiom to emerge in which different categories - often products of the colonial episteme - spoke to one another.

REFERENCES

Banerjee, Sandeep and Subho Basu. 2015. "Secularizing the Sacred, Imagining the Nation-Space: The Himalaya in Bengali Travelogues, 1856–1901." *Modern Asian Studies* 49, no. 3: 609–49.

Chandra, Nandini. 2007. "The Pedagogic Imperative of Travel Writing in the Hindi World: Children's Periodicals (1920–1950)." *South Asia: Journal of South Asian Studies* 30, no. 2: 293–325.

Dalmia, Vasudha. 1997. *The Nationalization of Hindu Traditions: Bhāratendu Hariśchandra and Nineteenth-century Banaras*. Delhi: Oxford University Press.

Dube, Rameshwardayal. 1940. *Himālaya ke antarāl meṁ* [In(side) the Himalayas]. *Sudhā*, October, 391–98.

Gupta, Charu. 2020. "Masculine Vernacular Histories of Travel in Colonial India: The Writings of Satyadev 'Parivrajak'." *South Asia: Journal of South Asian Studies* 43, no. 5: 836–59.

Gupta, Jayati. 2020. *Travel Culture, Travel Writing and Bengali Women, 1870–1940*. London: CRC Press.

Gupta, Siyaramsharan. 1939. *Himālay kī Jhalak* [A glimpse of the Himalayas]. *Sudhā*, November, 349–55.

Ludden, David. 2003. "Presidential Address: Maps in the Mind and the Mobility of Asia." *The Journal of Asian Studies* 62, no. 4: 1057–78.

Machwe, Prabhakar. 1998. *Rahul Sankrityayan*. New Delhi: Sahitya Academy.

Majchrowicz, Daniel. 2020. "Malika Begum's Mehfil: The Lost Legacy of Women's Travel Writing in Urdu." *South Asia* 43, no. 5: 860–78.

Mukhopadhyay, Aparajita. 2014. "Colonised Gaze? Guidebooks and Journeying in Colonial India." *South Asia: Journal of South Asian Studies* 37, no. 4: 656–69.

———. 2018. *Imperial Technology and 'Native' Agency: A Social History of Railways in Colonial India, 1850–1920*. London: Routledge.

Nijhawan, Shobna. 2012. "At the Margins of Empire: Feminist Configurations of Burmese Society in the Hindi Public (1917–1920)." *Journal of Asian Studies* 71, no. 4: 1013–33.

Orsini, Francesca. 2015. "Booklets and Sants: Religious Publics and Literary History." *South Asia* 38, no. 3: 435–49.

Prasad, Ritika. 2012. "Smoke and Mirrors: Railway Travel and Women in Colonial India." *South Asian History and Culture* 3, no. 1: 26–46.

Rajendrasinha, Bhyohar. 1939. *Śimlā kī kalaṅk* [Shimla's Stain]. *Sudhā*, August, 67–71.

Singh, Shalini. 2005. "Secular Pilgrimages and Sacred Tourism in the Indian Himalayas." *GeoJournal* 64: 215–23.

Statistical abstract relating to British India from 1910–11 to 1919–20. London: His Majesty's Stationary Office, 1922. http://dsal.uchicago.edu/statistics/1910_excel/index.html. Accessed on 13 February 2025.

Tandan, Lakshminarayan 'Premi'. 1940. *Merī nainitāl-yātra* [My Travel to Nainital]. *Sudhā*, November, 468–96.

———. 1941a. *Sārnāth kī madhur smṛti* [Reminiscences of Sarnath]. *Sudhā*, January, 677–80.

———. 1941b. *Merī rājgṛh-yātrā* [My Travel to Rajgrih]. *Sudhā*, March, 141–46.

———. 1941c. *Merī hardvār-yātra* [My Travel to Hardwar]. *Sudhā*, June, 427–36.

———. 1941d. *Sevāgram meṁ kuch ghaṇṭe* [A Couple of Hours in Sevagram]. *Sudhā*, August, 43–54.

FOUR

Race, Religion, and Enumeration: Configurations of Hindu Nationalism in India, 1910–1947

SAYORI GHOSHAL

> The Mahomedans have a future and they believe in it – we Hindus have no conception of it. Time is with them – time is against us. At the end of the year they count their gains, we calculate our losses. They are growing in number, growing in strength, growing in wealth, growing in solidarity, we are crumbling to pieces. They look forward to a united Mahomedan world – we are waiting for our extinction. (Mukerji 1909, 97)

In 1909, Upendra Nath Mukerji published a monograph on the declining condition of the Hindu; the title of Mukerji's work circulated like an apocalyptic prediction – *A Dying Race*. Mukerji was a doctor trained in Edinburgh and worked with the Indian Medical Services since 1884. He derived his theories and conclusions primarily from the national census data. He claimed that the Muslim race, which was 'in a minority of 4 lakhs' thirty years ago, 'had not only made up the deficiency, but were nearly 25 lakhs more numerous than the Hindus' (1909, 1). He was not unique in his time for penning communally divisive arguments; nor was he a fanatic, espousing *irrational* religious sentiments. His work influenced Swami Shraddhananda, founder of the Punjab Arya Samaj, when the two met in Calcutta in 1912. Mukerji impressed on Shraddhananda the thesis of the 'dying race' and the argument that 'within the next 420 years the Indo Aryan race would be wiped off the face of the earth unless steps were taken to save it' (Shraddhananda 1926, 14).

While in the 1870–1880s, 'Muslim' and 'Hindu' became increasingly consolidated and mutually exclusive categories, by the early twentieth century, Hindu and Muslim nationalisms turned into organising principles for public politics. Multiple factors went into the consolidation of pan-India Hindu and Muslim identities. For instance, in the case of Muslims, religious revival movements in the 1880s played a major role (Ahmed 1981); and the data collection initiated with the censuses contributed to the rise of Hindu nationalism (Cohn 1987; Datta 1999). Even the colonial mode of documenting inter-community conflicts among the various Indian groups led to Hindu–Muslim 'communalism' (Pandey 1990). However, what remains under-theorised is how Hindu and Muslim identities were also constituted, besides religious reforms and the census, by notions of biological difference and enumerative reasoning in general.

The rise and entrenchment of Hindu right-wing politics in Indian governance and public life in the last decade warrants a critical engagement with the long history of Hindu nationalism. In order to critically engage with the present configuration of Hindu nationalism, mapping the constitutive strands of Hindu nationalism becomes urgently crucial. Analysing these historically constitutive and changing strands of Hindu nationalism, I argue that Hindu nationalism cannot be perceived only as an intersection of religion and politics. Rather, what needs to be equally considered is how other identity categories, especially race and caste, as well as secular categories, such as statistical reasoning, informed the consolidation of Hindu nationalism and helped construct India as Hindu.

Hindu Nationalism as *Religious* Nationalism

In most theories of nationalism, religious nationalism is considered an aberration. The modern nation-state is construed to be either equidistant from all religious faiths or as relegating religious practices to the private and personal.[1] Other scholars argue that religious nationalism is not opposed to or the precursor of modern nationalism since secularism is not integral to the definition of nationalism. The predominant thrust of the latter approach is that religious nationalism is neither an outright oxymoron nor a premodern carryover into modern nationalism. Desirable or not, religious nationalism in this framework is considered just as modern as secularism (Friedland 2002). Several scholars working on India conceive of religious nationalism as a modern, specifically colonial, construct. Partha Chatterjee (1993) has demonstrated how the beginning of national history was also the beginning of the Hindu fundamentalist rhetoric in India. Peter van der Veer (1994), following Gyan Pandey (1990), argues that just as secular nationalism was an import through imperialism from modern Europe, communalism or religious nationalism too was formed via orientalist, colonial worldviews of the colony as essentially premodern, religious and irrational. Going against academic and public advocates of secularism, van der Veer in fact emphasises how the political will and colonial/enlightenment origin of both secular nationalism and communalism are similar. Ashutosh Varshney argues that the 'ideological trend' of Hindu nationalism can be traced back to the anticolonial desire to 'resurrect India's cultural pride' (1993, 232). If secular nationalism is based on territory and culture, Hindu or religious nationalism is based on territory and religion (Varshney 1993, 235).

In this regard, most scholars seek to examine the relation between secularism and religious nationalism through the specific case of Hindu nationalism; Hindu nationalism is thus studied in contrast to secularism and as *religious* nationalism. Although from the nineteenth century onwards, 'nationalism in India has fed upon religious identifications', how did *Hindu* (and *Muslim*) nationalism come to be seamlessly translated into *religious* nationalism? (Veer 1994, 2) What other aspects, ideas

[1] Some examples are Ernest Gellner (2006), Benedict Anderson (1991) and Eric Hobsbawm (1990).

and practices went into the production of such nationalisms, other than religious or theological differences – that is, other than differences of faith; and what is thereby lost or remains unexamined in such an equation? For instance, how would an argument like Mukerji's – which is framed through elaborate statistical calculations, which imagines the Hindus and Muslims as 'races', and which concludes that Hindus were endangered and might actually become 'extinct' – contribute to the conceptual history of 'religious' nationalism? Within the public discussions on the questions of Hindu identity, the Hindu's weakening condition, and perceived threat from other communities, the racial-qua-biological was as much a part of the vocabulary, rhetoric and contentions as were questions of faith and religiosity. To understand religious nationalism then, especially the history of Hindu nationalism in this early formative phase, it becomes crucial to examine how notions of race and religion 'co-constituted' this history, as well as how sustenance for these conflicts were drawn from practices of science (physical anthropology and statistics), just as from governmental administrative technologies (for example, census).

There have been attempts to read race into Hindu communalism, but in such accounts, the focus remains mostly on the terminological usage of race by Hindu nationalists (Baber 2004). Christophe Jaffrelot (1995) argues, for instance, that although Hindu nationalists drew from the European science of racism, they could not reconcile the politics of exclusion with the traditional Indian politics of domination, that is, the caste system. Although the racism of extermination was replaced by domination in the Indian context, biological racism continued to be operative and was formative of the Hindu nationalist discourse.

'Hindu' and 'Muslim' were relevant identities in the pre-colonial world, but were always striated by conjoined identities of caste, linguistic communities and class. The national censuses and the reformist movements which aimed at people across class boundaries produced the Hindu or the Muslim identity in terms of the 'imagined community', where the close-knit boundary of the neighbourhood was transcended to enable identities across regions, class, caste and languages (Anderson 1991). But in this transformation, it was not just religious faith that served as the basis of the imagined homogeneity of Hindu (or Muslim or Christian) community. The possibility – even if not a definite affirmation – of racial homogeneity within these communities increasingly earned a central place among advocates of Hindu nationalism. Thus, the 'Hindu', as it came to refer increasingly to a religious and faith-based community (that is, across class, caste and languages) in the early twentieth century simultaneously came to incorporate racial, caste and numerical congruity.

Race in 'Religious' Difference

Unlike religion, which is unequivocally understood as a *social* (and not natural) category and where the question is whether it can be considered ahistorical or a modern construct,[2] the contention regarding race has to do with the question of its 'natural' basis or a (purported) reality in nature.[3] Although scholarship on modern race and racism locates its origin in the late eighteenth-early nineteenth centuries, the assumption remains, even if implicit, that there is some correspondence of the broad categories of racial types (which remain actually quite consistent through the nineteenth century from Johann Friedrich Blumenbach to Paul Topinard in France and Herbert Risley in India), with those in 'nature'. Thus, despite the decline of popularity of race science from the 1920s (Stepan 1982; Barkan 2003), the biologism of race continued to remain unchallenged in several quarters – for instance, in physical anthropology which continued to flourish in postcolonial India (Mukharji 2015).

In the 1920s colonial India, race had a significant presence not just among the colonial administrators with regard to their surveys and policies for the colonised but also, even if with varying

---

[2] As one of the initial proponents of this debate, see Wilfred Smith (1978).

[3] Here 'race' refers to 'a new context for the study of man' that emerged within 'the modern, biological and human sciences' in the early nineteenth century (Stepan 1982, x).

connotations and implications, among the different communities in India. In such public perception, the racial connotation – in contrast to religiosity – was the aspect of both biological origin as well as physical prowess as an inherent character of a community. There certainly were techniques and knowledges of difference between the self and other in the pre-modern world (some of which might even have used the term 'race'), but the modern notion of race was novel due to the 'fact that "science", the body of knowledge rationally derived from empirical observation, then supported the proposition that race was one of the principal determinants of attitudes, endowments, capabilities, and inherent tendencies among human beings' (Curtin 1965, 29). The understanding of race – almost always deployed in terms of racial *difference* – in these public debates on sectarian rivalry, comparison and conflict drew on the knowledges produced in the anthropological and biological sciences (Bates 1995). Regardless of the veracity quotient of these 'sciences', what is significant is the recurrence of such an understanding of race in these sectarian debates; and this comes through when a seemingly faith-based community (for example, 'Muslims') is essentialised through certain 'inherent' and 'hereditary' physical and physiological characteristics. This imperative of race, along with ideas of religiosity and a politics of enumeration, constituted Hindu nationalism in India. Therefore, despite the consensus on discarding race and race science, we still need to account for the remnants of such an understanding of race – because it continued to be used and deployed to understand the 'Other'; critiquing the colonial project of racialising Indians cannot imply that we ignore how such understandings became popular among – at the least – the Hindu upper castes.

In the Indian subcontinent, scholars have understood 'race' to be the *modus operandi* for 'the rule of colonial difference' (Chatterjee 1993). Produced within scientific theories, the notion of racial difference was deployed as a political trope for the colonisers to govern the subject population – through medical science, biological science, sanitation measures – as well as to regulate the boundaries of their own imperial privilege (Sinha 1995; Stoler

2002). The only attention 'racial difference' receives as a principle of hierarchy *within* the colonised population is in the discourse of caste; especially, with regard to how the imperial administration restructured it from 'fuzzy' to a more rigid, enumerated structure (Kaviraj 1992). Caste and religion became the 'sociological keys to the understanding of Indian people' (Cohn 1987, 242) and the essentialised principle through which all knowledges and practices of Indians were thereafter distilled and comprehended (Dirks 2001).

Herbert Risley (1891), who was the most important advocate of anthropometry and race science in India and conducted the ethnographic survey of Bengal, suggested that race was the organising basis of caste hierarchy. He applied the European science of anthropometry for the first time in the subcontinent to classify the Indian population (1908). Although some of the other administrators challenged Risley's racial theory of caste, 'it should not therefore be forgotten that the [colonial discourse on castes and tribes] was situated in a political order in which concepts of race were habitually used quite instrumentally' (Bates 1995, 30). In fact, for many of the colonial ethnographers, 'the new, progressive and scientifically-verifiable insights of race theory outweighed or at least sharply modified notions of "caste" as a fundamental fact of Indian history or Indian social organisation' (Bayly 1995, 170). Colonial epistemology and governance thus rigidified caste hierarchies along the lines of racial hierarchy (Bandyopadhyay 1985); where, race served as a lens through which the imperial regime could comprehend, classify, and govern the subject population (Fuller 2017). But how did race and the implications of racial difference figure in the discourses generated by Indians themselves? How was race used as a parameter to understand a community's predicament vis-à-vis, not only the coloniser but, other communities that ranked closer to one's own and yet had to be perceived as an unassimilable Other? The public debates on Hindu nationalism, as we see in Upendra Nath Mukerji and Jatindra Mohan Datta's works, were discursive sites where race featured as a constitutive factor.

In the late nineteenth century, the formulation of the dichotomy of the 'manly Englishman' and the 'effeminate Bengali' was in order to maintain the colonisers' racial privileges (Sinha 1995). The same 'scientific' reasoning from European and Anglo-Indian race science structured the Hindu ideas of racial difference from the Muslims; however, it was not a simple reversal of the hierarchical structure, where Hindu nationalists would claim their racial superiority over Muslims. During the first half of the twentieth century, several anticolonial Indian intellectuals, such as Brajendranath Seal, Sarat Chandra Roy and Biraja Sankar Guha developed race science as a modern science, specifically applicable and useful for understanding the subcontinent's anthropological diversity (Mukharji 2023; Ghoshal 2024). These epistemological developments show that race science was neither rejected by nationalists as merely a colonial tool nor accepted and uncritically applied to the Indian context.

Within the institutional context of advancing race science, knowledge about race as a biological and hereditary feature was simultaneously used to construct a discourse on why the Hindus were on the decline physically and physiologically, why their population was dwindling and, thus, why they were degrading 'in their own land' whereas the Muslim as a racial and religious outsider was flourishing (Mukerji 1909).[4] The charge of effeminacy served a double purpose for the Hindu; owing to the Muslim's sexuality, virility and physical strength, this Other became at once a model for emulation and an object of contempt. Thus, the attempt to understand the declining condition and 'religious-mindedness' of the Hindu, was necessarily embroiled with the question of the community's biological and physiological condition (Datta 1946a). Although Indian writers, statisticians and anthropologists did not advocate for racism per se, the preoccupation with the racial origin of the non-Hindu communities or the Hindu's

---

4 Such a reading of the Hindu nationalist discourse also serves the purpose of moving beyond, as Ishita Banerjee-Dube suggests, 'a clear separation between the "colonizer" and the "colonized"' (2014, 141).

degenerating reproductive and mortality rate over the decades, foregrounds the racial-qua-biological basis of Hindu nationalism. Given these specific configurations, race and religion cannot be distinguished as if 'one was historically older or more natural than the other…religion and race [were] contemporary, indeed, coextensive' (Anidjar 2008, 28).

The Dying Hindu Race

The colonial practice of decennial census was a major source of ideas about Hindu identity as distinct from and threatened by the non-Hindu others (Jones 1981; Datta 1999; Bandyopadhyay 1992). The published censuses reported the statistical data as well as provided descriptions of the 'caste system, the religions of India, fertility and morbidity, domestic organisation, and the economic structure of India' (Cohn 1996, 8). The public preoccupation with census data began with the publication of the census findings in 1891. Based on the 'slower growth rates of Hindus', the Census Commissioner, C. J. O'Donnell calculated 'the number of years for Hindus to disappear altogether' (Datta 1999, 24). This thesis – which became the basis for Mukerji's book – continued to be harped on and circulated in the public domain. Herbert Risley evoked this idea again around the 1901 census operation (Datta 1999).

The next major public discourse about comparative demographics between Hindus and Muslims erupted with the partition of Bengal, in 1905. The dominant population in the new province of Eastern Bengal and Assam turned out to be the Muslims, much to the Bengali Hindus' despair and anxiety (Bandyopadhyay 2015). Mukerji's thesis of the Hindus as a 'dying race' and the discussions it generated, can be read against this background; it was conditioned by anxiety around demographics and its sociopolitical implications for the communities. However, only a preoccupation with demographics originating in the colonial census, certainly cannot explain the racialisation of 'religious' differences. Race was not used in these debates as merely a rhetorical device, or interchangeably with religion or community or nation, nor was it an additive factor to simply entrench the *already* given differences between Hindus and Muslims. Rather, notions of racial and religious differences equally constituted the discourse of Hindu nationalism. And, as discussed below, when the purpose of enumerative reasoning shifted radically with the rise in representational politics, the obsession with racial difference altered but did not dissipate.

Mukerji's *A Dying Race* contains articles that were initially published in the newspaper *The Bengalee* (founded in 1862, Calcutta) indicating a wider circulation than a published monograph might accrue.[5] His treatise comprises numerical figures, percentages and demographics, accompanied by passionate and anxious laments over – what he conceives as – the 'dramatically' increasing numbers of 'Mahomedans' and the rapidly declining numbers of Hindus. After several citations from the decennial censuses between 1872 and 1901, he remarks: 'The question that strikes one is, why two communities, living side by side, practically under the same conditions, should show such disparity in their respective rates of growth' (1909, 2). He recalls that various groups across the world 'have dwindled and finally disappeared from their own country' and concludes that a similar thing was happening to the Bengali Hindus 'in their own land' (1909, 2). Given these historical instances, he finds that, Bengali Hindus 'are also a decaying race', and that, 'Year after year they [Bengali Hindus] are being pushed back, the land once occupied by them is taken up by the Mahomedans and their relative proportion to the population of the country is getting smaller and smaller' (1909, 4–5).

[5] Moving the discussion away from figures like V. D. Savarkar and M. S. Golwalkar to U. N. Mukerji and Jatindra Mohan Datta challenges the exclusive focus on the *institutional* historiography (from RSS and Hindu Mahasabha to the contemporary Bharatiya Janata Party) of Hindu nationalism. The ideas that would engender and sustain Hindu nationalism were not restricted to the political institutions and discourses, but significantly shaped the 'secular' popular as well.

When Mukerji delves further into his sources (census reports, district reports, popular publications, and personal experience) for the major causes of increase in the Muslim population, he comes across a reality overdetermined by poverty and caste hierarchies for most Hindus. In several cases, lower-caste Hindu widows are found to 'desire' Muslim men. This idea can be traced back to the nineteenth-century Hindu reformers who advocated widow remarriage on the grounds of 'untrammeled sexuality' of Hindu widows (Datta 1999, 30). As Pradip K. Datta points out, Mukerji differs from the agenda of these reformist projects insofar as he relocates the object of reform from Hindu women to Hindu men (1999). Mukerji observes that Hindu widows remarry and convert to the Islamic faith to escape poverty and caste oppressions: 'She has no other alternative but to marry a Mahomedan, who is generally better off than a Hindu of the cultivating class, unless she takes to an immoral life' (1909, 7). After this discussion of caste restrictions and polygamy,[6] matters which could be said to relate directly to questions of faith and religious practices, he moves on to discuss the 'superior physique of the Mahomedans as compared with that of the Hindus'. He claims that, 'Very few Bengali Hindus work as porters. Their poor physique stands in the way. One can get a fair idea of the physique of the two communities by looking at the Mahomedan porter and the Hindu sweetmeat-seller on the Railway platform' (1909, 8).

Mukerji explains this by turning an 'anthropological' eye towards his neighbours: 'a colony of Mahomedan duftries' who place higher value on health as their 'only asset', spend more on food than their Hindu counterparts; this, in turn, is possible only because land in Bengal now 'practically belongs to' the Muslim (1909, 11). In another essay in this book, Mukerji analyses the absence of Hindus in certain professions. Discussing in detail the history of one profession – carpentry – he remarks that most of the men working in this trade are Muslims. He notes that only Hindus

[6] Going against the stereotype, Mukerji in fact claims that polygamy is largely absent among Muslims in Bengal (1909, 8).

from a certain caste take up carpentry. Although lower castes like Namasudras and Bagdis could enter the trade, as a matter of fact they tend not to. Moreover, the Muslims work for a lower wage than the Hindus. The latter – to their disadvantage – believe that they were better workers than their Muslim competitors and consequently demand higher wages. According to Mukerji, the Hindu assumption was not completely baseless, but he cautions that '[h]ereditary dexterity, if not an entire myth, has been greatly exaggerated' (ibid., 19).

Describing the Hindu carpenters' quarters and their habits as almost inverse, Mukerji also comments on how deeply religious the Muslims are: 'Early in the morning and in the evening when they come back from their work, one can hear them reading their sacred books from almost every hut' (ibid., 21). The Hindus have no religiosity, are regular drinkers, and are illiterate. Besides, as a doctor, Mukerji also claims the advantage of seeing and being able to compare Hindu and Muslim physiologies who he treats as outpatients in a dispensary. By the time they are thirty, Hindus seem to become 'a physical wreck', clearly owing to their illiteracy, and eating and drinking habits. Here, Mukerji connects the physiological to the religious. He attributes the systematic physiological degradation of the Hindus to their addiction to drugs and drinking. This habit, in turn, is seen to sprout and spread among Hindus, given their lack of religious rigour. In contrast, Muslims, irrespective of their social class, are members of religious congregations where religious and moral teachings are regularly imparted, resulting in their thriving physical health (ibid., 70). For Mukerji 'the chauvinistic anxiety produced by a declining proportion of Bengalis, is relocated in the Muslim' (Datta 1999, 31), through the use of religion, biology, caste, and numerical demographic calculations such as birth rates and death rates.

It is the notion of the 'body' where the religious and the racial are arguably intertwined. As Mrinalini Sinha has demonstrated, 'enfeebling diet' of the (Hindu) Bengali was often cited in colonial discourses about the effeminacy of the Bengali men. Although she does not bring the racial aspect of 'religious' communities to bear on this discourse of diet, effeminacy and 'degeneration of contemporary Indians' (1995, 20–21), it can be suggested, building on this argument, that this concept of effeminacy was to some extent not only internalised by the Hindus vis-à-vis the coloniser but also to a large extent mapped on to the discourse of racial difference vis-à-vis the Muslims. Physical habits of working, eating or drinking – stemming from religious prescriptions – are considered to have direct effect on the physiological, biological constitution of the individuals of a community. The biology of the individuals of a community, in turn, is mapped on to an imagined – in the sense of calculated – body of a ('religious') collective. The condition of this collective biological body can then be referred to in terms of demographics and reproductive rates, birth rates and mortality rates. These terms of measurement pervade the nationalism debates in the 1920–1930s.

The focus on diet and physiology expands the politics of enumerating demographic strength into a question of quantifiable racial difference. Whereas the calculation of representational politics based on the numbers in a community is about the present, the relation between rates (of reproduction, mortality, etc.) and the assumptions of physiological health and physical prowess is based on heredity and a calculated projection into the future. Here, the concern is not just with the current demographics of Hindus (and Muslims) but – significantly – with the reproductive (or other) *rate* of the community. Measures of rate within a population group indicates 'phenomena that occur over a period of time, which have to be studied over a certain period of time; they are serial phenomena. The phenomena addressed by biopolitics are, essentially, aleatory events that occur within a population that exists over a period of time' (Foucault 2003, 246). 'Rate' then, given its very specific career in modern politics, exceeds the here-and-now concerns of representational politics and explicitly enters the domain of heredity and (purportedly) racial lineage. Inculcating 'good' eating habits, cultivating physical strength and physiological health of a community presumes a notion of a community that is hereditary (and thus biological) and not based strictly on questions of religious faith, which theoretically is subject to changes through conversion or renunciation.

The Changing Racial Imperative

As mentioned above, Mukerji was a voice that stood out not for being exclusive but for being representative of the public political common sense[7] which drew simultaneously from theories of contemporary race science, enumerative practices like the census, and notions of religiosity to measure and compare communities. These derivations then became the grounds on which Hindu nationalism came to be formulated during the first half of the twentieth century. A sense of continuity of the preoccupation with race is conveyed by Jatindra Mohan Datta – a Hindu Mahasabha member as well as a fellow at the Royal Statistical Society in London, who published extensively in the 1930s and 1940s in both English and Bangla. He wrote quite regularly for particularly the *Modern Review* – a widely circulating Calcutta periodical, founded in 1907 by Ramananda Chatterjee and popular among the English-educated Bengali reading public. By the time Datta engaged with the question of Hindus, Muslims and their respective nationalisms, the political terrain had altered in at least one major way.

The Morley-Minto Reforms had begun the process of granting separate electorates and seats in the legislative assembly for Muslims in 1909. The Government of India Act of 1919 and 1935 further strengthened 'communal' representation in governing bodies. British Prime Minister Ramsay Macdonald's Communal Award of 1932 offered proportionate representation to communities and further extended the provisions of separate electorates to communities, besides the Muslims. This was replaced by the Poona Pact the same year (agreed to by B. R. Ambedkar and M. K. Gandhi) which removed the provision of separate electorates and retained reservation of seats for 'lower' castes in

[7] Kishori Lal Sarkar (1911) and Sakharam Ganesh Deuskar (n.d.) published monographs in response to Mukerji's thesis. Several others also responded in the journal *Modern Review* (1911).

the electoral system. In this move towards self-government and rise of representational politics, the significance of numbers for communities continued; although, unlike in the earlier decades, it was now crucial to establish the numerical strength of Hindus rather than their weakening or declining condition, in order for that to be translated into political leverage. 'Race' continued to be a primary factor for producing the Self and the Other in Hindu nationalism; but now it was more important to foreground the racial sameness of Indian Muslims rather than their 'alien-ness'. Thus, the renewed attempt in the public sectarian debates was to establish that Indian Muslims were Hindu converts and – assuming that religious conversion failed to affect racial change – the point was to consider Muslims as Hindus who should thus be ineligible for separate political and legislative representation. Despite the extreme contrast in the way the role of demographics and enumeration altered, the preoccupation with determining the racial origin of Bengali Muslims persisted.

Datta argued that 'an overwhelmingly large number' of contemporary Muslims were descendants of Hindu converts; and that the 'foreign element in them is exceedingly small, and whatever foreign element there may be, it is diluted by repeated intermarriages with the native element in course of centuries'(1931b). Elsewhere, Datta construed Bengali Muslims as distinctly different from the Hindus in terms of 'public spirit', 'religious-mindedness', heroism, language, and on 'where their loyalties truly lie', in this essay, Datta – in order to invalidate all political claims by the Muslims in India, especially Bengal – chose to demonstrate that the,

> Bengali Muhammadan is not essentially different from the Bengali Hindus, either by race or by language. His claim to a separate recognition is untenable…His religion is but skin-deep; he has got no past and his past is not glorious. He tries to shine in the reflected glory of the Pathan or the Mughal conquerors, forgetting that it was his ancestors who were conquered; that it was his father who was oppressed and, perhaps, forcibly converted./ His attempt belongs to the same plane of absurdity if the Santal Christian convert were to

> claim that his ancestors came with Clive and conquered Bengal on the glorious field of Plassey in 1757. (1931b)

Besides dismissing conversion in an off-hand gesture as unsubstantial, Datta rejects any biological basis of difference between the Muslims and the Hindus of Bengal. However, in doing that and in bringing together the Santal Christian and the Bengali low-caste Muslim, he unwittingly demonstrates the inevitability of the question (and the possibility) of racial difference of other communities vis-à-vis the dominant Hindus. In fact, the almost sudden introduction of Santal Christians, to establish the 'absurdity' (besides perhaps underlining that Bengali Muslims shining 'in the reflected glory of the Pathan or the Mughals' is not so absurd by itself) of Bengali Muslims, clearly states the greater value of racial over religious affiliation. Datta plays to his readers' sensibilities by making this unwarranted comparison; it is not difficult to surmise that he meant to invoke the stereotype figure of the dark-skin Santals and the white European (the 'true' Christians) to drive home the absurdity of imagining that the two share the same lineage. In rendering the Other's religion as 'skin-deep', he implies that race, instead of being about skin colour, goes deeper to one's blood and physiology. Thus, religious conversion cannot override one's racial history. The varied writings of Datta reveal the change from entrenching the Hindu–Muslim *difference*, to *assimilating* the Indian Muslim as essentially – that is racially – Hindu. Such changes in Hindu nationalism's position vis-à-vis the Indian Muslim signal the inevitable evolution of the 'meanings, salience and dimensions' of community identities with changes in the politics and needs of the national and majoritarian identity.

A Style of Reasoning

A focus on the prevalent use of numbers in these public sectarian debates reveals how enumeration was not only a 'modality' (Cohn 1996) for colonial administrative purposes but was also a 'style of reasoning' (Hacking 1985), of deriving conclusions and constructing claims, within the arena of public politics. The prevalence of an enumerative form of public reasoning is exclusively related to the rise of representational politics and the popularity of the colonial census (Cohn 1987; Kaviraj 1992; Appadurai 1993; Dirks 2001). Despite generating insightful arguments about how the colonial practice of census was more 'productive' of identities and not merely documenting what was already on the ground, what is missed is how Hindu nationalists came to mobilise enumerative evidence, so abundantly and credibly, in the service of political arguments such as racial and religious difference.[8] Although the census was undoubtedly a major source of data for these public intellectuals, the enumerative common sense was not contained by it. In fact, this public form of reasoning was, at least partly, also informed by the simultaneously emerging discipline of statistics. These early-decade (Hindu) nationalist statisticians were invested in questions of racial and religious difference of communities.[9] Using statistical methods (and anthropometric data), they attempted to establish measurable differences – in terms of racial origin, racial mix and purity, and degree of religiosity – between various non-Hindu communities. This rise in a statistical way of thinking, to argue for political motives, produced a vocabulary of enumerable categories within the sectarian discourse.

The rates of reproduction, percentages of demographic change, numerical figures in public organisations, public welfare and education made up major portions of these debates. Therefore, beyond absolute demographic numbers of the various populations, the style of calculative reasoning itself enabled these intellectuals to calculate qualitative group features such as national loyalty and religiosity. For instance, Ramesh Chandra Banerjee (1934)

---

[8] Arjun Appadurai (1993) demonstrates how numbers, not just the census, became an integral part of the colonial imagination; but he does not refer to the nationalists.

[9] A significant example is Prasanta Chandra Mahalanobis (1893–1972) who is considered the 'father' of Indian statistics. His work on anthropometry continued into the late 1940s and was published in a well-reputed academic journal *Sankhya* (contrary to scholarly view but for exception see Projit Mukharji 2015).

argues that, since the Muslims were demanding a share in Bengal's administrative structure, it was only justified that one compares the contribution of Hindus versus Muslims in various branches of public work. Banerjee compares endowments given to Calcutta University for disbursal to students in the form of scholarships, stipends and prizes. He notes that there are 266 endowments by Hindus and that 'some...are of very substantial value' (ibid., 312), omitting to mention the exact amount. The Muslim endowments are five in number; he carefully differentiates that four of them total to a meagre Rs. 6000; and merely footnotes that the other one, alone amounts to Rs. 5000. The numerical endeavour continues. In terms of the proportion of students who benefit from these endowments, he remarks that of the five Muslim endowments, three are 'such that Muslim students have the best chance of securing their advantages' – and stops short of qualifying it any further. For the Hindus, he states clearly that out of the 266 endowments, 259 are open to all students, irrespective of caste and creed. Additionally, non-Governmental schools opened by Christians is 30, by Muslims is 37, and 1006 by Hindus. Since 'a community's claim to superior Govermental [sic] powers can only be justified by its superiority in the field of public service', Banerjee concludes that the Hindus have a (numerically substantiated) greater percentage of 'public spirit' than the Muslims; thus debunking the Muslim demand for a greater role in the administration (1934).

Datta writes about religious favouritism in Bengal administration. He states, 'In the Bengal Legislative Council, out of a total of 140 seats, thirty-nine are occupied by members returned by the Muhammadans on a communal basis' (1931a). To refute the legitimacy of the Muslim demand for reservation of legislative seats, he decides to bring to light the already existing Muslim bias, not just in the main administrative bodies but in the 'by-ways of administration'. He turns to the estates in Bengal that are managed by the Court of Wards. He claims that in the case of the five Dacca Nawab family estates (which are understood to be Muslim-owned), the government charges 1¼ per cent of the gross income for its supervision. For the Bhawal estate, which is

Hindu, the rate charged is 1¾ per cent of the gross income (1931a). Datta also compares the proportion of Hindus and Muslims who had received the Victoria Cross, awarded to Indian soldiers by the British Empire for bravery. Comparing these figures against the total population of each community, respectively, he concluded that 'the Hindus are *twice* more ready to defend India; they are *twice* more courageous and brave than the Muhammadans ... the higher the level of heroism the lesser becomes the number of Muhammadans' (1946b).

Measurements of blood dilution and admixture of Muslim 'foreign' ancestry feature as part of several statistical and anthropological works. The question of Muslim racial origin – whether Indian Muslims were converts from the local Hindu population or were 'descendants of those who originally came from Arab lands' – had provoked speculation among the British and evoked responses from some Muslims since the first national censuses (Vishwanathan 1998, 156). The British soon settled this question in favour of conversion; as Gauri Viswanathan remarks, this definitely helped the British dismiss separatist claims of Muslims. However, there is a resurgence of the question of Muslim racial origin in significantly different terms, in the 1920s–1930s. No longer restricted to the domain of colonial administration, the questions of racial origin of Indian Muslims and the degree to which their blood had mixed and been diluted with 'local' Hindu lineage are taken up by Indian anthropologists and statisticians.

For renowned anthropologist Dhirendra Nath Majumdar (1947), the furthest extent to which racial admixture can take place is best represented through the serological data for the Indian Muslim population. Conversion would yield, according to the discipline's premise, same anthropometric measurements as the communities they live amongst or marry within. Admixture, meanwhile, would yield serological and anthropometric results that exhibit lineages of the various races mixed. Communities with demonstrated admixture would not be able to claim racial purity or any biological distinction from other adjacent communities nor would they be considered part of the dominant race with which the admixture took place. The theory of racial fusion thus keeps at bay the danger of racial purity turning into the logic of racial superiority; but, at the same time, it makes it possible through the science of anthropometry and serology (and genetics later on) to trace the varied lineages and to 'reveal' foreign elements in such races (Mukharji 2023).

Enumeration became central to the Hindu nationalism discourse; and going beyond the framework of comparative demographics, produced a normative vocabulary that could rationalise and mobilise the Hindu anxiety of decline as numerically demonstrable. In discussions of religiosity and racial difference – which constituted the discourse of Hindu nationalism – the use of numerical calculations allowed certain Hindu nationalist claims as secular reasoning.[10] Further, instead of using data directly from existing administrative records, these public figures were inventive in their use and analysis of numerical figures – and even went so far as to rewrite familiar social and affective categories as numerical and therefore comparable. The statistical language, in the form of proportions and rates were applied to a wide range of categories: from the degree of blood admixture to 'religious-mindedness' and 'public spirit'. For the first time perhaps, heroism, religiosity, and loyalty became numerically measurable and comparable categories used to hierarchise communities. Moreover, this practice of perceiving the social through the statistical made religious difference and racial difference interchangeable registers of identification.

Conclusion

In the context of the twentieth-century public debates among Hindu nationalists, one could say then that religious distinctions

[10] On statistical thinking as secular reasoning see Talal Asad (2018). In European historiography, the simultaneous rise of race science and statistics has been extensively explored; for example, Ian Hacking (1990) and Alain Desrosières (1998). In the Indian context, this conjunction has not been adequately engaged with; as exception, see Mukharji (2015).

'hide the most persistent remnants of a history of racism' (Anidjar 2008, 20). The attempt here has been to re-examine the relation of religion and race, in the specific context of Hindu nationalism. The specificity of the 'dying Hindu' discourse from the early twentieth century additionally shows how dated and misleading the Hindutva claim is that 'Hindu khatre mein hain'. The problematic and xenophobic idea that Muslims have a higher growth rate in comparison to the Hindus originated in these century-old debates. Over the last several decades, Muslim growth rate has not increased as predicted by the early twentieth century Hindu nationalists and yet the discourse has become popular again. Turning to the history of this discourse enables us to understand how calculative reasoning and numbers, despite being flawed, can be generative of affective states which can lead to communal solidarity and antagonism towards the perceived Other.

Focusing on how claims and notions from race science – in terms of biological categories and physiological conditions of communities – permeated communal politics, I have suggested that the history of Hindu nationalism is constituted as much by ideas of racial as by religious differences. Although scholars have studied race as used by religious nationalists, the relation between race and religion has remained historically and conceptually separated. In most instances, the claim has been that religious propagandists have *used* race to further their religious nationalist agendas. Instead, religious identity and racial difference, far from being operative on separate registers, were in fact produced in conjunction, such that the implications of being Hindu and Muslim were as much about faith and ritual, as about biology and heredity. Moreover, with changes in representational politics and corresponding changes in Hindu nationalist politics, the anti-Muslim stance also shifted between separation and assimilation. And in order to do that, religious difference and racial similarity between Hindus and Indian Muslims came to be alternately foregrounded. But, significantly, through these varied emphases, Hindu nationalism consistently produced the cultural, racial and political imagination of the nation as Hindu. Drawing from the logic and content of race science and enumerative technique from statistics, Hindu nationalists did not merely construct a Hindu version of racism; they reconfigured Hindu nationalism itself through the triangulation of race, religion and enumeration. Unequivocally equating Hindu nationalism to religious nationalism, therefore, misses other strands that make up the former. Highlighting these strands shows that combating Hindu nationalism with modernist principles such as secularism might be limiting. In a nation where the cultural, racial, political and religious ideals remain implicitly Hindu, secular ideals also come to be informed by these Hindu ideals. Thus, instead of reducing Hindu nationalism to its religious aspects, in this chapter, I have argued for prising apart the multiple domains in which the nation came to be structured as Hindu.

References

Ahmed, Rafiuddin. 1981. *The Bengal Muslims, 1871–1906: A Quest for Identity*. New York: Oxford University Press.

Anderson, Benedict R. (1983) 1991. *Imagined Communities: Reflections on the Origin and Spread of Nationalism*. London: Verso.

Anidjar, Gil. 2008. *Semites: Race, Religion, Literature*. California: Stanford University Press.

Appadurai, Arjun. 1993. "Number in the Colonial Imagination." In *Orientalism and the Postcolonial Predicament*, edited by Carol Breckenridge and Peter Veer, 314–40. Philadelphia: University of Pennsylvania.

Asad, Talal. 2018. *Secular Translations: Nation-State, Modern Self, and Calculative Reason*. New York: Columbia University Press.

Baber, Zaheer. 2004. "'Race', Religion and Riots: The 'Racialization' of Communal Identity and Conflict in India." *Sociology* 38, no. 4: 701–18.

Bandyopadhyay, Sekhar. 1985. "The Raj, Risley and the Tribes and Castes of Bengal." *India Past and Present* 2, no. 1: 41–52.

———. 1992. 'Construction of Social Categories: The Role of Colonial Census'. In K. S. Singh (ed.), *Ethnicity, Caste and People*, 26–36. Delhi: Manohar.

———. 2015. *From Plassey to Partition and After: A History of Modern India*. New Delhi: Orient Blackswan.

Banerjee, Ramesh Chandra. 1934. "Hindu and Muslim Public Spirit in Bengal." *Modern Review* 55, nos. 1–6: 312–16.

Banerjee-Dube, Ishita. 2014. *A History of Modern India*. Delhi: Cambridge University Press.

Bates, Crispin. 1995. "Race, Caste and Tribe in Central India: The Early Origins of Indian Anthropometry." In *The Concept of Race in South Asia*, edited by P. Robb, 219–59. Delhi: Oxford University Press.

Bayly, Susan. 1995. "Caste and 'race' in the colonial ethnography of India." In *The Concept of Race in South Asia*, edited by P. Robb, 165–218. Delhi: Oxford University Press.

Chatterjee, Partha. 1993. *The Nation and Its Fragments: Colonial and Postcolonial Histories*. Princeton: Princeton University Press.

Cohn, Bernard. 1987. "The Census, Social Structure and Objectification." In *An Anthropologist among the Historians and Other Essays*, 224–54. Delhi: Oxford University Press.

———. 1996. *Colonialism and Its Forms of Knowledge: The British in India*. Princeton: Princeton University Press.

Curtin, Philip D. 1965. *The Image of Africa: British Ideas and Action, 1780–1850*. London: Macmillan.

Datta, Jatindra Mohan. 1931a. "Communalism in the Bengal Administration." *Modern Review* 49, no. 1: 45–49.

———. 1931b. "Who the Bengali Mohammedans Are?" *Modern Review* 49, no. 3: 303–09.

———. 1946a. "An Analysis of the 'Religious-Mindedness' Among the Hindus." *Modern Review* 79, nos. 1–6: 365–67.

———. 1946b. "Relative Heroism of the Hindus and the Muhammadans of India." *Modern Review* 79, nos. 1–6: 463–64.

Datta, Pradip. 1999. *Carving Blocs: Communal Ideology in Early Twentieth-Century Bengal*. New York: Oxford University Press.

Desrosières, Alain. 1998. *The Politics of Large Numbers: A History of Statistical Reasoning*. Massachusetts: Harvard University Press.

Dirks, Nicholas B. 2001. *Castes of Mind: Colonialism and Making of Modern India*. Princeton: Princeton University Press.

Foucault, Michel. 2003. *Society Must Be Defended: Lectures at the Collège de France, 1975–76*. New York: Picador.

Friedland, Roger. 2002. "Money, Sex, and God: The Erotic Logic of Religious Nationalism." *Sociological Theory* 20, no. 3: 381–425.

Fuller, C. J. 2017. "Ethnographic Inquiry in Colonial India: Herbert Risley, William Crooke, and the Study of Tribes and Castes." *Journal of the Royal Anthropological Institute* 23, no. 3: 603–21.

Gellner, Ernest. 2006. *Nations and Nationalism.* Malden: Blackwell Pub.

Ghoshal, Sayori. 2024. "Experts of Identity: Race, Ethnicity, and Science in India, 1910s–1940s." *Isis* 115, no. 1: 84–104. https://doi.org/10.1086/729014.

Hacking, Ian. 1985. "Styles of Reasoning." In *Postanalytic Philosophy*, edited by J. Rajchman and C. West, 145–64. New York: Columbia University Press.

———. 1990. *The Taming of Chance.* New York: Cambridge University Press.

Hobsbawm, E. J. 1990. *Nations and Nationalism since 1780: Programme, Myth, Reality.* New York: Cambridge University Press.

Jaffrelot, C. 1995. "The ideas of the Hindu race in the writings of Hindu nationalist ideologues in the 1920s and 1930s." In *The Concept of Race in South Asia*, edited by Peter Robb, 327–54. Delhi: Oxford University Press.

Jones, Kenneth W. 1981. "Religious Identity and the Indian Census." In *The Census in British India: New Perspectives*, edited by G. Barrier, 73–102. Delhi: Manohar.

Kaviraj, Sudipta. 1992. "The imaginary institution of India." In *Subaltern Studies: Writings on South Asian History and Society VII*, edited by Partha Chatterjee and Gyanendra Pandey. Delhi; New York: Oxford University Press.

Majumdar, Dhirendra N. 1947. *Racial Problems in Asia.* New Delhi: Indian Council of World Affairs.

Mukerji, Upendra Nath. 1909. *A Dying Race.* Calcutta: Mukerjee and Sons.

Mukharji, Projit. 2015. "Profiling the Profiloscope: Facialization of Race Technologies and the Rise of Biometric Nationalism in Inter-War British India." *History and Technology* 31, no. 4: 376–96.

———. 2023. *Brown Skins, White Coats: Race Science in India, 1920–66.* Chicago, IL: University of Chicago Press.

Pandey, Gyanendra. 1990. *The Construction of Communalism in Colonial North India.* New York: Oxford University Press.

Risley, Herbert H. 1891. *The Tribes and Castes of Bengal.* Calcutta: Government Press.

———. 1908. *The Peoples of India.* London.

Shraddhananda, Sanyasi. 1926. *Hindu Sangathan: Saviour of the Dying Race.* Delhi: Arjun Press.

Sinha, Mrinalini. 1995. *Colonial Masculinity: The 'Manly Englishman' and the 'Effeminate Bengali' in the Late Nineteenth Century*. Manchester; New York: Manchester University Press.

Smith, Wilfred Cantwell. 1978. *The Meaning and End of Religion*. New York: Harper & Row.

Stepan, Nancy. 1982. *The Idea of Race in Science: Great Britain, 1800–1960*. Hamden: Archon Books.

Stoler, Ann. 2002. *Carnal Knowledge and Imperial Power: Race and the Intimate in Colonial Rule*. California: University of California Press.

Varshney, Ashutosh. 1993. "Contested Meanings: India's National Identity, Hindu Nationalism, and the Politics of Anxiety." *Daedalus* 122, no. 3: 227–61.

Veer, Peter van der. 1994. *Religious Nationalism: Hindus and Muslims in India*. California: University of California.

Viswanathan, Gauri. 1998. *Outside the Fold: Conversion, Modernity, and Belief*. Princeton: Princeton University Press.

FIVE

The Public and the Person: Religion and Competing Legal Personhoods in Today's India

Esha Meher

In February 2016, the Public Works Department of the Bihar State Government approached the court of the sub-divisional magistrate, seeking summons against a party that had encroached upon public property. The Public Works Department alleged that a portion of a public road was blocked, creating hassle for commuters as well as traffic policemen. The magistrate admitted the petition and issued a summons to the alleged encroacher. But the personnel entrusted with delivering the summons were in a dilemma: the mischief monger in question was none other than the Hindu deity, Lord Hanuman, who stood in full glory within the precincts of his temple. Since the recipient of the summons was a deity, the personnel proceeded to face the deity and pinned the piece of paper on his 'person' before leaving the premises (Pandey 2016). The deity, smeared in vermillion paint and with the summons stuck on his chest, stood in silence while the locals looked on.

The attempted eviction of Lord Hanuman shows the deep entanglement between Hindu deities, public spaces, and the law in contemporary India. Not only do deities physically occupy public spaces – roads, buildings under construction, riverbanks and alcoves under flyovers – but they also have a specific legal standing. The interests of deities, and even material comforts (like using air conditioners in sanctums of temples), are regularly discussed when laws regarding temples are made, enacted and upheld in society. This entanglement of deities as persons and state legislation has given rise to a peculiar problem. On the one hand, the management of temples is often regulated by the state, in the manner of other institutions like schools, trusts, or hospitals (Dhavan 1987). On the other hand, enforcement of laws regarding deities is also subject to legal measures against blasphemy, obscenity, and 'hurting public sentiments' (Nair 2023; Scott 2023). While courts treat deities at par with human litigants (they can sue and be sued, be made to depose under oath, furnish evidence, be held liable for perjury, and the like), the veneration and sanctity of deities seem, in many ways, to be above the law. It goes without saying, for instance, that the court cannot imprison or punish deities like human subjects, in light of the public outcry that would follow. In other words, although deities enjoy the same rights as human litigants, they are practically not subject to the same liabilities. This peculiar position with respect to legal rights and implicit immunity has placed Hindu deities in a unique position in the Indian public sphere. The importance of the personhood of Hindu deities has been upheld by India's 'secular' legal system and the judiciary multiple times; most recently in the Supreme Court's 2019 judgement on the Ram Janmabhoomi dispute in Ayodhya, which upheld the claims of the deity Ram Lalla over the Sunni Waqf Board on the contested site of the Babri Masjid (*M. Siddiq v. Mahant Suresh Das*, 2020).

How, then, does the legal personality of Hindu deities set them apart in the religious–political landscape of contemporary India? What, in particular, is different in the case of the personhood of Hindu deities, especially in relation to parallel institutions in other religious communities? In this chapter, I examine the relationship between religion and the public sphere in India by focussing on the peculiar *legal personality* of the Hindu deity in the contemporary Indian state. I argue that the construction of legal personhood of the Hindu deity by the colonial and post-colonial Indian judiciary has put the Hindu deity in a unique position in the Indian public space. It is this position that allows property claims made in the name of Hindu deities to have a great deal of comparative advantage over those by other religious institutions, like mosques or churches. In the first part of the chapter, I trace the particularity of the Hindu deity with respect to the tool of legal personhood. In the second part, I compare the legal personhood of the Hindu deity with that of the Islamic *waqf* and the Christian Church to highlight the skewed effects of the application of legal personhood to the religious–legal landscape in India.

The (Divine) Person and the Public

To analyse the circumstances that led to the Hindu deity becoming a legal person, we need to understand the nature of the relationship between Indian litigants and the judiciary in colonial India. Several studies on the 'litigious' character of Indians in colonial and post-colonial India (Cohn 1965; Rudolph and Rudolph 1967; Mendelsohn 1981; Dhavan 1987; De 2018) suggest that it was fairly common for the Hindus to approach the colonial judiciary for adjudication of disputes of a religious character. At the same time, however, colonial judges as well as litigants expected that resolutions on questions of Hinduism would be based not on English law but on scriptural authorities like the *Dharmashastras*. Hindu pundits had assisted the colonial state since the late eighteenth century in compiling treatises, based on their interpretations and commentaries on the *Dharmashastras*, laying the groundwork for what would be known as Anglo-Hindu law (Halhed 1776; Colebrooke 1802; Morley 1858; see also Vidyasagar 2012). Given their routine invocation by litigants and judges, the *Dharmashastras* have continued since to be the most authoritative source of Hindu law in the late colonial period, and even, to a great extent, to the present day (Kane 1930; Derrett 1968; Davis 2010; Rocher 2012). The point to note here is that judges and legal commentators of the colonial and post-colonial judiciary have played a critical role in preserving the *Dharmashastras* as a source of law.

Why did Hindus choose to approach the colonial judiciary for the settlement of their religious disputes? It is important to remember here that the legal landscape of colonial India was a diverse one: even the colonial state allowed *pundits* and *qazis* authority to issue advisory opinion, as well as adjudicate disputes using religious laws (Morley 1858, 177–201). Litigants, in other words, had a degree of choice in deciding whom to approach for the settlements of religious disputes. That they chose to approach the colonial court (as opposed to the traditional authorities like the *pundit*) was an instance of forum shopping. One possible reason for Indians to approach colonial courts was the belief that they had more room to manoeuvre multiple legal systems, since colonial judges drew upon both English law and shastric interpretations. Such manoeuvring was not uncommon in the legal landscapes of empires: Sergio Serulnikov, for one, has shown how indigenous litigants in Potosí chose to approach colonial courts over traditional authorities to take advantage of the complex webs of colonial and indigenous legal systems to pursue their claims (Serulnikov 1996; see also Benton 2012). The act of choosing the colonial judiciary over traditional authorities, therefore, was a deliberate choice by litigants.

While there was an initial overlap between traditional and modern legal systems in colonial India, by the late nineteenth century, colonial judges were delivering verdicts on Indian religious matters without the advice of traditional religious authorities. Pundits and qazis were initially employed to guide the English judges through disputes concerning a 'religious' character or question. These experts, however, soon understood the importance of their position and began manoeuvring the cases to suit their strategic – and monetary – interests. Upon spotting this disturbing trend, the colonial state began controlling and gradually reducing the power and jurisdiction of religious authorities in the legal process (Galanter 1989). What eventually remained of their authority was confined to a tiny fraction of disputes pertaining to 'personal' laws of family and inheritance (Stephens 2018). The reducing power of traditional experts meant that the colonial judiciary was increasingly drawn into directly adjudicating Hindu law. Despite the Queen's 1858 Proclamation, which overtly promised non-interference in religious matters of her Indian subjects, colonial judges continued to hear cases concerning religious governance (for instance, *Mullick v. Mullick*, 1925).

Questions of governance, however, were not necessarily questions of faith. The most common dispute regarding 'governance' of Hindu institutions tended to be administrative in nature and often carried a commercial significance. Such matters included the ability of the deity, separate from the temple, to claim exemption from taxes; whether the deity had the right to alienate its 'own' wealth, received through donations, for the welfare of the temple; technical disputes over *shebaits* being a separate category of caretakers with proprietary interests in the deity's wealth; and whether women could be 'caretakers' of family deities (Mukherjea 1952). At the heart of these disputes lay clarifications on contractual relations, debts, and the rights of buying and selling property – in short, matters of a *public* nature. I use the term 'public' in its specific legal sense, to mean that the disputes per se have little to do with the specifics of the Hindu faith. Similar disputes, as one can expect, arose with regard to Muslim institutions and endowments as well, particularly on the nature of the *waqf*, its subtypes, beneficiaries and the purposes for which a *waqf* could be instituted (Kozlowski 1985; see also *Abdul Fata v. Russomoy*, 1894). Such public disputes, in other words, need not be necessarily adjudicated through 'religious' laws like the *Dharmashastras*; the usual laws on contracts, trusts and endowments could take care of them, as they did for other public institutions.

The tool of legal personhood was used in the adjudication of religious disputes in India, in part, because such disputes were considered to be property disputes of a public nature. The common use of legal personhood in Europe was to govern companies and ships: the tool was seen as a 'legal fiction' that helped protect private property, adjudicate complex jurisdictional disputes, and navigate liability. Take, for example, ships that were arrested for trespassing into territorial waters. If the liability was pinned on the owner of the ship, there was little chance that he would come, knowingly accept arrest and criminal liability, and release the ship. The typical consequence was the ship stranded in a harbour with its cargo going to waste (for the crew would usually flee). Instead, once the ship was recognised as a legal person, the owners would be more amenable to negotiation, knowing that they faced no chances of arrest or personal criminal liability. The same is true for companies: key directors and decision-makers are protected from personal criminal liability should the company be engaged in commercial default (see Geldart 1925). Thus, when colonial courts were faced with the multitude of religious institutions in India, each having its share of wealth and endowments, they saw it as a battle among multiple stakeholders – the *shebait*s, *archaka*s, priests, *mahant*s, worshippers, *mutawali*s, *imam*s, and trustees – each claiming their legitimacy through religious scriptures. Legal personhood was a convenient tool to adjudicate these disputes: the *waqf* already acted like a legal person in Islamic law; the colonial courts imposed personhood on the Hindu deity as well (see *Tambekar v. Govindram*, 1888).

Imposing legal personhood on the Hindu deity was different from using the tool in case of ships and companies. In such cases, the point of legal personhood was to protect the owner by imposing liability on the object: the ship could be arrested so that the owner could go free. But that could not be the case with the deity. Imposing liability on the *deity* – such as the charge of tax evasion or criminal trespass – to protect the human persons involved in the case was not accepted by any party. The deity, unlike the ship and the company, is an object of worship, and, to a degree, enjoys a higher status over its human adversaries (like the priests and caretakers). In other words, the law that was used to govern the Hindu deity, including the manner and method of imposition of legal personhood, was not purely English law. It was a curious and hybrid form of law that claimed to derive its legitimacy from the Crown and its roots from the *Dharmashastra*s. I have shown elsewhere how this particular process of shaping the legal personhood of Hindu deities took shape through a series of judgements in colonial India (Meher forthcoming). Here, I want to emphasise that the status of the Hindu deity as a legal person is of great consequence, both legally and politically, in its position in public space. While both *waqf* and deities are treated as legal persons, the *waqf* is not a sacral object in the manner of the deity and is rarely politically mobilised in the name of hurt sentiments.

It is in this tussle between the persons of the Hindu deity and the *waqf* that we need to understand the outcome of the Babri Masjid demolition dispute. The 2019 judgement of the Supreme Court of India (*M. Siddiq v. Mahant Suresh Das*, 2020) was more than a thousand pages long, and has many complicated aspects that are not relevant for our purposes. The point is that, keeping aside the major political ramifications of the matter, the legal issue was a property dispute that fell within the boundaries of public law. The issues covered a wide variety of classic property claims: adverse possession, invocation of the law of limitation, and the application of the concept of *res judicata*. Yet, it was the status of litigants as rights-bearing human beings on one side (the Muslim parties) and *deities* in possession of legal personality on the other (Ram Lalla Virajman and Asthan Ram Janmabhoomi) that gave this dispute its own distinct colour. The Hindu deity's possession of legal personhood in contrast to the lack of personhood of the Muslim mosque or any object of worship gave this dispute a lopsided character. At the very heart of the dispute was the claim that the historic mosque built during the Mughal era was built at the birthplace of the Hindu God, Ram. The Hindu community made a historical–legal claim to the site. This dispute showed the inherent contradictions within the existing body of jurisprudence governing questions of religion and public life in India.

State governance of religious institutions is a reasonable concept and action as long as all religious actors are placed on the same level-playing ground. It is here that the case of India takes an interesting turn. While mosques, *waqfs*, churches, gurudwaras and their respective property are treated as institutions with a set corpus, the Hindu deity claims an exceptional status of a legal person. This element of legal personhood seems to be a benign legal tool employed for effective administration. But upon closer inspection, one sees its chequered history in this brand of religious adjudication. This tool single-handedly gives the Hindu deity an exceptional status with a lopsided bargaining power over religious institutions of other faiths.

Unequal Equality

To evaluate the significance of this exceptionality of the Hindu deity, I will now take a comparative look at the use of legal personhood in managing Christian and Muslim religious property in colonial and post-colonial India. Much like the image of the Hindu deity, the Church and the Islamic *waqf* (trust) claim legal personhood, and routinely receive money and land. But there is a crucial difference that sets apart the use of legal personhood in these two minority religions from that of the Hindu deity – while Indian courts have reached no consensus on imposing personhood in Christian and Muslim institutions, they have put the Hindu deity above all such scriptural and legal debates. This difference, giving a rather wide berth to the Hindu divine image with respect to the *waqf* and the Church, has been a key factor in tilting the balance in favour of acquiring contested spaces in the name of Hindu deities.

In Christianity, canon law imposes personhood on the body of the Roman Catholic Church, although not in non-Catholic or other secular constitutions. Canon 100 in the *Code of Canon Law* lays down the hierarchy of personhood within the institution of the Roman Catholic Church, stating that the Church, being the highest authority, gains personhood from God (*Code of Canon Law*, c. 100). For any other religious entity within the Order, such personhood is conferred only through special decree for a well-defined purpose like religion or charity (*Code of Canon Law*, c. 279, §1). It must be noted that neither Christ nor the Cross is ever made the subject for conferral of legal personhood. The Austrian jurist Edmund Bernatzik proposed a typology of Church administration in terms of property: the *dominium proprietaris* (property) of the Church belonged to nobody, the *dominium absolutissimum* (absolute) to God, the *dominium directivum* (right of supervision) to the State, and the *dominium possessionis* (right of administration and maintenance) to the clergy (Bernatzik 1890).

While Bernatzik argued that the ownership of Church property belonged to no one, others have ascribed ownership of church goods to the Pope and the Holy See, who effectively had the power to sell such property (Byrnes 2017). All over the Christian world, in other words, there is significant consensus on the conditions of imposing legal personhood on the Church.

In India, however, there continues to be no consensus on the legal personhood of the Church. The confusion is most apparent in a series of cases dealing with the effective management of Church property, beginning with the *Rev. Fr. Farcisus Mascarenhas v. State of Bombay* (1960), on whether the Bombay Public Trust Act applied to Roman Catholic Churches. The Bombay High Court distinguished between the Hindu deity and the Roman Catholic Church despite both being closely related to faith: Hindu deities, unlike the Church, were 'conceived as individual persons', and therefore did not need any recognition by law to be conferred with legal personhood. Drawing on the jurist Savigny's distinction between Roman polytheism and Christian monotheism, the court held that Hindu gods, like Roman ones, were conceived to resemble 'individual visible men that one sees around one', and that indeed 'nothing was more natural than that each of them should have his own personal property' (*Mascarenhas v. Bombay*, 1960). Note that Hindu gods being legal persons was not rigorously argued based on theology or law, but was simply based on their perceived 'natural' appearance. A similar argument could not be made for Christianity, where God is divine and does not have a human manifestation, and articles of faith therein needed express recognition of the law to be called a legal person. The court did consider a range of authorities, from the Magna Carta to Legal Digests from England and the United States, to understand the role of the Church and its different components, the role of rituals like consecration, and the people who exercise authority on behalf of the church. Yet, after much deliberation, the court held the Church to be a public trust and not a legal person – a decision that departed from canon law, which holds the Catholic Church to be a person.

Far from settling the question of the Church's legal personhood in India, the Bombay High Court's judgement in *Rev. Mascarenhas* only served to complicate the issue, reaching no conclusion based on either canon or secular law. Two years later, the Kerala High Court, in *James Chinamma v. Joseph Abraham* (1962), while judging whether the Church could be called an agriculturalist, revisited the same question. This time, the Court based its judgement not on canon law, but instead relied, for reasons not altogether clear, on the definition of person within the colonial legal framework, specifically the General Clauses Act of 1897. It concluded that the Church was a legal person – not because of any scriptural or legal sanction, but simply as a matter of convenience. The judges accepted as much, confessing that the imposition of personhood on the Church was simply the 'best mode' for addressing the question (*Chinamma v. Joseph Abraham*, 1962). Given this history of opposing judgements without clear legal or scriptural backing, the jurisprudence on the legal personhood of the Church and the management of Church property continue to be contradictory to this day. On the one hand, there is a set of case laws, which ascribe to the view held by the court in *Rev. Mascarenhas* to hold that the Church does not have personhood since ecclesiastical law is not the law of the land in India. On the other hand, there exists a parallel set of case laws, led by *James Chinamma*, which hold that 'there is no legal impediment in treating the Church as a person' (*Chinamma v. Joseph Abraham*, 1962).

The significance of this contradictory jurisprudence on the personhood of the Church in India is that it only serves to reinforce the Hindu deity's exceptional claim to personhood, and, thereby, to property. Courts in India have left the conferral of legal personhood on the Church undecided, hanging on the cusp of ecclesiastical and secular law. But no such indecision remains around the Hindu deity, which, as the *Rev. Mascarenhas* judgement maintained, is assumed to have personhood simply by virtue of its 'nature'. As we have seen, there is nothing natural about this conclusion, given that the Hindu deity's journey to personhood had more to do with an idiosyncratic array of colonial judgements than with either theological or legal reasoning. Yet, this 'naturalness' of the Hindu deity's personhood is not only considered to be above debate but has also come to serve, in post-colonial Indian jurisprudence, as the yardstick to judge personhood in other religions. Both Christianity and Islam have extensive debates on the question of personhood in their legal traditions, yet Indian courts have routinely chosen to ignore them, instead of evaluating them in light of the Hindu deity's personhood. This discrimination was blatant in *Rev. Mascarenhas*, where the court disregarded canon law and rejected the Church's personhood in comparison with the 'naturalness' of the Hindu deity. It is this curious mode of legal reasoning that has further weakened the case for minority religious institutions in secular Indian law, for the solid legal support for the Hindu deity's personhood can be routinely deployed to challenge and undermine competing claims of Christian and Muslim institutions.

The problem is even more acute for Muslim institutions than Christian ones, for, in contrast with canon law, the notion of legal personhood is hotly debated in Islamic law. On the one hand, scholars like Joseph Schacht have argued that such a concept simply does not exist in Islam – given Islam's origins as a monotheistic religion against the backdrop of a polytheistic Arab regime, there was no room for any legal status to be attached to Allah or his manifestation of divinity (Schacht 1964). On the other hand, the likes of Mahdi Zahraa have argued that corporations, trusts, and other similar associations, while not expressed in those terms, have long been granted legal personhood (*dhimma*) in Islamic jurisprudence (Zahraa 1995). Indeed, as Zahraa shows, the doctrine of *dhimma* – defined as a presumed or imagined repository that contains all the rights and obligations relating to a person – was developed in conjunction with the doctrine of legal capacity (*ahliyyah*) and both doctrines have been well defined in order to serve the concept of legal personhood and clarify its elements. The crucial point here is that legal personhood in Islamic law, while existing under various names, is always perceived as a *secular* legal instrument, with no relation to the divine.

This ambiguity on personhood in Islamic law translated into yet another conundrum in the Indian legal system in 1940 when the Privy Council refused to classify a mosque as a legal person. Instead, it characterised the dispute strictly in terms of property law and redirected focus on questions of legal title and access. In the case of *Masjid Shahid Ganj v. Shiromani Gurudwara Prabandhak Committee Amritsar* (1940), involving a contested site between Muslims and Sikhs in Punjab, the Privy Council neither supported nor rejected the view that the mosque was a legal person. It only held that the mosque was 'at best a *caput mortum*,' where 'human agency is always required to take delivery of the property and apply it to the intended purposes' (*Masjid Shahid Ganj v. Shiromani Gurudwara*, 1940). The metaphor of a *caput mortuum* to describe a mosque stood in stark contrast to the continued insistence on the naturalness and humanity of the Hindu deities and the reasoning of the Privy Council goes a long way to show their reluctance in ascribing independence to the corpus of the mosque.

It was this indecision of the colonial Privy Council that the Supreme Court deployed in the Ayodhya judgement of 2019, when it interpreted that *Masjid Shahid Ganj* had rejected the legal personhood of the mosque. Although the Privy Council had not stated this point clearly in 1940, the Supreme Court seized upon the words of George Rankin, one of the colonial judges who had voiced his apprehensions in classifying the mosque as a legal person (*M. Siddiq v. Mahant Suresh Das*, 2020). While one previous judgement had interpreted mosques to have legal personhood (*Shiromani Gurudwara v. SomNathDass*, 2000), the Supreme Court was intent on dismissing all such contrary opinions outright. It justified such dismissals by using a range of arguments – that previous decisions of the court recognising the mosque as a legal person were confined to the Punjab region, or that in all but one (*Maula Bux v. Hafizuddin*, 1926) of those cases the mosque was not made a party to the suit. The court instead agreed with Rankin in saying that if a mosque is conferred with legal personhood, it deprives the site of its fundamental character of being an immovable property. The consequences of such an action, as the court saw it, were grave in terms of property rights, since the contested site would no longer be subject to conditions stipulated in title deeds, law of limitations, adverse possessions, and other legal safeguards that are imposed on immovable properties to ascertain ownership in case of a dispute (*M. Siddiq v. Mahant Suresh Das*, 2020). Simply put, the property ceases to be owned and becomes the *owner of other properties*, and the court would not allow that for the mosque.

Yet, this reasoning did not matter when it came to the Hindu deity. In the same judgement, the Supreme Court ascribed legal personhood to the same site, just not to the now-demolished Babri Masjid, but to the image of Ram Lalla, which was placed on the site of the birthplace. Unlike the mosque, which was just property, Ram Lalla was a person and therefore the owner of properties. It simply did not matter that the Muslims had had uncontested legal title to the land for centuries, or that they were in possession of the site. Once the personhood of Ram Lalla was invoked, rehearsed through decades of colonial and post-colonial judgements, the Hindu deity's exceptional claim to the contested site had been solidified. Since the mosque was denied personhood, all that the Muslim parties could claim was merely the title to the property, a claim that was easily overridden by the exceptional position of Ram Lalla. The exceptional personhood of the Hindu deity, buttressed by the ambiguity of colonial and post-colonial jurisprudence around Muslim and Christian institutions, now could be confidently used to legitimise the dispossession of minority religious institutions.

Conclusion

The entanglements of religion and the law in India have been chequered since the days of its colonial past. The British have struggled to understand the nature of faith and bonds of co-existence between the inhabitants of this region. Having understood the crucial place of religion in the lives of their Indian subjects, the colonial state often claimed to limit its reach to matters of 'public interest': taxation, crime management, administration and governance. However, what they did not understand or purposefully overlooked was the very nature of religion that prevailed over every item of public life and socialisation itself. Matters of the 'family' consisted of alienation of property, the structure of a Hindu Undivided Family affected the nature and incidence of taxation, and the participation in public life and occupation of public space was influenced by the faith one adhered to. In a situation like this, the colonial government did what it was known for doing best – undertook a series of administrative and legal actions devoid of in-depth knowledge or reasoned decisions to guide its working principles. The law itself was chiselled in an ad hoc fashion creating disturbing inequalities between religious institutions of different faiths. The Christian church and the Muslim mosque were treated with a half-baked adherence to canon law and shari'ah. But the Hindu deity, in contrast, was a legal person as opposed to a mosque or a church which retained its status as 'property' of individuals or incorporated associations. This exceptional status of the deity enabled it to acquire 'property' that may belong to other institutions including Muslim and Christian ones.

The public 'space' in India is already fraught with inequalities. Fanned by political winds and economic interests, the relationship between religious communities stands on an ever-delicate thread. The role of the law and the legal enforcement system is vital in these cases. Religious minorities have time and again found themselves before courts seeking justice and reiterating faith in the written words of the law. However, it is the law itself that leaves ample room for a majoritarian takeover of the public space and discourse. Be it the question of land acquisition or cessation of fundamental rights of one community in favour of another, the courts have enough room to uphold the majoritarian (and often politically motivated) view, jeopardising the interests of equality and justice and whatever remains of Indian secularism.

List of Cases

Abdul Fata Mahomed Ishak v. Russomoy Dhar Chowdhury, 1894 ILR 18 Cal 399

James Chinamma v. Joseph Abraham, 1962 KLT 240

M. Siddiq (Dead) Thr LR & Ors. v. Mahant Suresh Das & Ors., (2020) 1 SCC 1, para 196

Maula Bux v. Hafizuddin, (1926) 13 AIR Lah 372

Masjid Shahid Ganj v. Shiromani Gurudwara Prabandhak Committee Amritsar, AIR 1940 PC 116

Pramatha Nath Mullick v. Pradyumna Kumar Mullick, AIR 1925 PC 139

Rev. Fr. Farcisus Mascarenhas v. State of Bombay, (1960) , 62 BOMLR 790

Shiromani Gurudwara Prabandhak Committee Amritsar v. Som Nath Dass, (2000) 4 SCC 146

Manohar Ganesh Tambekar and Ors. v. Lakhmiram Govindram and Ors. (1888) ILR. 12 Bom. 247

References

Benton, Lauren. 2012. "This Melancholy Labyrinth: The Trial of Arthur Hodge and the Boundaries of Imperial Law." *Alabama Law Review* 64: 91–122.

Bernatzik, Edmund. 1890. "Kritische Studien über den Begriff der juristischen Person und über die juristische Persönlichkeit der Behörden Insbesondere." *Archiv Des Öffentlichen Rechts* 5, no. 2: 169–318.

Byrnes, Timothy A. 2017. "Sovereignty, Supranationalism and Soft Power: The Holy See in International Relations." *The Review of Faith and International Affairs* 15, no. 4: 6–20.

Code of Canon Law Latin-English Edition. Washington, DC: Canon Law Society of America, 1983.

Cohn, Bernard. 1965. "Anthropological Notes on Disputes and Law in India." *American Anthropologist* 67, no. 6: 82–122.

Colebrooke, Henry Thomas. 1802. *A Digest of Hindu Law, on Contracts and Successions: With a Commentary by Jagannatha Tercapanchanana*, in 3 vols. Calcutta: Printed at the Honourable Company's Press.

Davis, Donald R., Jr. 2010. *The Spirit of Hindu Law*. Cambridge: Cambridge University Press.

De, Rohit. 2018. *A People's Constitution: The Everyday Life of Law in the Indian Republic*. Princeton: Princeton University Press.

Derrett, Duncan J. 1968. *Religion, Law and the State in India*. London: Faber and Faber.

Dhavan, Rajeev. 1987. "Religious Freedom in India." *The American Journal of Comparative Law* 35, no. 1: 209–54.

Galanter, Marc. 1989. *Law and Society in Modern India*. Edited with an introduction by Rajeev Dhavan. New Delhi: Oxford University Press.

Geldart, William Martin. 1925. *Legal Personality*. Oxford: Clarendon Press.

Halhed, Nathaniel Brassey. 1776. *A Code of Gentoo Laws, or, Ordinations of the Pundits: From a Persian Translation, made from the Original, Written in the Shanscrit Language*. London.

Kane, Pandurang Vaman. 1930. *History of Dharmasastra (Ancient and Medieval Religious and Civil Law)*, in 7 vols. Pune: Bhandarkar Oriental Research Institute.

Kozlowski, Gregory C. 1985. *Muslim Endowments and Society in British India*. Cambridge: Cambridge University Press.

Meher, Esha. Forthcoming. "Courting the Divine." In *Rethinking Hinduism in Colonial India*, edited by Lucian Wong, Avni Chag, and Arun Brahmbhatt. Albany: State University of New York Press.

Mendelsohn, Oliver. 1981. "The Pathology of the Indian Legal System." *Modern Asian Studies* 15, no. 4: 823–63.

Morley, William H. 1858. *The Administration of Justice in British India; Its Past History and Present State: Comprising an Account of the Laws Peculiar to India*. London: Williams and Norgate.

Mukherjea, B. K. 1952. *The Hindu Law of Religious and Charitable Trusts*. Calcutta: Eastern Law House.

Nair, Neeti. 2023. *Hurt Sentiments: Secularism and Belonging in South Asia*. Cambridge, MA: Harvard University Press.

Pandey, Geeta. 2016. "When Gods were Hauled into Indian Courts." *BBC News India*, 29 February 2016. https://www.bbc.com/news/world-asia-india-35629805. Accessed on 10 April 2025.

Rocher, Ludo. 2012. *Studies in Hindu Law and Dharmaśāstra*. Edited by Donald R. Davis. London: Anthem Press.

Rudolph, Lloyd I., and Susan Hoeber Rudolph. 1967. *The Modernity of Tradition: Political Development in India*. Chicago: University of Chicago Press.

Schacht, Joseph. 1964. *An Introduction to Islamic Law*. Oxford: Clarendon Press.

Scott, J. Barton. 2023. *Slandering the Sacred: Blasphemy Law and Religious Affect in Colonial India*. Chicago: University of Chicago Press.

Serulnikov, Sergio. 1996. "Disputed Images of Colonialism: Spanish Rule and Indian Subversion in Northern Potosí, 1777-1780." *Hispanic American Research Review* 76, no. 2: 189–226.

Stephens, Julia. 2018. *Governing Islam: Law, Empire and Secularism in South Asia*. Cambridge: Cambridge University Press.

Vidyasagar, Ishvarchandra. 2012. *Hindu Widow Marriage: An Epochal Work on Social Reform from Colonial India*. Translated with an introduction by Brian A. Hatcher. New York: Columbia University Press.

Zahraa, Mahdi. 1995. "Legal Personality in Islamic Law." *Arab Law Quarterly* 10, no. 3: 193–206.

SIX

Racial Citizenship and the 'Tribal Other' in Northeast India

ROLUAHPUIA

Introduction

This chapter draws upon Nira Yuval-Davis' (1997; 1999) insightful analysis of citizenship and belonging as 'multi-layered' and hierarchical concepts in order to explore the intricate issue of citizenship of the 'tribal' communities of northeastern India. Instead of considering citizenship exclusively in terms of the nation-state, defined by horizontal comradeship and homogeneity, it locates the different layers of belonging at the local, ethnic, national and state levels, and situates the process of violent 'othering' of 'tribal' communities within the long history of racialisation of the region and its peoples. The effort is to offer a better understanding of the recent attempt to reconfigure citizenship in India through the enactment of new laws such as the National Register of Citizens (NRC) and the Citizenship Amendment Act (CAA), 2019,[1] that seek to deprive

[1] The NRC is the register containing the names of Indian citizens, which was first prepared in the year 1951. The demand for NRC means the updating of the list to identify legal citizens, and today, it is conceived as an exercise to count citizens in the northeastern state of Assam as a measure to detect, detain, and deport 'illegal immigrants' from Bangladesh. The CAA was passed by the Parliament of India on 11 December 2019 by the BJP government; it provides citizenship pathway for religious minorities belonging to Hindu, Christian, Sikh, Buddhist and Parsi refugees from Afghanistan, Bangladesh and Pakistan who enter India on or before 31 December 2014.

or deny citizenship and a sense of belonging to the country's minorities, including the 'tribal' peoples of the northeast.[2]

The visible consequence of such attempts has been the redrawing of citizenship and belonging along religious lines. This has put the northeast at the centre-stage of the debate around the NRC and CAA, viewed primarily as the Bharatiya Janata Party (BJP)'s attempt to redefine citizenship in India (Barbora 2019; Dutta 2021; Roy 2022). The question of citizenship, however, is entangled with dominant regional politics whose dynamics are shifting owing to new regional political alignments following the expansion of the BJP in the northeast.[3] In Assam, this has resulted in new forms of targeted violence, particularly for the state's Muslim population,[4] who are now at the receiving end of the NRC.

The racial profiling of 'tribal' communities of the region at the national level makes them targets of violence as 'suspicious' Others. At the regional level, they are excluded and marginalised by dominant groups who label them as 'illegal' and 'non-indigenous'. Furthermore, the characterisation of the region by the post-colonial Indian state as a 'troubled periphery' (Bhaumik 2009) has instituted a regime of violence that seeks to integrate recalcitrant subjects into citizens through the imposition of laws such as the Armed Forces Special Powers Act (AFSPA),1958, a law that gives sweeping power

---

[2] Northeast India comprises eight states, viz. Assam, Manipur, Meghalaya, Mizoram, Nagaland, Tripura, Sikkim and Arunachal Pradesh. At the time of Independence, it was only Assam with two princely states, viz. Manipur and Tripura, but by 1986, the region was reorganised into seven states and Sikkim was officially made part of the northeast only in 2002.

[3] Since 2014, the BJP has gained an increasing presence in the region by entering into alliances with regional parties such as the Asom Gana Parishad (AGP), National Peoples Party (NPP), and National Democratic Progressive Party (NDPP), while it has been able to singularly wrest power in the state of Assam, Tripura, Manipur, and Arunachal Pradesh. This is against the long history of the Congress's dominance of the region, which has more or less maintained a one-party dominance.

[4] As per the 2011 census, out of the state's 3.12 crore population, 61.47% were Hindus, 34.22% Muslims and 3.7% Christians.

to the military from allowing security forces to search premise and make an arrest without a warrant to authorising the right to shoot on mere suspicion.[5] Most importantly, the Act protects the military personnel from legal suits without the sanction of the Union Government. Therefore, the powers given to the military are what make the law 'draconian' and hence, a critique of the law as 'unconstitutional' and 'undemocratic' (McDuie-Ra 2009). The law was aimed at suppressing the Naga armed rebellion in the early 1950s, but later on, it was imposed in other parts of the northeast, such as in Manipur, Mizoram, and Assam, with periodic extensions to this day. While ethnic groups such as the Nagas and Mizos question the national integration policy of assimilation and homogenisation, several other groups and communities vie for autonomy within the Indian Constitution (Biswas and Suklabaidya 2008; Roluahpuia 2023). The counter-insurgency measures adopted by the Indian state to quell the several armed movements vitally affect the way local communities view the Indian state as an institution imposing the interest of dominant groups by taking recourse to continual military action. A discussion on citizenship and contemporary politics of the state in the region needs to take into account this history of violence and militarisation and how issues of citizenship are complicated by national and regional dynamics of 'othering'.

Such a distinct understanding of space and its people is complemented by racialised notions of citizenship – a categorical sorting of populations on the basis of race that groups people in accordance with certain physical traits they are meant to share.

---

[5] AFSPA is based on the 1942 British ordinance that give special powers to the colonial armed forces to suppress the Indian national movement, particulary the Quit India movement. Under it, several leaders such as Mahatma Gandhi and Jawarharlal Nehru among others were imprisoned. In postcolonial India, the law was re-introduced in areas declared as 'Disturbed Areas' by the Home Ministry; under this law, normal civil and political rights can easily be suspended, with the law providing impunity to the military. The law remains highly controversial with movements and demands by various human rights organisations and civil societies to repeal the same.

Tribal migrants from the northeast in metropolitan cities such as Delhi are routinely abused as 'Chinky' or 'Nepali' (McDuie-Ra 2012). The state, in turn, brings them under constant surveillance and treats them as the 'national other' (Thirumuthy 2019). Racialised citizenship indicates how groups and communities are granted and denied access to citizenship, and how such racialised notions of belonging permeate the politics of inclusion and exclusion, of who 'belongs' and 'who does not belong'. As several scholars have noted, even though the conferral of citizenship means that the state assures and grants rights to its legally sanctioned equal members, their equal safety and security is not safeguarded. The discourse and experience of northeastern tribal communities highlight how racial othering is coupled with ethnic othering as primitive, backward 'tribals' who work to reinforce their 'cultural inferiority' and bolster 'internal othering' as well as their 'outsider' status.

Race, racism, violence, militarisation, and the new legal regimes of citizenship – NRC and CAA – have a long history of intersection and interaction. It was the British colonial officer Olaf Caroe who first conceptualised the region as India's 'Mongolian Fringe' given its proximity to China and Southeast Asia, distinct from the inhabitants of 'India proper' (Baruah 2020). If this offers a telling story of the geopolitical and racial anxieties of the colonial state with regard to a frontier region (Gergan and Smith 2022), it also highlights Indian nationalist leaders' inheritance of the colonial gaze in their perception of the region as an insecure frontier, whose inhabitants are only dubiously 'loyal'. Even today, suspicion and anxiety continue to inform the relationship between the Indian state and the region (Gergan and Smith 2022).

It is from this vantage point that I seek to explore and discuss the issue of citizenship in contemporary India and what it means for the vast majority of India's 'tribal' communities. If we follow Gianfranco Poggi (2003), the vantage point is essential since it determines how we understand the relationship between states and citizens, taking into account 'the importance of context in terms of place, space, and time' (Siim and Stolz 2024, 4). I use race and the histories of violence in the northeast in the making of the post-colonial nation-state to fill a lacunae in scholarship on citizenship studies that has almost completely erased the experience of 'tribal' communities.

'Tribes' constitute the majority in the states of Meghalaya, Mizoram, Nagaland and Arunachal Pradesh. In contrast to many other parts of India, these societies are largely non-caste societies in terms of their social organisation, and most of their members have embraced Christianity, following missionary proselytisation during colonial times.[6] While 'tribe' is largely viewed as an administrative category introduced by the colonial state (see the chapter by Sanghamitra Misra), the idea of 'tribe' has acquired a new significance as a mode of identity where communities classified as Scheduled Tribes (STs) have internalised that identity to empower themselves against their marginalised condition.[7] This embracing of tribal identity follows a challenge of the stereotypical notion associated with the term, but also questions how different groups, notably the right-wing groups in India, including scholars, view[8] and understand tribal communities (Xaxa 2005).

---

[6] Tribal population in Meghalaya, Mizoram, Nagaland and Arunachal Pradesh are 86.1%, 94.4%, 86.5% and 68.8%, respectively. Also, they are highly heterogenous in terms of their population where there is internal diversity across the states with significant variation in terms of culture, language and religion. While a significant percentage of them follow Christianity, many of the tribal communities continue to practice their traditional religion.

[7] Specifically in the northeast, there are now rising demands for ST status such as in the state of Assam and Manipur. Often, this has resulted in confrontation among local communities, but most importantly, the assertion also follows how regionally dominant groups are able to appropriate the categories of 'tribe' and 'indigenous', as in the case of Manipur and how this is used to suppress the protection granted to those already recognised as STs. I discuss this in the later part of the chapter.

[8] There is a longstanding view among several scholars including right-wing groups that tribes are 'Backward Hindus'. This idea of tribes as 'Backward Hindus' follows the logic of tribes as belonging to the wider Hindu religion, and this idea is now advanced to bring back many of those converted and un-converted to the fold of Hinduism.

The discourse and debate on citizenship, particularly in the context of NRC and CAA, have focused almost singularly on the question of religious minorities and their violent 'othering'. While this remains significantly critical against the backdrop of majoritarian nationalism at the national level, it does not adequately represent the multilayered nature of citizenship, where regional and local politics shape the category of the 'other'. My exploration of the 'othering' of northeastern 'tribal' communities, establishes a vital link between citizenship and race. The danger of any form of 'othering' is its consequence, where violence is justified, and those who are 'othered' become vulnerable to abuse and physical violence. I examine the politics of 'othering' at the national and regional levels that underlie the NRC–CAA, and their strident use by dominant regional groups through a focus on Manipur.

Citizenship and the politics of belonging

India's northeast is a borderland. The history of it 'becoming a borderland' (Misra 2011) goes back to the colonial period – the annexation of kingdoms and tribal territories and the administrative re-ordering that implanted the modern notion of borders for the first time. Various stages of colonial incorporation produced fluctuating borders and contested borderlands (Pachuau and van Schendel 2016), which are entrapped in the history of the imposition of borders and mapping of the region. What is today Northeast India is a product of a culmination of events and upheavals such as the first partition of Bengal (1905), India and Myanmar (1937), and the Partition of India (Bengal and Punjab) in 1947 up to the independence of Bangladesh in 1971. With independence, India's landlocked northeast came to be surrounded by five different countries (China, Nepal, Bangladesh, Bhutan and Myanmar). Many of the regions inhabited by 'tribal' communities came to be demarcated as the peripheral zone of territorial borders of the newly independent states. Different groups and communities that inhabit the region, such as the Garos (India and Bangladesh), Nagas (India and Myanmar) and Mizos (India,

Myanmar and Bangladesh), were compelled to live and adopt new citizenship and identities, frequently multiple national identities (Bal and Chambugong 2014; Roluahpuia 2020; 2023).

This creates an intriguing situation since citizenship normally signifies belonging to a single nation-state and acknowledges the citizen as a full member of the broader 'imagined community' of the nation (Anderson 1991). Prevailing understandings of citizenship obscure internal differentiation and hierarchies around social and cultural identities and ignore the problems of national belonging and identity of those living in borderlands or enclaves (van Schendel 2002). This is partly due to the statist notion inherent in citizenship, where states and national communities are assumed to be congruent, and members of the national community share contiguous territories separated by neat borders. This territorial dimension of citizenship, however, is complemented by its cultural constructions that produce hierarchies and inequality in the integration of citizens (Roy 2010). As such, citizenship falls short of capturing the experience and sense of belonging of those living at the borders of the nation-state. Citizenship as an idea and practice has been an ever-evolving and contested concept appropriated both by the dominant and the marginal who deploy it to challenge their exclusion.

The Partition of India and the subsequent events have crucially shaped narratives and definitions of citizenship and belonging. The debates in the Constituent Assembly underscore the severe tussle between the two rival principles of birth (*jus soli*) and blood-based descent (*jus sanguinis*) in defining citizenship. The Assembly agreed that *jus soli* citizenship – or an individual's descent was considered to be a form of 'enlightened, modern, civilized' and democratic citizenship against the latter, which it considered as a form of racialised citizenship (Jayal 2019, 34). The Citizenship Act of 1955 underlies this, and under Articles 5 to 8 of the Constitution, the Act allows the following categories of persons to be citizens of India from the date of the commencement of the Constitution: (1) those domiciled and born in India; (2) those domiciled, not born in India but either of whose parents was born in India; (3) those domiciled, not born in India, but ordinarily residing in India for more than five years; (4) those residents in India, who migrated to Pakistan after 1 March 1947 and returned later on resettlement permits; (5) those residents in Pakistan, who migrated to India before 19 July 1948 or those who came afterwards but stayed on for more than six months and got registered; and (6) those whose parents and grandparents were born in India but were residing outside India. With this, everyone who was residing in India at the time of independence automatically became an Indian citizen (Roy 2010). With the signing of the Assam Accord in 1986, a new clause was inserted under Section 6A, which allows foreign migrants who came to Assam before 1 January 1966 and who are ordinarily residents of Assam to be considered Indian citizens and those who entered Assam after 1 January 1966 but before 25 March 1971 and have been detected to be foreigners would be considered citizens only after ten years from the date of their detection as a foreigner.

Since then, Assam has been the centre of the debate on citizenship in the northeast with 'illegal migration' from Bangladesh being the principal issue. Since the colonial period, Assam has witnessed an intensive migration where peasants and labourers were recruited from different parts of the then-British Indian Empire to work in plantations and other factories. Beyond this, international borders remained fluid and porous, enabling a continuous cross-border movement, as well as licit and illicit movement of people and goods. Tripura and Mizoram also witnessed cross-border migration and resettlement of refugees. This makes the location of the states important in the definition of 'insider' and 'outsider', 'citizens' and 'immigrant', and makes 'border' supremely significant in the articulation of belonging as indigenous citizens. Many 'tribal' communities living at the border make use of their ethnic identification of kinship and historical connections, to claim a privileged status. In contemporary India, however, a shared ethnicity across the border has been deployed to victimise communities as 'immigrants' whose histories and identities are 'foreign' to the nation-state.

Over time, more and more social groups belonging to marginalised sections are being denied citizenship on account of their identity, religion and gender. Assam and Manipur cultivate this targeting of the minority religious and tribal communities as the 'other', producing over time a perception of such groups as 'illegal immigrants' at the societal level. Dominant groups and communities make use of such social perception to create a bloc of homogenised 'legal' residents against the 'illegal others'. This lies at the core of the new citizenship regime under CAA and NRC, where the social existence of communities is reduced to the status of an 'outsider'.

'Tribes' as racialised subjects

The emergence, if not the introduction, of the category 'tribe' in India and its use by the British was influenced by the racist anthropometry of the late nineteenth century that categorised populations along an evolutionary schema prevalent in colonial anthropology. Tribes were relegated to the lowest rung in the civilisational order on account of their 'primitive' and backward ways of life and economic practices. They were also described as 'animists' and 'forest dwellers'. Such notions and classification found their way into the policies of the post-colonial Indian state that retained the colonial demarcation of Scheduled Tribes (STs) as 'backward' (Jenkins 2003) and extended state protection to them.

Such classification and state policy simultaneously integrated and 'othered' the tribes as citizens distinct from the 'mainstream'. The view of tribes as isolated, primitive and backward, culturally and economically, are all entangled with the idea of tribes as wild, savage and forest dwellers, or *jangli* (Skaria 1997; Xaxa 2008). In the context of northeastern tribes, racialisation follows their physical and regional categorisations as 'Mongoloid'. This marker of difference provides ground for everyday violence, both symbolic and physical, and for communities that are under heavy military rule, counter-insurgency measures bring these racialised subjects under routine violence (Roluahpuia 2023).

One may argue that India does not use race as a ground for assigning citizenship. Nor does it use the racial principle to hierarchise citizenship. However, if one is to look, if not abide by the understanding of citizenship in legal terms, this does not explain the persisting issue of race or the racial question in India. In the case of the northeastern communities, discrimination goes hand in hand with a questioning of their nationality, where their 'Indianess' is questioned (Ngaihte 2014). In protest by student groups and communities from the region in metropolitan cities, there is a strong claim of being 'Indian'. Hurling abuse and racial slurs such as 'Chinky', 'Chinese' and 'Nepali' relegate their belonging as foreign nationals.

Many of the 'tribal' communities in the northeast belong to the 'Mongoloid' race, and their cultural and social habits, including everyday life, are viewed as 'un-Indian'. In outlining this, Wouters and Subba (2013, 127) noted how the 'Mongogloid' phenotype is excluded from what they call the 'Indian Face' that makes the northeastern tribals 'lesser Indians'. Such withholding of equal recognition of 'Indianness' works to subjugate and marginalise them. Furthermore, the mainstream perception of 'tribes' intersects with the caste notions of purity and pollution, where the food habits and social life of the communities are perceived as foreign, making them cultural 'outsiders'. Fermentation, or fermented foods, is widely practiced and common across tribal communities, and in most tribal societies, there is no segregation of vegetarian and non-vegetarian food. Food is also not ordered as a marker of social status, unlike in caste societies. As such, the smell of fermented foods such as *bekang/akhuni* (fermented soybean) or *tuaithur* (bamboo shoot) produces a scent that disrupts the odour in neighbourhoods in metropolitan cities, where caste is inscribed in space and sensoria (Lee 2017; Kikon 2022).

While the issue of race studies is recent (McDuie-Ra 2012; Kikon and Karlsson 2019), it has rarely been addressed or treated as a political problem. For instance, in 2014, the Government of

India constituted the Bezbaruah Committee to look into the issue of racial discrimination against northeastern migrants in India's metropolitan cities. The constitution of the committee came against the backdrop of protest and solidarity movements in New Delhi, the nation's capital, against the murder of Nido Tania, a young college migrant from Arunachal Pradesh in Delhi. The recommendation by the committee reduced racism to a 'cultural' issue and a problem of national integration. The report notes:

> The strength of the Indian nation is its wide diversity. All our recommendations for increasing two-way exchange and understanding of the people of the northeast and the rest of India have one primary objective, i.e., the ethnic and cultural differences of the northeast should be a cause for celebration and not for raising barriers. They are meant to integrate the northeast with the rest of India and not to segregate. (Bezbaruah Committee 2014, 5)

The suggestion by the committee does not address the 'anxiety' and 'insecurity' (Krishna 1999) and the tension it produces.

To elaborate, in the early years of independent India, Laldenga, the Mizo political leader, locates the Mizo desire for *zalenna* (freedom) as a racial problem. In his reply to the root cause of the insurgent problem in northeast India to *India Today*, he notes:

> In India there are three distinct races – Aryan, Dravidian and Mongolian. When more than one race live together, racial prejudice is bound to come because the ways of life differ. In the South also such problems crop up, like the language issue and now the whole North-east region – where the Mongolians live – is in turmoil, because their existence as Assamese, as Meiteis, Nagas, Mizos, Meghalayans, is threatened. This feeling of insecurity sparks the movement. (Louis 1980)

In the same interview, he further notes how racial difference is more than a mere 'difference' but a problem rooted in power relations of dominance and hierarchy. To quote him again:

> The Mizos and Nagas were ahead of them as they were in a compact area. So, the feeling came earlier, the feeling of being submerged by other populations, their domination … This feeling is enhanced by the misbehaviour of many service personnel who are sent to that

> area by Delhi. It seems their racial prejudice is taking the upper hand and the general feeling in the North-east is that the white sahib has gone but the brown sahib has come. These officials behave as if they came to the dominion. Their attitude seems to say: 'We are your lord and master. Unless you obey us and crawl at our feet, we will crush you under the heel of the Indian Army.' It is a human problem, not just law and order. It should be tackled as such. (ibid.)

Race and racism, therefore, play an important role in the contemporary manifestations of national 'othering' of tribal communities. This 'othering' is pervasive and institutionalised, and efforts to solve the problem are couched in the language of national integration, a recommendation echoed by the Bezbaruah Committee, rather than aiming 'to build a genuinely democratic polity that recognizes tribal and non-tribal individuals as equal citizens' (Chandra 2013, 161).

NRC–CAA and the new citizenship regime

The NRC is about 'counting citizens' (Barbora 2021) while identifying 'illegal' citizens. In Assam, it has been a longstanding demand and remains a contested political issue. It was part of the 'Sons of the Soil' movement (Weiner 1978), which is popularly known as the Assam Movement (1979–1985), which demanded the detection and deportation of 'illegal immigrants' through the updating of the National Register of Citizens (NRC), 1951. Scholars locate this demand within the long history of the state, which saw population movement from the erstwhile East Pakistan, the settling of peasants, particularly Muslim peasants, by the British in their bid to convert 'wasteland' into 'cultivable land', and the Partition of India that saw resettlement of Hindu refugees in the state (Dutta 2021). The argument is that Assam's concerns need to be understood against the backdrop of its specific history and geography. The public and political discourse in Assam is centered around the issue of 'illegal immigrants', and over time, this discourse has now shifted to the targeting and labelling of every Muslim as 'Bangladeshi'. The suspicion has caused anxiety and insecurity for the state Muslim population, particularly the poor and marginalised, who live in fear of being disenfranchised and hence made 'stateless'.

The coming of the BJP into power both in the state and center has intensified the process of NRC implementation. It has also emerged as a major political plank of the party, which turns the demand for NRC into an issue of Assamese *jatiyotabaad* (nationalism) politics where the intention is to save *jati-mati-bheti* (community, land, hearth). In fact, the BJP in Assam has been able to bring together Assamese nationalistic aspirations of *jati-mati-bheti* and Hindutva politics of *Akhand Bharat* (One India) (Das 2023). This means a shifting discourse regarding the politics of who is 'illegal', where the 'immigrant' and the 'citizen' discourse is increasingly drawn along the axis of religious lines. The response to the published list of NRC and the CAA is a testament to this. In 2019, the Government of Assam published its final NRC list which excluded almost 1.9 million people. As in the case of CAA, it singled out Muslims while removing barriers for communities from other religions, such as Hindus, Sikhs, Buddhists, Jains, Parsis, and Christians from the neighbouring countries of Afghanistan, Bangladesh and Pakistan who arrived in India on or before 31 December 2014 from acquiring Indian citizenship. It has eased the extension of citizenship to such groups to qualify as citizens with a minimum of six years of residence as opposed to eleven years.

Jayal (2019) captures this moment thus: 'The march from a *jus soli* to a *jus sanguinis* conception of citizenship is also simultaneously a march from civic-nationalism to ethno-religious nationalism, from a universalist and inclusive form of nationalism to an exclusionary form that renders difference as graded hierarchy'. This shift marked a reconfiguration of the inclusive and civic ethos of Indian citizenship towards faith-based citizenship, where the eligibility for acquiring citizenship is now graded hierarchically around religion. The case of CAA and NRC has brought into stark relief the violence of the new citizenship regime. On the ground, the implementation of NRC follows the setting up of detention centres across the state, where those whose names are excluded from the NRC list are identified as 'D' voters and referred to the Foreigners Tribunals that will determine if they are to be deported or not. This detention affirms the stereotypes and violent process of exclusion of the state's linguistic and religious minority, and in the process, what one finds in the detention centres turns into a zone of death. Those detained suffer from the severe psychological trauma of trying to prove their citizenship, not to speak of the ordeals of the tribunals and the bureaucratic constraints and practices that have been embroiled with religious preferences and prejudices (Punathil 2022).

What the NRC and CAA set to achieve is to either grant or deny citizenship to select religious groups. The two are integrally linked in their logic to reverse the idea of equal citizenship. By rewarding citizenship to persecuted minorities from select religions, the BJP intends to make Assam 'safe'. However, one cannot undermine the electoral calculations. This was evident when the BJP changed its position soon before the release of the final list of NRC in 2019, as it feared that many genuine citizens, implying Bengal Hindus, would be left off the list, the party's major vote bank. It also goes against the party's ideological standpoint; hence the demand for re-verification of the NRC list. However, what is often missed is the exclusion of a large number of tribal communities within the NRC. The final publication of NRC on 31 August 2019 was a testament to this, where different communities across religions, including Hindus, Muslims, Sikhs and Christians, were excluded. Of this, Scheduled Tribes (STs) constituted a large number, cutting across religions, including 25,0000 Bodos, 12,000 Reangs, 8,000 Hajongs and 55,0000 other tribal communities (Dungdung 2020). Stories of family members' names missing from the list, followed by the detention of such members, have caused disruption and distress in the family. The case of Naresh Koch, a detainee in the Goalpara detention centre in Assam who breathed his last in 2014, is a testimony of the violent process of the NRC (ibid.). As several scholars have argued, the violence of the NRC lies in the very 'process' itself, where administrative biases, prejudice, and selective victimisation have made those excluded from the list precarious (Mathur 2020; Punathil 2022).

Citizenship anywhere is a 'documentary citizenship' (Sadiq 2008). And in the wake of NRC–CAA in India, documents have emerged as more vital than ever. The failure to produce documents and prove legacy has proved fatal and catastrophic for those detained. Today, as the line of distinction between 'citizen' and the 'immigrant' is increasingly drawn, in this reading, the NRC is one of the largest projects of disenfranchising marginalised groups – from right-bearing citizens to stateless beings (Mathur 2020). Beyond this, the CAA and NRC should not be seen merely as a state agenda of institutionalising a new regime of citizenship. It has found wide appeal and support even among dominant regional groups. Several groups and communities view the NRC as a solution to tackle the issue of border control and immigration, as the call for a nationwide NRC is gaining traction within the northeast and across the country.

Manipur and the invention of the new 'other'

On 3 May 2023, violence broke out in Manipur and spread like wildfire across the state, particularly in the Meitei-dominated valley districts and the Kuki-Zo[9]-dominated districts.[10] A common reading of the violence suggests that it was a spontaneous reaction to the rally organised by the All Tribal Students Union Manipur (ATSUM), a conglomerate of tribal student organisations, against the Meiteis demand for Scheduled Tribes (STs) status. Media

[9] The term Kuki-Zo gained popularity after the violence where different tribal groups such as Zou, Simte, Hmar and Mizo, among others, have accepted to be used as a pan-ethnic category.

[10] In Manipur, the valley areas are largely dominated by the Meiteis, who are also non-tribals with majority of them practicing Hinduism while the hill areas are dominated by different tribal communities belonging to the Nagas, Kukis, Mizos, and several others, who are predominantly Christian. In fact, there are 33 communities who are identified as Scheduled Tribes (STs) in the state while sections within Meiteis are recognised as Other Backward Classes (OBCs) and Scheduled Castes (SCs).

commentators and the mainstream discourse viewed the conflict in ethnic terms or as a 'clash between two ethnicities' (Banerjee 2023) and in a state where ethnic polarisation runs deep, such explanations are convenient. Of course, while the state has witnessed violence or ethnic conflict in the past, such as the Naga–Kuki conflict (1992–96) or the Kuki–Zomi conflict (1997–98) (Haokip 2013; Roluahpuia 2017), the current violence in the state is a by-product of a concerted political mobilisation by various sections of Meiteis, wrapped in the language of protecting the rights of 'indigenous people', who are faced with the danger of 'illegal immigrant' from Myanmar, herein the Kuki–Zo community. The return to power by the BJP in the state assembly in 2022 has bolstered the confidence of Biren Singh, the state's Chief Minister, who has valiantly pursued the targeting of the Kuki–Zo community of the state. What has drawn the attention of media, civil societies and academicians is the scale and intensity of violence, which is evident in the number of casualties – loss of lives, displacement, the destruction of properties in Imphal, the valley, and the hill districts such as Churachandpur, Chandel and Kangpokpi.

Since the early 2010s, Manipur began to witness new political dynamics where local majoritarianism was gaining ground among the Meiteis. This culminated in several efforts on the part of the state government to appease majoritarian anxiety and aspirations by passing three bills, viz. The Protection of Manipur People Bill, Manipur Land Revenue and Land Reforms (Seventh Amendment) Bill, and Manipur Shops and Establishments (Second Amendment) Bill. The state's tribal communities viewed these laws as an attempt to infringe on their land rights while redefining the idea of belonging by putting the cut-off date as 1951 to determine 'Manipur People', which would inadvertently label everyone unable to prove their identity as 'non-indigenous'. The tribal communities of the state, particularly the Kuki–Zo protested, resulting in violence and death, with strong electoral implications for the then-ruling Congress government which saw them being ousted in the upcoming state assembly elections by the BJP and its allies. In 2017, the BJP, under the new leadership of Biren

Singh, a former Congressmen was ruling the state for the first time with the support of coalition partners such as the Naga People's Front (NPF). By the 2022 assembly elections, BJP was able to gain a foothold and emerge victorious with an absolute majority by winning 32 seats in the 60-assembly house. After the formation of the new government, there remains a sense of unease among the tribal populace against the several initiatives taken by the Government of Manipur. The first of these initiatives came in the form of the inauguration of Maharaja Chandrakirti Memorial Park in the border village of Tonzang, Churachandpur District. The stone inscription in the park claiming the Meitei King's victory over the Lusei chiefs, which Mizo historians have refuted as an event that has never happened in history,[11] has filled the tribal communities with unease. While this inauguration of the park is projected by the state government as a way to honour the Meitei Maharaja Chandrakirti, there is suspicion among the tribal populace that the state government will use it as a pretext to lay claim upon tribal lands under its territorialisation project of expanding its foothold in the hills. The park was inaugurated on 14 October 2022 under a high-security presence by Biren Singh. As Hausing (2017) notes, the initiative by the CM is 'unmindful of history' as the park for the tribal communities symbolises the celebration of the violent subjugation of their chiefs and communities by the British, aided by the Meitei kings. In fact, there is now a harping on the Meitei's history, which has taken the form of ethnic revivalism to restore the lost glory of the kingdom. In their bid to capitalise on this, the BJP has nominated Leishemba Sanajaoba, the titular king of Manipur as its candidate for the lone Rajya Sabha in 2019 from the inner constituency in Manipur. This is a symbolic move as the King symbolises the long and glorious history of the Meitei while also yielding a strong emotional and historical connection with the erstwhile Kingdom. In this historical narrative, Meiteis are an indigenous community with a distinct religion, culture and civilisational history.

[11] Mizo History Association (MHA) Memorandum [No. MHA 2020/2] to the Archaeological Survey of India (ASI), 4 June 2020.

In its existence as a post-colonial federal state, Manipur has witnessed several ethnic mobilisations, either in the form of public protest or armed mobilisations. For several Meitei armed groups, the history of the kingdom as a sovereign state and the contested nature of the merger under the Indian Union, the 'other' has been the *mayang* (plainsmen) and the Indian state, with periodic attacks on central security forces by the armed groups. This targeting of the *mayang* in the state involves the making of a distinction of their 'outsider' status. Over the years, there has been a sense of imagined victimhood among the Meiteis, where they are denied their rightful claim and protection as a community. For a long time, this was directed against migrants from the mainland, that is, the *mayang*, which to an extent has been contained with the extension of the Bengal Eastern Frontier Regulation (BEFR), 1873, or Inner Line Permit (ILP) as is commonly known, in Manipur from the year 2019 to prevent continued migration and control of the economy. While it is another matter that BEFR was specifically introduced to protect and safeguard the 'tribes' by the British, there is a clear shift in how the discourse has taken a turn, where the Kuki–Zo community emerged, if not were made, the new 'other'.

The state government began to weaponise the law by using forest regulations to target the Kuki–Zo communities. In the process, a new vocabulary began to enter, which often labelled the Kuki–Zo communities as 'illegal' and 'encroacher'. In Churachandpur District alone, there are two Reserved Forests (RFs) and two Protected Forests (PFs) where the state government incessantly undertook a policy to drive the tribals out of such areas. In one incident in K. Songjang village in Churachandpur District, JCBs were deployed by the state to clear villages, terming them as 'encroachers'. This news was soon picked up by the media, where the tribals of the state were targeted as engaging in destruction and degrading of the environment, indulging in illicit activities such as poppy plantation, where the Kuki–Zo communities were again singled out as ‘poppy planters’. Following this, the state government raised concerns about the rising population of the Kuki–Zo people and villages, casting doubt on the legality of their settlements. As per the dominant narrative, what has led to this is the increasing demographic growth of the Kuki–Zo people, who have ‘illegally’ migrated from the neighbouring country, Myanmar. In short, it follows the same logic and pattern where the state and various civil societies were engaged in selective targeting and targeting while dehumanising a particular community.

In the process, there is a growing as well as an abiding hostility against the Kuki–Zo communities in the state, with majoritarian sentiments mobilised against them. There was a concerted agenda where the narrative of ‘illegal’ and ‘outsider’ was being made by the state and non-state actors, citing abnormal growth of Kuki villages, demographic invasion from Myanmar, and the destruction of the environment due to poppy cultivation and encroachment of forests that reduce them as the problematic ‘outsiders’. This narrative has been officalised by the state actors, whereby the entire Kuki-Zo community began to be viewed as the internal ‘Other’ (Hausing 2024). It is this that permits the wide participation of the local population in the violence since 3 May 2023. Alongside, there was direct physical violence and an ethnic massacre of anyone other than ‘Naga’ tribals, who remain outside of the current conflict and who are considered, if not accepted as ‘indigenous’ to Manipur. Soon, homes and properties of the Kuki–Zo communities in the valley were targeted, with hundreds massacred and killed in a span of few days while thousands sought shelter in military camps. Several Naga and other communities living in Imphal marked their homes and properties using their tribal names or any specific tribal identifications while there were also cases of Kuki–Zo homes being identified and marked against other tribal homes. A significant aspect of the violence is the targeting of churches and religious establishments, and in a short span, close to 220 churches across the state have been vandalised, desecrated and burned down (ZSF and KSO 2023). The violence also became symbolic with the hosting of *salai taret*[12] on top of the churches to signify victory and the re-christening of old Meitei cultural symbols by armed militias such as Arambai Tenggol.[13]

In the current political context, the targeting of Kuki–Zo as 'illegal' is legitimated in the wake of the military coup in Myanmar, with a large number of ethnic minorities, including the Kuki–Zo, fleeing the country to India in search of safety and shelter. Since then, there have been repeated drives in Manipur to detect and detain illegal migrants with an enhancement of surveillance and securitisation of borders. The government of Manipur has also deported those who are detained and identified as citizens of Myanmar. This military coup in Myanmar was used as a pretext for intensifying the surveillance of its own citizens, and all village chiefs and authorities were instructed to record the biometrics of all the villagers as a part of the 'verification drive'. Also, there are increasing calls to introduce and implement NRC in the state as a way to curb the problem of illegal immigration in the state. In short, the issue of illegal encroachment is cocktailed with illegal immigration that painted the Kuki-Zo communities as 'refugees' and 'immigrants' from Myanmar, hence denying their indigenous as well as citizenship status.

Conclusion

With the politics of citizenship taking centrestage in northeast India, the local notion of belonging and politics are redefined, and the 'outsider' or the figure of the 'illegal' shifts in response to

12 A flag formed by seven colours that represents the seven clans of the Meitei. These flags become popularised as part of the ethnic mobilisation campaign led by *Arambai Tenggol*.

13 The Arambai Tenggol (AT) has become an important part of the conflict where the group is leading the war front in attacking the Kuki-Zo communities. For details about the group, see Greeshma Kumar. 2024. 'Saviour Complex: Why the Biren Singh government gives a free hand to Arambai Tenggol'. The Caravan, 15 April. Accessible online at https://caravanmagazine.in/conflict/biren-singh-gives-a-free-hand-to-arambai-tenggol-militia-imphal-manipur

regional and local politics. In other words, within the region, the distinction between 'citizen' and the 'immigrant', the 'indigenous' and the 'outsider' takes different and multiple forms where the 'other' – the 'immigrant' and the 'illegal' also shift. If it is religion in Assam, it has taken an ethnic and tribal turn in Manipur. Yet, the logic in terms of the end goal remains the same, which is the targeting and labelling, a dehumanisation and humiliation of the 'other'. It follows a systemic process of labelling where the 'other' is identified and named, and the media and civil society, needless to say, the state apparatus, are conjoined in manufacturing this consent. In the end, this produces a form of violence, either direct or symbolic, where targeting the 'other' is justified to cleanse the nation from intruders. It remains to be seen how the recently elected regime without the single party majority of the BJP will deal with majoritarian citizenship and proceed with the NRC and CAA.

REFERENCES

Anderson, B. 1991. *Imagined Communities: Reflections on the Origin and the Spread of Nationalism.* London/New York: Verso.

Bal, E., and T.C. Chambugong. 2014. "The Borders that Divide, the Borders that Unite: (Re)interpreting Garo Processes of Identification in India and Bangladesh." *Journal of Borderlands Studies* 29, no. 1: 95–109.

Banerjee, Shoumojit. 2023. "Manipur clashes primarily ethnic, nothing to do with counter-insurgency: Chief of Defence Staff Anil Chauhan." *The Hindu*, 31 May 2023. https://www.thehindu.com/news/national/challenges-in-manipur-will-take-some-time-to-settle-cds-anil-chauhan/article66910854.ece. Accessed on 11 April 2025.

Barbora, S. 2019. "National Register of Citizens: Politics and Problems in Assam." *Explorations: E-Journal of the Indian Sociological Society* 3, no. 2: 3–28.

———. 2021. "Counting Citizens in Assam: Contests and Claims." *The South Atlantic Quarterly* 120, no. 1: 220–31.

Baruah, S. 2020. *In the Name of the Nation: India and Its Northeast.* Redwood City, CA: Stanford University Press.

Bezbaruah Committee. 2014. "Report of the Committee under the Chairmanship of Shri M.P Bezbaruah to Look into the Concerns of the People of the Northeast Living in Other Parts of the Country." Report submitted to the Ministry of Home Affairs, New Delhi.

Bhaumik, S. 2009. *Troubled Periphery: Crisis of India's Northeast*. New Delhi: Sage.

Biswas, P., and C. Suklabaidya. 2008. *Ethnic Life-Worlds in North-East India. An Analysis*. New Delhi: Sage.

Chandra, U. 2013. "Liberalism and Its Other: The Politics of Primitivism in Colonial and Postcolonial Indian Law." *Law & Society Review* 47, no. 1: 135–68.

Das, B. 2023. "NRC, 'Jatiyotabaad' and Citizenship Crisis in Assam." *South Asia Multidisciplinary Academic Journal* 1, no. 30.

Dungdung, Gladson. 2020. "Indian citizenship laws have deep impact on Adivasis." *International Working Group for Indigenous Affairs* (IWGIA). 05 February 2020. https://www.iwgia.org/en/india/3536-nrc-impact-adivasis.html#:~:text=If%20the%20NRC%2FCAA%20is%20enforced%20in%20all%20states%20of,documents%20to%20prove%20their%20existence. Accessed on 11 April 2025.

Dutta, A. R. 2021. *Hindutva Regime in Assam: Saffron in the Rainbow*. New Delhi: Sage.

Gergan, M.D., and S.H. Smith. 2022. "Theorizing racialization through India's 'Mongolian Fringe'." *Ethnic and Racial Studies* 45, no. 2: 361–82.

Haokip, T. 2013. "The Kuki–Naga conflict in the light of recent publications." *South Asia Research* 33, no. 1: 77–87.

Hausing, K. K. S. 2017. "Unmindful of History: On Biren Singh and Manipur." *The Hindu*, 29 December 2017. https://www.thehindu.com/opinion/op-ed/unmindful-of-history/article22320391.ece. Accessed on 11 April 2025.

Hausing, K. K. S. 2024. "1 Year of Manipur Violence: Biren Singh Has Ruptured the State's Shared Space." *The Quint*, 3 May 2024. https://www.thequint.com/opinion/one-year-of-manipur-meitei-kuki-violence-biren-singh-has-ruptured-the-states-shared-space#read-more. Accessed on 11 April 2025.

Jayal, N.G. 2019. "Reconfiguring Citizenship in Contemporary India." *South Asia: Journal of South Asian Studies* 42, no. 1: 33–50.

Jenkins, L. D. 2003. "'Another People of India' Project: Colonial and National Anthropology." *The Journal of Asian Studies* 62, no. 4: 1143–170.

Kikon, D. 2022. "Dirty Food: Racism and Casteism in India." *Ethnic and Racial Studies* 45, no. 2: 278–97.

Kikon, D., and B. G. Karlsson. 2019. *Leaving the Land: Indigenous Migration and Affective Labour in India*. New Delhi: Cambridge University Press.

Krishna, S. 1999. *Postcolonial Insecurities: India, Sri Lanka and the Question of Nationalism*. Minneapolis: University of Minnesota Press.

Kumar, Greeshma. 2024. "Saviour Complex: Why the Biren Singh government gives a free hand to Arambai Tenggol." *The Caravan*, 15 April 2024. https://caravanmagazine.in/conflict/biren-singh-gives-a-free-hand-to-arambai-tenggol-militia-imphal-manipur. Accessed on 11 April 2025.

Lee, J. 2017. "Odor and Order: How Caste Is Inscribed in Space and Sensoria." *Comparative Studies of South Asia, Africa and the Middle East* 37, no. 3: 470–90.

Louis, Arul B. 1980. "We can make Ho Chi Minhs in Mizoram also: Laldenga." *India Today*, 17 January 1980. https://www.indiatoday.in/magazine/indiascope/story/19800731-we-can-make-ho-chi-minhs-in-mizoram-also-laldenga-821295-2014-01-17. Accessed on 11 April 2025.

Mathur, N. 2020. "'NRC se Azadi': Process, Chronology, and a Paper Monster." *South Asia Multidisciplinary Academic Journal* 1, nos. 24/25.

McDuie-Ra, D. 2009. "Fifty-year disturbance: the Armed Forces Special Powers Act and exceptionalism in a South Asian periphery." *Contemporary South Asia* 17, no. 3: 255–70.

———. 2012. *Northeast Migrants in Delhi: Race, Refuge and Retail.* Amsterdam: Amsterdam University Press.

Misra, S. 2011. *Becoming a Borderland: The Politics of Space and Identity in Colonial Northeast India.* New Delhi: Routledge.

Ngaihte, T. 2014. "NidoTaniam and the Fraught Question of Racism in India." *Economic and Political Weekly* 49, no. 11: 15–17.

Pachuau, J. L. K., and W. V. Schendel. 2016. "Borderland Histories, Northeastern India: An Introduction." *Studies in History* 32, no. 1: 1–4.

Poggi, G. 2003. "Citizens and the State: Retrospect and Prospect." In *States and Citizens: History, Theory, Prospects*, edited by Q. Skinner and B. Strath, 39–50. Cambridge: Cambridge University Press.

Punathil, S. 2022. "Precarious Citizenship: Detection, Detention and 'Deportability' in India." *Citizenship Studies* 26, no. 1: 55–72.

Roluahpuia. 2017. "Media in Conflict or Conflict in Media: Examining Media Coverage of Conflict in Northeast India." *Asian Ethnicity* 18, no. 4: 488–504.

———. 2020. "Whose Border Is It Anyway? Control, Contestation, and Confluence in Indo-Myanmar Borderlands." *Contemporary South Asia* 28, no. 1: 74–85.

———. 2023. *Nationalism in the Vernacular: State, Tribes, and the Politics of Peace in Northeast India.* New Delhi: Cambridge University Press.

Siim, B., and P. Stoltz. 2024. "Intersectional and Transnational Approaches to Gender and Citizenship: Contributions and Contestations." In *The*

Palgrave Handbook of Gender and Citizenship, edited by B. Siim and P. Stoltz, 1-24. London: Palgrave Macmillan.

Roy, A. 2010. *Mapping Citizenship in India.* New Delhi: Oxford University Press.

———. 2022. *Citizenship Regimes, Law, and Belonging: The CAA and the NRC.* Oxford: Oxford University Press.

Sadiq, K. 2008. *Paper Citizens: How Illegal Immigrants Acquire Citizenship in Developing Countries.* New York: Oxford University Press.

Skaria, A. 1997. "Shades of Wildness Tribe, Caste, and Gender in Western India." *The Journal of Asian Studies* 56, no. 3: 726–45.

Thirumuthy, Priyanka. 2019. "Chennai cops mistook us for Tibetans: North-East Indians detained for Modi-Jinping meet." *The NEWS Minute* 16 October 2019. https://www.thenewsminute.com/tamil-nadu/chennai-cops-mistook-us-tibetans-north-east-indians-detained-modi-jinping-meet-110642. Accessed on 11 April 2025.

van Schendel, W. 2002. "Stateless in South Asia: The Making of the India-Bangladesh Enclaves." *The Journal of Asian Studies* 61, no. 1: 115–47.

Weiner, M. 1978. *Sons of the Soil, Migration, and Ethnic Conflict in India.* Princeton: Princeton University Press.

Wouters, J. J. P., and T. B. Subba. 2013. "The 'Indian Face', India's Northeast, and 'The Idea of India'." *Asian Anthropology* 12, no. 2: 126–40.

Xaxa, V. 2005. "Politics of Language, Religion and Identity: Tribes in India." *Economic and Political Weekly* 40, no. 13: 1363–370.

———. 2008. *State, Society, and Tribes: Issues in Post-colonial India.* New Delhi: Pearson.

Yuval-Davis, N. 1997. "Women, Citizenship and Difference." *Feminist Review* 57: 4–27.

——— 1999. "The Multi-Layered Citizen." *International Feminist Journal of Politics* 1, no. 1: 119–36.

Zomi Students Federation (ZSF) and Kuki Students Organisation (KSO). 2023. "The Inevitable Split: Documents on State Sponsored Ethnic Cleansing in Manipur", Vol. 1. Lamka: ZSF and KSO.

SEVEN

The Hindu Right and the Erasure of Kashmir

ANURADHA BHASIN

The Jammu and Kashmir Reorganisation Act passed in 2019 altered the erstwhile state of Jammu and Kashmir politically and geographically, fundamentally transforming Kashmir's[1] relationship with the Indian Union. Subsequent legal modifications by the Indian state that metamorphosed the socio-economic and development models within the region highlight the contrasting transition from the 'Naya Kashmir', whose foundations were laid in the 1950s, to the second 'Naya Kashmir' post-2019, and the consequent impact on the economy and civil rights of the residents of Jammu and Kashmir.

In this chapter, I examine the multifaceted transformation of Kashmir and its relationship with India under a Hindu Right-wing state through several interconnected lenses. I begin with the constitutional–legal landscape, focusing on Article 370 watered down in August 2019 and its subsequent modifications. Next, I delve into the realm of development, comparing and contrasting two distinct 'Naya Kashmir' schemes and their impacts, including the ecological fallout on the region. The economic and civic dimensions are then scrutinised, with particular attention to the pressing issues of unemployment and media suppression. While these challenges are not unique to Kashmir, they are a precursor

[1] The word 'Kashmir' can have multiple connotations. It is interchangeably used to denote both Kashmiri ethnicity and as an abbreviated form of the state of J&K (as it stood on 15 August 1947) in its entirety. In this chapter, the word Kashmir denotes the state of J&K unless otherwise specified.

to similar broader trends across India where governmental influence over media outlets also intersects with greater corporate control of media. I analyse these broad sweeping changes in the dismantling and erasure of Kashmir using Lal Chowk – a symbolic and historical political epicentre that encapsulates the ongoing efforts to rewrite Kashmir's narrative, as a metaphor for the broader attempt to supersede historical legacies, including that of Jawaharlal Nehru, and a deliberate invisibilisation of Kashmiri people, culture and politics. This comprehensive exploration is aimed to provide a nuanced understanding of the complex forces at play in shaping contemporary Kashmir.

Article 370's Trajectory: From Autonomy to Siege

On 5 August 2019, the Indian government led by Prime Minister Narendra Modi stripped J&K of its autonomy by revoking Article 370 and Article 35A, dismembered and downgraded it by dividing it into two – Union Territory of J&K and Union Territory of Ladakh. The autonomy enjoyed by Jammu and Kashmir, under Article 370, which was also a constitutional link to India, was ended through an Act of Indian Parliament, called the Jammu and Kashmir Reorganisation Act 2019 (PTI 2019), without consultation or concurrence of the people of Jammu and Kashmir. In December 2023, the Supreme Court upheld the Act.[2]

Article 370, which outlined the legal and constitutional arrangement between Jammu and Kashmir and India, was inserted into the Indian Constitution keeping in view Jammu and Kashmir's history and the circumstances under which it became a part of India. Any decision pertaining to its continuance should have factored in both the legality as well as the history.

The verdict of the Supreme Court of India, however, chose to discard both. The 476-page verdict that was delivered turned out to be a saga of historical distortions, selective amnesia and legal interpretations without the application of logic. In declaring Article

[2] In Re: Article 370 of the Constitution. Writ Petition (civil) 1099 of 2019 in the Supreme Court. https://api.sci.gov.in/pdf/LU/article_370.pdf

370 to be temporary, the court noted that it served two purposes: One was the war-like conditions, and second was transitional – to provide for an interim arrangement until the Constituent Assembly of Jammu and Kashmir could frame its own constitution.

This is far from the truth. The Constitution, of which Article 370 was a part, was unanimously adopted in 1949. Shyama Prasad Mookherji, who later became the Jana Sangh founder, also gave his consent.[3] The war was long over by then. The sole purpose of Article 370 was to provide a legal and constitutional bridge between India and Jammu and Kashmir, owing to the unique circumstances in which the state had acceded to India and in accordance with the complexity of the aspirations of the people of Jammu and Kashmir (Bhasin 2022). It recorded a solemn pact between leaders of the Union of India and Jammu and Kashmir. It was inevitable in view of the state's exceptional history and the circumstances under which it acceded to India (Noorani 2013, 15–16). At the same time, it offered certain protections and granted special status to Jammu and Kashmir.

This arrangement was meant to be temporary only until the time the J&K Constituent Assembly could ratify Article 370 and adopt it while framing a separate constitution for the state. J&K Constituent Assembly's approval of the same sealed the finality of Article 370 and J&K's special status, its own constitution and flag. The task of the J&K Constituent Assembly was to draft a separate constitution and take a call on accepting or rejecting Article 370.[4] The notion that such an exercise was undertaken only to finally discard Article 370, the special status, and the Constitution of J&K, reflects not just ignorance of history but also lack of knowledge of jurisprudence.

Autonomy under Article 370, it bears pointing out, has been immensely eroded in the past through several presidential orders – starting from the Presidential Order of 1954, allowing

[3] An interview by the author with Krishan Dev Sethi at his house in Jammu in the afternoon of 5 August 2019. Sethi was a member of the J&K Constituent Assembly and a witness to Indian Constituent Assembly debates in 1949.

[4] Interview with Krishan Dev Sethi, 5 August 2019.

the extension of almost the entire Indian Constitution to Jammu and Kashmir: 94 out of 97 entries in the Union List were already applicable to Jammu and Kashmir; 260 out of the 395 Articles of the Constitution; as well as 7 out of the 12 Schedules of the Indian Constitution were extended to the state before Article 370 was completely decimated on 5 August 2019. However, all these dilutions were done with the concurrence of the Jammu and Kashmir legislature.

Article 370 (1)(b) limited the power of the Parliament to make laws for Jammu and Kashmir in relation to 'matters in the Union List and the Concurrent List which, in consultation with the Government of the State, are declared by the President of India to correspond to matters specified in the Instrument of Accession' or 'such other matters in the said Lists as, with the concurrence of the Government of the State'. There is an emphasis on the concurrence of the state. The sub-article 3 of Article 370 lays down that for the President to declare that this Article shall cease to be operative or shall be operative, the recommendation of the Constituent Assembly would be mandatory (Noorani 2000).

Thus, while there was a possibility of extending central laws to Jammu and Kashmir, provided there was concurrence of the state legislature, Article 370 could not have been made inoperative since the J&K Constituent Assembly was disbanded in 1957. A. G. Noorani, a noted lawyer and an expert on the constitutional history of Jammu and Kashmir, states unequivocally that Article 370 could not be amended at all (2019). He points to Article 370 (3) which states that Article 370 could cease to be operative through a President's notification provided that this is done on the recommendation of J&K Constituent Assembly. He writes that this power could not be transferred or modified. He further elaborates:

> A constituent assembly is a body wielding constituent powers as a *sovereign* body. It itself establishes a legislative assembly with limited powers it defines. J&K's constituent assembly ceased to exist on January 20, 1957. The assembly it created in J&K's Constitution survives still (Article 46). How can you endow it with constituent

> power to accord its concurrence to the Centre to destroy the state's autonomy? (Noorani 2019)

Presidential Order 272, that enabled the passing of the J&K Reorganisation Act, amounted to the Central Government taking its own consent to amend the Constitution and nullify Article 370: it modified 'constituent assembly' to mean 'legislative assembly' and then delegated all powers of the legislative assembly to the Governor – who was the Centre's nominee. The Supreme Court, however, has overlooked these aspects as trivial.

Technically, Article 370 was amended, not revoked, in 2019; it was neutered and made inoperative. By virtue of this dilution, all the Presidential Orders since 1950, including Article 35A that defined who a permanent resident is, protected the Muslim-majority status of the state as well as the exclusive land rights of all its citizens, stood invalidated. The Indian Constitution was extended to the state of Jammu and Kashmir, truncated and demoted into two union territories in toto.

The Constituent Assembly of Jammu and Kashmir did not exist on 5 August 2019. The legislative assembly was dissolved on 21 November 2018. No consultations were ever held with any of the stakeholders, turning this exercise into one that invoked a sense of humiliation among its citizens. Not only were the people's special status rights snatched, but they were also divided and granted a status that was deemed much lower than the status of a fully integrated state in this forced integration process as per the J&K Reorganisation Act that was subsequently passed on 9 August 2019.

Effectively, the people of Jammu and Kashmir had not been consulted about their future prior to the circumvention of constitutional provisions. Before the Union Home Minister moved the legislation, 13–14 million people whose fate the Parliament was deciding were virtually put under siege with the imposition of Section 144, excessive militarisation and internet ban (Wani 2019). With sweeping arrests and detentions and civil rights kept under prolonged suspension, what was abrogated were the last remaining vestiges of democracy in Jammu and Kashmir (Waheed

2019). A smooth transition from autonomy to complete integration was ensured by trampling the civil rights of its 14 million people under the sheer weight of military jackboots.

Even the pretence of democracy was discarded during this siege, leading to the residents of Jammu and Kashmir feeling emasculated, humiliated and disenfranchised. The actions of the Indian government since 2019 including the exacerbation of repressive policies and an aggressive economic and development agenda, to the detriment of the region's ecology, betray that the disempowerment of the residents of Jammu and Kashmir – the erstwhile only Muslim-majority state of India – was the intended motive.

The Transformation: A Saga of Two 'Naya Kashmirs'

Within minutes after the Act was passed in the Parliament through a voice vote with hardly any debate, Amit Shah, the Union Home Minister and Modi's close aide 'congratulated the nation' and tweeted: 'This historic decision will usher in a new dawn of peace and development in J&K and Ladakh region' (PTI 2019). Subsequently, the Indian government rolled out the blueprint of the new 'Naya Kashmir' dismantling the entire state, altering land laws, and bringing upheavals in economic policies and development models in a complete reversal of the old 'Naya Kashmir'.

The 1940s marked a pivotal moment in Jammu and Kashmir's history with the introduction of the Naya Kashmir (New Kashmir) document by the National Conference under Sheikh Abdullah's leadership. This visionary manifesto outlined a socialist framework for the state, later serving as the foundation for the Jammu and Kashmir Constitution and several groundbreaking laws. These transformative legislations, including the Jammu and Kashmir Big Landed Estates Abolition Act (BLEAA), debt reconciliation measures, and other land-related reforms, were designed to fundamentally restructure society along egalitarian lines. Their primary aim was to rectify the long-standing injustices stemming from years of oppression, including the inhumane practice of forced labour (*begar*), arbitrary land acquisitions and unjust taxation. Sheikh Mohammad Abdullah, J&K's first Prime Minister, and his close associates acted swiftly to draft and implement these revolutionary land reforms. The cornerstone of this initiative was the historic BLEAA of 1950, which effectively ended landlordism and paved the way for rural prosperity. This Act imposed a ceiling of 22.5 acres on landholdings, with surplus land transferred to tillers without compensation to the original owners.[5]

These land reforms were bolstered by tenancy reforms, creating a comprehensive protective framework that addressed the skewed land ownership patterns in Jammu and Kashmir. The primary beneficiaries were Muslims and lower-caste Hindus, who had long been marginalised under the previous system. To safeguard the interests of the newly empowered tillers and prevent exploitation, a series of additional laws were enacted. These included the prohibition of land transfers to non-permanent residents, strict regulation of land alienation by agricultural classes under the Jammu and Kashmir Alienation of Land Act, 1938, restrictions on converting agricultural land for non-agricultural purposes, limitations on land transfers without government permission to prevent fragmentation of holdings, and strict regulation of tenancy and prohibition of sub-tenancy to eliminate intermediary interests. These measures were designed to ensure that redistributed land remained with the tillers-turned-landowners, protecting them from potential harassment by former landlords and land speculators. The reforms also aimed at preventing the re-emergence of exploitative agrarian practices through backdoor channels. The comprehensive nature of these reforms represented a radical departure from the previous system, setting Jammu and Kashmir on a path toward greater economic equality and social justice. By addressing the fundamental issues of land ownership and agricultural rights, these changes laid the groundwork for significant improvements in rural prosperity and social mobility.

---

[5] The Jammu and Kashmir Big Landed Estates Abolition Act, 2007 (1950 A. D.) (Act No. xvii of Samvat 2007), https://www.indiacode.nic.in/bitstream/123456789/4128/1/Big_Landed_Estates_Abolition_Act.pdf

The land reforms in Jammu and Kashmir, while ambitious in scope and revolutionary in intent, encountered significant hurdles that impeded their full implementation and impact. These challenges stemmed from various quarters, creating a complex web of obstacles that diluted the reforms' effectiveness. Administrative complacency emerged as a primary stumbling block. The bureaucratic machinery, tasked with executing these sweeping changes, often lacked the necessary drive and efficiency. This lethargy in implementation allowed for gaps and delays that undermined the reforms' potential. Compounding this issue was the spectre of corruption that permeated various levels of the administrative structure. Instances of graft and misuse of power not only diverted resources but also eroded public trust in the reform process. Perhaps the most significant challenge lay in the socio-economic landscape of the intended beneficiaries. The majority of those who stood to gain from these reforms were the illiterate and socially backward, lacking the awareness and means to fully comprehend and claim their newly granted rights (Bhasin 2022). This knowledge gap created a disconnect between the legislative intent and ground-level realities, often leaving the most vulnerable unable to capitalise on the opportunities presented by the reforms. The entrenched power structures and vested interests of the old order also posed formidable resistance. Former landlords and influential figures, reluctant to relinquish their privileged positions, often employed various tactics to subvert or delay the implementation of reforms. This resistance manifested in legal challenges, social pressures and exploitation of administrative loopholes.

Despite these multifaceted challenges, it is important to note that the land reforms did manage to alter the lives of many, albeit not to the extent originally envisioned. The mixed legacy of these reforms serves as a testament to both the transformative potential of progressive legislation and the intricate difficulties involved in reshaping deeply ingrained social and economic structures. Economist Jean Dreze has pointed out how Article 370 and J&K's unique system of land laws ensured that Jammu and Kashmir, contrary to the myths being peddled by the Modi-led Indian government, was far ahead of many states including Gujarat in the economic and social indicators. *The Telegraph* reported:

> The economist cited 2015–2016 figures of life expectancy, under-five mortality rate, total fertility rate and the percentages of girls aged 15–19 with eight years of schooling, underweight children, adult women with low body mass index and fully immunised children. He also cited 2011–12 figures for rural poverty and the wages of rural labourers. Kashmir scored better than Gujarat in all the indices. (Vincent 2019)

After the residents of Jammu and Kashmir lost their constitutional protections under Article 370 and Article 35A with the passage of the J&K Reorganisation Act in 2019, the Narendra Modi-led BJP government brought in legal changes, most of them stealthily, to alter Jammu and Kashmir's economic and development structures completely.

In a late-night move on 31 March 2020 the Indian government officially announced the notification called the Jammu and Kashmir Reorganisation (Adaptation of State Laws) Order, 2020, which introduced the domicile clause in the J&K Civil Services Recruitment Act. According to this, anyone who has resided in J&K for 15 years or has studied in the territory for seven years, and appeared in either Class 10 or Class 12 examination, will get residency rights. They will then be eligible for various government jobs (Muzaffar 2020). The notification's timing, one week after India announced a countrywide lockdown to contain the COVID-19 outbreak, was odd. While a lockdown in the rest of the country became a safety measure in the fight against a virus, in Kashmir it assumed a different meaning. It was a lockdown within a lockdown that had been partially in place since 5 August 2019.

The new domicile rule, and its timing, stirred up anxieties, particularly among the J&K youth, irrespective of their ethnic and communal identities or their political ideologies, since it meant that they would be losing government jobs they earlier had a monopoly over, to outsiders. The government was one of the biggest employers of fresh graduates in the region and ahead of this notification a number of recruitment processes were stalled, prompting suspicions that this was done intentionally to allow outsiders who qualified for domicile under the new rule to apply as well. Many recruitment processes since 2020 have been mired in controversies with aspirants complaining about sluggishness and wrongdoings. In 2023, the premier recruitment agency, the Jammu and Kashmir Service Selection Board (JKSSB) has been caught in the eye of the storm over the recruitment process for Police Sub-Inspectors (PSIs), Junior Engineers (JEs) in various engineering departments, and Finance Account Assistants. These recruitments had been lingering on for almost two years (KTNS 2024).

Far more damaging legal changes were made with respect to land ownership and development. The Union Territory of Jammu and Kashmir Reorganisation (Adaptation of Central Laws) Third Order and the Jammu and Kashmir Reorganisation (Adaptation of State Laws) Fifth Order, 2020, repealed twelve Acts and amended fourteen laws related to land on 26 October 2020. The changes enacted were to allow non-residents to purchase and own immovable property in Jammu and Kashmir. The notification also allowed the transfer of agricultural land for non-agricultural purposes, but only after a government permit. The BLEAA was struck off the statute. So was Jammu and Kashmir Tenancy Act, 1980, that had stayed all applications or proceedings relating to ejecting tenants. The order also did away with the Jammu and Kashmir Common Lands (Regulation) Act, 1956, which regulated the rights of common land such as roads, streets, lanes, pathways, water channels, drains, wells, tanks, or any other source of water supply to villagers. The Jammu and Kashmir Alienation of Land Act, 1938, a law related to the transfer of agricultural land for non-agricultural purposes, also ceased to exist. The Jammu and Kashmir Agrarian Reforms Act, 1976, and the Jammu and Kashmir Land Revenue Act, 1996 were also scrapped. The law that prohibited the conversion of land into orchards and existing orchard land for other uses, without prior government permission, termed the

Jammu and Kashmir Prohibition on Conversion of Land and Alienation of Orchards Act, 1975, was also repealed.[6]

The changes entail that the locals can be stripped of their possession and ownership of land – in the name of development, economic activity, public welfare, NGO activities or strategic reasons – with far-reaching economic, political, social and ecological impact. The laws enable large-scale conversion of agricultural and forest lands and offer innumerable ways in which land can now be forcibly acquired with much greater ease than before, giving sweeping powers to the bureaucracy to adjudicate matters in the most arbitrary ways.

These have by and large changed the nature of land laws. For instance, J&K had its own land-related laws where the state was the biggest owner of land but also the protector of people's rights. Lands were often given on leases to people for residential, agricultural or business purposes. Land reforms in the 1950s had given land to the tiller, subsequent laws had offered extra protection to the agrarian communities. The impact of these changes on the socially and economically oppressed communities who benefited from the previous reforms has yet to be fully understood.

Besides, the amended laws make it easier for the government to acquire huge land holdings in the name of security or development and though the Fair Compensation Act for land acquisitions has been extended, this is not being adhered to. Lands which were earlier earmarked for certain purposes – but had not been fully

---

[6] The other Acts that are no longer effective in the UT are the Jammu and Kashmir Consolidation of Holdings Act, 1962; the Jammu and Kashmir Flood Plain Zones (Regulation and Development) Act; the Jammu and Kashmir Land Improvement Schemes Act, the Jammu and Kashmir Prevention of Fragmentation of Agricultural Holdings Act, the Jammu and Kashmir Right of Prior Purchase Act, the Jammu and Kashmir Utilization of Lands Act and the Jammu and Kashmir Underground Public Utilities (Acquisition of Rights of User in Land) Act. In their place Central laws like the Real Estate (Regulation and Development) Act (RERA), 2016, aimed at boosting real estate industry and adjudicating speedy property dispute resolutions were extended to the one-year-old Union Territory.

regularised because of complacency or corruption that was always there – are now being declared as state lands and people are being evicted and their homes demolished without any adequate notice or without giving them a chance to be heard. People are being declared encroachers and land grabbers without an investigation.

Livelihoods, Economy, Ecology and Liberties

This massive restructuring is, thus, paving the way for forcible and large-scale acquisition of agricultural lands for development purposes, rendering residents homeless or deprived of their sole source of income. Since 2022, in multiple districts of Jammu and Kashmir, the district municipal corporation, state revenue authorities, and police have worked together to demolish houses and properties of residents (Chakraborty 2023). News reports indicate that numerous residents claim they were not given any advance notice by the administration (Zargar 2023). Many also assert they possessed ownership documents for their properties but were not afforded an opportunity to present their claims before their homes were bulldozed (Zutshi 2024). The reckless acquisition of land for aggressive development purposes involves not only forcible evictions and demolitions but also has major ecological implications, rendering agricultural lands barren or unfit for use. For instance, the construction of a Ring Road around Srinagar city has waterlogged agricultural fields and orchards, raising concerns of the farmers and the environmentalists (Bhat 2024).

The models of development being employed involve excessive focus on unsustainable tourism, aggressive building of infrastructure like roads and tunnels, and tapping of Jammu and Kashmir's rich resources including water and minerals with deleterious impacts on its already fragile Himalayan ecology.

For instance, India discovered 5.9 million tons of lithium in Jammu and Kashmir, potentially making it a top global holder. This could boost India's electric vehicle industry and energy independence. However, environmental risks include potential harm to local ecology, water resources and deforestation.

Security implications are also heightened due to the discovery in a militarised, disputed area, which could exacerbate tensions (Allison 2023).

A 2021–22 J&K government report states that 224 out of 247 'minor mineral blocks' in Kashmir valley's streams and rivers were e-auctioned for mining. However, in violation of rules and environmental norms, heavy machinery is being used for mining in major Jhelum tributaries, including the Rambiara, Vishaw and Sukhnag rivers, thus damaging river ecosystems and altering river hydrology (Shabir 2024).

Major infrastructure projects in the Pir Panchal region are causing significant environmental and social impacts. Land subsidence, landslides and ecological damage have resulted from railway construction, highway expansion and hydroelectric projects (Andrabi 2023). Notable incidents include house collapses in Duksar village and Thathri, and fatal accidents on the Jammu–Srinagar highway.

In March 2024, climate activist Sonam Wangchuk led a massive protest in Leh, fasting in sub-zero temperatures to highlight Ladakh's environmental crisis. He warned of impending climate disaster due to unchecked industrial development and military activities. Ladakh's glaciers are rapidly receding, threatening water supplies for millions. Local pollution, exacerbated by militarisation and the India–China standoff, worsens the situation, Wangchuk pointed out and emphasised Ladakh's global importance, as its mountains are part of the Greater Himalayas, affecting over 2 billion people. He also highlighted the loss of pastureland to industrial plans and Chinese encroachment, impacting local nomads and shepherds (Associated Press 2024).

These are just some of the many manifestations of the aggressive and unscientific development plans in Jammu and Kashmir since 2019 that are not only disempowering individuals and communities but also evoking serious ecological concerns.

Yet, these stories of dispossession and disempowerment are lesser heard because the institutions that could speak truth to power have been crushed and democratic spaces of dissent completely choked. The government has resorted to systemic and ruthless marginalisation of political voices, invisibilisation of the civil society and the silencing of the media.

Local political representation has been denied by demoting the state into a centrally controlled union territory and by not holding assembly elections. Kashmir's politics has been consistently manipulated since 1947, with New Delhi often violating democratic principles to install favourable leaders. Under Modi's BJP government, this trend has intensified. Non-BJP politicians were jailed or placed under house arrest for nearly a year, and continue to face pressure through terror and money laundering accusations. Other than this, constitutional norms were disregarded in the premature delimitation of J&K's electoral constituencies. The process ignored population size principles and introduced invalid criteria, resulting in gerrymandering that divides Muslim votes and consolidates Hindu votes. Furthermore, new and unknown political parties are being promoted through Delhi-based media. Despite these efforts to marginalise established politicians and engineer new faces, the BJP remains uncertain about achieving its goal of installing a Hindu chief minister in India's only Muslim-majority region. Consequently, J&K has not held elections since 2014.

Since 2019, Kashmir's civil society has been effectively silenced. NGOs and activists face intimidation through tax and money laundering cases, with some subjected to anti-terror raids. The arrest of renowned human rights activist Khurram Parvez in November 2021 under Unlawful Activities Prevention Act (UAPA, 1967) has particularly chilled activism in the region (Manecksha 2024). Previously, even during turbulent periods, civil resistance persisted through various non-violent means: street protests, sit-ins, art, poetry, writings and graffiti. A notable example was the Association of Parents of the Disappeared, led by Parveena Ahangar, which held monthly sit-ins seeking justice for those who disappeared in custody. Post-2019, these public expressions of dissent have vanished. Artistic resistance has gone underground, and public discussions on Kashmir are banned, not only in the region but across India. This represents an unprecedented suppression of civil society voices in Kashmir's recent history.

The stifling of the press and media has been a major contributor to the absence of democratic spaces in Jammu and Kashmir. Kashmir's free press has been effectively dismantled. Initially, an internet shutdown forced journalists to share limited government-provided resources, working under surveillance. As connectivity resumed, journalists faced new challenges: summons, raids, arrests and criminal charges. As of June 2024, four journalists remain imprisoned, some under anti-terror laws. The Kashmir Press Club has been shut down, many journalists are on no-fly lists and some have their passports revoked. This climate of fear has led to widespread self-censorship or resignation (Limaye 2023). Local newspapers now primarily publish government-approved content, incentivised by lucrative state advertisements.

Half-Truths, Lies and Selfie-Points

The silencing of journalists, politicians and civil society has created a pervasive atmosphere of suppression. In this environment, the only narrative that thrives in Jammu and Kashmir is one that is either directly propagated or endorsed by the government, effectively stifling independent voices and diverse perspectives. Simultaneously, it paves the way for lies, half-truths and myths to be freely propagated by the government which is papering over the distressing level of disempowerment at the ground with a cacophony of the celebratory and jubilant note of the government narrative about 'prosperity' and 'tourism' in the new Naya Kashmir.

For instance, investment claims in Jammu and Kashmir have been inconsistent and often contradictory. In March 2022, the J&K administration claimed ₹33,000 crore in investments for 2021–2022, projecting ₹75,000 crore for 2022–2023 (Rashid 2022). However, the Ministry of Home Affairs (MHA) data in December 2022 showed only ₹376.76 crore for 2021–2022, down from previous years. The MHA later revised the figures, stating ₹56,000 crore in investments over three years, conflicting with earlier Lok Sabha data of ₹1,084 crore (*The Hindu* 2023). A

June Live Mint report (2023) cited ₹66,000 crore in investment proposals, not actual investments. These discrepancies raise questions about the accuracy of investment claims, the nature and location of investments, and their impact on local populations and ecology. The lack of transparency regarding new industries and investors fuels concerns among locals. Celebratory statistics from the government and some journalists lack evidence to support claims about development schemes. The absence of public information on these projects and their potential adverse effects on local communities and the environment is notable. This is why the discontent over the new development vision is emerging not only in Kashmir Valley but also in Ladakh and Jammu, suggesting widespread concerns about the current approach to regional development in Modi's Naya Kashmir. This Naya Kashmir is low on substance and high on symbolism, much in line with Modi's persona. It is showcased through aggressive tourism, hoisting of flags and 'selfie-points' in aggrandisement of Modi, while perpetuating many myths and camouflaging the ugly reality of disempowerment.

Though tourism in Kashmir has been robust since 2021, this is not something new for the region which has seen many ups and downs in tourism before and after insurgency broke out in 1990, receding tourism to the margins for almost a decade. Tourism revival began in early 2000s and by 2011, 10 lakh tourists including foreign tourists visited Jammu and Kashmir, besides 1 crore-plus pilgrims who visited Mata Vaishno Devi's shrine in Jammu province and the 6.75 lakh devotees who undertook the Amarnath Yatra in 2011 (Sharma 2012). In 2014, a record-breaking 11 lakh tourists visited Jammu and Kashmir, despite the devastating floods that inundated major parts of Srinagar under 20 feet water for several weeks (PTI 2014). According to government data, 1 crore tourists visited in 2023 and the projected tourists for 2023–24 are 20 million. The Jammu and Kashmir LG claimed that the region witnessed an 'unprecedented influx of 2.35 crore tourists' in 2024 (KashmirLife 2025). Prime Minister Modi during his visit to Kashmir in January 2025 also signalled a major boost in tourism and pegged the number over 2 crore. These are unrealistic figures. A breakdown of numbers and comparison with transportation and boarding-lodging infrastructure falsify the claims (KashmirLife 2025). Reports have pointed out that, unlike in the past, the government has begun to club the statistics of tourists and pilgrims to make it sound impressive (Sareen 2019). More importantly, how ecologically sustainable can this vast size of tourism be in a region that has 7–8 million people living in the fragile Himalayan belt? (Bhat 2023)

While the government publicises tourism as the high-point of economic activity, only 10–15 per cent local population is connected to tourism. All other traditional areas of economy, particularly agriculture and horticulture are in distress due to lack of government initiatives. Even with respect to tourism industry, several hoteliers are bearing the brunt of the new land laws and are facing eviction notices or have already closed down (Bhat 2023).

Some of the other symbols of normalcy proclaimed by the Modi government are the increasing number of national tricolours hoisted at public buildings, hotels and marketplaces, or the selfie-points with Narendra Modi life-size cut-outs. The flag posts are higher and questions have been raised about the aggressive multiplication of the Indian national flags. Politicians and workers unions have complained about government officials compelling people to buy and hoist flags. Mainstream politicians have called off the bluff of the government and maintain that the local regional parties had always kept the tricolour, along with the erstwhile state's flag, aloft in Kashmir. Yet, the government has turned every flag-hoisting ceremony into a spectacle. On Modi's first-ever visit to Kashmir after 2019, the venue of his event at Bakshi Stadium in Srinagar was draped in tricolour. Lal Chowk is one of the hot spots where the government often organises flag-hoisting events.

One of the most prominent selfie-points is also placed at Lal Chowk, the nerve of Srinagar city that has borne witness to many historic and political moments in the past. The selfie-point comprises a life-size cut-out of Prime Minister Modi next to a hoarding which depicts a young lady doctor attending to an elderly man. The theme of the campaign is *Buzurgon Ka Samman* (Respect for Elderly) written in Devanagari script which only a few Kashmiris can read. The selfie-point, bereft of any Kashmiri essence, is as good as a selfie-point in New Delhi or any other Indian city. The selfie-point with Modi cut-out where smiling tourists pose for a photograph and video reel has become a new tourism destination at Lal Chowk. The overhauling of Lal Chowk with flashy, ugly, garish lights and synthetic tiling signifies the appropriation of all of Lal Chowk – a historic site that has been witness to many a historic moment in Kashmir's history, starting from Nehru's promise in 1948.

Conclusion

The transformation at Lal Chowk is crucial in understanding the rest of Kashmir, particularly the Valley. The capture of this city square, where Sheikh Abdullah once stood with India's first Prime Minister Jawaharlal Nehru, who promised that the future of Kashmir would be resolved in accordance with the will of the people, with flags and Modi cut-outs marks the erasure of the place's history, its people, and culture.

In early June 2024, Yasmeen Khan, a Kashmiri video journalist, posted on X a video showing her argument with a cop who had stopped her from interviewing a woman at this site. She argued that if tourists could come and take selfies and shoot videos at Lal Chowk, why was she being stopped, but the cop does not relent and asks her to go talk to her boss. A few weeks before that, during the parliamentary elections, an Indian journalist Arfa Khannum Sherwani interviewed a man at Lal Chowk, asking him about the issues he would vote on. The moment he started speaking about 'youth frustration over unemployment', three cops including those in civvies encircled them and the interviewee clammed up.

Such rare videos highlight the reality of Lal Chowk and the rest of Kashmir, which beneath the glamour of the national tricolours, life-size Modi cut-outs, synthetic pavements and garish lights is forced into silence under harsh military repression that evinces itself not only in the form of arrests and police raids but also a systemic and cóntinuous system of surveillance and repeated verification of citizens, particularly civil society activists and journalists. Lal Chowk in its new avatar is an apt metaphor of the complete erasure of Kashmir – Kashmir as it exists, and Kashmir as it earlier existed.

The J&K Reorganisation Act was designed to erase Kashmir and re-create a new one minus its people. Jammu and Kashmir was the only Muslim-majority state prior to 2019. Over 68 per cent of the region's population is Muslim and Kashmir Valley, the epicentre of this project of erasure has 97 per cent Muslims. The reading down of Article 370, which granted special status to Jammu and Kashmir, was a significant move aligned with the Bharatiya Janata Party's (BJP) ideological goals for India's only Muslim-majority state. This action is seen as part of a broader strategy by the BJP and its ideological parent, the Rashtriya Swayamsevak Sangh (RSS), to reshape India's national identity by marginalising Muslims or reducing them to non-entities. The RSS has openly advocated for changing Kashmir's demography as a solution to its long pending dispute.

The diminishing of Kashmir's autonomy and the marginalisation of its population serve two primary purposes in this agenda. First, it aims to subjugate the Muslim majority by potentially altering the region's demographic balance, though the feasibility of such a change remains uncertain. This approach in Kashmir – of subjugating the Muslims – is a model that could be extended to other parts of India, potentially affecting the Muslim minority nationwide. Second, it allows for greater central control over Kashmir's natural resources and strategic assets. To achieve these goals, the strategy involves disempowering and marginalising the local population. This approach not only affects the Muslim majority but also impacts other communities in the region, including Jammu's Hindu population and Ladakh's Buddhist community, who are seen as collateral damage in this larger political strategy.

The broader implication of this approach is the potential for increased marginalisation and humiliation of Muslim communities across India, as the Kashmir model could be seen as a template for dealing with minority populations elsewhere in the country. This strategy raises concerns about India's secular fabric and the rights of minority communities in a diverse nation.

References

Allison, T. 2023, March 30. "India's Lithium Resources in Kashmir Highlight Conflict Risks Around Critical Minerals." Center for Climate & Security, 30 March 2023. https://tinyurl.com/mrx2chzn. Accessed on 11 April 2025.

Andrabi, R. 2023, July 31. "From Cracks to Catastrophe: Pir Panchal's Sinking Houses." *IndiaSpend*, 31 July 2023. https://tinyurl.com/44de2r9k Accessed on 22 January 2025.

Associated Press. "Protests in Ladakh Enter Third Week as Locals Seek Protection of Fragile Ecology." *VoA*, 24 March 2024. https://tinyurl.com/yc84xkfv. Accessed on 22 January 2025.

Bhasin, A. 2022. *A Dismantled State: Untold Story of Kashmir After 370.* New Delhi: Harper Collins.

Bhat, R. M. "Unregulated Tourist Influx: Kashmir Dreads the Final Straw That Will Break the Himalayas' Back." *Money Life*, 8 June 2023. https://tinyurl.com/7wje79p3. Accessed on 22 January 2025.

———. "Apple Orchards and Farmlands Inundated: Farmers in Chadoora Demand Compensation from NHAI Over Ring Road Project's Environmental Violations." *Kashmir Times*, April 2024. https://kashmirtimes.com/jammu-and-kashmir-news/apple-orchards-and-farmlands-inundated-farmers-in-chadoora-demand-compensation-from-nhai-over-ring-road-projects-environmental-violations#:~:text=Project's%20Environmental%20Violations-,Apple%20Orchards%20and%20Farmlands%20Inundated%3A%20Farmers%20in%20Chadoora%20Demand%20Compensation,among%20local%20farmers%20and%20environmentalists. Accessed on 22 January 2025.

Bhat, T. "How Kashmir's New Land-grant Rules Have Put Livelihoods in Jeopardy." *The Week*, 09 April 2023. https://tinyurl.com/4kknuw7c Accessed on 22 January 2025.

Chakraborty, K. 2023. "Kashmiris Are Living in Fear of Demolitions." *New Internationalist*, 24 May 2023. https://newint.org/features/2023/05/24/kashmiris-are-living-fear-demolitions. Accessed on 22 January 2025.

KashmirLife. "2.35 Crore Tourists Visit Jammu and Kashmir in 2024: LG Sinha." 13 January 2025. https://kashmirlife.net/2-35-crore-tourists-visit-jammu-and-kashmir-in-2024-lg-sinha-379526/ Accessed on 14 April 2025.

———. "Did 2 Crore Tourists visit Kashmir in 2024?" 13 January 2025. https://kashmirtimes.com/jammu-and-kashmir-news/did-2-crore-tourists-visited-kashmir-in-2024. Accessed on 14 April 2025.

KTNS. "J&K: Scams surface in Insurance schemes, recruitments in Police, Engineering and FAAs." *Kashmir Times*, 11 January 2024. https://kashmirtimes.com/jammu-and-kashmir-scams-surface-in-insurance-schemes-recruitments-in-police-engineering-and-faas-allotment-of-projects-in-2023. Accessed on 23 January 2025.

Limaye, Y. 2023, September 1. "'Any Story Could Be Your Last' – India's crackdown on Kashmir press." *BBC*, 1 September 2023. https://tinyurl.com/4rufcdee. Accessed on 22 January 2025.

LiveMint. "J&K's New Industrial Policy ropes in ₹2,200 crore investment, 10,000 jobs in one year." 10 June 2023. https://www.livemint.com/news/india/jammu-and-kashmirs-new-industrial-policy-2021-ropes-in-rs-2-200-crore-investment-10-000-jobs-in-one-year-11686386215449.html Accessed on 14 April 2025.

Maneckshа, F. "Empty Rooms, Silenced Voices: What Remains of Kashmiri Civil Society's Valiant Fight for Justice." *Scroll.in*, 20 March 2024. https://tinyurl.com/4nhu82xk. Accessed on 22 January 2025.

Muzaffar, R. "Government Opens J&K Jobs for All." *The Telegraph*, 1 April 2020. https://tinyurl.com/42dcpf3z. Accessed on 22 January 2025.

Noorani, A. G. "Article 370: Law and Politics." *Frontline*, 16 September 2000. https://tinyurl.com/38hastpp. Accessed on 22 January 2025.

———. 2013. Constituent Assembly Debates, 17 October 1949. In *The Kashmir Dispute 1947–2012*. New Delhi: Tulika Books.

———. "Murder of Insaniyat, and of India's Solemn Commitment to Kashmir." *The Wire.in*, 13 August 2019. https://tinyurl.com/3c72bbxn Accessed on 22 January 2025.

PTI. "Article 370 Abolished: 'No more do nishan, do samvidhan', tweets Amit Shah." *The Times of India*, 5 August 2019. https://tinyurl.com/ycyd8c2x. Accessed on 22 January 2025.

———. "President Gives Assent to J&K Reorganisation Legislation, 2 UTs to come into Existence on October 31." *India Today*, 10 August 2019. https://tinyurl.com/3xr69paa. Accessed on 22 January 2025.

———. "11 Lakh Tourists Visit Kashmir Despite Floods, Elections." *IndiaTVNews*, 29 December 2014. https://tinyurl.com/4935jshe. Accessed on 22 January 2025.

Rashid, Hakeem Irfan. "J&K gets Rs 33,000-cr investment last year, claims UT administration." *ETPrime*, 22 March 2022. https://economictimes.indiatimes.com/news/economy/finance/33000-cr-investment-in-jk-admin/articleshow/90361640.cms?from=mdr. Accessed on 14 April 2025.

Sareen, P. "Kashmir, a Tourism Hub? Numbers Tell a Different Story – Most Tourists are Pilgrims." *The Wire.in*, 27 October 2019. https://tinyurl.com/5n8zh3c4. Accessed on 22 January 2025.

Shabir, Z. B. "An Unregulated Mining Boom in Kashmir Is Degrading Rivers, Worsening Floods and Destroying Livelihoods." *Article 14*, 29 January 2024. https://article-14.com/post/an-unregulated-mining-boom-in-kashmir-is-degrading-rivers-worsening-floods-destroying-livelihoods-65b7288ced999. Accessed on 22 January 2025.

Sharma, A. "Record 10 Lakh Tourists Visited Kashmir Valley in 2011." *India Today.in*, 2 January 2012. https://tinyurl.com/25jmxcsr. Accessed on 22 January 2025.

The Hindu. "Mismatch between Home Ministry's report on J&K investments and its statement in Lok Sabha." 3 January 2023. https://www.thehindu.com/news/national/mismatch-between-home-ministrys-report-on-jk-investments-and-its-statement-in-lok-sabha/article66334247.ece Accessed on 14 April 2025.

Vincent, P. L. "Jean Dreze Contests Amit Shah with Gujarat Data." *The Telegraph*, 8 August 2019. https://rb.gy/asieol. Accessed on 22 January 2025.

Waheed, M. "India's Illegal Power Grab Is Turning Kashmir into a Colony." *The Guardian*, 14 August 2019. https://rb.gy/78ckfk. Accessed on 22 January 2025.

Wani, M. "Kashmir under Siege and Forced into Silence while India Decides Its Future." *Forbes*, 7 August 2019. https://rb.gy/e27kjf. Accessed on 22 January 2025.

Zargar, S. "Why a Demolition Drive has Sparked Panic and Anxiety in Jammu and Kashmir." *Scroll.in*, 9 February 2023. https://rb.gy/hh0obq. Accessed on 22 January 2025.

Zutshi, A. "Farmers in R.S. Pura Staging Protest Sit-in After Being 'Forcibly Evicted from Their Lands'." *Kashmir Times*, March 2024. https://rb.gy/5wz1b0. Accessed on 22 January 2025.

EIGHT

Screening Hindutva: Religion and Television in India

MARIBEL ELLIET ALVARADO BECERRIL

This chapter examines the different narratives of nationalism in India as seen in television news channels in English that analyse the intersection between media, especially television debates, and the triumph of the Hindu right wing with Prime Minister Narendra Modi. It also offers a look at how the religious/cultural construction of Hindutva is intertwined with the idea of a perfectly defined nation which allows the association between citizen participation, sense of belonging, as well as individual and collective identity. This chapter is based on the idea that media has a fundamental role, which offers a formal and narrative space for the articulation of specific national imaginations. Taking into account that popular culture is the most utilised scope to inform and discuss any topic, television programming has become an integral component of political culture which has been incorporated into the formal processes of electoral politics and governance (Jones 2005, 13).

The importance of religion is related to the dynamics of engagement between India's rapidly expanding news television and the growing Hindu nationalism which blends territorial unity with Hindutva, or the belief that India is fundamentally a polity by, for, and of the majority Hindu community. For this reason, the research focuses on the different symbolic elements and narratives of 'nationalism' used in news channels in English: New Delhi Television, Times Now and Republic TV.

This combination of politics, religion, culture and nation has conferred a unique meaning and authority to the parties of the Hindu right. Hindu nationalist agendas, speeches and institutions have gradually penetrated everyday life and acquired a growing and almost indisputable social respectability in contemporary Indian society (Hansen 1999). The goal of Hindu nationalism, based on the transformation of the country's public culture into a national culture rooted in the belief of a 'glorious Hindu past', is increasingly palpable.

An inherent element of the exercise of democracy is the possibility of having a space for interaction, deliberation or communication. Media has been a fundamental part of representative governments, turning freedom of opinion and access to information into pillars of their existence. Thus, the interconnection between information messages, political reality and public opinion, creates a selection of what should be communicated and how it should be done to fit the medium in question (press, radio, television, social networks, among others) or the types of genres and formats (news, reports, interviews, debates, entertainment, advertising, etc.).

> Through the relentless communication of the media, a 'commonly known reality' is being built, which can then be implicitly assumed as a background in all social interactions. This crystallises elements of social communication – such as 'knowledge'– and both facts and opinions on the facts to create a description of reality, a building of the world and a reality that orients the society. The funny thing is that this reality is not a mere 'reflection' of what is happening. It is actively built following the very logic of the system. (Vallespín 2000, 84)

In this way, popular culture[1] is completely intertwined with political communication. Jürgen Habermas (2006) considers that, within political communication,[2] the deliberative tradition of democracy emphasises both the political participation of citizens

[1] Popular culture has been considered the main component of cultural studies, as it encompasses the set of practices, beliefs and objects that embody the shared meanings of a social system. It includes elements from the media, entertainment and leisure, fashion, linguistic conventions, among others (Gokulsing and Dissanayake 2009).

[2] Political communication is an interactive process concerning the transmission of information among politicians, the news media, and the public (Norris 2014, 318).

and how public opinion is shaped, that is, political socialisation.[3] In this process of socialisation, media acquires relevance by generating and transmitting messages that help internalise certain political priorities and concepts. At the same time, media – especially television – offers a formal and narrative space for the articulation of particular national imaginations that helps to create the idea that communities have about themselves.

In India, news channels have become one of the main sources of information, in a context where news is not merely a media product but a vehicle for engagement in the democratic process, feeding off and into domestic policies and international relations (Thussu 2007, 2). India is a country with a population of 1.4 billion people, of which 836 million own a television. In 2018, 298 million households with television were registered with a range of 87% in urban areas and 52% in rural areas. As per the Broadcast India Survey, 98% of the 197 million TV homes in the country still have access to a single TV (Broadcast Audience Research Council India 2018, 1). According to the Federation of Indian Chambers of Commerce and Industry (FICCI), in 2019, the average time spent watching television increased to 3 hours 46 minutes per day, led by megacities, which had 4 hours 32 minutes and south markets, at 4 hours 14 minutes (FICCI 2019, 37). This consumption tends to increase among the youngest population, and it is mainly carried out in the company of another person in the prime-time zone, from 5:00 pm to 11:00 pm. The news genre, including talk shows and debate programmes, contributes 8% to the total viewers, becoming the third-largest genre in terms of audience, just behind the General Entertainment Channels (GECs) and movies.

From a cognitive perspective, Doris Graber argues that audiovisual materials are essential in individual learning about

---

[3] Political socialisation is the process by which individuals develop conceptions of themselves and their reality, encompassing the political sphere, including direct experiences, judgements and inferences about the knowledge they have at the time (Pinkleton and Weintraub 2001).

politics, causing the population to be actively involved when they process the transmitted information. The visual nature of television reinforces the degree of reality that is granted to the content presented and increases the credibility of what has been seen. Also, the studies carried out reveal that the images are memorised better and are accompanied by a greater emotional commitment on the part of the recipients (Graber 2001).

> Broadcasting may be thought of as an 'institution' in two different senses of the term. On the one hand, it is an industry for the manufacture of symbolic goods. It has various institutional sites of cultural production that are characterised by particular professional practices and by specific relationships to the state or the market. On the other hand, at the point of cultural consumption where those symbolic goods enter into the social settings which are inhabited by its audiences, broadcasting can also be understood as what is called an institution in everyday life – part of the social fabric that goes to make up our routine daily experiences. (Moores 2000, 12)

For sociologist Ron Lembo (2000), visual culture includes the formation of attitudes and opinions of people, who associate what they are seeing with other aspects of their lives, both textual and 'real'. Audiences decide to consciously participate with television when they believe that the stories are plausible, incorporating the speeches into their understanding of the world. This 'voluntary suspension of disbelief' implies the willingness to accept as certain the premises on which the received message is based, leaving aside the critical or rational sense and ignoring possible inconsistencies or limitations (Tomko 2013, 13).

As Sonia Livingstone (1994) has pointed out, the audience in front of the public formulation is really based on a series of assumptions of value in competition with the behaviours, practices, and state of the spectator, including consumers versus citizens, public versus private, rational versus emotional, disinterested versus biased, participatory versus withdrawn, shared versus individualised, visible versus hidden, and so on. As proof of this, there is what happened following the tweet published by Harbhajan Singh in June 2019.

'Some countries have the moon on their flags... While some countries having their flags on the moon. #Chandrayaan2theMoon', Harbhajan Singh wrote on X after the Indian Space Research Organisation (ISRO) launched its second moon mission from the Satish Dhawan Space Centre at Sriharikota (Andhra Pradesh) on 22 July 2019. He posted the flags of nine countries with the crescent moon and star – Pakistan, Turkey, Tunisia, Libya, Azerbaijan, Algeria, Malaysia, Maldives and Mauritania – and, in the next line, those of four nations with successful space programmes: United States of America, Russia, India and China.

Immediately, the former Indian cricketer received numerous compliments for his comment as it reflected pride in the country's achievement. However, certain others found it to be distasteful and called Singh a 'bigot', 'racist', 'communal' and 'Islamophobic'. Harbhajan's tweet went viral with nearly 41,700 re-tweets and 228,000 likes. It resulted in an extended controversy in the media, mainly on television, where many people took it as fun while others criticised it. Arnab Goswami, one of India's most controversial TV anchors, was the first to pick on this dispute for the prime-time broadcast of The Debate with Arnab Goswami on 23 July 2019.

During this episode, Arnab Goswami attempted to defend the former Mumbai Indians' captain from being labelled as a bigot, communal and Islamophobic. Goswami accused those who attacked Bhajji and anyone who is not proud of the country's accomplishments as 'anti-nationalist'. One of the panellists, filmmaker Ashoke Pandit, called them 'white-collar terrorists, urban-Naxals[4] and a *tukde-tukde* gang,[5] as they have been working

[4] The term 'urban-Naxal' remains undefined. It is best attributed to a book and a few essays by film-maker and social media opinion-maker Vivek Agnihotri. His book, *Urban Naxals: The Making Of Buddha in a Traffic Jam* was released in May 2018. A few TV news channels, and right-wing spokespersons use the term 'urban-Naxal' to label anyone – from academics to activists – who question the policies of the state or are perceived to be anti-establishment. They allegedly are covertly aiding those who are working to break India, such as Naxalite movement (Dutta 2018).

[5] On January 2018, Arnab Goswami coined the phrase '*tukde-tukde* gang' – the 'break gang' – to target people who were out to fragment India

against the country for the past many years. The anchor ended his debate by declaring 'Harbhajan Singh a nationalist, a patriot and a great supporter of the Indian army, whose heart beats only for India' (Goswami 2019).

These kinds of debates, broadcast on prime-time hours on news channels, are becoming more frequent. Most of the time they ensure the preference of the viewers and respond only to commercial interests; however, the aggressive campaign showed against the 'enemies of the nation' is increasingly linked to the agenda of the Hindu Right driven by the Bharatiya Janata Party (BJP).[6] Television channels, or at least some of them, seem to be making a coordinated effort to create a particular scenario and narrative, which adapts to governmental objectives (Bhatia 2019).

In recent years, the growing wave of Hindu nationalism has defied the secularism embodied in constitutional principles, unleashing endless discussions about the fundamental nature of India's political identity. The discourse of Hindu nationalism, as an enactment of literary modernity, had the narrative form at the heart of its operations. That is, it devolved stories that were, in the best instances, enunciated under the governance of the modern, setting up claims of authenticity in line with disciplinary protocols (Basu 2008, 243). Some controversies exacerbated this debate, including the event at Jawaharlal Nehru University (JNU) in 2016. On 10 February 2016, during the final minutes of the prime-time broadcast of The Newshour Debate, the former editor-in-chief of Times Now channel – Arnab Goswami – addressed viewers to reflect on this event.

(Goswami 2018). The term has been used to justify governmental actions against a range of people considered a threat to the nation.

[6] The Bharatiya Janata Party (Indian People's Party) was founded in 1980 and emerged from its precursor, the Bharatiya Jana Sangh (BJS). The BJS was founded in 1951 by Shyama Prasad Mookerjee, a member of the Rashtriya Swayamsevak Sangh (National Volunteer Organisation) which quickly developed into the largest Hindu nationalist movement and was intended not only to propagate the Hindutva ideology but also to infuse new physical strength into the majority community (Jaffrelot 2007).

> What we should do with a group of secessionists, anti-nationals, opportunists who masqueraded to be believing into a political ideology. They are simply pro-Pakistan elements and I wonder what the forces are which are behind them [...] Let us vow never to let something like this happen ever again, not just in a campus or any square inch of our soil. (Goswami 2016)

Weeks before this broadcast, JNU students proposed a cultural event entitled 'Poetry Reading – "The Country Without a Post Office"' to be held on 9 February. The posters presented an event showing solidarity with Kashmiri people's demand for their democratic right to self-determination and to criticise the 2013 execution of Afzal Guru, who was condemned for his involvement in the attack on Parliament in 2001 (Ray and Singh 2017, 254). Although respective arrangements were made to host the event, the university authorities cancelled the permission saying that the organisers had not provided detailed information regarding this event.

As a sign of disagreement and in protest, the assembled students began shouting slogans, some of which were perceived as allegedly 'anti-national', provoking a fight between the Akhil Bharatiya Vidyarthi Parishad (ABVP)[7] and leftist groups present at that venue. Demonstrations rapidly intensified, causing the police irruption on campus, followed by the emblematic speech by the president of the Jawaharlal Nehru University Student Union (JNUSU), Kanhaiya Kumar. On 12 February 2016, Kanhaiya Kumar was arrested under Section 124A of the Indian Penal Code on charges of sedition, imposing similar charges on other students for their organisation of, and participation in, an evening

[7] Akhil Bharatiya Vidyarthi Parishad (ABVP) is a student organisation affiliated with RSS, formalised and registered on 9 July 1949. It participates in joint activities with the official youth wing of the BJP, the Bharatiya Janata Yuva Morcha. It is India's largest student organisation with more than three million members who, 'inspired by the great culture and traditions of the world's oldest civilisation, wanted to reconstruct India into a powerful, prosperous and proud Nation' (ABVP 2018).

of poetry, speeches, talks, and song related to the execution of Afzal Guru (JNUTA 2017, 10).

The arrest of Kumar set off a series of strikes, marches and protests which immediately caught media's attention. In this extensive media coverage, television played a key role as, beyond the battle for rating points, it was a direct inter-channel confrontation around debating and addressing the meanings, stories, experiences and unresolved dilemmas of nationalism. Channels such as Times Now and Zee News were at one end of the spectrum, making value judgements and continuously repeating the dichotomies 'us versus them' and 'national vs anti-national'. New Delhi Television (NDTV) and CNN-IBN were at the other end, trying to broadcast the news as objectively as possible. Among them, the statements of two personalities – Arnab Goswami of Times Now and Ravish Kumar of NDTV – stood out and became the largest source of public opinion information (Bhushan 2016).

Once again, Arnab Goswami, known for calling himself 'nationalist', was the first to use this topic for his TV show. On 10 February, he invited JNU students to discuss anti-India slogans, which were shouted on campus. He openly called the student panellists 'anti-nationals' and allowed them to defend their stance and externalise their opinions only a couple of times. 'Being a nationalist is a prerequisite for being a journalist' said Goswami (2017), who, in the wake of these events, has contributed towards shaping and keeping the 'nationalism' narrative as the central attribute for assessing public life.

A few days later, in his Prime Time programme of 16 February, Ravish Kumar broadcasted live from a protest march in New Delhi. Journalists staged the protest against the violence that took place in Patiala House Court on 15 February. A mob of men, wearing lawyer's robe, assaulted some students, teachers, reporters and bystanders when JNU student leader, Kanhaiya Kumar, was to be presented before Metropolitan Magistrate Loveleen. Without mentioning names, Ravish lashed out at some presenters who, from his perspective, were not only suppressing freedom of expression but were polarising the audience. While walking along, he conducted some interviews and stated: 'It is good to see journalists showing solidarity and coming together but the problem is that there are still many journalists who have not united to fight against this' (Kumar 2016).

Extensive media coverage of the event included different narratives of nationalism; TV presenters had supporters and detractors who, from this moment on, placed at the centre of the general discourse the terms 'nation', 'nationalism', 'national' and 'patriotism'. It also showed how the anger of social media fuelled the 'outrage' created by conventional television systems and vice versa when they came together to launch a widespread attack on JNU.

In the political and cultural communication process, some news channels – through rhetoric and reason, performances, debates and public discourses, images and ideas – have been actively participating in spreading Hindutva ideas. Therefore, this chapter also queries whether television has reshaped the context in which religion is symbolised, screened and understood. News channels, or at least some of their prime-time shows, seem to be making a coordinated effort to create a particular environment and narrative that suits the government's goals.

Television in India

Television was introduced in India on 15 September 1959, as a project with the aim of speeding up the development process of the nation. The project – financed by the United Nations Educational, Scientific and Cultural Organization (UNESCO) and the Ford Foundation – was launched as a public broadcasting model committed to informing, educating and entertaining people. The then Prime Minister, Jawaharlal Nehru, gave the state government full control of these media. The All India Radio (AIR) handled the initial broadcasts, which consisted of educational programmes twice a week for half an hour each.

Daily transmission service began in Delhi in 1965 and, subsequently, branched out to other cities such as Bombay

(1972), Calcutta (1975) and Chennai (1975). With the separation of radio and television in 1976, the Ministry of Information and Broadcasting created *Doordarshan*, the public television company, whose goal was to increase coverage at the national level. In 1982, India achieved this goal with the broadcast of the ninth Asian Games, which was transmitted, for the first time, in full colour and via the INSAT 1A satellite.

Television in India developed as a medium whose educational purpose was supplemented by its utilisation as a spokesman for the Central Government and the ruling party. Promoting 'national integrity' was one of *Doordarshan*'s most important purposes and, as a result of movements in Punjab and Assam in the late 1970s and 1980s, this purpose became increasingly significant; any information that was transmitted about these regions was treated from the perspective of 'threats to the nation'.

> However, the project had a crucial contradiction produced possibly by the very form of mass media dissemination, the compulsive direct address to the people, and the onus of 'representation' through a 'visual' medium. The programmes were mainly compartmentalised fragments addressed towards different segments of people: agricultural programmes for farmers, news in English for the urban elite, quiz programmes for urban school-going children, literacy and awareness programmes particularly for the rural illiterate, folk performances from various parts of India. (Roy 2008, 31)

Furthermore, in January 1987, the secular character of television changed completely with the national broadcast of a Hindu epic series: *Ramayan*. On Sunday mornings from January 1987 to July 1988, around a hundred million Indians watched this 78-episode series directed by Ramanand Sagar (Kumar 2006, 38). *Ramayan*'s broadcast coincided with the strengthening of the Hindu nationalist movement, causing unexpected expressions of devotion 'with viewers performing purification rituals before the programme began and adorning television sets with flowers and incense, consecrating them as altars' (Mitchell 2005, 2).

Ramayan, along with other series such as *Mahabharat* (1988) and *Sri Krishna* (1993) made the Hindu gods extremely popular figures. In all these serials, a particular set of similar symbols was used to picture the Hindu religion, which introduced several implications. First and foremost, other practices were marginalised, and, within the national image, these were perceived as deviant and non-Indian. This situation resulted in a struggle that was no longer restricted to questions of specific religious rituals but was manifested in political struggles (Mitra 1993, 147).

Hindu nationalist parties cashed in on the success of these epics among people. The actors of these serials who had gained fame overnight and attained 'godlike' status extended this popularity from television to politics, joining parties such as the BJP. Even, 'the BJP's *rath yatra*, or grand tour in 1991, was in imitation of the chariot wheeled in by the god Krishna to war in the Mahabharat epic' (Pasricha 2014). Gods and goddesses were present in almost every political discourse of Hindu nationalism that would trigger the *Ram Janmabhoomi*[8] movement and end with the destruction of the Babri Masjid in 1992. After this event, television's influence on Indian politics became increasingly apparent.

---

[8] The campaign for demolition of a historic mosque constructed in 1528 was spearheaded politically by Hindutva forces to gain power. According to Hindu tradition, Ayodhya (Uttar Pradesh) is the birthplace (*Ram Janmabhoomi*) and capital of the god-king, Rama. Supposedly, in this site was a temple dedicated to the god Rama which was destroyed in the sixteenth century on the orders of Babur, the first Mughal emperor, and replaced by a mosque, the Babri Masjid. In the summer of 1989, with the logistical support of the RSS, the Rama Shila Pujan festivals were organised, which involved the worship of bricks (*shila*) printed with Rama's name. These sacred bricks would be used to rebuild the Ayodhya temple (Jaffrelot 2007, 20).

See also the writings which contests the mythologisation of Ayodhya as 'Ram Janmabhoomi': R. S. Sharma, *Communal History and Rama's Ayodhya*, 1990; Suraj Bhan, Athar Ali, R.S. Sharma and Dwijendra Narayan Jha, *Ramjanmabhumi-Baburi Masjid: A Historians' Report to the Nation*, 1991; Shireen Ratnagar, 'Archaeology at the Heart of a Political Confrontation. The Case of Ayodhya', *Current Anthropology*, 45 (2), 2004; and Romila Thapar, 'The verdict on Ayodhya: a historian's perspective', *The Hindu*, 2010.

In the 1990s, the Central Government, led by Prime Minister Narasimha Rao, implemented a series of economic and social reforms that allowed private and foreign broadcasters to enter the country. After three decades of state monopoly, television went from being a highly centralised one-way communication system, with a limited number of broadcasters' networks to a more diversified and decentralised broadcasting system. By 1992, the first private channels, local (Zee TV and Sun TV) and foreigners (CNN and Star TV), began their satellite broadcast.

It was not until 1998 that the private channels began broadcasting news 24 hours a day. Since then, the number of private satellite channels has considerably increased, reaching 869 in 2018, from which 382 broadcast news in 24 languages and 54 of them are in 24x7 format (Ministry of Information and Broadcasting 2018). Within the programming of these channels, different temporal and spatial relationships with the audience developed; the popularity and multiplicity of their debate programmes quickly excelled and 'constituted a space in which new discursive practices are developed in contrast to the traditional modes of political and ideological representation' (Jones 2005, 53).

Competition in the private channel market required the use of distinctive stylistic markers to create a new and more meaningful relationship with the viewers. Debate programmes offer alternative spaces to make sense of political reality 'while directly and indirectly questioning the vaunted place of journalism as the primary arbiter of political truth' (Jones 2010, 64).

Political Strategy of Hindu Nationalism

According to Christophe Jaffrelot (2010), the Jana Sangh,[9] and later the BJP, has maintained a policy that ranges between two strategies. A moderate line which involves positioning itself as a patriotic party in defence of national unity, often with populist

[9] The Jana Sangh formed in 1951 as the political arm of the RSS, the most prominent Hindu nationalist volunteer organisation, aimed at propagating Hindutva ideology.

connotations. The other is a more militant strategy based on ethno-religious movements and the promotion of an aggressive form of 'Hinduness', symbolised by the campaign to elevate Hindi to the level of India's national language and protection of cows, as well as the mobilisation around Ayodhya.

One of the main features of Hindu nationalist militancy is the presence of highly disciplined organisations, which promote different facets of the Hindutva. Daily attendance at *shakhas* is considered the core of the RSS activities and is a clear indicator of the organisation's spread. A report presented by RSS general secretary Suresh Joshi at the ongoing Akhil Bharatiya Pratinidhi Sabha notes that 58,967 *shakhas* operate in 37,190 locations across the country. In addition to *shakhas*, the RSS also has weekly and monthly meetings, as well as training camps for its volunteers (Pathak 2018).

Although the militant strategy was more in line with the wishes of the RSS, the Jana Sangh faced constitutional barriers which prevented it from expanding and establishing alliances with other parties. This strategy changed in the 1970s when it partnered with the Janata Party. With the creation of the BJP in 1980, the original ideology of the Jana Sangh was gradually diluted to become more acceptable in the party system allowing it to secure valuable allies (Jaffrelot 2010, 20). After winning the 1996 elections, Hindutva certainly did not disappear, but the coalition arrangement suggested that the BJP deemphasise those controversial social issues that might cause nuisances for its friends and partners. Once in power, the BJP's programme included some of the traditional elements of Hindu nationalism programme but found it was 'no longer in their interest to stoke communal fires' (Friedlander 2016, 77).

The National Democratic Alliance (NDA) ruled from 1998 until 2004, when it was surprisingly defeated and replaced by a coalition led by the Congress Party. Most members of the Sangh Parivar[10]

[10] The Sangh Parivar, the 'family of the [Rashtriya Swayamsevak] Sangh', refers to the collection of Hindu nationalist organisations, led by the RSS.

considered the defeat a consequence of Prime Minister Atal Bihari Vajpayee's moderate line. For them, the BJP-led government had betrayed the Hindus by not building the Rama temple they so longed for in Ayodhya. The coalition's political decisions hampered the Hindutva's agenda, prompting its division. It was only in May 2014, for the first time in more than thirty years, the BJP achieved without any coalition, a majority in Parliament and Narendra Modi became Prime Minister. The election broke a record in terms of the number of voters, candidates, political parties, participation and election expenses. Data from various surveys showed the enormous popularity of the new Prime Minister, calling this the 'Modi phenomenon'.

Satish Misra (2018) acknowledges that the BJP has been able to expand its political base in the country because of various elements, including (1) Financial Resources, (2) Expansion of Mass Base, (3) Centralised Decision-Making and, (4) Emphasis on Young and Hindutva Hardliners. The importance of television is a consequence of this last point. The debates broadcasted by news channels have been of great use in keeping alive the impulse of militant nationalism and the narrative of defending the fundamental interests of the majority community.

Screening Hindutva on News Channels

As the Hindu right strategy seems set to embrace a more militant Hindutva agenda as part of its core electoral strategy, TV news channels are increasingly being used and play a significant role in the formation of public opinion. However, any evaluation of the influence of Hindu nationalism in politics should take into account that it is a set of ideas or beliefs that are located in a much

---

The core group of the Sangh Parivar represents significant areas of the public sphere – the Bharatiya Janata Party in the political domain, the Rashtra Sevika Samiti (women's wing of the RSS), the Vanvasi Kalyan Ashram (for welfare of tribal groups), the Sewa Bharati (for the socially and economically weaker sections of the society), the Vidya Bharati (for a national system of education), and the Swadeshi Jagran Manch (for the economic area).

wider space than that represented by the BJP. With a growing need for an identity, belonging, representation and participation, Hindu nationalists seek to attack, in the name of the nation, any perceived weakness in and from faith.

Some news channels – through rhetoric and reason, performances, debates and public discourses, images and ideas – have been spreading this Hindutva ideology, playing a pivotal role in the political and cultural communication process. News channels, or at least some of their prime-time shows, have reshaped the context in which religion is symbolised, screened and understood. More than ever, they seem to be making a coordinated effort to create a particular environment and narrative that suits the government's goals.

NDTV, Times Now and Republic TV are the three most-watched English-language channels in India.[11] In addition to providing news, they broadcast numerous talk shows and debates that have strongly influenced public opinion and even politics. NDTV, founded in 1988 by Radhika Roy and Prannoy Roy, has pioneered Indian television, producing the first uninterrupted 24-hour news channel. At the Indian Television Awards (ITA), NDTV was named 'Most Popular English News Channel' in 2015 and 'Best English News Channel' in 2017. Its show 'We the People' also won the prize for 'Best English Debate Show' in 2016, granted by the Indiantelevision.com Awards.

NDTV in its prime time, from 07:30 pm to 10:30 pm, apart from presenting national and international news, has segments of business, finances, sports, climate, interviews, researches and debates, where experts discuss and opine about current issues. Their commitment is always to provide their viewers with reliable, honest and impartial programmes. 'NDTV is today the most-

[11] Broadcast Audience Research Council (BARC) is responsible for providing data on the rating of television channels through the measurement of 'impressions', that is, the number of individuals of a target audience who viewed an 'event', averaged across minutes. BARC published that, during the 52 weeks of 2018, Republic TV topped its lists as the most-watched English news channel, followed by Times Now and NDTV (BARC 2019).

watched, credible and respected news network in India and a leader in Internet' (NDTV 2019).

Similarly, Times Now is a leader in 24-hour English news broadcasting. The channel was presented by The Television Division of Bennett Coleman & Company Limited in January 2006, appointing Arnab Goswami as editor-in-chief. The channel has won several prizes in the Exchange4media News Broadcasters Awards of 2012, received 'News Channel of the Year Award', while Arnab Goswami won 'Editor-in-Chief of the Year Award'. In 2015, Goswami won the Red Impact Award as 'Editor of the Year', granted by The Press Club in Mumbai. 'It is a channel that stands for credibility and unbiased approach in bringing news and reportages to the viewers. Sharp, incisive and direct, Times Now is the nation's voice in the news' (Times of India 2017).

On 1 November 2016, Arnab Goswami resigned from his position at Times Now, broadcasting his iconic show The Newshour Debate for the last time on November 14. A few months later, Goswami founded Republic TV in May 2017. Since its opening week, Republic TV has ranked as one of the most-watched English news channels in India. The channel has nationalism as the core element, the search for truth as its guiding principle, and responds to the need to investigate, dig up and transmit that truth to millions of viewers. 'Being home to the youngest and most insatiable news team in India, Republic has broken the norms of traditional newsrooms and journalistic setups' (Republic TV 2019).

The rapid rise of 24-hour news television suggests that these channels play the role of mediators on contemporary political issues of great interest, especially for the middle class. News television's prominence has become influential in every aspect of an Indian's life as the medium has grown to be the primary source of information. Despite the transition to digital media, the print and television news industry in the country has continued to grow although at a not-so-fast pace. According to the India Digital News Report, with much of the population still offline, hundreds of millions of Indians still turn to newspapers, television and radio as their main sources of news.

> Among respondents over 35 years, online (38%) and television (34%) are about equally widely named as the main source of news, and print (27%) still more widely relied on than social media (19%). But among respondents under 35, online generally (56%) and social media specifically (28%) are named as the main source of news by many more than print (16%) and even television (26%). (Aneez et al. 2019, 12)

As time goes by, news television has been engaging with several dominant ideologies. In recent decades, the Hindutva ideology has been a dominant force in Indian politics, and its engagement with news television has been visible in the media narratives on various socio-political and cultural issues. NDTV, Times Now and Republic TV have numerous programmes in which religion, nationhood and identity are questioned and come into the debate. In programmes such as 'The NDTV Dialogues: Has Hindutva Replaced Secularism?', 'The Newshour Debate: The Hindutva Identity' and 'Sunday Debate with Arnab Goswami: What Is Secularism?', the spokespersons of Hindu nationalism attempt to redefine the Indian nation as Hindu, constructing audio-visual narratives that exalt the 'glorious' common past of the Hindus and heavily relying on the discourse of demonising the 'other' (Mankekar 1999).

Further, the simultaneous use of 'Hindu nationalism' and 'Indian nationalism' has blurred the difference between the two and has given a certain amount of legitimacy or credibility to Hindu nationalism. The interactions between the media and religion, leading to the greater participation of religion in the public sphere remain a crucial topic of investigation in a society where the state is losing its grip in the age of new media (Dwyer 2006). In this intersection, television constitutes spaces of cultural and social practices integrated into the cultural discourse, wherein identity is not just a variable separate from religion (Galal 2014, 97).

Several authors have indicated that television can be fundamental to the nation-building process (Barker 2005; Drummond et al. 1993; Louw 2005; Schlesinger 1991; Van den Bulck 2001). Television offers a formal and narrative space for the articulation of specific national imaginations, helping to integrate the idea that communities have about themselves. Their discourse ideologically guides the construction or reinforcement of the sense of identity, belonging, and collective identification with the 'nation', through the idea that 'the nation needs us'. The Hindutva's television public sphere, evoking religious feelings, has created a favourable environment and provided ideological support for the movement's sustenance.

For Hindu nationalism, media plays a crucial role in articulating Hindutva as the country's 'national identity' and the 'thread of unity' running through its diversities. In TV programmes such as 'Left, Right & Centre: Is India Moving Towards a "Hindu Rashtra"?', 'The Newshour Debate: Is BJP Appropriating Hinduism in Hindutva's Name?' and 'The Debate with Arnab Goswami: Should Religion Be Kept Out of Indian Politics?', members of BJP define their national identity through their religious identity and in so doing combine the religious with the cultural practices and values. Thus, viewers engage in the process of (re)identifying their own cultural bonds in relation to the 'others', enforcing a collective identity which evokes memories of shared history and geography.

In a crisis or during social or political change, 'nationalism' appears as a powerful agitation of feelings (Cullingford 2003, 22). In this regard, by analysing television discourse in the symbolic construction of 'nationalism', it is possible to identify the channelling of emotions and feelings towards daily social attitudes or behaviours. Nationalism consistently uses beliefs, representations, assumptions and practices to reproduce nations as the predominant form of political organisation in today's world (Jenkins 1995). Further, Grossberg (1998, 206) argues that the media has penetrated identity formations based on traditional understandings of location, profession and religion, among others.

> At the same time, the sense of unity among people, created by such powerful identities as were defined by religion, nationality, and work, have themselves been increasingly undermined by the powerful representations of difference that have come to define the media's

> cultural content, even as the media has come to shape social life. Ultimately, the media's ability to produce people's social identities, in terms of both a sense of unity and difference, may be their most powerful and meaningful effect.

In turn, ideologies, collective representations, habits, and social practices forge the identity. They are elements that help to reproduce the way of being in the social world and make it seem natural, ordinary and banal. In the words of Anderson (1983), with the information obtained from television, viewers can identify how, where and why they can be recognised and built as a community, as an imagined community. Likewise, the culturalist approach emphasises how the individual actively uses media as an integrated part of their social and cultural life. Television participates in the structuring of social consciousness through style, genre, schedule, images and language. When people interact with it, they become involved in a process that simultaneously connects them with different cultures, with remembered and imagined pasts and with sources of insight and meaning (Hoover 2006, 72).

The use of media and its integration in people's daily lives involves a number of parameters, material, social and individual elements. Although media does not determine identities, it does contribute towards the creation of symbolic communicative spaces (Schlesinger 2000) that either include or exclude, thereby affecting audiences' lives and discourses about their identities. Audiences use media to negotiate religious, national, regional, and many other forms of identity. As an inevitable aspect of television's participation in the mediatisation of identities, it takes part in collective processes of inclusion and exclusion. Hence, media becomes a tool for performing cultural and social ways of life, which become symbolic of belonging. These processes emphasise how religious identity intersects with ethnic and national belonging, and more importantly, how these intersections are inscribed with negotiations of power relations.

The excessive style of the television debates of these three channels is more than just a visual phenomenon; it is a mechanism to develop a permanence in the minds of viewers through its distinctive appeal. The viewer looks at the image from their own experience, from their own culture or social values and, it is from that perspective that each image is understandable through some informal and acquired cultural rules, but not entirely codified. Besides, anchors – such as Arnab Goswami, Sonia Singh, Sarah Jacob, Rahul Ravishankar, among others – are chosen on the basis of their personality and public reputation, not just by the genre of the show. The regular broadcast of debates around 'religion', 'nation', 'nationalism' and 'patriotism' is not merely a business-oriented tactic but is in tune with a broader strategy involving not only TV channels but also social media, fake news, troll armies[12] and bots.[13]

News channels focus on the immediacy and proximity of any event. Most of the time, the television is the only point of access to politics; it is the place for political meetings that precede, shape and sometimes determine greater participation. This medium does much more than provide information about political ideas, problems, events or participants; it is a container of images and voices, heroes and villains, sayings and slogans, facts and ideas that audience turn to make sense of politics. It also provides the constituent components of the narratives that viewers build to organise, interpret, explain, understand and mediate the realities and illusions found in their daily lives. News channels are melting pots with public life that help us know who and what we are as individuals, as a community, as a public, and as a nation (Jones 2009, 23).

[12] 'Trolling' refers to a specific type of malicious online behaviour, intended to disrupt interactions, aggravate interactional partners, and lure them into fruitless argumentation. A media troll is someone who creates conflict on sites like Twitter or Facebook by posting messages that are particularly controversial or inflammatory with the sole intent of provoking an emotional response from other users (Coles and West 2016, 233).

[13] A bot (short for 'robot') is an automated application that runs over the Internet, used to perform simple and repetitive tasks that would be time-consuming, mundane or impossible for a human to perform. Bots can be used for productive tasks, but they are also frequently used for malicious purposes (Dunham and Melnick 2008).

Arvind Rajagopal (2004) argues that media re-shapes the context in which politics is conceived, enacted and understood. He suggests that Hindu nationalists in recent times represented an attempt to create a populist language of politics, even on television, appealing to authoritarian rather than democratic values. This allows Hindu nationalism to fashion a range of different rhetoric outside the political sphere proper, and to suggest a homology between forms of consumption and voting behaviour, and between cultural identification and the requirements of electoral affiliation.

Conclusion

The euphoria that surrounded the elections in 2014 remains unaltered; indeed, Hindu nationalist sentiment has intensified, especially during election campaigns for the state assembly and the 2019 general election. In the 2024 general elections, the Bharatiya Janata Party (BJP), led by Prime Minister Narendra Modi, secured 240 seats, falling short of the 272 required for an outright majority. Consequently, the BJP formed a coalition with allies, notably the Telugu Desam Party (TDP) and Janata Dal (United) (JD(U)), bringing the National Democratic Alliance (NDA) to a total of 293 seats (Election Comission of India, 2024).

These developments suggest that the fervour of Hindu nationalism remains a significant force but is being tempered by voters' concerns over governance, economic stability and social welfare. While nationalist rhetoric continued to play a central role in the campaign, particularly through the promotion of cultural and religious symbols, the election results indicate that voters are increasingly prioritising tangible policy outcomes over ideological appeals. The 2024 elections have underscored the electorate's demand for effective leadership that not only upholds national identity but also delivers on economic growth, job creation and social development. This shift suggests that while Hindu nationalism remains influential, it must now coexist with broader governance and economic expectations from the public.

However, any assessment of the influence of Hindu nationalism in political terms must take into account that it is a set of ideas that are located in a much wider space than represented by the BJP. These ideas overlap and blend with other critical discourses on society, religion, culture and identity, which are manifested in a wide range of actions and political articulations.

The media have a role to play within representative democratic governments, but they also respond to a market logic that contrasts with the information principle. Religion has been a recurrent topic in the media. However, how the media addresses religion differs widely among nations and across public and private media. With a growing need to identify themselves, Hindu nationalists seek to attack a perceived weakness in and from the faith, the same vulnerability that many believe resulted in Islamic rule and British colonisation of the subcontinent. Through this broad vision, this nationalism presents a Hindu identity, which apparently offers a supposed unity, but in reality remains deeply fractured.

Considering that popular culture is one of the most widely used areas for informing and discussing any topic, television has become an integral component of politics, incorporated into the formal processes of the electoral and governance policy. In the debates, news channels often purposefully construct an intensely dramatic narrative, particularly in times of national conflict or crisis, which has a positive relation with audience approval, reflected through consistently high rating points (Pandit and Chattopadhyay 2018).

The news television has emerged as the main source of information in India. While trying to keep its momentum with the market demands, news channels have not been immune to sensationalism. The debate programmes have taken the public sphere and the 'imagined community' to a new level. The mystification, glorification and romanticising of value systems of the past amply prove that the media can be biased or can be used as a consolidating tool for empowering communal norms. The growth of the Hindutva movement was catapulted by the media explosion, which helped them hugely to form even transnational Hindutva communities. The recent history of the Hindu nationalist movement in India provides a good illustration of how modern media technology qualitatively changes the politics of religious diversity and mobilisation (Eisenlohr 2011).

Television is a significant medium for the relationship between audiences and politics; through its narratives, political action is given meaning when discussing, reflecting or working on the information provided. When television gives visibility to the members of the Hindutva public sphere, which is firmly rooted in sociopolitical structures, it leads to its further expansion and extension of the Hindutva public scope across the country. Television, giving visibility to the campaigning activities and the public demonstrations of the Hindutva public, helps them in their attempt to compel the state to act in favour of their ideology. It is in this sphere that official discourses about the nation can be identified.

News television does not explain every political change in contemporary India, but it recognises and manifests the changes in the language of political discourse. So, in a country where the political landscape is full of happenings, television's contribution to the democratic processes and the political discourse cannot be ignored.

REFERENCES

Akhil Bharatiya Vidyarthi Parishad. 2018. *History*. Mumbai: ABVP. https://www.abvp.org/history

Anderson, Benedict. 1983. *Imagined Communities. Reflections on the Origin and Spread of Nationalism*. London: Verso.

Aneez, Zeenab et al. 2019. *Reuters Institute: India Digital News Report*. Oxford: Reuters Institute for the Study of Journalism / University of Oxford.

Barker, Chris. 1999. *Television, Globalization and Cultural Identities*. Buckingham: Open University Press.

Basu, Anustup. 2008. "Hindutva and Informatic Modernization." *Boundary* 35, no. 3: 239–50.

Bhatia, Sidharth. "Indian TV Media's Blatant Endorsement of Hyper-Nationalism Is Shameful." *The Wire*, 28 February 2019. https://thewire.in/media/indian-tv-medias-blatant-endorsement-of-hyper-nationalism-is-shameful. Accessed on 23 January 2025.

Bhushan, Sandeep. "How Television Media Uncritically Reproduced the Sangh's Narrative of 'Nationalist' versus 'Anti-nationalist'." *The Caravan*, 27 February 2016. https://caravanmagazine.in/vantage/media-uncritically-reproduced-nationalist. Accessed on 23 January 2025.

Broadcast Audience Research Council India. 2018. *Impact of Co-viewing on TV Viewership*. Mumbai: BARC.

———. 2019. *TV Audiences. Weekly Data*, Mumbai: BARC. https://www.barcindia.co.in/statistic.aspx. Accessed on 23 January 2025.

Chandhoke, Neera. 2005. "Exploring the Mythology of the Public Sphere." In *Civil Society, Public Sphere and Citizenship*, edited by R. Bhargava and H. Reifeld, 327–47. New Delhi: Sage Publications.

Coles, B. A., and M. West. 2016. "Trolling the Trolls: Online Forum Users Constructions of the Nature and Properties of Trolling." *Computers in Human Behavior* 60, no. 1: 233–44.

Cullingford, Cedric. 2003. *El prejuicio en los jóvenes. De la identidad individual al nacionalismo*. Madrid: Alianza Editorial.

Drummond, P., R. Paterson, and J. Willis, eds. 1993. *National Identity and Europe: The Television Revolution*. London: British Film Institute.

Dunham, Ken, and Jim Melnick. 2008. *Malicious Bots: An Inside Look into the Cyber-Criminal Underground of the Internet*. Florida: Auerbach Publications.

Dutta, Prabhash K. "Urban Naxals: Know the original Naxals." *India Today*, 30 August 2018. https://www.indiatoday.in/india/story/urban-naxals-know-the-original-naxals-1327316-2018-08-30. Accessed on 23 January 2025.

Dwyer, Rachel. 2006. "The Saffron Screen? Hindi Movies and Hindu Nationalism." In *Religion, Media and the Public Sphere*, edited by B. Meyer and A. Moors, 273–89. Bloomington: Indiana University Press.

Eisenlohr, Patrick. 2011. "The Anthropology of Media and the Question of Ethnic and Religious Pluralism." *Social Anthropology* 19, no. 1: 40–55.

Federation of Indian Chambers of Commerce and Industry. 2019. *A Billion Screens of Opportunity. India's Media & Entertainment Sector, March 2019*. Kolkata: FICCI/Ernst & Young LLP.

Friedlander, Peter. 2016. "Hinduism and Politics." *Routledge Handbook of Religion and Politics*. Abingdon: Routledge.

Galal, Ehab, ed. 2014. *Arab TV-Audiences. Negotiating Religion and Identity*. Frankfurt: Peter Lang Academic Research.

Gokulsing, K. Moti, and Wimal Dissanayake. 2009. *Popular Culture in a Globalised India*. London: Routledge.

Goswami, Arnab. 2016. "Tribute To Afzal Guru at JNU – Students Crossed All Lines?" [TV Show], *The Newshour Debate*. Mumbai: Times Now, 10 February 2016.

———. 2017. "Arnab Is Back!" [TV Show], *Republic TV*. Mumbai: Republic TV, 06 May 2017.

———. 2018. "Republic TV Exposed the Tukde-Tukde Gang" [TV show], *The Debate with Arnab Goswami*. Mumbai: Republic TV, 05 January 2018.

———. 2019. "Lobby Goes After Harbhajan Singh Over Chandrayaan 2" [TV show], *The Debate with Arnab Goswami*. Mumbai: Republic TV, 23 July 2019.

Graber, Doris A. 2001. *Processing Politics. Learning from Television in the Internet Age*. Chicago: University of Chicago Press.

Grossberg, Lawrence, E. Wartella, and Whitney D. Charles. 1998. *Media Making Mass Media in a Popular Culture*. California: Sage Publications.

Habermas, Jürgen. 2006. "Political Communication in Media Society: Does Democracy Still Enjoy an Epistemic Dimension? The Impact of Normative Theory on Empirical Research." *Communication Theory. International Communication Association* 16, no. 4: 411–26.

Hansen, Thomas B. 1999. *The Saffron Wave. Democracy and Hindu Nationalism in Modern India*. Princeton: Princeton University Press.

Hoover, Stewart M. 2006. *Religion in the Media Age; Media, Religion and Culture*. London: Routledge.

Jaffrelot, Christophe. 2007. *Hindu Nationalism; A Reader*. Princeton: Princeton University Press.

———. "Hindutva's Politics of Denial." *The Caravan*, 31 August 2010. https://caravanmagazine.in/perspectives/hindutvas-politics-denial. Accessed on 23 January 2025.

Jawaharlal Nehru University Teachers' Association. 2017. *What the Nation Really Needs to Know: The JNU Nationalism Lectures*. Noida: Harper Collins Publishers India.

Jenkins, R. 1995. "Nations and Nationalism: Towards More Open Models." *Nations and Nationalism* 1, no. 1: 369–90.

Jones, Jeffrey P. (2005) 2009. *Entertaining Politics. New Political Television and Civic Culture*. Maryland: Rowman & Littlefield Publishers.

———. 2010. *Entertaining Politics Satiric. Television and Political Engagement*. Maryland: Rowman & Littlefield Publishers.

Kim, Sebastian. 2005. *In Search of Identity. Debates on Religious Conversion in India*. Oxford: Oxford University Press.

Kumar, Ravish. 2016. "Journalists March to Protest Against Attacks on Media Personnel" [TV Show], *Prime Time*. New Delhi: NDTV, 16 February 2016.

———. 2006. *Gandhi Meets Primetime: Globalization and Nationalism in Indian Television*. Chicago: University of Illinois Press.

Lembo, Ron. 2000. *Thinking through Television*. Cambridge: Cambridge University Press.

Livingstone, Sonia, and Peter Lunt. 1994. *Talk on Television: Audience Participation and Public Debate*. London: Routledge.

Louw, Eric. 2005. *The Media and Political Process*. London: Sage Publications.

Mankekar, Purnima. 1999. *Screening Culture, Viewing Politics Television, Womanhood and Nation in Modern India*. New Delhi: Oxford University Press.

Ministry of Information and Broadcasting. 2018. *Master List of Permitted Private Satellite TV Channels as on 30.09.2018*. Delhi: Government of India. https://mib.gov.in/sites/default/files/Master%20List%20of%20Permitted%20Private%20%20statellite%20TV%20Channels%20as%20on%20%2030.09.2018.pdf. Accessed on 23 January 2025.

Misra, Satish. 2018. "Understanding the Rise of the Bharatiya Janata Party." *Observer Research Foundation Issue Brief No. 258*. New Delhi: Observer Research Foundation.

Mitchell, Jolyon. 2005. "Christianity and Television." *Studies in World Christianity* 11, no. 1: 1–8. Edinburgh University Press.

Mitra, Ananda. 1993. *Television and Popular Culture in India*. New Delhi: Sage Publications.

Moores, Shaun. 2000. *Media and Everyday Life in Modern Society*. Edinburgh: Edinburgh University Press.

New Delhi Television. 2019. *About the Company*. Delhi: New Delhi Television Limited. https://www.ndtv.com/convergence/ndtv/corporatepage/index.aspx. Accessed on 23 January 2025.

Norris, Pippa. 2014. "Political Communication." In *Comparative Politics*, edited by Daniele Caramani. Oxford: Oxford University Press.

Pandit, Sushmita and Chattopadhyay, Saayan. 2018. "Coverage of the Surgical Strike on Television News in India." *Journalism Practice* 12, no. 2: 162–76.

Pasricha, Anjana. 2014. "Hindu Mythologies Rule Indian Television." *Al Jazeera*, 30 January 2014. https://www.aljazeera.com/indepth/features/2014/01/hindu-mythologies-rule-indian-television-20141179558915889.html. Accessed on 23 January 2025.

Pathak, Vikas. 2018. "RSS Reports Sharp Rise in Shakhas in 2018." *The Hindu*. 09 March 2018. https://www.thehindu.com/news/national/rss-reports-sharp-rise-in-shakhas-in-2018/article23009796.ece. Accessed on 23 January 2025.

Pinkleton, Bruce E., and Erica Austin Weintraub. 2001. "Individual Motivations, Perceived Media Importance, and Political Disaffection." *Political Communication* 18, no. 3: 321–34.

Rajgopal, Arvind. 2004. *Politics After Television. Religious Nationalism and the Reshaping of the Indian Public*. Cambridge: Cambridge University Press.

Ray, Shovana and Jitendra Kumar Singh. 2017. "Discourse Analysis on Nationalism Debate Reported in India Print Media During Feb-Mar 2016." *International and Multidisciplinary Journal of Social Sciences* 6, no. 3: 251–80. Barcelona: Hipatia Press.

Republic TV. 2019. *About Us*. Mumbai: Republic World. https://www.republicworld.com/about-us. Accessed on 23 January 2025.

Roy, Abhijit. 2008. "Bringing up TV: Popular Culture and the Developmental Modern in India." *South Asian Popular Culture* 6, no. 1: 29–43.

Schlesinger, Philip. 1991. *Media, State and Nation. Political Violence and Collective Identities*. London: Sage Publications.

———. 2000. "The Nation and Communicative Space." In *Media Power Professionals and Politics*, edited by Harold Tumber, 99–115. London: Routledge.

The Times of India. "TIMES NOW Marks Its Presence in 100 Countries." *The Times of India*, 28 March 2017. https://timesofindia.indiatimes.com/brandwire/media-entertainment/tv-radio-ooh/times-now-marks-its-presence-in-100-countries/articleshow/57036050.cms. Accessed on 23 January 2025.

Thussu, Daya Kishan. 2007. *News as Entertainment; The Rise of Global Infotainment*. London: Sage Publications.

Tomko, Michael. 2015. *Beyond the Willing Suspension of Disbelief*. Bloomsbury Publishing.

Vallespín, Fernando. 2000. "La Crisis del Espacio Público." *Revista Española de Ciencia Política*, no. 3: 77–95.

Van den Bulck, H. 2001. "Public Service Television and National Identity as a Project of Modernity. The Example of Flemish Television." *Media, Culture & Society* 23, no. 1: 53–69.

NINE

Revisiting the Cow Protection Discourse: Gender, Caste and Labour at a North Indian *Gaushala*

RIDHIMA SHARMA

The political and analytical impulse for this chapter comes from a familiar and oft-encountered place – one of discomfort, with historical and contemporary ways of framing and interpreting the 'cow protection movement' or *gauraksha* in India. I argue that the dominant mode of analysing cow-politics in India, in its overwhelming association of the cow with Hindu nationalism both in symbolic and material terms, pays necessary but disproportionate emphasis on a certain kind of hyper-visible, spectacular violence. This deeply informs the construction of a purported linear and teleological 'movement' in the name of the cow as if all heightened, finite episodes of cow-related violence, their varied textures notwithstanding, add up to produce a coherent 'cow protection movement'. This conception of the 'cow protection movement' I posit, obfuscates not only the everyday process of mobilising of the cow into a potent Hindu politico-religious symbol and the intimate relationship between the 'everyday' and the 'event' (of violence) but also obscures the manner in which gendered and caste-marked routinised practices of labour have come to constitute a 'movement' in the name of the cow. Making a departure from the commonly deployed method of analysing spectacular modes of violence such as cow-related 'riots' and 'lynchings', this chapter uses an ethnographic engagement with the space of a *gaushala* or cow-shelter as a way of entering the cow protection discourse.

The first section sets the stage for my claim of *gaushalas* as a significant constitutive site in the making of the 'cow protection movement' and introduces the *gaushala* in which my ethnographic inquiry would be located. The second section provides a historical view of the scholarly construction of a linear 'movement' in the name of the cow and its analytical effect in the reading of the 'cow protection movement'. The third section, the kernel of the ethnographic engagement, explores the manner in which gender, labour and caste shape symbolic, material and discursive practices at the *gaushala* to produce simultaneously the figure of the *gausevak* (loosely translated as 'one who serves the cow') and the *gaumata*; the feminised and revered cow who is at once, the mother, the goddess and the nation. I also reflect briefly here on the politics of my own presence as a researcher in the field. The final section reiterates the political and analytical value of a *gaushala* as a point of entry into the cow protection discourse which I argue, can in fact, enable a feminist retelling of the story of cow protection.

Why *gaushalas*: Introducing the Shree Gopal *gaushala*

The story of cow protection in India has conspicuously omitted *gaushalas* as active constitutive spaces in the making of the 'cow protection movement'. While there is some information available on the role played by cow protection societies or *gaurakshini sabhas* that began to sprout in nineteenth-century North and West India, in the culmination of 'cow-based riots' (Freitag 1980; Pandey 1981; Robb 1986), *gaushalas* are mentioned, if at all, cursorily as mere 'asylums' for cows in the northern parts of the country (Yang 1980). One of the most significant reasons for this cursory treatment of *gaushalas* in the otherwise verbose story of cow protection, I submit, is that the very idea of 'cow protection' is over-determined by the imagination of a certain kind of spectacular violence, leaving little space for a *gaushala;* which is presumed to be a benign charitable space engaged in an innocent form of *seva* or charitable service. The *gaurakshini sabhas*; which were explicitly militant and aggressive in their demand to ban cow slaughter and have been held responsible for the cow protection 'riots' of the late nineteenth and early twentieth centuries fit far more easily into the violence-ridden story of cow protection, than the generous *gaushalas* that 'merely' shelter hapless, old and ailing cows.

Adcock (2019) in her insightful research on cow protection has pointed towards the need to visit afresh those institutions, actors and practices that have been marked as 'secular' or even apolitical in the making of the cow protection discourse. The *gaushala* is one such space which on the one hand needs to be brought into the fold of the religiously marked cow protection story while on the other, also provides the opportunity to explore the more seemingly 'secular' workings of religion that may not necessarily be wholly explained by placing it in the framework of Hindu nationalist violence. What constitutes the bedrock of this chapter is my argument that a *gaushala* can enable us to go beyond the 'exceptional' events of heightened violence (which are arguably becoming a present 'everyday reality'), to capture the makings of the cow protection discourse, helping us understand how the two intimately relate to and construct one another.

Part of the current interest in *gaushalas* can be attributed to the investment of the present Hindu nationalist government, which first came to power in 2014, in the setting up and maintenance of *gaushalas*. As per news reports, the Bharatiya Janata Party (henceforth, BJP)-led government spent INR 5.8 billion on the construction and maintenance of *gaushalas* in the period from 2014 to 2016.[1] In mid-2014, soon after coming to power at the Centre, the BJP started the Rashtriya Gokul Mission, a national programme to build 'havens for retired, ailing and barren bovines'.[2] In May 2016, a national conference was held on *gauvansh* (cow-clans) and *gaushalas* in the national capital with a 'three-pronged agenda' to discuss (a) the challenge of increasing cows' productivity,

1 See https://www.bloomberg.com/news/articles/2016-07-17/cow-urine-can-sell-for-more-than-milk-in-india. Accessed on 27 January 2025.

2 Ibid.

(b) steps to ensure better care of cows, and (c) security 'against smugglers and other cruel incidents'.[3] In the same year, Baba Ramdev's Patanjali Ayurved declared its plan to invest INR 500 crore in four 'mega', 'scientific' *gaushalas* across the country.[4] This governmental interest in *gaushalas* at the contemporary moment when cow-based lynchings have come to constitute a category of violence in itself, presents the need to examine further the linkages between the *gaushala* as a site and a heightened, spectacularly gruesome event like lynching.

My ethnographic inquiry is located at the Shree Gopal Gaushala (henceforth SGG) in the town of Faridabad, in the north Indian state of Haryana, nearly thirty kilometres from the national capital. SGG is one of the four registered *gaushalas* in Faridabad district. Founded by the Vishwa Hindu Parishad (VHP) in 1995 and run by those principally identifying as VHP *karyakartas* or 'activists', SGG self-identifies as a 'religious organisation', unlike other *gaushalas* in the town which refer to themselves as 'animal shelters' or related variants. Even though this *gaushala* is one of the oldest in the city, it began to acquire visibility only towards the middle of 2015. This is true of *gaushalas* in general in Faridabad; their existence was a rather lesser-known fact before 2014–15 when the current dispensation first came to power. It was around this time that two trusts, namely the Som Prakash Charitable Trust and the Kailash Devi Trust, started the service of running cycle rickshaws across the city to collect food and other supplies for the cows housed in the *gaushalas* in Faridabad, thereby familiarising many residents with the existence of the *gaushalas* in the first place. The knowledge of SGG (procured through these very cycle rickshaws) made it convenient for my family to perform the Brahminical ritual of *gaudaan* or 'cow donation' at SGG, upon

[3] See http://www.hindustantimes.com/india/government-to-introduce-special-protection-for-desi-cows/story-b6Dbk75ICmv6HyG0QbSaKN.html. Accessed on 27 January 2025.

[4] See http://m.rediff.com/money/report/patanjali-to-spend-rs-500-crore-on-cow-protection/20160814.htm. Accessed on 27 January 2025.

the death of my long-ailing grandmother. A month before her passing away, a cow from SGG was made to perform *vaitarani*, a Brahminical ritual where 'a cow is first worshipped and then its tail grasped with both hands … in preparation for that terrible event after death in which the dead have to cross the fetid river of death on the opposite bank, on which the kingdom of the dead is found' (van der Veer 1994, 87). Thus, my familiarity with the SGG was mediated by a familial encounter. In a forthcoming section, I shall dwell on how this kind of mediation shaped my presence in the field.

Situated at Surajkund Road, Faridabad, SGG with its stated objective 'to encourage people to respect cows', housed nearly 840 cows as of December 2017. Of these, roughly 150 were milk-producing, 170 were male (referred to as *nandis*), 200 were old, 60 were blind, 20 were accident-striken and/or were disabled and the remaining were calves and unproductive cows.

The number of paid workers at SGG, both men and women, all from Bhil, Gond and Sahariya tribes who migrated largely from VHP-mobilised districts of Madhya Pradesh, was around 40, with nearly 30 men among these. All women workers were wives of the men working at the *gaushala*. In addition, there were a few volunteers who visited the *gaushala* regularly and provided financial assistance in times of requirement. The workers resided in the premises of the *gaushala* itself, making the home the same as the workplace.

SGG is owned and run by VHP *kuryakurtas*, men from middle-class Brahmin-Baniya backgrounds, who occupy all leadership roles at the *gaushala*. The leadership and the trustee board are therefore entirely male, dominant caste and middle class. The manager at SGG is a young Jat man in his thirties who also worked part-time as an insurance agent (at the time of fieldwork).

The Cow Protection Movement: A Historical Overview

The relevance of the cow in India has been at the centre of much academic conversation, especially since the 1960s. Anthropologists, economists, ecologists, historians and geographers have engaged with various strands of thought pertaining to the bovine (Korom 2000). An important debate was initiated in the 1960s by Marvin Harris' controversial thesis that the sanctity of cow in India must be understood as largely a 'techno-environmental' issue, a taboo grounded in scientific principles which helps maintain a 'low-energy, small-scale, animal-based ecosystem' (van der Veer 1994, 87). Harris argued that the problem of the 'holy cow' is found to unravel itself not in the domain of the religious, but, the economic–ecological – its functional importance to the Indian peasant-farmer. He further upheld the Hindu logic of the cow's sanctity as economically and ecologically sound and asserted that the Hindu practices reflect a level of economising that is not appreciated by the Western standards of saving and husbandry (Harris 1974). Harris' functional approach was severely criticised for reducing the complex cattle question to a mere 'calculus of calories' (Glucklich 1997). In an attempt to 'correct' the 'imbalance' resulting from a disproportionate emphasis on the economic and environmental, Simoons, Simoons and Lodrick (1981) placed the 'sacred cow concept in a broader cultural perspective by examining its varied and interesting expressions in Hindu religion, folk thought and everyday behavior' (Simoons, Simoons and Lodrick 1981, 121).

In the 1980s, scholarly attention shifted to the sacred status granted by Hindus to the cow and the manner in which this 'sanctity', defined in religious terms, affected the sociopolitical landscape of India. This body of work, most of which came from historians, dates the cow protection 'movement' to the late nineteenth and early twentieth century cow-related 'riots' (Yang 1980; Freitag 1980; Pandey 1983; Robb 1986), the formation of cow protection societies or *gaurakshini sabhas*, and the efforts undertaken by Arya Samaj's Dayanand Saraswati to prevent cow slaughter and protect the *gaumata*. One of the most rigorously documented aspects of cow protection is the period around the 1880s when a large number of *gaurakshini sabhas* began to emerge and the reformist Arya Samaj's Dayanand Saraswati actively took up this agenda (Freitag 1980; Robb 1986, Van der Veer 1994; Pinney 1997). Scholars have held the activities of the *gaurakshini sabhas*, along with the efforts undertaken by an army of *gau swamis*, that is, 'agitators, emissaries, lecturers, paid agents, penniless adventurers, preachers and propagandists' (Yang 1980, 586) who toured different parts of the country (though largely limited to the northern belt), chiefly responsible for a series of 'communal riots' that broke out in almost all of North India in the 1880s–90s and 1900s.

While this body of work is insightful in its description of the causal mechanisms and structures of violence that erupted in the name of the cow as early as the nineteenth century, it suggests a linear history of the 'cow protection movement' and conflates the spectacle of violence with the process by which the cow was made to become the charged symbol of the *gaumata*.[5] I seek to caution against this uniform and linear conceptualisation of the 'cow protection movement' and argue that the sanctity of the cow draws from a range of symbolic, discursive and material practices, across multiple spheres – economic, ecological, religious and political and it is these aspects that are called upon discreetly and distinctly at various points in history to (re)cast the cow as *gaumata* and activate 'her' as a powerful politico-religious symbol.[6]

---

[5] Many significant political actors took public positions on the matter of cow protection in the late nineteenth to the early twentieth centuries. Since these do not directly pertain to my argument in this chapter, I do not delve into their intricacies here but mention a few examples to indicate certain positions. Gandhi (1909) for example, in line with his belief in non-violence harboured a love for the cow but was against a legislative ban on cow slaughter. Ambedkar (1948) argued that the declaration of beef-eating as sacrilegious was rooted in the tussle between Brahminism and Buddhism. Jha (2009) has shown through archaeological evidence that Hindus, including brahmins and even deities consumed beef in ancient India. Interestingly, Savarkar, known for his 1923 work *Hindutva,* was opposed to the notion of the cow's divinity. The Kukas, a millenarian Sikh sect, despite their belief in Hindu-Sikh distinctions thought of cow slaughter and beef consumption as *mleccha* or 'impure' (Oberoi 1992).

[6] I have demonstrated this at length elsewhere by (re)visiting several moments in a rather long period, from the mid-1700s to the 1890s, when the figure of the 'holy' cow had been made to (re)surface at distinct points.

In the following section, I dwell on my ethnographic experience at SGG to understand the ways in which it constructs the notions of *gaumata* and *gauseva(k)*, which I argue are central to the present project of cow protection. Exploring the manner in which the *gaushala* is built and presented as a space and place – I examine the spatial organisation of SGG; its motivations of founding, structure and organisation with an emphasis on the division of labour (between the leadership and the workers in general as well as between the men and women workers); the way in which the cow is recast as *gaumata* and the Adivasi worker as her *sevak*; and, lastly, my own gendered position in the *gaushala* as well as the larger project as a researcher.

The Production of *(gau) seva(k)*: The Spatial Organisation of SGG

The spatial organisation of SGG exemplifies one of the material practices that orders the *gaushala* in specific ways to produce a gendered discourse of *gauseva* and regulate the construction of masculinities and femininities in that space. Underlying this approach is the idea that challenges a static or reactionary conceptualisation of space, as if time/history plays itself out against an inert, homogenous and unchanging space (Massey 1993). I intend to show instead that the space of the *gaushala* itself is central to the production of the practice of *gauseva* and the figure of the *gausevak*, within the rubric of which we must understand the cow protection movement. 'Space', therefore, is not the background against which the action of cow protection can be plotted; it is the protagonist of the story of cow protection that positions both materially and symbolically, some actors at the

I posit that the vignettes described at length, some of which can be dated to the eighteenth century, must not be seen as the components or parts that simply add up together to produce a singular, cohesive 'whole' of the 'cow protection movement'; instead, it would be productive to see them as pieces of varying shapes and textures that are embedded in their own contexts and histories and can tell us only partial and situated stories of cow protection.

centre of the cow protection discourse as the legitimate *gausevaks* and marginalises and vilifies others as *gauhinsaks* (perpetrators of violence against the cow).

Upon entering SGG, the first area to make itself visible is the shed for milch cattle on the extreme left and the office area on the right, with a sizeable parking lot in between. The milch cows' shed is the most valuable section of the *gaushala*, placed right at the front, as it houses the productive female cows. Right next to it is a huge expanse, designated for the construction of the Shani Temple (a temple dedicated to Shani, the Hindu god for justice and death). In the office on the right, is the seating area of the manager (and sometimes, the visiting trustees and other guests) along with a small shop which sells various cow-based products along with neatly lined Patanjali[7] products and a few books on Hindu religion and culture, most of which are Gita Press publications.[8] Adjacent to the office is a huge, well-maintained temple where idols of various gods of the Hindu religion reside. This is also where *bhandaras* or 'religious feasts' are held almost on a daily basis by visitors as part of rituals on occasions such as birthdays, anniversaries, death of a loved one, etc. Behind the temple are more sheds for disabled (mostly, blind) cows, with a shed for bulls and buffaloes adjacent to it. Next to it is the open shed for calves. Removed from the rest of the sheds is a dispensary where accident-stricken and seriously injured/sick cattle are brought in and attended to by the in-house vet. Right next to the dispensary, in keeping with the government guidelines, is a separate shed for cattle suffering from various kinds of illnesses, where they are housed during the duration of their

[7] Patanjali Ayurved Limited is an Indian consumer goods company with Baba Ramdev at the helm, who started out as a 'yoga guru'. The company claims to rely on the wisdom of using 'native Hindu' ingredients and takes pride in its purportedly Hindu ethos thus setting itself apart from 'western' companies and products. Known for its herbal products, the company has also been mired in multiple controversies for not meeting quality and hygiene standards.

[8] Gita Press is the world's largest publisher of Hindu religious texts set up in 1923 in Gorakhpur in the North Indian state of Uttar Pradesh.

recovery. Amidst these sheds is a single room that is often locked and opened only in the event of a need – this is where numerous notebooks are stocked, to be borrowed by visitors only to write 'Ram' innumerable times, as they chant the god's name as a sign of their devotion to him and once done, return the notebooks to be kept in the same room. This room then is an embodiment of Ram bhakti (worship of Ram) demonstrated by the *gaubhakts* (cow worshippers). On the extreme periphery of the *gaushala* are the staff quarters that I was politely denied access to. This is where the migrant Adivasi workers reside, some with their families (See Figure 9.1 for an illustrative depiction of SGG).

This spatial mapping illustrates the manner in which the *gaushala* is structured and hierarchised on lines of gender and caste. The area of most value is the sheds of the milch cows – it is the milk obtained from these cows that also becomes the chief source of revenue. It is therefore not surprising that the milk-producing cows are regarded as *gaumata* and worshipped in literal terms every morning, right before the day starts at SGG. They are, in fact, placed at maximum distance from those who may be a threat to their (re)productive capacity and/ or purity – bulls in general and disabled and accident-stricken bulls in particular. The practice of mating is crucial and needs to be regulated. For instance, Mr Tyagi, one of the senior VHP *karyakartas* would often stress the fact that one of the major strengths of SGG over other *gaushalas* was that it houses only native breeds that are far superior to Western breeds like Jersey, which do not even qualify as the sacred *gaumata*. He stressed, 'We have here many cow breeds that have been referred to in Vedic literature – the *kamadhenu* (the wish-fulfilling cow), *surbhi* and *kapila* cows which cannot be seen in most *gaushalas* around.' He noted further that one of the missions of SGG is to restore the purity of *gaumata* through *nasal sudhaar* or breed improvement. Notably, he dated the emergence of the 'sin' of cross-breeding in India only after the Muslims invaded India. In conversation, he elaborated:

> Just as there is the concept of the *gotra* or clan among humans, with prohibition of marriage within the same *gotra*, there had been the

> notion of a *gotra* among cows with stringent injunctions against mating within bulls from the same lineage, or else their quality and productivity is adversely affected. This malpractice of mating of intra-familial cows started with the Mughal rule and it is precisely this sin of the Muslim which has caused a decline in productivity of cows today.

The *gaumata* therefore emerges as akin to the ideal Hindu-Brahmin woman, another figure carved in the image of the 'mother' – the generous, self-sacrificing woman who nurtures her (Hindu) sons and the (Hindu) nation at large through her (re)productive capacity and her milk; she is on the one hand a nurturer, a protector but is also in constant need of protection herself, against the 'cow-slaughtering' or 'beef-eating' 'other' – the Muslim and the Dalit. Her purity, which is inextricably tied with notions of honour and respectability, therefore must be maintained by a strict control over her sexuality, the principle through which caste is maintained in the Hindu social order. SGG's pride in housing indigenous 'pure' breeds as opposed to 'mixed' or 'foreign' breeds is pertinent, for it not only gestures towards Brahminical Hinduism's preoccupation with notions of purity but mirrors caste-marked hierarchies intrinsic to the Hindu order. Yamini Narayanan (2018) argues that the dominant Hindu discourse which ascribes excessive importance to the bovine is critical in the production of what she calls 'casteisedspeciesism' – a hierarchised order that regards native Hindu breeds as epitomes of Hindu purity and culture while buffalo and crossbred or Jersey cows are 'exposed to exploitation and oppression comparable to the situation faced by Dalits' (Narayanan 2018).

Apart from the aforementioned references to the able-bodied and 'productive cows' housed in the front-most sheds, the other recurring reference is to the 'scientific and research-based' activities undertaken there – manufacture of various products like phenyl, shampoo, eye-drops, etc., which are also sold on a small scale within the front-facing office area of SGG. Most of these 'experiments' are undertaken by Tyagi, who has learnt much of his work at the RSS-run *gaushala* at Nagpur, Maharashtra. Visitors at SGG are often greeted with heavy verbal catalogues of how visitors have benefitted from cow-based products like *panchgavya*.[9]

Founding and Organisational Structure of SGG

The story/ies around the founding of SGG are central to understanding its social and political ethos, motivations and proclivities. While more than one version with minor variations were narrated to me, I recount here the broad contours of what was told to me by senior *karyakartas* and the manager:

> After some thinking and assistance from the VHP, Baislaji, one of our *karyakartas* started a small *gaushala* on a piece of land in Sector 8 in Faridabad. The Congress was in power then. We were, very soon, driven out of there and this was when Baislaji, one of senior leaders, inaugurated his own 1.5-acre land, right here, with a *BhoomiPujan*. Nearly 240 cows were given to us then by the Municipal Corporation. At that point, we were struggling to make sheds but the lord showed us the path once again. Out of nowhere, a Jain female ascetic came to the *gaushala* one day. She was terribly angry on seeing the state of the *gaushala*, and how much we were struggling with taking care of the cows. She reprimanded us a lot and we listened. After all, she was an ascetic. But then, she emptied a bag of more than 70,000 rupees before us. 'Take this and make use of it to serve *gaumata*', she instructed. That very week, another *bhakt* from the Jain samaj, a businessman, donated another lakh. This amount became the foundation on which the *gaushala* was built and today, we can say with pride, that this is one of the superior *gaushalas* in not just Faridabad but all of Haryana.'

Many questions remained unanswered despite my polite insistence on responses. Who informed the VHP *karyakartas* about the transport of cattle and how exactly did they come to know of it? How exactly were the cows 'rescued'? What happened to the *kasai*

---

[9] *Panchgavya*, a concoction of cow dung, urine, milk, curd, and ghee is regarded as one of the most significant and beneficial products obtained from the cow. Repeated insistence on the useful properties of *panchgavya* recurs in the cow protection discourse and is one of the refrains at SGG.

or butcher who was taking them for slaughter? The question of land for the construction of SGG seemed to have been easily resolved too, just as the question of the initial funding. These absences in Dagras's story are as critical to its construction as the elements that overtly constitute it. In the case of the story of founding, as in the general context of my work, the recovery of an 'authentic truth' is not the motivation this work is guided by; it is, in fact, the self-fashioning of the story of cow protection that I am interested in. It is in this specific regard that this story becomes significant. What emerges most strongly is the continuation and consolidation of the trope of the Muslim 'other', given a material-visual image as the dangerous *kasai* threatening the *gaumata*. A large part of the verbal interaction and visual representation at SGG builds on the notion of the *kasai* as representative of the entire Muslim community. Even though there is no Muslim presence at SGG, among the leadership, workers or even visitors, the Muslims occupy an important place in the cow protection discourse at SGG, either as the threatening *kasai* or by way of occasional references to the 'good Muslim' who is 'accommodating of and respectful to' Hindu values and beliefs. Mr Tyagi once told me, 'I will welcome Muslims with open arms as long as they are as reverent to the *gaumata* as we are.'

Labour is an important structuring category to understand relationships and networks at SGG. As mentioned earlier, the Board of Trustees as well as the leadership at SGG is entirely male, Brahmin and Baniya. It is composed mainly of senior VHP *karyakartas* who supervise the overall functioning of SGG, look into financial matters and serve as the connecting bridge between the VHP and SGG. The physical work is undertaken by the workforce, composed of Adivasi men and some women. The manager is the point of contact between the leadership and the workers. It is the manager who the workers report to. He oversees the three teams of 10–15 persons each, headed by a team head who is always male. An ordinary day at the *gaushala* begins at 4:00 am with the feeding of the cows followed by milking the cows. The selling of the milk takes place 6:30 am onwards, a process managed by the team heads and overseen by the manager. After this, all the 11 *wadas* or sections are cleaned thoroughly by the women workers. The cows and calves are then separated and placed in different *wadas*. In the evening, around 4:00 pm, this process is repeated and milk is sold again, 6:00 pm onwards. The entire process is supervised and assisted by the team heads. Women are responsible for cleaning the *wadas*, the temple in the compound of the *gaushala* and the room of the temple's pandit. Among the workers, duties and areas of work are interchanged periodically. When the women workers are not doing '*gaushala* work', they are involved in cooking, cleaning, taking care of their children and other household tasks. It is significant to note that the men workers are regarded as 'full time workers' with a wage of INR 10,000 per month, while the women workers are given a 'part time' wage of INR 5000 per month. This is an exemplification of one of the ways in which women's labour is devalued, compounded at the *gaushala* by the fact that there is a hazy distinction, if any, between 'home' and 'workplace'. My argument is that the deification of the productive cow into the *gaumata,* who must be elevated by ritual worship and protected, is sustained by the simultaneous recasting of the Adivasi *karmachari* or worker into the *gausevak.* The discourse of *seva* therefore becomes important in marking the contours of the current cow protection discourse.

'*Gauseva*' and the making of the '*gaumata*'

Dating the emergence of *gaumata* as a loaded symbol of the Hindu nation to the late nineteenth to the early twentieth centuries, Gupta argues that the cow had the 'potential to be represented as the mother of all Hindus and of a Hindu identity and nationality, requiring protection from non-Hindus' because of its transcendent appeal (Gupta 2001, 4295). The *gaumata* was akin to the Brahmin domestic woman as well as the goddess whose chastity and honour needed to be guarded against 'external' penetration, as metonymic of the nation that had to be protected against the non-Hindu invasion (Oberoi 1992; Gupta 2001). This iconography of the cow as mother–nation–goddess was central to her construction as sacred. The association of the cow with the loaded image of the mother was further solidified by giving it a concrete material base – the economic usefulness of the cow in terms of its productivity and capacity to provide milk, curd, ghee, etc. was repeatedly emphasised. The *gaumata* then, much like Bharat Mata or Mother-India is almost always in a fragile position of threat and in need of militant protection against the ever-present danger of violation of her honour at the hands of the 'outsider'. The extent and intensity of the danger must constantly be reinforced to arouse 'her' virile Hindu sons who must dedicate themselves to the cause of her protection, or else face the disgrace of emasculation.

If the dominant discourse of cow protection takes shape through the violent *gauraksha*, *gauseva* with its dual aim of rearing of 'ailing and helpless cattle' and the 'upliftment of the downtrodden Adivasis' is a seemingly more benign project. The political and ideological construction of both is, however, inextricably tied with the gendered project of rescuing the *gaumata* from the villainous *kasai* and/or the filthy beef-eater, thus consolidating communal and caste-based antagonisms. At the *gaushala*, we witness a specific manner in which the practice of *gauseva* enjoins the Brahmin-Baniya leadership and the Adivasi workers or *gausevak*s in mutually constitutive or even seemingly reciprocal ways – while the leadership can appropriate the workers into a benign project without necessarily having to eliminate them through the violent *gauraksha* as typified in the 'riot' or the 'lynching', the workers are imparted dignity for labour that is otherwise regarded as filthy or dehumanising through a systematic recasting of working with cattle as the noble, virtuous and sacred *gauseva*. Freitag (1980) has eloquently demonstrated the manner in which 'lower' castes, Chamars, for instance, have been historically kept outside the fold of the 'sacred' cow protection while also being assigned the physically demanding and 'impure' labour of working with animals' bodies. More recently, Singh (2017) has also pointed out the irony of the exclusion and vilification of Dalit-Bahujans from the Brahminical fold of cow protection when the labour of cattle rearing has historically been the task of the Ahir community. I argue that *gauseva,* therefore, emerges as a relatively more sanitised means of ensuring Adivasi and Dalit-Bahujan co-operation in a Brahminical project with the appearance of granting them a 'better' life while also keeping them in 'their place'.

The appearance notwithstanding, the project of *gauseva* is built on fundamentally unequal terms. Analysing *seva* as a concept and practice, Srivatsan (2014) argues that it has come to constitute one of the most significant strands of voluntary activism. *Seva,* in its very structural mode, encodes beneficiaries of charity bound in a hierarchical relationship with the *sevak*-saviour, where any attempt to criticise or challenge what the saviour has chosen to offer will be marginalised. In other words, *seva* consolidates the hegemony of the elite while also providing them an ethical supremacy. He points out how an activism of this nature is founded on the view of the disadvantaged as the 'sinful wretch' who needs to be uplifted. In the context of cow protection, the 'wretch' is also seen as 'dirty', in need of purification through bodily work that involves coming in contact with *gaumata,* the work that simultaneously dirties and purifies him. This kind of *seva* is fundamentally and qualitatively different from a view that looks at entry to schools, libraries, etc., as civic rights. Srivatsan's observation of the sevak-saviour's attitude seems especially accurate in the light of the statement made by Dagra who once casually mentioned to me, 'The workers' children are really not interested in studying or for improving their life prospects in general. They just like to while away their time, sitting around, doing nothing. We ask them to work at the *gaushala,* help around with something or the other so they realise the value of work and learn to do something!' Dagra's utterance makes clear his view of the workers' children who he posits, are not just in a social and economic crisis but a moral one.

The notion of *gauseva* at the VHP-run SGG is also informed significantly by the VHP's use of *karseva* in the Ram Janmabhoomi movement, in semantic and discursive terms.[10] The idea of *karseva* was used originally by Sikhs in the context of the restoration of the Golden Temple in 1984 when it had been damaged in the face of military action by the then-Indian government (Chopra 2010). *Kar* (meaning 'hands') and *seva* (meaning 'service') evokes an idea of 'selfless service' or 'voluntary labour' that is religious in nature – a 'labour of love' performed in service of religion with humility (Virdee 2006). *Karseva,* then, is associated simultaneously with both 'worship' and 'service', in ways that sometimes make them one and the same. In 1989, the VHP appropriated the erstwhile Sikh notion of *karseva* to mobilise Hindu activists to demolish the mosque and build the Ram temple (Jaffrelot 1996). Incitement of violence as a means of protection was an intrinsic part of this imagination of *karseva.* At the centre of this protectionist discourse then was the figure of Ram (imagined as male but also feminised in certain visual and symbolic repertoires of Hindu tradition), metonymic in a larger sense of Hindu religion and nation.[11] In the distinctive couching of *karseva* at SGG into *gauseva* (and its intimately porous relationship with *gauraksha*), the feminised

[10] In 1984, the VHP and its affiliates launched an agitation to demolish the Babri mosque at 'Ram Janmabhoomi' (the birthplace of the Hindu god, Ram) in Ayodhya in order to erect a Ram Temple instead. The 'Ram RathYatra' organised by the BJP and led by its then president, L. K. Advani, was launched in September 1990 to accomplish the mission of building the Ram Mandir at the site of the Masjid. The Yatra triggered serious violence and led to riots across the country, where hundreds lost their lives. Both with regard to the history of Hindu–Muslim relations in the country and the political career of the VHP, the 'Ram Janmabhoomi agitation' marked a defining moment. Last year, on 22 January 2024, the Ram Mandir was inaugurated and opened to the public in a spectacular ceremony, where Prime Minister Narendra Modi took upon a priestly role, leading its consecration, and announced it as the beginning of a 'new era'.

[11] For a detailed analysis of the various meanings ascribed to Ram through the VHP's organisation and ideology during the Ramjanmabhoomi movement, see Datta 1991. Also see early, foundational work on the ideological origins and institutional modes of working of Hindu nationalism (Hansen 1998; Jaffrelot 2007)

figure of the *gaumata* who at once embodies the mother, the goddess and the nation becomes the object of protection, in whose service, the labour of Adivasi men and women must be deployed. The SGG leadership in this specific rehashing of *gauseva* also sees itself as engaged in *samajseva* (social service) and *deshseva* (service to the nation), not only for the role it views itself as playing in cow protection but also in the 'upliftment' of disadvantaged sections.

In one of my interactions with the manager at SGG, he emphasised repeatedly the 'pious' nature of *gauseva*. This emphasis on piety and religious virtuosity becomes important in the project of the sanitisation of the otherwise supposedly 'dirty' labour of working with cattle, which needs to be spiritually elevated in order to be devalued and appropriated. The differentially hierarchised positions at SGG – the Brahmin-Baniya men who occupy leadership roles and the Board of Trustees; the young Jat manager who supervises the workers; the Adivasi men who are regarded as 'full time' *gausevaks*, and the Adivasi women, their wives who are viewed as 'part time' *gausevaks* with no representation in both the SGG core bodies or the workers' teams, is an illustration of Ambedkar's argument of the caste Hindu order manifesting not as a mere division of labour but the division of labourers. The devaluation of women's work is pertinent to the blurry distinction between 'work' and 'home'. Gopal (2013) has argued that the mechanistic distinction of 'work' into the compartments of formal, informal and domestic reflects the superficial and artificially imposed distinction charted out between production and social reproduction and that a

> ...significant aspect of social reproduction, as reflected in the subsistence and socially necessary activities done by women as well as the numerous degraded tasks performed by women/workers in the informal sectors, also fall under the rubric of caste-based labours. Thus caste hierarchies, as much as gender hierarchies, contribute to the segmentation and devaluation of labours'. (Gopal 2013, 92)

While devaluation of labour is central to the production of stigmatised labouring bodies, the *gaushala*'s fashioning of the discourse of *gauseva* through symbolic and material practices stigmatises as it claims to spiritually elevate – which, as Srivatsan argues, *seva* as a form of voluntary activism has historically allowed for.

The Politics of My Presence at SGG: A Brief Note on Methodology

Arguably, my own social and political-analytical location informed not only the ways in which I navigated the space of SGG but also what I 'saw' and 'was allowed to see' in the course of my fieldwork.

A large body of feminist scholarship on ethnography has been tremendously useful in challenging the dualisms of the 'subject and object, thought and feeling, knower and known and political and personal' as well as the 'arbitrary boundaries of traditional academic disciplines' (Stacey 1988, 21). At the same time, there has been hesitation to place uncritical faith in the feminist principles of empathy and mutuality as the necessary analytical and ethical frameworks to do ethnographic research, with the fear that purportedly feminist research may actually pose a greater risk of abandonment and betrayal than even positivist research (Stacey 1988; Abu-Lughod 1990; Woolf 1993). In this context, conversations around the methodological aspects of working with what Nigel Fielding (1993) has termed 'unloved groups', have been especially rich and insightful. As a feminist-identified, dominant caste, university-trained women's study scholar researching a *gaushala* founded and run by a militant Hindu nationalist organisation, I grappled with several concerns about accessing the field, performing various roles at SGG (of which that of the researcher was but one) and walking the tightrope between my privilege which gave me access to the *gaushala* as well as my vulnerabilities within that space which invoked fear and at many points, the genuine possibility of threat.

I came in touch with SGG through a familial encounter and my access to it was mediated significantly by my father, who though not from the VHP or its circles in any manner was seen as 'one among us' in certain ways by the *gaushala*'s leadership, given his gender, caste-class and political position. Joseph (1996) has referred to access of this nature, facilitated by figures of authority whose own positions are often oppositional to the researcher's own as 'patriarchal connectivity'. Further, women researchers have written about the invisibility or even the erasure of their researcher-selves in the field. In her contribution to *Women Fielding Danger* that deals with the methodological challenges faced by women researchers, Schwandner-Sievers notes that, '... as a woman working on my own that the greatest threat was not the violence toward me, but rather not being taken seriously as a researcher' (2009, 1). In SGG's view, I was the daughter of a respectable Hindu middle-class man, curiously interested in the cow but largely a politically insignificant actor, given my age and gender, both different from the SGG as a larger constituency. I was also the 'brahmin *beti*' (Brahmin daughter) interested in learning about the SGG's investment in another Brahminised-feminised figure – that of the *gaumata*. While this perception undermined my researcher-self, it is also what facilitated my access to the space. In many ways, I was not a consequential presence by virtue of not being aligned with their notion of an influential man of power. However, suspicion and distrust were far from completely eliminated. On my very first day at SGG, my father's personal and professional details were noted (mine were not), and reticence and hesitation coexisted with the insistence on transparency and benevolence. The former was at its strongest in the context of my interaction with the workers; all my conversations with them took place in a highly supervised environment and were therefore limited in many ways. SGG then would often manifest for me as a disorienting space where rehearsed politeness and a seemingly welcoming disposition would uncomfortably sit with fear, suspicion and strategic revelation and concealment by all parties. As Sehgal (2009) points out in the context of her ethnographic work with the RSS:

> I began to see that my own covertness was matched by that of the Hindu nationalist interlocutors ... [E]ach of us was subtly and covertly 'bargaining' for our interests on the basis of what we perceived to be the identity and social location of the other ... I discovered that the Hindu nationalists and myself each held assumptions about, and goals for, the other that were not always totally true and usually not fully explicit. (2009, 11)

I therefore build on the suggestion that feminist methodological principles of honesty, trust and empathy cannot be called upon simplistically or worse, eulogised as essential to doing 'authentic' research. Ethnographic identities in the field play out in far more complex ways than the polarities of overt–covert, honest–dishonest, all powerful–subservient, disclosure–concealment can capture or allow for. It is in these complex webs of relationships and networks in the field that various truth-claims are operationalised.

Conclusion: Joining the Dots

I have argued in this chapter that the cow protection discourse has been reductively and, in my view, wrongly viewed as a coherent 'movement', with emphasis on spectacular violence that is episodic in nature. The epistemic offshoot of this approach is the production of a linear, uniform cow protection movement that climaxed into the 'riot' in the late nineteenth and early twentieth centuries and the 'bovine lynching' in the contemporary moment. Making a departure from this mode of analysis, I place at the centre an ordinary and benign space like a *gaushala* and examine its everyday symbolic, material and discursive practices to understand the manner in which the 'everyday' and the 'event' are both intimately related and mutually constituted. The fashioning of the discourse of *gauseva* and the making of the *gaumata* at SGG bring to the fore the ways in which gender, labour and caste shape and collapse the fine distinction between the violent *gauraksha* and the charitable *gauseva*.

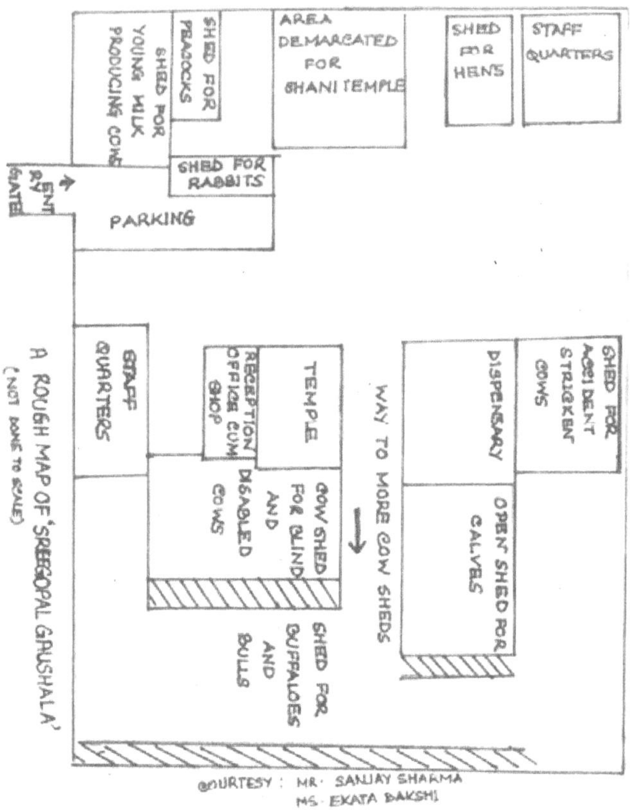

Figure 9.1 Spatial Layout of SGG (Source: Ridhima Sharma)

REFERENCES

Adcock, Cassie. 2019. "'Preserving and Improving the Breeds': Cow Protection's Animal-Husbandry Connection." *South Asia Journal of South Asian Studies* 42, no. 6: 1–15.

Ambedkar, B. R. 1948. *The Untouchables: Who Were They and Why They Became Untouchables.* New Delhi: Amrit Book Company.

Chopra, Radhika. 2010. "Commemorating Hurt: Memorializing Operation Bluestar." *Sikh Formations: Religion, Culture, Theory* 6, no. 2: 119–52.

Datta, Pradip. 1991. "VHP's Ram at Ayodhya: Reincarnation through Ideology and Organisation." *Economic and Political Weekly* 26, no. 44: 2517–526.

Freitag, Sandra. 1980. "Sacred Symbol as Mobilising Ideology: The North Indian Search for a 'Hindu' Community." *Comparative Studies in Society and History* 22, no. 4: 597–625.

Gandhi, Mohandas Karamchand. 1909. *Hind Swaraj or Indian Home Rule.* Ahmedabad: Navjivan Publishing House.

Glucklich, Ariel. 1997. *The End of Magic.* Oxford: Oxford University Press.

Gopal, Meena. 2013. "Ruptures and Reproduction in Caste/Gender/Labour." *Economic and Political Weekly* 48, no. 18: 91–97.

Gupta, Charu. 2001. "The Icon of Mother in Late Colonial North India: 'Bharat Mata' 'Matri Bhasha' and 'Gau Mata'." *Economic and Political Weekly* 36, no. 45: 4291–299.

Hansen, Thomas. 1998. *The Saffron Wave: Democracy and Hindu Nationalism in Modern India.* Princeton University Press.

Harris, Marvin. 1966. "The Cultural Ecology of India's Sacred Cattle." *Current Anthropology* 7, no. 1: 51–59.

———. 1974. *Cows, Pigs, Wars, and Witches.* New York: Vintage Publishers.

Jaffrelot, Christophe. 1996. *The Hindu Nationalist Movement and Indian Politics.* C. Hurst & Co. Publishers.

———. 2007. *Hindu Nationalism: A Reader.* Princeton University Press.

Jha, Dwijendra Narayan. 2009. *The Myth of the Holy Cow.* New Delhi: Navayana Publishing.

Joseph, Suad. 1996. "Relationality and Ethnographic Subjectivity: Key Informants and the Construction of Personhood in Fieldwork." In *Feminist Dilemmas in Fieldwork*, edited by D. L. Wolf, 107–121. Boulder, CO: Westview Press.

Korom, Frank J. 2000. "Holy Cow! The Apotheosis of Zebu, or Why the Cow Is Sacred in Hinduism." *Asian Folklore Studies* 59, no. 2: 181–203.

Narayanan, Yamini. 2018. "Cow Protection as 'Casteised Speciesism': Sacralisation, Commercialisation and Politicisation." *South Asia: Journal of South Asian Studies* 41, no. 2: 331–51. doi:10.1080/00856401.2018.1419794. Accessed on 27 January 2025.

Oberoi, Harjot. 1992. "Brotherhood of the Pure: The Poetics and Politics of Cultural Transgression." *Modern Asian Studies* 26, no. 1: 157–97.

Pandey, Gyanendra. 1981. "Rallying around the Cow: Sectarian Strife in the Bhojpuri Region, c.1888–1917." In *Subaltern Studies II*, edited by Ranajit Guha, 1–95. New Delhi: Oxford University Press.

Pinney, Christopher. 1997. "The Nation (Un) Pictured? 'Chromolithography' and Popular Politics in India." *Critical Inquiry* 23, no. 4: 834–67.

Robb, Peter. 1986. "The Challenge of Gau Mata: British Policy and Religious Change in India, 1880–1916." *Modern Asian Studies* 20, no. 2: 285–319.

Sehgal, Meera. 2009. "The Veiled Feminist Ethnographer: Fieldwork among Women of India's Hindu Right." In *Women Fielding Danger: Negotiating Ethnographic Identities in Field Research*, edited by M.K. Huggins and M.L. Glebbeek, 325–52. Lanham: Rowman & Littlefield Publishers.

Simoons, Frederick J., Frederick I. Simoons and Deryck O. Lodrick. 1981. "Background to Understanding the Cattle Situation of India: The Sacred Cow Concept in Hindu Religion and Folk Culture." *Zeitschrift für Ethnologie* 106: 121–37.

Singh, Asha. 2017. "Cow, Backwardness and Bahujan Women." Round Table India. https://www.roundtableindia.co.in/cow-backwardness-and-bahujan-women/ Accessed on 24 April 2025.

Srivatsan, R. 2014. *Seva, Saviour and State: Caste Politics, Tribal Welfare and Capitalist Development.* New Delhi: Routledge.

Stacey, Judith. 1988. "Can There Be a Feminist Ethnography." *Women's Studies International Forum* 11, no. 1: 21–27.

Schwandner-Sievers, Stephanie. 2009. "Securing 'Safe Spaces': Field Diplomacy in Albania and Kosovo." In *Women Fielding Danger: Negotiating Ethnographic Identities in Field Research*, edited by M.K. Huggins and M.L. Glebbeek, 325–52. Lanham: Rowman & Littlefield Publishers.

van der Veer, Peter. 1994. *Religious Nationalism: Hindus and Muslims in India.* Berkeley: University of California Press.

Virdee, Gurmit Singh. 2006. "Labour of Love: Karseva at Darbar Sahib's Amrit Sarover." *Sikh Formations: Religion, Culture, Theory* 1, no. 1: 13–28.

Yang, Anand. 1980. "Sacred Symbol and Sacred Space in Rural India: Community Mobilisation in the 'Anti-Cow Killing' Riot of 1893." *Comparative Studies in Society and History* 22, no. 4: 576–96.

TEN

Gender and Hindutva: A Study of Jnana Prabodhini Women[1]

Swati Dyahadroy

The rapid and fascinating transformation of women as subjects and as a category from invisibility to visibility over the past two decades has drawn scholarly attention. Such transformation, instead of being lauded as a great success, is often considered to be a problem (Tharu and Niranjana 1994). 'Issues rendered critical by feminism are now being invested in by projects that seem to endorse and extend feminist demands yet harness them to initiatives that an egalitarian feminism would find unacceptable' (ibid., 93). The emergence of new forms of politics, the acceptance of neoliberal policies, and an increasing influence of Hindu nationalist groups over the nation in post-2000 India have raised new and complicated political and cultural questions. A rich body of work that explores the complex relationship between globalisation, Hindutva, and gender emphasises the need to understand the success of the Hindu-right by paying close attention to its changing strategies of mobilisation. Contemporary Hindutva is not only popular but also significantly different from its earlier forms and constituents (Hansen and Roy 2022).

This chapter examines the Hindu-right strategy of collective mobilisation and ideological engineering (Hansen and Roy 2022) from the perspective of gender (Basu and Sarkar 2022). It studies Jnana Prabodhini, a Hindu-right organisation located in Pune, by focussing on its women's wing and the work done by middle

[1] I would like to thank my colleagues and friends at the department of Women and Gender Studies for their comments and sustained support. I would like to thank my students of the course on Gender and Nation/ Nationalism: Focus on Everyday Lives, with whom I developed my arguments on gender and Hindutva. Forever indebted to Sharmila.

class women members. These women work untiringly to expand the base of the establishment with absolute belief in its cause. A close analysis of how and why organisations such as Prabodhini appeal to women by allowing them the opportunity to offer *seva* (service) to the nation, reveals how gender ideology is developed and reimagined, recast and expanded to strengthen the vision and the programmes of Hindu-right organisations. Moreover, an exploration of the contemporary mobilisation of urban middle-class women in Prabodhini enables an understanding of their perceptions of *stree-shakti*[2] and offers insights into the vital role they play in the wide proliferation of Hindutva.

A proper understanding of the rapid transformations in economic, sociocultural and political processes in India since the 1990s requires close attention to the specific intersections of caste, class, gender and community as well as the sustained work of different fractions of Hindu nationalist groups. The work of Hindu nationalist organisations in the fields of health, education and culture through which Hindutva has widened and consolidated its base, has involved active and wide participation of women; particularly middle-class women. By offering women a space to express themselves and find a meaningful and constructive way to serve the Hindu *rashtra* (nation-state) by reinforcing Hindu roots and culture, organisations such as the Prabodhini confer on women an agentive role where they can make themselves visible as valuable citizens and make use of individual opportunities opened up by the neoliberal economy.

Jnana Prabodhini is based in Pune, a city known for its orthodoxy and predominance of Brahmins, a second home for the Rashtriya Swayamsevak Sangh (RSS) as well as a growing urban middle class struggling to be modern and neoliberal while being worried about rootlessness. Prabodhini offers them a space

[2] The idea of *stree-shakti* was proposed as an Indian/Hindu alternative to women's power derived from Hindu culture with the idea of women's emancipation rooted in Hindu traditions by the women's wing of different Hindutva organisations and was further developed by the women's wing of Jnana Prabodhini by taking references of Sarda Devi and Sister Nivedita.

that is distinct from the orthodox RSS, yet one that sustains and bolsters their Hindu identity. Prabodhini is representative of the changing strategies of mobilisation that account for the growing legitimacy of the Hindu-right from the local to the national level.

My exploration of the women's wing of the Prabodhini will locate it in the larger context of the work of other right-wing women's organisations such as the Durga Wahini and Rashtra Sevika Samiti, and in conversations with scholarship on them (Basu 1993; Bachetta 2004; Sarkar 1993; Tyagi 2022; Bedi 2016; Warrier 2003). That will provide an overview of the continuities in ways these organisations have addressed women through particular constructions of the Hindu woman and the constitutive role she can play in building the Hindu nation, as well as the difference represented by organisations such as the Prabodhini. The discontinuity/difference that makes Prabodhini unique is the fine blending of scientific Hindutva, discipline, and critical acceptance of modern values where women create a space where they feel relevant for society and the nation while being rooted in the 'private' familial space as wives.

The first section of the chapter offers a brief introduction to the establishment, ideological roots and the location of Jnana Prabodhini; the second section examines the programmes and activities of the women's wing of the Prabodhini that includes the magazine *Samatol* published by the Stree Shakti Prabodhan group, which plays an important role in the consolidation, dissemination and formulation of the ideology. The final section analyses how the ideas of *stree-shakti* (woman's power), seva/service, and the construction of gender are woven together in the ideology and programmes of the women's wing that serve to construct a strong Hindu nation.

Jnana Prabodhini: Its Organisation, Ideology and Practices

'Jnana Prabodhini: A New Experiment in Education' was founded in 1962 by Dr Vinayak Pendse (1916–86), popularly known as Appa Pendse, who was a member of the Rashtriya Swayamsevak

Sangh till the time he was expelled from it.[3] Appa Pendse was born in a Chitpavan Brahmin[4] family of Pune. His indoctrination and training in the RSS inspired him to launch Jnana Prabodhini as an experimental education that was to groom generations of leaders to serve the cause of the Hindu nation-state.

The work and the values cherished by Prabodhini acknowledge the influence of the ideology of Swami Shradhnanda, Vivekananda, Sri Aurobindo and Sister Nivedita. The founder was motivated by Vivekananda's idea of placing importance on spiritual Hindutva rather than political Hindutva, and focused mainly on the organisation of dispersed Hindus. The early influences of Vivekananda and Savarkar together with that of Bal Gangadhar Tilak as a national leader and his training in *balchar sena* (a form of drill, established by Lala Lajpat Rai) and later in the RSS, helped Pendse to construct his own idea of Hindutva and the Hindu nation. He wanted to create an organisation that would make Hindus and Hindutva homogenous, disciplined and dynamic, and could form proper leaders of the Hindu nation.

The ideas and different projects undertaken by the Prabodhini are not only diverse in terms of the constituency it wants to address, but carefully worked out to mark its distinctiveness from other educational institutions as well as other Hindutva organisations. This is reflected in the very architecture of the edifice of Jnana Prabodhini – with Hindu temple spires constantly punctuating the view, onlookers are reminded that it is a temple of learning in contrast to other educational structures. The school was one of the first in Pune to be affiliated with the Central Board of Secondary Education. The IQ testing for admissions created the image of a 'scientifically oriented' school with stated aims and ideology and

---

[3] He was expelled from RSS as he distributed milk powder at the time of influenza against the orders of the chief and he had differences of opinion in terms of how to expand the activities of sangha post-ban period. Of course, Prabodhini in later period was doing collaborative activities with RSS and Samiti, but always kept its identity separate from both.

[4] Chitpavan is a sub-caste amongst Brahmins who trace their lineage to Parshuram.

as a school for 'gifted' children as against others where admissions were based either on a first-come-first-serve basis or on political/ social influence or on donations. The distinctive markers of the school were its insistence on speaking 'pure Marathi' (*namaskar* instead of 'hello'; *udwahak* instead of 'elevator' and *vastu* for 'building'), and *churidar, kurta* and *Gandhi topi* for boys and *churidar, kurta, dupatta* for girls as school uniform. Prabodhini introduced compulsory training in traditional physical activities (three times a week) and extracurricular activities that were related to the civic life of the city. They included offering voluntary service during Ganesh *utsav*, performing *barchya* (a combination of folk Lezim and drill) during the Ganesh idol immersion[5] procession, selling crackers, participating in relief work at the time of natural disasters, organising summer and winter camps for students during holidays, and study tours to rural areas or the northeast region of India. Its geographical location in Pune and within Pune, in Sadashiv Peth, with a concentration of upper caste Hindus, especially Chitpavan Brahmins, is significant.

Prabodhini's founding in the 1960s coincided with the post-ban revival of the RSS.[6] Internal debates on its vision and plans for expansion, mainly in terms of how to make it relevant in post-independent India, were underway. This was also the period when citizens were hopeful about building a better future for themselves, expectations from the state were high, and the burden of the colonial past pre-empted any critique of the state. The establishment of Prabodhini may be located at the intersection of diverse factors – the tensions within the RSS in the post-ban period over how to expand it and whether the RSS should be an umbrella

[5] Over the last decade, the participation of men and women from middle-class upper castes in the Ganesh immersion procession and beating drums has increased considerably. There is overwhelming support for women's participation in it, seemingly occupying the masculine space and task (for instance beating drums/riding the horse/driving a bike, particularly a Bullet).

[6] The RSS was banned in February 1948 following the assasination of Mahatma Gandhi by Nathuram Godse, one of its members and a Chitpavan Brahmin, on 30 January 1948. It was lifted in July 1949.

organisation; the strong presence of anti-caste movements; the anti-Brahmin riots following the assassination of Gandhi forcing the migration, especially to Pune, of Chitpavan Brahmins from Konkan; Dr Ambedkar's conversion to Buddhism along with his Dalit followers; and the Brahmin–Maratha alliance at the time of the Samyukta Maharashtra movement.[7] Another crucial factor that influenced the establishment of the organisation was the unease of the Brahmins with changes in the sociocultural world, especially the consolidation of the Maratha educational elites and the increasing presence of educated Dalits, as a result of development and special policies for the deprived classes and castes.

In the late 1960s, the Nehruvian model of development was seriously questioned by the new social movements inspired by socialist and Marxist ideals, while the 1970s witnessed a severe interrogation of the nation-state and of the Indian National Congress in the aftermath of Indira Gandhi's autocratic decision to impose a state of national emergency. This was also a time when the Hindu-right was slowly gaining presence in the political mainstream. The Prabodhini was launched with an explicit aim of all-round development of physical, mental and spiritual qualities of students, especially the 'gifted' ones:

> Jnana Prabodhini is not a common level educational institution imparting education based on textbooks... Development of virtuous behaviour, truth in action, studiousness, industriousness, nationalistic character, nationalistic spirit, pride in golden Indian cultural past, pride in tradition, spontaneity, self-motivation etc are the main tasks of Jnana Prabodhini. (JP 1972)

Prabodhini believes that through education alone, one can create leaders who will accept the role of being selfless servants of the Hindu nation and work with a purpose to build this nation-state. With this ideological base and stated aims, Prabodhini's first activity – *Prabodhshala* – was introduced in 1962 for boys selected

[7] The Samyaukta Maharashtra movement was aimed at creating a separate Marathi state with Mumbai as its capital. It faced violent repression by the state.

through IQ testing. After seven years of experimenting, a full-time school for the selected 'intellectually gifted' male students was started in 1969. In 1972, *Prabodhshala* started a special course for selected girls. The participants of this course pushed the demand for a full-time school for girls which was materialised in 1975 (International Women's Year). Prabodhini, however, has not been co-educational. By the mid-1980s, the school came to occupy an important place on the educational map of Pune on account of the concurrence of the aims of the school and aspirations of the growing middle classes to acquire skills of scientific leadership to build a Hindu nation.

The four volumes published by the Probodhini that review its activities and explain its ideology, plans and practices geared towards adapting to new challenges and contemporary demands, give a clear picture of its vision and programmes. Founded upon Vivekananda's philosophy of strengthening the spiritual basis of individual and social life, the Prabodhini lays stress on collective and individual meditation/prayer as a way to enhance the inner power of the individual and his capacity to work and think. It pays attention to organising youth power, encouraging young men to serve the nation, and helping people in times of natural or human-made disaster.

Appa Pendse gave clear instructions to the enrolled youth on the vows to take:

> (1) I shall not feel content if I do not do anything spectacular. Therefore, a) I will not accept anything without labouring for it, b) I will not postpone the work to tomorrow, c) I will not pass on my work to someone else, and d) I need to make progress/grow. (2) My life will be incomplete till I excel in life. Hence, I will not compromise on quality. (3) My life will not be happy till I get new ideas, so I need to get new ideas every day. (4) I will be flexible to accept the changes in my surroundings and to retain them for most of my life. For that, I will a) meditate every day, and b) in all my work, I will think about the well-being of others. (JP 2021)

Along with running the school, Prabodhini conducted research and development work that included setting-up manufacturing units in rural areas. Together, these activities consolidated its ideology of constructing and serving a Hindu nation.

It is time now to turn to the Prabodhini's work directed at women: its programme 'Samvadini' that aims at developing *stree-shakti* to consolidate a strong Hindu nation culturally and educationally; and its magazine *Samatol* published from the 1990s. By means of an analysis of the content of some issues of *Samatol*, I wish to highlight how texts produced by individuals offer visions of the ideals and values that a group believes in, allowing the researcher thereby to move beyond the world of individuals (Leavy 2007). The attempt is to comprehend the construction of a new Hindu woman, and her work and purpose in life and through that understand Hindutva's gender.

Samvadini: From Self-awareness, Self-confidence to Self-respect: Unravelling Hindutva's Gender

The programme for women started when a group of women in their mid-forties or early fifties, rooted in their families, had an overwhelming feeling that they were not utilising their capacity to the full, especially in terms of what they could contribute to society. The society, conceived completely as Hindu, was to be enriched by the work of moral and social construction of dedicated women. The 'urge of these women to serve the society paved the way for Samvadini' (Lavlekar 2021, 36). Samvadini was formed and developed as a platform for women who wanted to serve society through meaningful activities, including singing devotional songs collectively, and assembling women who were not alumni of Prabodhini. The initial work had begun from 1990, when women active in other programmes of the Prabodhini had made efforts to organise women and young-adolescent girls to give shape to their nascent idea of *stree-shakti*. Based on the idea of inner-awakening derived from Hindu cultural roots, proponents of *stree-shakti* sought to forge alliances with different groups working on women's issues. A short-lived group named *samwedana* (empathy) was started, and lectures and recitations for women were organised during the religious festival of Navratri.[8]

Samvadini [9] started in Pune in January 2000 when a group of women associated with Prabodhini started meeting once a month to discuss social issues and/or do field visits to a specific area. By 2010, Samvadini had a total of 13 projects, 9 of which were socially oriented and others designed to develop the skills of its members. A detailed review of the activities indicates that the women's wing has developed its own distinct identity and they contributed to Prabodhini's ideological constitution. Samvadini has now spread to rural and semi-urban areas outside Pune and some parts of Mumbai and Solapur.

Women members of Samvadini are part of Jnana Prabodhini and the two are structured hierarchically (Bacchetta and Power 2002). Most members of Samvadini are married and continue to live with their families, unlike some other right-wing organisations where primarily single/unmarried/unattached women ask other women to be 'good wives' in their conjugal life. It remains to be seen whether the participation of good wives, such as that of the Samvadini women, in social work and Hindu nation-building has brought about any significant shift in the gender division of roles within middle-class families.

Different activities of the Samvadini include monthly meetings that discuss personality development, health, life skills and social skills as four pillars of the organisation; running a *Wall Magazine* directed at generating health-related awareness among rural women; *Samatol*, a women's magazine initiated by the *stree-shakti* Prabodhan group and taken over by Samvadini; and engaging in dialogue with adolescents by means of workshops that offer lessons on sexuality and emphasise the importance of equality between the

[8] The festival which is celebrated to honour Hindu goddess Durga. In recent years in Maharashtra this festival is also celebrated as a symbol of women's power.

[9] The name indicates that the forum aimed at developing communicative leadership by allowing all participants to offer their opinion before a decision is taken centrally.

sexes. These workshops do not only target adolescents of different age groups, but also train a large number of workers to conduct the workshops. Counselling groups for adolescents emerged as a follow-up of the workshops with adolescents. In addition, children from underprivileged groups were brought within the range of Samvadini's activities through Palavi; a programme that provides opportunities for children to get additional training through extracurricular activities that indoctrinate them with Hindu culture. The constructed Hindu ritual of *vidyavrat* was started in 2011 as a part of the agenda to 'Change the face of the nation' by introducing school children to Indian/Hindu culture; develop their physical, mental and intellectual skills along with their souls to serve the nation-state; and activities to develop different skills of growing children, and prepare them to become good citizens of the Hindu state. Alongside, there are study tours, meetings and annual gatherings that allow the children, adolescents and the organisers to meet their counterparts from different parts of India, discuss contemporary issues and pressing problems in an attempt to find solutions and strengthen the Hindu nation. These meetings also serve as tools for the recruitment and training of volunteers/*sevaks* for Hindu-right organisations. Weekly prayers allow all members of the Samvadini to come together, meditate and introspect.

Even though the Samvadini is structured hierarchically within the Prabodhini, Lavlekar, one of its main protagonists claims that:

> Samvadini is a thought and action-based movement. Every participant is working on an entirely voluntary basis with a sense of social responsibility. There is no hierarchy and everyone is an equal member. This work is expanding, just like a candle lighting another candle. Samvadini has come up as a platform for using women's hidden power for social good by developing their leadership abilities through changing their self-image and awakening their sense of self. (Lavlekar 2021, 43)

This overview of the activities of the women's wing underlines that this seemingly local organisation is not only leaving its mark on the social and cultural map of Pune, but is also playing an important role in making Hindutva a norm rather than the exception (Hansen and Roy 2022), by extending its ideology and activities among women, adolescents and children of underprivileged groups and of rural and semi-urban areas of Maharashtra. The firm belief in *sangathan* (association) of selfless volunteers, dedicated to serve the cause of a Hindu nation-state and society, enables Samvadini women to assume a central role in diffusing the ideology of Hindutva among individuals, families and communities, and of making themselves visible without overstepping the norms and boundaries set for good wives.

The activities of Samvadini women suggest that they are neither external nor an appendix to the main organisation. In a manner similar to women members of other right-wing organisations, they have created an important space for themselves within Prabodhini and work in conjunction with other right-wing organisations across Maharashtra.[10] The participation of women sustains the claim of right-wing organisations that they are not orthodox or regressive in nature, even though 'the gendered fractionalisation of Hindu nationalist discourse is ultimately a function of its unifying praxis' (Bacchetta 2004, 52).

'*Samatol*': *Stree-Shakti* and its *Sevak*

The *Samatol* magazine, published by the Stree-Shakti Prabodhan Group, was initially intended for internal circulation as a mouthpiece for the platform and a medium through which the idea of *stree-shakti*, women's power/empowerment of women, could be discussed and disseminated.

> 'Stree-Shakti Prabodhan' is a priority of the Jnana Prabodhini. This is a movement and wants to reach to all sections of the society. Stree

[10] The women's wing of Prabodhini collaborates with the Pune unit of Rashtra Sevika Samiti, Drushti: Stree Shakti Prabodhan, and Baya Karve Women's Studies and Research Centre, Pune. Activities such as seminars, lecture series and small surveys are collectively conducted. These organisations are collectively building the base and ideological foundation for right-wing women.

> shakti Prabodhan is 'behavioural pattern, way of thinking' … Stree Shakti Prabodhan is fundamental thought, what is the perspective of women about themselves, what it needs to be, at the same time how men look at themselves and about women, what it could be, what changes are required … Stree shakti needs to work towards that. Women and men as individuals and as a group need to make some fundamental changes in attitude and we need to make an effort. (*Samatol* 1998)

A series of three articles and other regular writings by the key founder member Anagha Lavlekar of the Stree-Shakti Prabodhan, and other articles by important members reflect the care taken in dealing with the arguments of feminist scholars from within and outside India, in order to reinforce and uphold Hindu ideals on *stree-shakti* emphasised by Vivekananda, Aurobindo, Savarkar and Sister Nivedita.

The ideology of *stree-shakti*, as developed through *Samatol*, combines theories on the origins of women's subordination with the concept of their 'inner self-development.' It draws from Sarada Devi's (addressed as Mataji) teachings, which elucidate that the differences between the sexes and the discrimination based on them are not natural. It also incorporates Betty Friedan's neoliberal position, which advocates going beyond gender to analyse contemporary issues, such as women in the workforce, pay disparity, and the challenges women face in balancing domestic responsibilities with professional work. Additionally, it refers to the international NGO categorisation of strategic and practical gender needs, to further consolidate its position on the condition of women. For *Samatol*, even though both strategic and practical needs are equally important, fulfilment of strategic needs gains priority as a necessary pre-condition for *stree-shakti* (Lavlekar 2000). Strategic needs include an understanding of the diverse problems and challenges faced by women at present, and a discussion of the problems with a wider audience. *Samatol* analyses gender discrimination, tries to explain the origin of such discrimination, and comments on the situation of women workers in different sectors. 'Overwhelming feeling is that as women started working injustice is done to children but probably answer to this is changes/adjustment in the familial responsibilities between men and women' (Lele 2006, 6). After reviewing different sectors, it suggests that voluntary organisations or organisations based on the no-profit principle are best suitable for women since they offer the best opportunities for *seva*. '... the flexible and family-oriented work-sector is the need of women that can be facilitated by this voluntary sector'. (ibid.)

At the same time, special articles published by *Samatol* consider pressing contemporary issues such as domestic violence, sex selection, good touch/bad touch, love jihad, challenges in parenting, motherhood, marriage, changing family structures, women's contribution to different sectors and effects of globalisation, among others. Reports of visits/study tours to different parts of India by members of Samvadini individually and collectively form an important part of the magazine: they contribute to the consolidation of Hindu identity which goes beyond the local/regional boundaries to bind this otherwise 'imagined' heterogenous community into a unified, concrete Hindu community. They also help build a network with other institutions and individuals, generate confidence among members that the organisation and its programmes form a part of the broader agenda of building a Hindu nation and encourage them to aspire to serve society and achieve a sense of fulfilment without challenging gendered norms.

Another set of articles focuses on ideals of *stree-shakti* propounded by Vivekananda, Sister Nivedita and Savarkar along with a discussion of contemporary challenges and possible answers/solutions that can be found in their writings. These articles not only aim at developing an informed opinion about important issues; they underline the significance of Hindu 'traditional' ideals in dealing with problems of contemporary times. It is interesting to note that articles and editorials refrain from making any declarative statements or offering seemingly regressive statements; they persuade the reader about the openness and seriousness of their effort. This becomes very evident in the exploration of themes on family and motherhood where one expects a possible subscription to a glorification of both. A close reading reveals that there is an ambiguity in accepting the critique put forth by feminist scholars and struggles and suspicion is expressed about the validity of such critiques in the Indian (read Hindu) context. Editorials and articles stress the need to develop a valid Indian/ Hindu thinking about contemporary problems by returning to Hindu roots and effecting a change in the situation. For instance, while critiquing the family and violence against women within it, an editorial raises the concern about increasing cases of violence against women and the whole issue is discussed in the context of tradition and modernity.

> In the last 125 years, there was rapid transformation in the status of women. Mindset/psyche of women has changed from being conscious of the self to find self-respect and social status, women moved from being nowhere on the horizon to being at the forefront. However, after being enslaved for long when freedom has been granted it is obvious that one will take time to find balance ... One can fall into bad habits. There is a growth in violence against men by women ... But with time it is guaranteed that the society which is beautiful and where one can live fearlessly will be created... (Lavlekar 2012)

This indicates that *Samvadini* as a group is inclined towards maintaining balance (*samatol*) by displaying an acceptance of the gradual change in women's thought and action but insisting on the necessity of temperate behaviour on their part. This was conscientiously argued in other articles on the theme of family and motherhood. A close reading of these articles helps us understand the constant negotiation of 'tradition' and modernity, Hindu and Western culture by women members of the Prabodhini. The discussion on motherhood avoids glorification and extends its social and cultural context by highlighting the significance of the mother in the raising of virtuous citizens who will contribute to the project of building a Hindu nation-state. Thus, orthodox ideas about motherhood which consolidate patriarchal ideas are ostensibly denounced, while they are charged with the responsibility of raising children by instilling pride in Hindu culture along with modern education. Such prescriptions for women reinforce and extend RSS leader M. S. Golwalkar's idea that mothers need to set an example by putting the needs of the family and society above everything else and by conforming to Hindu beliefs and practices (Basu and Sarkar 2022). Mothers are conferred with the task of reproducing the nation and society biologically and strengthening it through their inner power – *matru-shakti.* The idea that mothers are not only nurturant but can also build the nation by promoting Indian/Hindu culture is consolidated through various essays and articles.

> 'The institution of family which is the soul of Indian (Hindu) culture is slowly collapsing. The meaning attached to women's liberty and freedom is changing. On this background professing 'mother's power' (Matru-shakti) is the need of the hour. (Kalyani 2011, 3)

> 'Women are excellent housewives, ideal mothers but they also perform the role of good researcher, scholar, teacher…manager, friend…If we know this, we need to kindle the inner strength of women and need to enlighten them...' (ibid.)

The emphasis on *matru-shakti* expresses how the inner strength of mothers can contribute to the construction of a healthy, solid Hindu nation. Real-life mothers who have reproduced national heroes/protagonists such as Shivaji/Vivekanand/Ramkrushna Paramhans as well as mothers who are fighting against all odds – financial, social, cultural – to support their children are valorised. Motherhood is intertwined with the interests of the nation, community and society. Such projections offer women a space to enhance the self (that goes beyond the self-centred idea of the individual) on account of the qualities of generosity, nurturance and care they possess and their ability to work selflessly that can be channelled into service of the poor and needy and in instilling a sense of pride in society.

The activities of the Prabodhini and the articles in *Samatol* give Prabodhini women an opportunity to reconfigure *stree-shakti* that in turn provides them with a political purpose and identity that far surpasses their role of a housewife. This opportunity to be relevant to society reconfigures the domestic space (Basu and

Sarkar 2022). Prabodhini women, like Samiti women, practice Hindutva in their everyday lives and disseminate it in society, the workplace, the neighbourhood, and their programmes and actions. The centrality of women in right-wing organisations often stands in contrast to the relative insignificance of women in other political or non-political organisations.

Prabodhini women are another example of how Hindutva provides women a space to seamlessly unite the domestic, public and political and to play an agential and critical role in promoting Hindutva for a particular section of urban, middle-class women with transnational exposure.

Right-Wing Women: Activism and Agency

In conclusion, it is important to note that an exploration of the role of Prabodhini women offers insights into the form and substance of an iteration of Hindutva which appears less orthodox. The developmental narrative syncs well with the neoliberal era of choice. It leaves an individual with the feeling that she can and does play an agentive role. Prabodhini allows women to feel relevant for the family and society and retain their individuality as an educated, cultured self, committed to the welfare of the community and the nation. Women in right-wing groups in general and Prabodhini women in particular contribute to upending assumptions about women's role in Hindutva organisations and their role in popularising Hindutva by seamlessly stitching it onto the fabric of everyday social and cultural life, normalising Hindutva for different class groups. These women reimagine the binaries of public–private, local–global, national–international, and reconfigure it to suit neoliberal times. They impel us to reframe old questions of whether they contradict the ideology of Hindutva or whether they play a decisive role in spreading Hindutva.

Prabodhini women, like other women in right-wing organisations, are promoting the idea of *stree-shakti* which can be read as an attempt to propose a solution to the dilemma of advocating a greater involvement of Hindu women in furthering

Hindutva without overriding their primary responsibility towards domestic life and family (Saluja 2022). The participation of middle-class women is significant as this class has been vital in the project of nation-building from the beginning. In a capitalist society, the middle class is not only an amorphous and large group but also plays a politically and ideologically important role (Sridharan 2011). The Prabodhini women represent a particular section of the middle class that specialises in the practice, regeneration and legitimation of Hindutva by means of varied social and cultural programmes (Deshpande 2003).

The legitimacy that Hindu-right-wing women have created and the legitimacy generated for middle-class women's participation in the project of Hindu nation-building, needs to be located in the context of the hegemonic role assumed by the middle class in the developmental state. Prabodhini eases the anxiety of middle classes of the neoliberal era about preserving social status and cultural hegemony while accessing the benefits associated with liberalisation (Fernandes 2006). Women in organisations like Prabodhini display less concern about the control exercised on them by their organisation and have less friction with it. Unlike women in other right-wing organisations, they are less prone to 'militarise' or establish themselves through 'violent' means. The insistence on a seemingly studied approach and a constant reminder about the importance of constructive work for the society allows women to assume their role as cultural reproducers of a Hindu nation and advocates of self-disciplining for the development of their inner strength, *stree-shakti*. While this grants Prabodhini great control over women, it also makes its women members feel that they have the autonomy to decide and act out of their own volition.

References

Bacchetta, Paola, and Margaret Power, eds. 2002. *Right-Wing Women: From Conservatives to Extremists Around the World*. New York: Routledge.

Bacchetta, Paola. 2004. *Gender in the Hindu Nation: RSS Women as Ideologues*. New Delhi: Women Unlimited.

Basu, Amrita. 1993. "Feminism Inverted: The Real Women and Gendered Imagery of Hindu Nationalism." In *Woman and the Hindu Right: A Collection of Essays*, edited by Tanika Sarkar and Urvashi Butalia, 158–80. New Delhi: Kali For Women.

———. 1999. "Hindutva Women's activism in India: The Question it Raises." In *Resisting the Sacred and the Secular: Women's Activism and Politicised Religion in South Asia*, edited by Patricia Jeffery and Amrita Basu, 167–84. New Delhi: Kali for Women.

Basu, Amrita, and Tanika Sarkar. 2022. *Women, Gender, and Religious Nationalism*. New Delhi: Cambridge University Press.

Baviskar, Amita, and Raka Ray. 2011. *Elite and Everyman: The Cultural Politics of the Indian Middle Class*. New Delhi: Routledge.

Beckerlegge, Gwilym. 2003. "Saffron and *Seva*: The Rashtriya Swayamsevak Sangh's Appropriation of Swami Vivekananda." In *Hinduism in Public and Private: Reform, Hindutva, Gender and Sampradaya*, edited by Antony Copley, 31–66. New Delhi: Oxford University Press.

Bedi, Tarini. 2016. *The Dashing Ladies of Shiv Sena: Political Matronage in Urbanizing India*. New York: State University of New York Press.

Bhole, Bhalchandra, and Kishor Bedkihal, eds. 2002. *Badalta Maharashtra* (Marathi). Mumbai: Lokvangmay Gruha.

Chaudhuri, Maitrayee, ed. 2004. *Feminism in India*. New Delhi: Kali for Women.

Copley, Antony. 2003. "Introduction: Debating Indian Nationalism and Hindu Religious Belief." In *Hinduism in Public and private- Reform Hindutva, Gender and Sampraday*, edited by A. Copley, 1–27. New Delhi: Oxford University Press.

Deshpande, Satish. 2003. *Contemporary India: A Sociological View*. Viking New Delhi.

Fernandes, Leela. 2006. *India's New Middle Class: Democratic Politics in an Era of Economic Reform* (NED-New edition). University of Minnesota Press. http://www.jstor.org/stable/10.5749/j.ctttsjgt. Accessed on 23 January 2025.

Gokhale, Jayashree. 1990. "Dalit Consciousness in Maharashtra." In *Dominance and State Power in Modern India: Decline of Social Order* (Vol II), edited by F. Frankel and M. S. A. Rao, 212–77. New Delhi: Oxford University Press.

Hansen, T., and Srirupa Roy. 2022. "What is New about New Hindutva." In *Saffron Republic: Hindu Nationalism and State Power in India*, edited by Thomas Blom Hansen and Srirupa Roy, 1–24. New Delhi: Cambridge University Press.

Hansen, T. 2004. "Politics as Permanent Performance: The Production of Political Authority in the Locality." In *The Politics of Cultural Mobilisation in India*, edited by J. Zavos, A. Wyatt and V. Hewitt, 19–36. New Delhi: Oxford University Press.

Iveković, Rada and Julie Mostov, eds. 2002. *From Gender to Nation*. New Delhi: Zuban.

Jeffery, Patricia and Amrita Basu, eds. 1999. *Resisting the Sacred and the Secular: Women's Activism and Politicised Religion in South Asia*. New Delhi: Kali for Women.

Jnana Prabodhini: A Novel Experiment in Education (JP). 1972. Volume I. Pune: Jnana Prabodhini.

———. 1980. Volume II. Pune: Jnana Prabodhini.

———. 1988. Volume III (Marathi). Pune: Jnana Prabodhini.

———. 2021. Volume IV, Part IV (Marathi). Pune: Jnana Prabodhini.

Kalyani, A. 2011. "Samwad Matrushaktishi" (Marathi). *Samatol*, Year 2, Issue No. 3, pp. 3–4.

Lavlekar, A. 2000. "Shiva aani Shakti ek Anawashyak Sangharsha" (Marathi). *Samatol*, Year 3. Issue No. 4, pp. 5–6.

———. 2012. "Samwad" (Marathi). *Samatol*, Year 3, Issue No. 3, pp. 5–6.

———. 2021. "Iwalese Rop" (Marathi). *Jnana Prabodhini: A Novel Experiment in Education*, Vol. 4, Part 4, pp. 35–43. Pune: Prabodh Udyog.

Lele, Y. 2006. "Bhasheteel Swadeshi" (Marathi). *Samatol*, Year 10, Issue No.1, pp. 3–5.

Leavy, Patricia Lina. 2007. "The Feminist Practice of Content Analysis." In *Feminist Research Practice: A Primer*, edited by S. N. Hess-Biber and P. L. Leavy, 223–48. New Delhi: SAGE Publications.

Patel, Sujata. 2018. "Seva, Sangathana and Gurus: Service and the Making of the Hindu Nation." In *Religion, Community and Development: Changing Contours of Politics and Policy in India*, edited by Gurpreet Mahajan, Surinder S. Jodhka, 102–28. New Delhi: Routledge.

Samatol. 1998 (Diwali Special). Year No. 2, Issue No. 3.

Sangari, K. 2007. "Shaping Pressures and Symbolic Horizons: The Women's Movement in India." In *At the Cutting Edge: Essays in Honour of Kumari Jayawardena*, edited by De Mel Neloufer and Thuvchadran S., 36–67. New Delhi: Women Unlimited.

Sarkar, Tanika. 1991. "The Woman as Communal Subject: Rashtrasevika Samiti and Ram Janmabhoomi Movement." *Economic and Political Weekly* 26, no. 35: 2057–62.

———. 1995. "Heroic Women, Mother Goddesses: Family and Organization in Hindutva Politics." In *Woman and the Hindu Right: A Collection of*

Essays, edited by T. Sarkar and U. Butalia, 181–215. New Delhi: Kali for Women.
Sridharan, E. 2011. "The Growth and Sectoral Composition of India's Middle Classes: Their Impact on the Politics of Economic Liberalism." In *Elite and Everyman: The Cultural Politics of the Indian Middle Class*, edited by Amita Baviskar and Raka Ray, 27–57. New Delhi: Routledge.
Srivatsan, R. 2006. "Concept of 'Seva' and the 'Sevak' in the Freedom Movement." *Economic and Political Weekly* 41, no. 5: 427–38.
Tharu, Susie, and Tejaswini Niranjana. 1994. "Problems for a Contemporary Theory of Gender." *Social Scientist* 22, nos. 3/4: (March– April), 93–117.
Tyagi, Astha. 2022. "Spinning the Saffron Yarn: Lessons of Ideal Girlhood in Hindu Nationalist Storytelling." In *Women. Gender and Religious Nationalism*, edited by A. Basu and T. Sarkar, 125–46. New Delhi: Cambridge University Press.
Warrier, M. 2003. "The Mata Amritananadamayi Mission." In *Hinduism in Public and Private: Reform, Hindutva, Gender, and Sampraday*, edited by A. Copley, 254–89. New Delhi: Oxford University Press.
Yuval Davis, Nira. 1997. *Gender and Nation*. London: Sage.

ELEVEN

The Nation and the Hero

MANJIMA CHATTERJEE

'Modi ek insaan nahin, ek soch hai', says the character Narendra Modi in the hagiographical film *PM Narendra Modi*. Modi is not a human being, he is an idea. In the India of 2026, Modi is considered to be both man, and more-than-man: a *lauhapurush* (iron man) and a *yugpurush* (millennial man). Barely twenty-four years from being considered the architect of one of the worst massacres in recent history, he is projected as the son, the saviour and 'hero' of the Indian nation in the third decade of the third millennium. Like the proverbial duck, Modi has come through accusations of supporting riots, rape, bigotry, divisiveness and even bringing into question the very idea of India. Today, almost a decade into his rise to power, even as the economy tries to lurch back to recovery in the wake of the global COVID pandemic, Modi himself continues to be viewed as the only clear leader available to lead this nation of 1.4 billion and growing. How did this come to be?

In the course of this chapter, I chart the phenomenal rise of Narendra Modi as a media-led journey by way of newspaper reports and op-ed articles. In the years since his journey to stardom began, there have been several works – critical as well as hagiographic – that have sought to explain the so-called 'Modi wave'. The impact of these works cannot compare with the constant media limelight on Modi, the man. While TV channels and a large section of the print media have been openly fawning, some sections of print and Internet-based news agencies have tried to keep a critical eye on Modi and his cohort, focusing on the impacts of his government and his use of media to cover up his numerous gaffes and dreadful decision-making. When I was writing the first version of this chapter, Kashmir had been under curfew for over a month, with Article 370 repealed and its right to be deemed a state taken away. The impacts of demonetisation were being felt all around the country, and the steady economic slowdown which had had the country in its grip since 2012 was threatening to reach its nadir, with large industries laying off workers and the automobile industry, particularly, on the verge of a total collapse. Yet, in the face of all the joblessness and despair, Modi's star continued to shine brightly. Today, 6 years down, the Kashmir situation is not much improved, the country has seen one of the harshest, most terribly managed pandemic lockdowns followed by the world's third-highest death rate (particularly exacerbated during the cruel months of April and May 2021), and an economic situation that can only be described as struggling. Yet, Modi is the man who cannot but be celebrated for the many real and fictional achievements of the government, even as many other leaders drop by the wayside on account of their involvement in corruption, open bigotry and scandals.

What is most surprising to many liberals is how a large portion of India's population worships Modi as a 'hero'. This is not the hero of our epics, not the ones we expect to see in the movies, or the comic book superheroes that are increasingly taking over the world of entertainment (although there have been hilarious echoes of both in works by Modi *bhakts*), but rather a home-grown version of the nationalist hero who lives, breathes and speaks for the nation. He is a martyr to the cause of nationhood, having, by his own claims, sacrificed days and nights and a family life for it: this particular aspect endearing him to the undifferentiated masses – at least over 33% of the voting public across state boundaries, genders, and age or professional groupings – and reminding them to forgive all his lapses. In India, a society that has traditionally recognised and sought a balanced life between the four aspects of *dharma, artha, kama* and *moksha*, the man who opts out of family life cannot be corrupt, because he has already conquered the *maya* of earthly desires. In modern India, a society at the brink of overwhelming changes, when such a man speaks with authority, 'daring', so to speak, to lead by the dint of his self-proclaimed immense capability (and his 56-inch chest), he has no trouble becoming the people's, and the media's, hero.

Building up the hero

> 'Slogans can be uttered by all, but the "punch line" always belongs to only one man — the hero.'
>
> *Economic Times*, 24 December 2007

While he had been steadily climbing the ranks of the Bharatiya Janata Party (BJP) from the mid-1980s on, Narendra Modi came into the spotlight when he was appointed Chief Minister (CM) of Gujarat to handle the mess created by Keshubhai Patel's health-related absences in the face of the earthquake that hit Gujarat in 2001. An RSS (Rashtriya Swayamsevak Sangh) man through and through, he had a reputation as a strong organiser and a man with some degree of personal charisma. Less than a year into his rule, in February and March 2002, Gujarat was beset by riots which left up to 2000 people dead, and a further 3000 injured or missing. Many stories abounded about the nature of these riots, often denoted as an organised pogrom against the Muslims of the state. As the serving Chief Minister of Gujarat, Narendra Modi's career should have suffered a severe blow. Instead, this event became the catalyst that propelled his career in politics, giving him a voice and stature that no RSS man since L. K. Advani had enjoyed.

Soon after the riots, the BJP leadership made a big noise about investigating the events, with its serving Prime Minister, Atal Behari Vajpayee, advising Modi to uphold 'Raj Dharma' and 'not discriminate on the basis of caste, creed or religion' (Venkitesh 2013) while working on reparations following the riots. Soon, however, the criticism dwindled in favour of praise for the development work being done by the Chief Minister of Gujarat. Even as whispers confirmed the regime's ruthlessness and appetite for vendetta, the government received praise from many quarters for presenting an energetic, pro-development face focussed on ease of business.

One interesting fact about most of the praise coming Modi's way from 2002 up to the present time has been the consistent disregard for facts. At a conference in 2013, as shared by a member of the BJP's partner in the National Democratic Alliance, Janata Dal (U), Sivanand Tiwari, Modi talked vigorously about undoing the evil done by several years of Congress misrule in Gujarat and claimed for himself the success of Amul Dairy (established in 1946). This was something of a joke, especially because of the humiliation Modi had heaped on Verghese Kurien, the engineer who had saved Amul Dairy from closing down due to internal strife, on account of the latter's being widely perceived as a Congressman (Thakkar 2009). Tiwari also talked about the relentless use of PR machinery, which had successfully managed to highlight the 'Gujarat Development Model' by covering up several facts, such as the following:

> how the public health infrastructure in Gujarat is in a shambles; how the rate of decline in Gujarat's infant mortality rate is much lower than the national average; how project implementation has plummeted from 73 per cent in 2003 to 13 per cent in 2011; how Gujarat is lagging behind in per capita income, gross domestic product and foreign direct investment inflows; or the pathetic state of malnutrition and the gender ratio. (Venkitesh 2013)

The Press also came to recognise that most of the 'punch' in Modi's speeches came not from facts, but from well-constructed punchlines. In December 2007, the *Economic Times* ran an article with a sub-heading which read: '"Punch dialogue" now will have a new mascot – Gujarat CM Narendra Modi' (*ET* 2007). The article goes on to give examples of Modi's strategic use of statements that stick within the public domain. In one speech, it quotes Modi as saying: 'Main aaliya, maliya, jamaliya, mafia, tapori/ In sab ko Gujarat ki dharti se bhaga doonga.' (roughly, 'I will get rid of all the aaliya, maliya, jamaliya' – all surname endings associated with Muslims – 'mafia and rowdies from the land of Gujarat'). In the same speech, he draws attention to his 56-inch chest, which grants him the unique ability to take on his detractors with panache. In other words, he asserts himself as the new strongman of Hindutva, the alpha male all set to teach a lesson to anyone who poses any sort of challenge.

Of all the personal qualities that his supporters and rivals have, variously, admired and criticised, the 56-inch chest seems to hold a special place. First reported around the year 2007, Modi and his supporters have continued to mention this apparently impossible chest size as indicative of his strength and capability. For instance, in response to a challenge thrown at him by Samajwadi Party leader Mulayam Singh Yadav in 2014, Modi said, 'Do you know what making another Gujarat requires? ... It requires a *chhappan inch ki chhati* (56-inch chest)' (*Press Trust of India* 2016). In 2016, after the so-called surgical strikes in Uri and Pakistan, the Chief Minister of Madhya Pradesh, Shivraj Singh Chouhan, said that the 56-inch chest was now 100 inches wide! (*Financial Express* 2016). Most recently, in 2019, after the strikes on Balakot by the Indian Air Force, Modi's right-hand man, Amit Shah, went on record to say that, by this action, Modi had proven that he was a man with a 56-inch chest (*The Hindu* 2019).

The Hero as Sex Symbol

The magical 56 inches seem to have garnered Modi an unexpected boost in support from women, who, it is reported, are quite taken up by the attributes of Modi the man. His overt masculinity and tendency to be seen as a man's man seemed to make him even more attractive to the female electorate. Newspaper reports point out that women tend to see him as a powerful man who makes 'tough decisions' (*The Print* 2019) and has the strength to withstand their cost or impact. In all his oratory, his decision-making or actions, the one thing Modi does not display is doubt. He refuses to question his team's or his own speech or actions, preferring silence in murky areas, and constantly attacking some well-identified opponents. It seems that this 'decisive' posturing works well with female voters, who see him as a man who can be relied upon in crises. This ties in with female preference in the animal kingdom for powerful males who can potentially protect their families (*Terradaily* 2011). The conversation around the

56 inches adds to this overall image of machismo. But while the core reasons for Modi's popularity among women may be related to animal instincts, there are various paradoxical aspects of his life which ought to distance the female electorate. By his own admission, he abandoned his wife and maintained a distant, though respectful relationship with his mother as long as she was alive (mediated annually by TV cameras). He commands a troupe of loyal female party members whom he abandons at the slightest sign of trouble and, in a well-known incident, used the heft of state machinery to stalk the young daughter of a friend, apparently at the friend's own request (Simha 2019).

It is possible to argue that it is, in fact, these very attributes that make Modi attractive to women. They are interpreted as the attributes of a man who is virile, but controlled, and independent of female influence. In a country like India, where patriarchy continues to dominate thought and mediate private and public spaces alike, where women continue to be blamed for inviting rape and turning men gay, among other things, this is hardly a revelation. In a country where, moreover, women are increasingly turning out to vote, with over 65% of women voting in the general elections of 2014 and over 66% in 2019, it makes sense to woo the conservative female voter (Pachauri 2019).

Accordingly, the government since 2014 has put out schemes that target women, particularly in rural areas. The Ujjwala scheme, Jan Dhan deposits in the name of women, the Swachh Bharat toilet-making scheme, the Jan Aushadhi sanitary pad distribution scheme, and land registries in the name of women are all schemes that, effective or not, make a clear pitch to woo women voters. These are not always successful, and the gaps are glaring in some cases: a rise of almost 27% in crimes against women, the increase in prices of cylinders rendering the Ujjwala scheme practically toothless, the low (and lowering) female Labour Force Participation Rate, which is currently lower than those of Bangladesh, Nepal and Sri Lanka, and far below East Asian nations (Khongwir and Sathyan 2022). There is, also, a growing voice against injustice. We saw this in the case of the Unnao rape case survivor and also in the protest raised by female wrestlers, many of whom had been vocal supporters of the BJP prior to going on hunger strike in protest against the sexual exploitation by Brij Bhushan Singh, a powerful Member of Parliament of the ruling party. Sexual exploitation in sports was for a while the spotlight of the hour, with photographs of the indignities suffered by the female wrestlers occupying the front pages on newspapers to almost the same degree as those of the women sitting in at Shaheen Bagh in December 2019 or the female farmers leading the protest at Delhi's borders a year later.

But the propaganda machine finds a way to make a comeback. With the news of the Indian Men's Cricket Team gaining a gender tag so as to allow the Indian Women's Team to be viewed at par, and the Board of Cricket Control in India (the Secretary of which is Jay Shah, son of Amit Shah, the Prime Minister's second-in-command) further announcing equal pay scales for both, much of the tar left behind by the wrestlers and boxers was wiped out and the gloss reapplied over Sports Shining under PM Modi. In the era of 24-hour news deluge, a shining, smiling Modi appears relentlessly in advertisements, news, posters, banners, and even on ticker parades over video games and entertainment sites in India, his smile wider and his face glossier as though seeking to blind any potential critic with its glaze. Additionally, a news report from 2013 pointed out, Modi's look, in recognition of the positives to be gained from his unexpected sex symbol status, had undergone a sea change since 2007 – 'the half-sleeve kurta is of the finest linen, not the humble khadi, Gucci stoles are casually flung around his neck, and a suspiciously generous pelt of hair has appeared on Modi's pate' (Hebbar 2013). The 56-inch association was further popularised by songs[1] and even food that celebrated the 'Modi myth'.

---

[1] For instance, see https://littleletterslinked.com/this-election-try-modi-jis-56-inch-thali for a description of the 'Deshbhakti Thali' or '56-inch Thali'. The conflation of Modi with deshbhakti or patriotism is deeply entrenched within the business class, in particular. The film *PM Narendra Modi*, which sought to present the man as a hero of our times at par with the likes of Gandhi, had a song, 'Namo, Namo', which played on the preferred short form of his name.

Modi's detractors, too, have kept the conversation going on this numerical reference, with ex-Minister of the UPA government Kapil Sibal going so far as to compose a satirical rhyme on Twitter: '*56 inch ki chhati, 58 ka rupaiya; kahan gayee woh chhati, kahan gaya rupaiya*' (The chest is 56 inches, the value of the rupee is 88 [against USD]; where is the chest now, where is the rupee now) (Shekhar 2015). News reporters have sought to demolish the myth by trying to prove that the chest is in fact only 44 inches (Sandhu 2014) or perhaps 50 inches wide (*ScoopWhoop* 2016). Most recently, the 56-inch chest and the so-called 'muscular nationalism' were called into action by his critics to defend the government's easy acceptance of large swathes of territory being taken over by China in the Ladakh region (Siddiqui 2023), and Mahua Moitra, a vocal critic from the Trinamool Congress, insisted that one didn't need it to be a strong leader, citing the examples of Naveen Patnaik (CM, Odisha) and Mamata Banerjee (CM, Bengal). One way or another, the 56-inch chest continues to remain newsworthy.

The Hero as Performer

A number of the features that make up the 'Modi myth' can be found in hero myths in other parts of the world. The 56-inch chest finds resonance in the stories about the physical attributes or sexual prowess of Alcibiades, Napoleon, or even Hitler, even though the last, just like Modi, worked hard to propagate the idea that he was 'married to the state'. The status of a sex symbol is useful as a channel for the adoration that the hero inspires. It further allows for humans of either sex to venerate the hero while allowing him to remain approachable. Like the 56-inch chest, the hero is an imaginable, yet unattainable dream.

In her book, *Heroes* (2006), a study of eight remarkable men who shocked as well as enthralled their societies, Lucy Hughes-Hallett points out that 'heroes are not required to be altruistic, or honest, or even competent. They are required only to inspire confidence and to appear, not good necessarily, but great'. Alcibiades, Napoleon, Hitler, all inspired admiration and disgust in equal measure. All were acknowledged by intellectuals in their time to have committed dastardly acts, and all were known to be unpredictable and wild. All were, almost immediately, forgiven in the light of their hero-worthiness. Having said that, all were acknowledged as heroes in the light of their deeds. Their people's confidence in them arose on the basis of what they had already achieved and therefore, what they could potentially achieve in the future.

If one looks at Modi's achievements over 13 years of leading Gujarat and 9 years of leading India, one is led to wonder once more at the development of the aura. Sivanand Tiwari was neither the first nor the last of Modi's friends and foes to call attention to his dismal record as Chief Minister. Yet, as Salil Tripathi pointed out in his essay in *The Caravan* magazine in 2014 (before Modi opened his first innings), the best of Indian minds seemed to be more than happy to praise and validate him even as he gave clear indications of going the way of Indonesia's President Suharto and China's Deng Xiaoping. Like the two East Asian dictators, Modi had a history of repression of the media, hounding of civil rights activists, artists and union leaders that went hand in hand with the acclaimed 'Gujarat Model of Development', which, as shared above, was always highly suspect.

What were the achievements of the 'Gujarat Model of Development'? It was widely acknowledged that the state had good roads and that there was ease of doing business there. Also, very importantly, Gujarat's bureaucracy is decentralised, responsive, and supportive of trade and innovation. Given the difficulty of working with government offices in almost any part of India, most Indians will appreciate that this is a major achievement. One of the main planks of Dr Manmohan Singh's United Progressive Alliance government was the cleaning up of the bureaucracy and issuing of single-window clearance options wherever possible. However, Dr Singh was widely regarded as a political pushover and was not able to complete this task over two terms. Enter Modi, the *baahubali* (strong man), who firmly asserted that he was successful because he did what needed to be done and did not allow silly things like the bureaucracy or due process to get in his way. He did not seek permission; he did not need to. He hammered his chest and acknowledged that he simply steamrolled anyone who got in his way.

And who decided what needed to be done? Why, Modi himself! He was judge, jury and executioner: a vigilante in the PM's chair. This presented a peculiar conundrum before the ordinary citizen: a PM who claimed to despise and belittle the very institutions he had sworn to protect. Here, then, was a democratically elected leader who had no respect for democracy or its tools and support systems. This was a monarch in the making, a man who allowed his associate, Sakshi Maharaj, to go on record to say that there would be no elections in India after 2019, because there would be no need for them after Modi's second victory (*Economic Times* 2019). This refusal to apologise or be seen as apologetic, coupled with a chest-beating flair for the controversial, is a trait we find in a number of world leaders today, most spectacularly the ex-Presidents (and also current President) of the USA and Brazil. Interestingly, all have a strong female following, despite (or perhaps because of?) their blatantly misogynistic comments and actions in public. In a country which is almost entirely patrilineal in its family structure with just a few pockets of geographically scattered alternates, Modi is seen as the patriarch, the *bade papa* ('big father' – the name given to the eldest male figure in northern and north-western Indian families) whose decisions propel us forward, whose word must be respected for he is the One-Who-Knows, and must be carried out by the good women of India, in accordance with the role traditionally played out in Indian families generation after generation. Such a figure could be seen as making a mistake, sometimes, but to call him out for it? – unthinkable.

Here, then, we have a 'hero' whose rise was powered by praise and criticism from his contemporaries by way of a single event – the Gujarat riots of 2002 – followed by a development model that was highly suspect. He pushed himself ahead as the decisive saviour India needed, but by itself this was not enough to keep the wheels of the public relations machinery turning. Modi was seen as the strong 56-inch-chested man capable of brushing everyone aside to achieve his goal, even the democratic process itself, but it was all the more laudable because of his humble beginnings. He claimed to be the son of a humble *chaiwalla* – a tea vendor – who had barely managed to complete his education before dedicating his life to the service of the nation. He represented the aspiration of the regular man on the street to rise to power and achieve his dreams – '*Modi hai to mumkin hai*' ('It is possible with Modi'). For such a man, of course, the opposition would be offered up by the established powers – the political establishment, the bureaucracy, the literati – all those who sought to uphold the old value system. In the story he likes to tell, time and again, the 'hero' emerged triumphant over a sea of opposition, and had the panache to do this with a wink and a nod for the man on the street. Witness, most recently, the reading down of Article 370, or the Balakot affair which followed the Pulwama strikes, or the most recent 'victory' of having passed the Women's Reservation Bill with the caveat that it will only come to pass in time for the elections of 2029, if at all it does. Even the much-reviled re-organisation of New Delhi's Central Vista – and the resultant destruction of the erstwhile Parliament House and the National Museum, among other heritage structures – is being projected as an outcome of India's leap into a shining future, and desire to move away from its colonial past. The message is clear – India is being reshaped to fit Modi's vision, and the capital needs to reflect the same. Even the erstwhile Ashokan era benign lions have been reinterpreted and placed all along the way from the city to the Delhi airport as snarling figures representing the aggressive new India of Modi's dreams (Kamal 2022; Pande 2023).

One needs to watch any one of Modi's public speeches to see how much of his aura derives from his performance. As most Indians irrespective of social background will affirm, good leader or not, there is no performer quite like Modi. Even as voices rose seeking reports for the first 5 years of Modi's rule, the question dominating his re-election campaign was: 'If not Modi, who?' Who else could be as entertaining, as witty, as ruthless in decimating his rivals as Modi was? Who else could be quite as good a storyteller? True, the story was mythical, facts were thin on the ground, the achievements were questionable, but who else could be the hero that India needed? When Modi performs, the facts cease to matter. All that matters is the way in which he uses propaganda to rouse the gathered crowds at an emotional level. As Hitler understood only too well, 'the more modest its intellectual ballast, the more exclusively it takes into consideration the emotions of the masses, the more effective [propaganda] will be' (Hitler 1943). Modi has learned at the feet of masters such as Alcibiades and Hitler, and more recently, Vladimir Putin. Here is a hero given birth by a nation that was eagerly awaiting one. Here is the charismatic *bade papa* who will take charge of the Great Indian Family. Here is, not a hero who inspires *bhakti* (devotion), but one who was created by the needs of the *bhakt* (devotee).

Globalisation and the changing face of *bhakti*

In the last few years, the world over, countries have seen a backlash against globalisation and the free market economy. Russian President Vladimir Putin, in an interview in July 2019 with the *Financial Times*, pointed out that one of the major contributory factors to Donald Trump's victory was the disillusionment of the middle classes with globalisation, which had benefited only the leading US companies – 'the companies, their managers, shareholders and partners'. The middle classes, he said, were 'left out when this pie was divided up'. It was from this group of disillusioned voters that Trump's call to 'Make America Great Again' got the maximum support (*Financial Times* 2019).

A similar thing happened in India. Globalisation, making a return after Indira Gandhi's protectionism, opened up new vistas for the rich and the upper middle classes, and created new benchmarks of aspiration for the upwardly mobile youth. It added more glitter and shine to the urban landscape, but remained mostly absent from rural India. Where it did enter, it piled up a heap of disasters, from the tragedies inflicted by genetically modified crops to the attempts at forcibly taking over agricultural and forest land for industrial manufacture and mining. For those who were already at mid-career or past the mid-point, globalisation meant the loss of the familiar and the stripping away of trust in national institutions such as banks and medical and communication services. The marketplace had changed, both literally and figuratively, and, while the promise of more jobs and opportunities available not just nationally but worldwide was tempting, it also brought about a crisis of identity, an empty space that the 'cultural nationalists' were raring to fill.

As we opened up to multinational corporations after a few decades of protectionism, Indian society also opened up considerably to liberal ideas in the last thirty years, with several taboos around sex and gender lifting, female roles within and without the family being queried and overhauled, and the very definition of family changing. The seismic shifts caused by these changing attitudes have led to considerable anxiety, reflecting in the rise of superstition and the grand performance of rituals (such as *jagrans*) and, predictably, rapes. Increasingly, Indians are turning to the judicial system to seek relief from oppressive social practices. While the Supreme Court's landmark judgement in *Navtej Johar vs Union of India* ruled that Section 377 of the Indian Penal Code was unconstitutional insofar as it sought to criminalise homosexuality, and could be viewed as a big win for the queer community in India, the more recent judgement in *Supriyo vs Union of India*, seeking to legalise queer marriages, makes it clear that the Court 'cannot either strike down the constitutional validity of Special Marriage Act (SMA) or read words into the SMA because of its institutional limitations', passing the buck to a BJP-majority Parliament. The BJP, dedicated towards preserving the traditional patriarchal family structure, is unlikely to fight in favour of any kind of change, and the largely conservative Indian voting public will most likely continue to approve.

We are reminded here of Erich Fromm's assertion, in *Escape from Freedom* (2013), of how freedom, though it may bring the individual independence and rationality, '...made [human beings] isolated and, thereby, anxious and powerless. This isolation is unbearable...' and the easier alternative facing them is frequently the one that involves escaping into new dependencies and surrendering their choices. This is made easier when a leader steps forward who is assertive and very willing to take choices out of the hands of individuals.

As Romila Thapar has observed, the idea that the religion of a community constitutes its identity is a British colonial one, which swamped the subcontinent and left a bloodbath in its wake, and continues to plague us in the present day (Thapar 2014). In an older time, the definition of a Hindu may have been closer to that of, say, a Greek – imbued with a sense of continuous historical presence within a geographical area over millennia, or with reference to this experience, and a sense of shared culture and what may loosely be termed a texture of living. The Hindus, in this sense, always worshipped a pantheon of gods who fought each other to seek supremacy and struggled to find a place in the caste hierarchy. Allah and Christ soon joined the pantheon, along with others such as Vailankanni (a version of Mary) and various cross-over goddesses such as Bandebi and *pirs* such as Manik and Badar Pir. For the longest time (and even now, in many parts of India), 'Muslim' and 'Christian' have been aspects of *jaat* rather than names of different 'national' identities, even though recent surveys would suggest that this is changing. When this writer first came to Delhi, she was privileged to be the house guest of a lady who was a Goan Christian, and who referred to herself as a 'Brahmin' on account of having Portuguese blood flowing through her veins. How shocked Aunty Fatema would have been to learn that she did not belong to the Hindu nation and therefore had no right to call herself Brahmin!

What will follow now is a very brief overview of the events I believe have significantly contributed to the creation of the 'Hindu identity' as we know it today and its proliferation, especially in north India. The events are too vast and too many to be handled within the dimensions of a single book, leave alone a chapter, and I must, therefore, beg forgiveness if some of the writing in the next few paragraphs seems facetious.

It was Bharatendu Harishchandra who, in the 1870s, campaigned with a vengeance for the switch from Urdu to Hindi and fought to prove that Hindi was the language of India and of 'Hindus'. The germ of the idea that periodically threatens to overtake the idea of India now was implanted only a hundred and fifty years ago. Despite the years of relentless campaigning, to this day, the language spoken on the streets of Delhi and Lucknow continues to be a mixture of Hindi, Urdu and dialects. The purported 'purity' of languages remains a dream to be achieved by 'nationalists' whose colonial ideal of nationhood, however, has been, and continues to be, drilled into the minds of the Indian public every passing day.

The development of the notion of the 'Hindu' identity, the project of a few business- and literary-minded men inspired by Bharatendu Harishchandra, was initiated in the early twentieth century and grew exponentially, inspired as it was by the ideology and imagery of the burgeoning Swadeshi movement. The journey of one iconic institution that played a pivotal role in this project has been studied by Akshaya Mukul in the brilliant *Gita Press and the Making of Hindu India*. Mukul closely examines how the Gita Press, over the 90-odd years of its existence, has been instrumental in laying down the principles that have served to define the identity of the average middle-class person in the Hindi belt – arguably the largest common-language-defined region in India. The works of the Gita Press and others of its ilk, put out with the clear intent of uniting all 'Hindus' within a common moral universe, received approbation and support from M. K. Gandhi and various other political leaders and social reformers and played a role in upholding the Swadeshi movement and the Indian identity. However, its editors were always more connected emotionally and ideologically with the politics of the Rashtriya Swayamsevak Sangh – a 'cultural nationalist' organisation – than with that of the larger independence movement, tending to look at reform that focussed on the removal of Islamic influences rather than political independence from the British, who were viewed as progressive and a positive influence. One of the major tasks that this group of 'Hindu revivalists' set out for itself was the popularisation of the Ramayana, and the version written by Tulsidas, *Ramacharitmanas*, was chosen for a very interesting reason – the promotion of the 1938 *Manas Ank* – a special issue of the *Kalyan* magazine published by the Gita Press (Mukul 2015). The *Manas Ank* was a lavish work with gold-embellished paintings, which soon became a coveted family heirloom – over 6 million copies of this issue have been printed so far. The popularisation drive for the *Manas Ank* involved regular readings of sections of the Ramayana within mid-sized community gatherings, most popularly the *Sundar Kand*, which prominently featured the character of Hanuman.

The figure of Hanuman, believed by some historians to have been the appropriation into the north Indian Ramayana tradition of a South Indian tribal deity, started gaining a more prominent role in oral retellings around the tenth century, possibly as a reaction to the rise of Vaishnavism in the north. Hanuman, traditionally a Shaivite, came to be seen as the biggest devotee of Ram, the avatar of Vishnu, thus making peace between the two feuding religious groups. The Bhakti period brought renewed interest in the 'Monkey God' as the epitome of devotion and obedience, and the embodiment of the belief that, literally, faith can move mountains. The *Hanuman Chalisa*, a poem of 40 lines celebrating the qualities of Hanuman and written by Tulsidas, had been popular in parts of the Hindi belt ever since the sixteenth century. With the targeted popularisation of the *Sundar Kand paath* in the late 1930s, the recitation of the *Hanuman Chalisa* on a daily basis became almost mandatory for men and women alike across the Hindi belt. Ram, the *Maryada Purushottam*, was an unattainable ideal. The aim, as reiterated over and over by priests and preachers across the region, was to be like Hanuman – devoted to faith, honest, reliable, brave and strong; a servant and soldier, not a king. The Bajrang Dal, a militant youth group formed by the Vishwa Hindu Parishad to protect its leaders during the Shri Ram Janaki Rath Yatra of 1984, took on this name with the clear intent of positing itself on the side of Ram. To this day, the group aims to support and protect the VHP and the RSS in their works and anyone with leadership aspirations must move from this group to its parent body, as its stated aim is to nurture workers, and not leaders.

Unless we acknowledge this background of decades of cultural indoctrination, it is impossible to understand the wave of humanity that turned up in support of L. K. Advani's *rathyatra* in 1990, or the Babri Masjid demolition that followed it, or, indeed, the growing support offered to the RSS and its allies, such as the Bajrang Dal and the Durga Vahini. It is with respect to this background that we look at the rise of Narendra Damodardas Modi.

The Importance of Hanuman

Before plunging into the modern-day political implications of a myth, it is important to look at the character of Hanuman and its various implications. Interestingly, the only mainstream deity to be worshipped across India and beyond, who is, to all intents and purposes, entirely an anthropomorphic animal – down to his tail – Hanuman is also considered to be immortal and, therefore, alive in the present time. This belief has led to the possibility of creating a huge amount of fiction, including cartoons and films centred around the character, which has only added to its popularity, introducing it to new generations of Indians as a fun, friendly character, even as it continued to serve in its primary role as protector.

Stories of the mighty Hanuman may be found, with important focal variations, all across the country. While the Hindi belt as well as many parts of southern India have had a long tradition of Hanuman worship, in the east, where I grew up, he was always regarded as a character that added humour to the rather sombre Ramayana story. In the annual Ramleela plays, Hanuman would be played usually by a young boy, whose jumping and prancing around would lead to the comic relief in the play. In the early days of television in the 1980s, Ramanand Sagar's TV series version, *Ramayan*, featured the erstwhile wrestler and action movie star of the 1960s, Dara Singh, in the role of Hanuman, played as an imposing, yet kind-hearted figure with a perennial twinkle in his eye. Up until the early 2010s, the benevolent figure of Hanuman could be seen guarding many a street crossing, and 'Sankat Mochan' Hanuman temples were open to all seeking protection from their troubles.

It was around 2016 that the image that came to be known as 'Angry Hanuman' started appearing on posters and car stickers. The young Malayali artist who had created this image claimed to have had no idea that it would take off in quite the way it did; he had, he said, intended to create an image that had 'attitude', but it came to signify aggression: the anger, as it were, of the person on the street (Bose 2018). Almost overnight, Hanuman started to assume his more dangerous incarnation, that of the formidable enemy who defeated magical monsters by sprouting five heads or changing his size at will. This was the almost one-man army that is considered to be the power that brought about *Ram Rajya*.

The one aspect of Hanuman that seems to have always endured is his undeniable maleness. In Hindu stories, the male celibate is considered to have tremendous power, and not everyone is believed to be capable of containing it. *Tapas* or immersive meditation is believed to be the only way to contain *tejas*, or the built-up heat of unreleased semen. This seminal energy is then transferred to other parts of the body, all of which become imbued with immense potential. Therefore, despite being a life-long celibate, Hanuman has a son called Makaradhwaja, born of a crocodile living in Lanka's waters which had swallowed a drop of Hanuman's sweat as he flew above. The notion of celibacy as an ideal to be pursued for the sake of heightened masculine energy is one that has influenced, for instance, the training of wrestlers, who worship Hanuman as their guiding deity. It is also an underlying factor in the celebration of men such as Atal Behari Vajpayee and Narendra Modi, who claim to be life-long celibate or to have abandoned their sexual partners in order to be 'married to the state'. Similar parallels exist with the Buddha, who abandoned his wife and child in search of higher truths, and was therefore able to dedicate himself in service to a higher cause. These are the parallels drawn, directly and indirectly, by the BJP in the case of the present Prime Minister. Modi, so the myth goes, is able to take tough decisions and make the impossible happen because he is dedicated to the nation, has no attachments and boundless energy, apparently working up to twenty hours a day. In comparison, the first Prime Minister of India, Pt. Jawaharlal Nehru, the only leader whom Modi's supporters are willing to discuss [since the leader in history whose personal style of leadership was nearest to Modi's was Indira Gandhi, a woman and therefore, not worthy of discussion], is constantly reviled on account of his purported fondness for women and cigarettes. A popular lyricist, in a staged 'casual talk' in London, famously asked Modi this difficult question: 'How do you work so hard? Don't you ever get tired?' This celebrated tirelessness in the service of the nation – a straightforward parallel to Hanuman's dedication to the service of Ram, his self-proclaimed title of Pradhan Sewak or chief servant, the constant claim to hold India in his heart – drawing attention to the image of Hanuman tearing open his chest to reveal Ram and Sita within it – are all strategic socio-emotional triggers planted to direct the populace towards an epiphany: the nation is the body of Ram, the public are His devoted servants, and Modi, as their leader, is Hanuman himself.

The *bhakt* and the Hero

The promise of *Ram Rajya* has been the plank on which the BJP has fought every election since the early 1990s. It took the disillusionment with globalisation, however, to truly rouse the latent *bhakt*. To quote Amit Bhaduri, 'Economic globalisation challenges the political authority which the nation-state had attained by undermining gradually many of the norms of the traditional civil society' (Bhaduri 2000). The 'sovereignty' of the nation – a neo-Hegelian view of the absolute authority of the state – is seen as being at stake in the face of rapid alterations of urban aspiration and changing lifestyles. Mark Juergensmeyer points out that the increasing porousness of boundaries and acceptance of other identities has led to the nation-state being viewed as a weak institution, and the 'vulnerability of the nation-state, in turn, has been the occasion for new ethno-religious politics to step into the breach and shore up national identities and purposes' (Juergensmeyer 2019). This phenomenon has been steadily on the rise in India since 1992. Increasingly, over the past three decades, the middle classes and small towns have voted in favour of reducing personal liberties and increasing community-based policing. Mob-lynching is on the rise, *khap* panchayats are gaining more ground even as the courts condemn their diktats. Hanuman is out protecting the *maryada* of this land.

While the last statement above may be read as ironic, what is even more ironic is that this is the precise statement that has accompanied many a communal march in recent times. As Jawhar Sircar pointed out, Ram Navami marches with swords, guns and *trishuls* have become the norm in the past few years in areas such as Bengal where Ram worship has never been practised heretofore. Hanuman Jayanti is being celebrated in places which were hitherto quite unconcerned with the circumstances of Hanuman's birth (Sircar 2018). Shivratri celebrations regularly involve *kanwariyas* taking over entire National Highways and city arterial roads for a month and more in North India. The more hooliganistic the display of religious fervour gets, the more acceptance it seems to receive from a citizenry that is entirely happy to serve the greater cause of 'rescuing' Hinduism from the threat of others. What the BJP did very successfully for over twenty years was to convince the populace to take up the role of *bhakt*. This is interesting because the characteristic image of the *bhakt* now is no longer that of a jobless male from a certain socioeconomic background and with limited educational opportunities – which was the case generally around the time of the Babri Masjid demolition and subsequent riots. The *bhakt* now may be a blue-collar worker or an entrepreneur, a teacher or a doctor; often employed and upwardly mobile, and frequently female. The fear of the educated 'Other' whose religion purportedly requires them to propagate without control and, therefore, become a threat to future generations of 'Us' is a fear that now plagues many countries across the world and has been successfully used to win elections, notably in the US, Brazil and in

India. The fear we speak of is not merely an economic one – 'our jobs are under threat' – but more importantly an emotional one: 'the very fabric of the nation and society is in danger'.

The 'Nation in need of a Saviour' theme, prepared for twenty years, then, became the perfect receptacle for Narendra Modi. This is how, in the face of Gujarat riots, Narendra Modi shone like a beacon for the *bhakt*. Here was a man who refused to apologise for his deeds, who insisted that what he had done was right and he had taught a lesson to all those who needed to be disciplined, and who somehow found a way to slip by the nagging arm of the law. He lost some of his shine when, in 2005, the US refused to offer him a visa in the light of the investigations which implicated him for communal crimes, but gained it back soon enough through persistent attempts and a dogged refusal to allow anything to besmirch him. In 2023, Modi became the first Indian leader to address the US Congress twice, and one of only a handful of global leaders to have done this more than once. Under his leadership, India hosted the G-20 meet the same year. While the leadership is rotational, and India's turn was bound to come sooner or later, the narrative spin that has been given is clear – this is a Modi victory. Further, in a world where financial corruption – particularly in political parties – seemed to be the norm, Modi was the one politician who gave the impression that he was not interested in money. This, coupled with his mysterious preening powers, that did not allow any allegations to stick, gave him the aura of an invincible survivor. Even those who did not like him felt that they had to admire him. And thus, the hero was born out of the needs of the *bhakt*.

The Nation and the Hero

As we have seen so far, the resistible rise of Narendra Modi bears a close resemblance to the rise of the authoritarian personality that is outlined in the works of Erich Fromm and others. There is a clear relationship based on emotional dependence; I follow Fromm in calling it a sado-masochistic relationship. A popular comic strip depicts the Indian public seeking jobs, food and clothing, while Modi gives them grand gestures – demonetisation; Sardar Patel's immense statue; the overnight overhauling of Kashmir's status and rights. In the comic, he finally loses his cool that the public isn't appreciative of his grand gestures and keeps whining for staples. A number of people 'liked' the strip but, as it turned out, about half of them claimed to understand the Modi-cartoon's frustration with an ungrateful public, and sent messages of support to the Prime Minister.

Our anxieties and emotional dependence go deeper still. In a country as diverse as India, the importance of asserting the national identity is a widely accepted opinion. Even the liberal who questions the need to play the national anthem before the screening of movies agrees that the Indian identity cannot be stressed enough. This makes the liberal deeply uncomfortable in the face of anti-India protests in Kashmir and Manipur, anti-CAA (Citizenship Amendment Act) protests in Assam, or when faced with a Muslim person who supports the Pakistani cricket team. This is the weak spot that the *bhakt* attacks again and again, relentlessly. When a Modi repeatedly calls out to the 'Hindu within us', or Bolsonaro says, 'We Brazilians don't like homosexuals', or a Putin reminds his audience that 'all of us live in a world based on biblical values', it is comforting to their listeners to be reassured that their world is, indeed, still recognisable, even though it may not feel that way. When Modi calls out to Hindus worldwide, he is reminding Indians that it is not merely the nation-state which is theirs, but that they have a trans-national existence which guarantees that their culture, and the Hindu nation, will persist, and triumph, in the face of all manners of cultural and economic threats. There isn't a hint of irony in these speeches, and they are, in fact, delivered with so much confidence, that in the twenty years or so that he has spent projecting himself as the Saviour, over a third of the voting population has been beguiled by the promise of Modi the hero. The fact that he hosts no press conferences and refuses to face the public unrehearsed does not seem to have dented his image as a man of wit and wisdom. Fawning interviews, cartoons featuring him as a superhero, films and songs released in his praise:

all have gone a long way towards building the 'Modi myth'. The parallels with Vladimir Putin, in particular, are obvious, down to the patented turns of phrase known variously as 'Putinisms' and 'Modiisms'. Even an accusation as serious as the one associated with the Rafale deal seems to have been 'handled' in the light of the party's victory in the 2019 elections. Modi, in keeping with the tradition of the heroes he seems to have modelled himself after, particularly Putin, is also very clear about ignoring what he can and ruthlessly repressing those he cannot. In recent times, Putin's incursion into Ukraine has served to distract the general populace from the economic issues that have beset the nation's economy over the past decade, and, in the face of global criticism, helped them to rally together in defence of the regime. This attitude is further helped along by the presence of harsh statewide repression of protests and opposition which makes it nearly impossible to consolidate popular opinion in any form, let alone organise an uprising. Modi's India is fairly similar, to the extent that people have been arrested for screening the BBC documentary which dared to question Modi's role in the Gujarat riots, or even for commenting negatively on the administration on X (formerly Twitter) and Facebook. Dare we say that Modi and Putin, good friends as they are, learn from each other?

In India, over the last few years, incidents of mob-lynching have been rising steadily, leading to a slew of protests, at the forefront of which have been artists. National-award-winning artists have returned their awards and citations, held protests and demonstrations and supported signature campaigns. This is natural, since the arts can only flourish where there is a certain amount of social stability, and vigilante mobs must be necessarily viewed as a threat to art and artists. For various reasons, the Modi government has an extremely uneasy relationship with the arts, which, in India, are the embodiment of the very intricate connectedness between various religio-cultural strands which the RSS questions. Even in their 'classical' forms, neither music nor dance nor theatre can claim to remember forms from an ancient past free of 'other' cultural influences, and the visual arts positively revel in varied cultural associations. Literature and film have been similarly guilty, even though the film community, perhaps conscious of the pitfalls of running a business with many lives depending on it, fawns over the powers-that-be irrespective of their politics. Choosing to address these discomforts directly would mean putting himself into a questionable spot, the kind of situation which Modi knows well to avoid. Instead, his publicity group has put together a clever strategy by way of which the questions put to the Prime Minister by artists are countered by accusations of anti-nationalism by other artists. Thus, serious, hard-hitting questions in the public space are degenerated into absurd cat-fights where all come out looking bedraggled and sorry, while the Prime Minister remains untouched. With Modi supporters having been named to every possible position of power in the country, and TV channels and newspapers having been frightened into submission by the threat of pulling out all government (and government favoured industrial groups') advertisements, now the artists, traditionally the conscience-keepers of the country, have been silenced. The other groups that have been a pain in the administration's neck are the social activists, particularly those working in the domain of civil rights and promoting rationality, and academics. The administration's answer to these worries is to cut off funding for civil rights groups across the country by making the process of securing foreign funding completely subject to the central government's whims, to imprison social activists on unbailable charges, such as the Unlawful Activities (Prevention) Act, and relentlessly replace the head of every government-funded academic institution, including universities, with supporters of the party. Tax raids and arrests on spurious grounds which wouldn't stand before a court of law, but would serve to harass the victim in the months or years before the cases reach India's overloaded courts, are another favoured mode of punishment for those who dare to speak up against the PM and his party. The Supreme Court, which has on occasion questioned or objected to some of the decisions taken by the present government, is sought to be bypassed through ordinances, or controlled by giving the Executive more of a say in the appointment of judges and, since the Court itself has not yet allowed this, by obstructing the appointments wherever possible.

The National Register of Citizens continues to be a potent weapon in the hands of the present government to determine who deserves to be termed a citizen of the nation. All those who oppose it are termed anti-national, and the Home Minister, Amit Shah, has made it very clear that the NRC will be used against those who are deemed as 'infiltrators', marking exceptions for 'Buddha (sic), Hindus and Sikhs' (*The Quint* 2019). This is very much in keeping with the expectations that people have from the party in power. In November 2019, a Supreme Court judgement helped deliver one of the BJP's core election promises: the permission to build a Ram Temple at the site of the destroyed Babri Masjid; a work in progress that has become a visual as well as metaphorical symbol of the rebuilding of the 'Hindu nation' on the ashes of its 'Muslim past' as per the narrative of the far Right. The NRC is presently on the backburner but will be revived, certainly, with the much-delayed Census exercise in 2026, to be followed by the delimitation of constituencies (Bharati 2023). Are we headed for another 'territorial reorganisation for administrative efficiency' on the lines of the British government's Partition of Bengal in 1905? The much-vaunted Women's Reservation Bill, which the BJP is already claiming as a victory by way of its propaganda machinery, is set to debut after the delimitation exercise, in time for the elections in 2029 (Khan 2023). In the meantime, a new trend has begun: that of homes being bulldozed – of the poor who happen to belong to minority groups (Rajvanshi 2023). As more and more atrocities on minorities or underprivileged communities become the norm rather than the exception, small- and medium-sized riots keep happening in affected pockets across the nation, evil has become truly banal (Butler 2011), a matter of routine in middle-class India, and the vilification of 'others' is now part of the everyday irritants of middle-class urban living, clubbed together with the endless religious fairs and celebrations that lead to roadblocks and enforced school holidays. For the regular white-collar worker, fed on a daily narrative of screeching pro-Modi media houses, the farmers' year-long agitation, or the protests at the Nuh–Gurgaon border are evidences of the anti-development agenda of the Opposition. The last mainstream bastion of middle-of-the-road TV journalism, NDTV, was bought over last year by the pro-Modi Adani group, and has since then staunchly shied away from raising questions on the central government. The only questions that remain arise from subscription-run web journalism or street reporters operating on YouTube and other video-sharing sites. In the meantime, a phone-based Emergency Alert System purportedly set up to prevent disasters keeps everyone with a mobile phone on tenterhooks by shrieking intermittently through these devices (Bhati 2023). The Ram Temple was inaugurated with much pomp and show on 22 January 2024, a day declared as a holiday across BJP-run states. The inauguration itself was marred by protests from religious groups, including the highest temple spokespersons, the four Shankaracharyas, who said that consecrating an incomplete temple goes against Hindu scriptures (Lodhi 2024). There is more unrest coming, and we wait, as a nation, with bated breath.

Yet we take it all in our stride. The millions of pyres burning on the streets at the peak of India's atrociously managed COVID-19 lockdown (Alluri 2021), coming on top of the walk of migrant labourers across the country, denied basic food, shelter, medical, transport, or employment-related support by the administration, are distant memories now, and the middle class is today happy to discuss the reports of India's support to other nations for the vaccination drive following the lockdown. The last display of resistance arose when the central government took a disproportionately aggressive stance against the screening of the BBC documentary on Modi, with colleges and universities once again picking up the cudgels on behalf of free speech (Rajvanshi and Syed 2023). But everyone eventually needs funding to survive, and to not have to suffer endless tax raids or find their operation permits being arbitrarily suspended (Chauhan 2023). And so, the colleges and universities clamp down on student protest, and NGOs keep their noses to the ground so that they can at least perform the basic functions for which they were founded. This blatant abuse of power has now become the norm in India. The question is, how far are we, the Indian public, willing to go in our celebration of this man whom we have appointed as our hero? How deep does the fear of the Other truly go, that we are willing to surrender our free will to Him, who would protect us from that? At this juncture of history, it may be worth our while to ponder on the words that Shakespeare gave to Ulysses, as he warns the Greek leaders of the dangers of investing too much in an unpredictable hero:

Force should be right; or rather, right and wrong,
Between whose endless jar justice resides,
Should lose their names, and so should justice too.
Then everything includes itself in power,
Power into will, will into appetite;
And appetite, an universal wolf,
So doubly seconded with will and power,
Must make perforce an universal prey,
And last eat up himself.

Troilus and Cressida (Act I, Scene 3)

References

Alluri, Aparna. "India's Covid Crisis Delivers a Blow to Brand Modi." *BBC News*, 8 May 2021. https://www.bbc.com/news/world-asia-india-56970569. Accessed on 13 November 2025.

Bhaduri, Amit. 2000. "Nationalism and Economic Policy in the Era of Globalisation." Working Papers no. 188, WIDER, The United Nations University. https://www.wider.unu.edu/sites/default/files/wp2000-188.pdf. Accessed on 25 April 2025.

Bharati, Manoranjan. "Explained: What India Will Look Like After 2026 Delimitation." *NDTV*, 21 September 2023. https://www.ndtv.com/india-news/explained-what-india-will-look-like-after-2026-delimitation-4411700#. Accessed on 25 April 2025.

Bhati, Divya. "Indian Govt Just Sent Another Emergency Alert Making Millions of Phones Sound Alarm, Here Is What It Means." *India Today*, 12 October 2023. https://www.indiatoday.in/technology/news/story/indian-govt-just-sent-another-emergency-alert-making-millions-of-phones-sound-alarm-here-is-what-it-means-2446887-2023-10-10. Accessed on 25 April 2025.

Bose, Rakhi. "How a Kerala Artist's 'Angry Hanuman' Became a Rage on India's Roads." *News 18*, 9 April 2018. https://www.news18.com/news/buzz/how-a-kerala-artists-angry-hanuman-became-a-rage-on-indias-roads-1711807.html. Accessed on 25 April 2025.

Butler, Judith. "'Hannah Arendt's Challenge to Adolf Eichmann', The Big Ideas: Ethics." *The Guardian*, 29 August 2011. https://www.theguardian.com/commentisfree/2011/aug/29/hannah-arendt-adolf-eichmann-banality-of-evil. Accessed on 25 April 2025.

Chauhan, Neeraj. "Modified FCRA Rules: NGOs to Give Details of Assets Created from Foreign Funds." *Hindustan Times*, 26 September 2023. https://www.hindustantimes.com/india-news/modified-fcra-rules-ngos-directed-to-give-details-of-assets-created-from-foreign-funds-101695669428261.html. Accessed on 25 April 2025.

Fromm, Erich. 1941/1969 (2013). *Escape from Freedom*. New York: Open Road Media.

Hebbar, Nistula. "Sex Symbol Status: Narendra Modi Attracts Female Audience but Need to Show More Tenderness." *Economic Times*, 29 September 2013. https://economictimes.indiatimes.com/news/politics-and-nation/sex-symbol-status-narendra-modi-attracts-female-audience-but-needs-to-show-more-tenderness/articleshow/23216479.cms. Accessed on 25 April 2025.

Hitler, Adolf. 1943. *Mein Kampf.* Translated by Ralph Manheim. Boston: Houghton Mifflin Company.

Hughes-Hallett, Lucy. 2006. *Heroes: A History of Hero Worship*. Anchor Books: New York.

Juergensmeyer, Mark. 2019. "How Globalisation Engenders Ethno-religious Nationalism." *Zocalo Public Square*, 30 April 2019. https://www.zocalopublicsquare.org/2019/04/30/how-globalization-engenders-ethno-religious-nationalism/ideas/essay/. Accessed on 25 April 2025.

Kamal, Asim. "Emblem Row: Historians Say 'Aggressive Lions' Lack Basic Essence of Ashokan Originals." *The Wire*, 17 July 2022. https://thewire.in/government/emblem-row-historians-aggressive-lions-essence-ashoka. Accessed on 25 April 2025.

Khan, Fatima. "What Is Delimitation & What Does Women's Reservation Bill Have To Do With It?" *The Quint*, 23 September 2023. https://www.thequint.com/news/politics/what-is-delimitation-and-what-does-women-reservation-have-to-do-with-it#read-more. Accessed on 25 April 2025.

Khongwir, Veronica Dudei Maia, and Devayani Sathyan. "Indian women's labour participation decades away from matching G20 peers, economists say: Reuters poll" *Reuters*, 22 July 2025. https://www.

reuters.com/sustainability/society-equity/indian-womens-labour-participation-decades-away-matching-g20-peers-economists-2025-07-22/#:~:text=A%20majority%2C%2080%25%2C%20of,urban%20areas%20are%20self%2Demployed. Accessed on 24 November 2025.

LiveLaw News Network. "Marriage Equality Case: Conclusions & Directions of Supreme Court Judgments." *LiveLaw*, 19 October 2023. https://www.livelaw.in/top-stories/marriage-equality-case-conclusions-directions-of-supreme-court-judgments-240529https://www.livelaw.in/top-stories/marriage-equality-case-conclusions-directions-of-supreme-court-judgments-240529. Accessed on 25 April 2025.

Lodhi, Areesha. "Why is India's Ram temple in Ayodhya controversial?" 22 January 2024. https://www.aljazeera.com/news/2024/1/22/why-is-indias-ram-temple-in-ayodhya-controversial. Accessed on 25 April 2025.

Mukul, Akshaya. 2015. *Gita Press and the Making of Hindu India.* Harper Collins: Noida.

Pachauri, Swasti. "Verdict 2019: Why Did Women Vote for BJP?" *Down to Earth*, 12 June 2019. https://www.downtoearth.org.in/blog/general-elections-2019/verdict-2019-why-did-women-vote-for-bjp--65030. Accessed on 25 April 2025.

Pande, Suresh K. Photo-Essay: "Why So Angry: Aggressive Lions on Display in Delhi for G-20 Decorations." *Outlook*, 10 September 2023. https://www.outlookindia.com/national/why-so-angry-lions-with-bared-fangs-installed-for-g-20-summit-decoration-photos-316816?photo-1. Accessed on 25 April 2025.

Pradhan, B., and S. R. Sen. "Religious Violence Threatens to Tar Modi's Image before G20." *Deccan Herald*, 4 August 2023. https://www.deccanherald.com/india/religious-violence-threatens-to-tar-modis-image-before-g20-1243715.html. Accessed on 25 April 2025.

PTI. "56 inch Chest is Now 100 inch: Shivraj Singh Chouhan." *Financial Express*, October 2, 2016. https://www.financialexpress.com/india-news/56-inch-chest-is-now-100-inch-shivraj-singh-chouhan/400909/. Accessed on 25 April 2025.

Rajvanshi, Astha. "How India's Bulldozers Became a Vehicle of Injustice." *Time*, 11 August 2023. https://time.com/6303571/how-bulldozers-became-a-symbol-of-anti-muslim-sentiment-in-india/. Accessed on 25 April 2025.

Rajvanshi, A., and A. Syed. "Why India Is Using Emergency Laws to Ban a Documentary About Prime Minister Modi." *Time*, 23 January 2023. https://time.com/6249393/the-modi-question-documentary-bbc-india-controversy/. Accessed on 25 April 2025.

Sandhu, Veena. "Who Can Boast about a 56-inch Chest?" *Business Standard*, 31 January 2014. https://www.business-standard.com/article/beyond-business/who-can-boast-about-a-56-inch-chest-114013101063_1.html. Accessed on 25 April 2025.

Scoop Whoop Staff. "PMO Office Exposes Modi's Lie of 'Chhappan inch ki chhati'." *Scoop Whoop*, 23 January 2016. https://www.scoopwhoop.com/No-More-Chhappan-Inch-Ki-Chhati-PM-Modis-Chest-Measures-50Inches/. Accessed on 25 April 2025.

Shekhar, Kumar Shakti. "When Kapil Sibal Wrote a Poem on Modi's 56-inch Chest." *Daily O*, 12 August 2015. https://www.dailyo.in/variety/kapil-sibal-trolled-modi-government-56-inch/story/1/5622.html. Accessed on 25 April 2025.

Siddiqui, Imran Ahmed. "Military Veterans Slam Modi's '56-inch chest' Boast, S Jaishankar's Comment on China." *The Telegraph Online*, 24 February 2023. https://www.telegraphindia.com/india/military-veterans-slam-modis-56-inch-chest-boast-s-jaishankars-comment-on-china/cid/1918541. Accessed on 25 April 2025.

Simha, Vijay. 2019. "The Women in Narendra Modi's Life." *Sify.com*. https://www.sify.com/news/the-women-in-narendra-modis-life-imagegallery1-features-oeoowCcfdccsi.html.

Sircar, Jawhar. "Using Ram and Hanuman for Violence and Votes." *The Wire*, 1 April 2018. https://thewire.in/politics/using-ram-and-hanuman-for-violence-and-votes. Accessed on 25 April 2025.

Staff Writers. "Standing up to fight." *Terradaily*, 23 May 2011. http://www.terradaily.com/reports/Standing_up_to_fight_999.html. Accessed 25 April 2025.

Syed, Armani. "India Banned a BBC Documentary Critical of Modi. Here's How People Are Watching Anyway." *Time*, 26 January 2023. https://time.com/6250480/bbc-modi-documentary-skirting-censors/. Accessed on 25 April 2025.

Thakkar, Mitul. "Verghese Kurien Faces Modi's Wrath, May've to Give up Basics." *Economic Times*, 30 January 2009. https://economictimes.indiatimes.com/industry/cons-products/food/verghese-kurien-faces-modis-wrath-mayve-to-give-up-basics/articleshow/4050549.cms?from=mdr. Accessed on 25 April 2025.

Thapar, Romila. 2014. *The Past Is Present*. Aleph: New Delhi.

———. "They Peddle Myths and Call It History." *The New York Times*, 17 May 2019. https://www.nytimes.com/2019/05/17/opinion/india-elections-modi-history.html. Accessed on 25 April 2025.

Tripathi, Salil. "How Some of India's Brightest Minds Have Bought into the Modi Myth." *Caravan*, 11 May 2014. https://caravanmagazine.in/vantage/minds-modi-myth. Accessed on 25 April 2025.

Venkitesh, R. "The Modi Myth." *Frontline*, 27 May 2013. https://frontline.thehindu.com/cover-story/modi-myth/article4666766.ece. Accessed on 25 April 2025.

TWELVE

'*Desh ka sawaal hai*': Shah Rukh Khan, the 'Global Indian' and the Problematics of Minority Citizenship in Contemporary India

Sreya Mitra

Introduction

Addressing the Rajya Sabha, the upper house of the Indian Parliament, Trinamool Congress (TMC) MP, Derek O'Brien waxed eloquent on Bollywood superstar, Shah Rukh Khan's latest blockbuster, *Pathaan* (dir. Siddharth Anand, 2023). Describing Khan as India's 'Global Ambassador', O'Brien lauded the efforts of the film's cast and crew in achieving something that even the nation's leaders had failed to do – the reaffirmation of India as a land of religious and cultural diversity, which underlines its uniqueness. The Trinamool MP was not the only one enamoured with *Pathaan*. For veteran journalist, Vir Sanghvi, it was more than just a Bollywood film, it was 'a battle for India' – 'Rarely has a film's release been so important in the battle for a tolerant India, free from hatred and communally charged bullying' (Sanghvi 2023). *Pathaan*'s success was perceived as not only a testament to Khan's superstardom, but more significantly, for many, it was also a reiteration of India's secular ethos, an aspect that was intrinsic to Khan's star text itself. Alluding to the right-wing Hindutva protests against the film's song, 'Besharam rang' ('shameless colour'), Sanghvi attributes it to how 'Part of the Hindutva section hates Shah Rukh and the manner in which his success embodies the triumph of Indian secularism' (Sanghvi 2023). With his Catholic school education, familiarity with Hindu festivals, a Hindu wife, and secular tenets, Khan is 'unmistakably a secular ideal, a Nehruvian child … an image of the nation itself' (Parasuraman 2023b). However, as the protests against the 'Besharam rang' song and the calls to boycott the film underline, Shah Rukh Khan's star text also reveals the problematic underpinnings of minority citizenship. By virtue of being a Muslim, the actor has been simultaneously celebrated as an icon of secularism and vilified as a figure of anti-nationalism.

For right-wing Hindutva extremists, 'Besharam rang', with the film's heroine in a revealing orange/saffron (symbolic of Hinduism) swimsuit and the hero in a chest-baring green (symbolic of Islam) shirt conjured up the imagery of 'Love Jihad', with the innocent Hindu girl being trapped by the unscrupulous Muslim boy. As incensed protestors lodged complaints with the Information & Broadcasting Ministry, demanded that the film be banned, and even threatened to burn theatres screening the film; it was a stark reminder of both the 'boycott culture' that has besieged the Hindi film industry in recent times as well as the right-wing Hindutva vitriolic hate that Shah Rukh Khan has been subjected to. This was not the first time that the actor had faced the wrath of Hindutva extremists and had his 'Indianness' questioned. In January 2010, prior to the release of *My Name Is Khan* (dir. Karan Johar, 2010), he was subjected to a similar experience, with incensed protestors burning his effigies and demonstrating outside his palatial Mumbai home, Mannat. Khan, who is co-owner of the Indian Premier League (IPL) cricket team, Kolkata Knight Riders, had voiced his dismay and disappointment that none of the teams had picked any of the eleven Pakistani cricketers who were up for bidding. His remarks earned him not only the ire of right-wing activists, but also the label of an anti-national and a traitor. Shiv Sena, the Maharashtra-based regional, right-wing political party, threatened to boycott the film and in a scathing editorial in the party mouthpiece, *Saamna*, Bal Thackeray, Sena's octogenarian supremo declared, 'Shah Rukh was, after all, no ordinary Indian; he was a Muslim' (Raina 2010). Sena spokesman, Sanjay Raut, exhorted a similar narrative, 'This is not Shah Rukh, but the

Khan in him that's saying all this. Let Shah Rukh go and stay in Lahore, Karachi or Islamabad. He is not needed in Mumbai' (Bhattacharjee 2010).

Similar allegations of his lack of patriotism would again emerge in 2015 when the actor, in interviews on the occasion of his fiftieth birthday, rued the growing intolerance and divisiveness in the country. Khan's comment, 'Religious intolerance and not being secular in this country is the worst kind of crime that you can do as a patriot' (Express News Service 2015) was perceived by many as an indictment of the ruling Bharatiya Janata Party (BJP), which had assumed power in 2014. BJP and other right-wing politicians were quick to condemn Khan and denounce him as a traitor. Kailash Vijayvargiya, BJP General Secretary, labelled the actor as 'anti-national' – 'Shah Rukh lives in India, but his soul is in Pakistan. His films make crores here but he thinks India is intolerant. If this is not anti-national, then what is it?' (HT Correspondent 2015). Sadhvi Prachi, from the right-wing Vishwa Hindu Parishad, echoed similar sentiments – 'Shah Rukh Khan is an agent of neighbouring country Pakistan as he reflects their (Pakistan's) ideology. Such a man should go to Pakistan' (HT Correspondent 2015). Khan's 'Muslimness', thus, marked him as inherently incapable of any loyalty and fidelity towards his country, consequently evoking the familiar rhetoric of the (unpatriotic) Indian Muslim's allegiance to neighbouring Pakistan.

In my discussion of Shah Rukh Khan's star text, I analyse how the actor's 'Muslimness' marks him both as the ideal citizen, and also as the Muslim 'Other', bringing into question his allegiance and loyalty to the national imaginary. In doing so, I also highlight the role of religion in framing questions of nationhood, belonging and minority citizenship in the contemporary Indian public sphere, particularly as it intersects with discourses of popular Hindi cinema and stardom. My analysis of Shah Rukh Khan's star text as the Global Indian and the (secular) Indian Muslim attempts to map the circulation and consumption of the Bollywood star to the sociopolitical and cultural rumblings of contemporary India. Central to my analysis is Khan's on-screen portrayal of the Indian

Muslim in *Chak De! India* (dir. Shimit Amin, 2007), *My Name Is Khan* (2010) and *Raees* (dir. Rahul Dholakia, 2017) as well as the religiously ambiguous protagonist in *Pathaan* (2023), and how his reel avatars embody not only the subjectivity of the Indian Muslim but also underline the susceptibility of Shah Rukh Khan's 'Muslimness' as an Indian citizen and a Bollywood star. Through a simultaneous engagement with the visual imagery of his films, particularly their Muslim protagonists, and Khan's off-screen text, I track the images of the nation and Khan's own articulation of his (Indian) Muslim citizenship and belonging.

Global India: The 'New Heroic Prototype' and the Muslim Superstar

In popular Hindi cinema's world of myth, romance and celluloid dreams, Shah Rukh Khan, or SRK, as the star is popularly known, occupies the place of a demi-god. Endowed with epithets such as 'King Khan' and 'Badshah of Bollywood', and with a filmography of more than hundred films, including some of Indian cinema's biggest blockbusters, the actor is phenomenally popular, inspiring fanatical adulation both at home and abroad (Dudrah et al. 2015). Khan's star text and media discourse often position him as the veritable 'outsider', the middle-class aspirant from Delhi, whose stardom is as much a story of chance and luck, as it is of hard work, dedication and perseverance. Prior to his film career, he had been active in Delhi's theatre circuit during his undergraduate years and had even gained a certain degree of success and stardom as a television actor (*Fauji*, 1988; *Dil Dariya*, 1988; *Circus*, 1989). Despite a rather tepid debut as a second lead hero, who makes his appearance only after the interval (*Deewana*, dir. Raj Kanwar, 1992), Khan quickly rose to prominence. Shah Rukh Khan's initial rise to stardom was marked by a series of 'psychotic lover' roles, where instead of cavorting with his heroines in picturesque locales, he terrorised and threatened them (*Darr*, dir. Yash Chopra, 1993; *Anjaam*, dir. Rahul Rawail, 1994), even at times remorselessly murdering them (*Baazigar*, dir. Abbas-Mustan, 1993). For the nation's cinematic public, Khan's 'psychotic hero', with his unbridled and all-consuming drive and passion, embodied their own unapologetic embrace of the new consumerist ontology, engendered by the 1990's economic liberalisation[1] and the utopian possibility of millennial India (Varma 1998; Mazzarella 2003). As Ranjani Mazumdar notes, this new anti-hero 'opened up new possibilities, the least of which is the changed architecture of *desire*, where the psychotic's action holds out the utopian possibility of breaking all boundaries' (Mazumdar 2000, 252).

Shah Rukh Khan's enunciation of the new national ideology would become further consolidated with his popular 'NRI films' – *Dilwale Dulhania Le Jayenge* (dir. Aditya Chopra, 1995), *Dil Toh Pagal Hai* (dir. Yash Chopra, 1997), *Kuch Kuch Hota Hai* (dir. Karan Johar, 1998), *Kabhi Khushi Kabhie Gham* (dir. Karan Johar, 2001) and *Kal Ho Na Ho* (dir. Nikkhil Advani, 2003). It was in these 'yuppie' romantic films, speaking to the cultural aspirations, anxieties, and travails of both the non-resident Indian (NRI) abroad, and the new (modern) middle-class Indian at home, that Khan achieved his superstardom and iconic fame. In his on-screen 'yuppie' incarnates, as *DDLJ*'s Raj Malhotra, or *Kuch Kuch Hota Hai*'s Rahul Khanna, Khan embodied post-liberalisation India's key mantra – 'Indian values are portable and malleable' (Chopra 2007, 73). His cinematic avatars, with their branded Gap and Calvin Klein apparel, swanky sports cars and high-tech gadgets, at once personified the new consumerist ontology of millennial India with its claim on global citizenship, and the emergent ethos of cultural hybridity, where tradition and modernity were expected to exist in complete harmony, devoid of any conflict or contradiction (Uberoi 2006). Signifying spaces that both embodied 'an expanding globalist imagination and where the global and the local encounter one another or are juxtaposed' (Srinivas 2005, 333), Khan's yuppie protagonist, despite the inherent globality,

---

[1] Economic liberalisation policies introduced by the Indian government in the early 1990s were instrumental in reducing bureaucratic red-tape, thus encouraging more fiscal growth and foreign investment. Consequently, the earlier emphasis on Nehruvian socialism and Gandhian frugality was replaced by an unapologetic endorsement of consumerism.

was 'marked as Indian rather than diasporic' (Dwyer 2015, 50), underlining his role as 'the global citizen' while reaffirming an 'uncompromising Indianness' (ibid., 63).

It is crucial to keep in mind that Khan's on-screen portrayal of the 'new heroic prototype' (Chopra 2007, 138) was inevitably not only Hindu, but also, specifically the Hindi-speaking, North Indian, upper-caste denizen, thus conforming to popular Hindi cinema's tradition of 'centralizing a north Indian hetero-normative Hindu male, upper middle class, and upper caste subject ... as national citizen' (Khan 2009, 128). Thus, as a Muslim superstar in a predominantly Hindu nation, embodying the (new) 'Global Indian' who is invariably coded as Hindu, Shah Rukh Khan's star text assumes crucial significance, particularly in the context of the hegemonic narrative of the Muslim 'Other'. Historian Mushirul Hasan has discussed how the exclusionary and violent diatribe of Hindu extremism 'conjured up the image of a community outside the "national mainstream"', in which Muslims figure as 'aggressive fundamentalists and *demonized* as descendants of depraved and tyrannical medieval rulers who demolished temples and forcibly converted Hindus to Islam' (Hasan 1996, 185). The slogans of Hindu extremist political outfits – '*Jo Ram ka nahin, woh hamara nahin*' ('He who does not worship Ram, does not belong to us'), '*Babur ki santaan, jao Pakistan ya kabristan*' ('Son of Babur, go to either Pakistan or the graveyard') – reiterate this familiar rhetoric.

While Shah Rukh Khan's (Muslim) religious affiliation marks him as more vulnerable to insinuations and accusations of unpatriotic behaviour, it also positions him, especially in the context of contemporary India's global, modernist ethos, as the ideal (secular) citizen. Khan himself has acknowledged this problematic (and contradictory) duality of his public persona:

> Whenever there is an act of violence in the name of Islam, I am called upon to air my views on it and dispel the notion that by virtue of being a Muslim, I condone such senseless brutality ... (And) I sometimes become the inadvertent object of political leaders who choose to make me a symbol of all that they think is wrong and unpatriotic about Muslims in India. (Khan 2013)

The actor's references to his religious beliefs and his 'Muslimness' in interviews function to further authenticate his star image, particularly his subscription to India's secular ethos. As Richard Dyer has mentioned, 'the value embodied by a star is as it were harder to reject as "impossible" or "false" because the star's existence guarantees the existence of the value s/he embodies' (1998, 20). Even though he maintains that he is primarily an entertainer ('Films are for entertainment, messages are for the post office',[2] 'I don't give messages, I try to entertain people'[3]), Khan is aware of the crucial significance of his role as a (Muslim) celebrity in the context of the Indian nation-state's claims of secular credentials and global ethos – 'Just being a movie actor has made me stand for a lot of values and iconic things … one of the things that I suddenly stand for is that I am a Muslim in a Hindu country'.[4]

Khan is undoubtedly the perfect spokesperson for millennial India's global persona and its secular agenda. Critiquing Islamic fundamentalists and exhorting the youth to combat communalism and uphold the principles of Indian secularism[5] ('There is an Islam from Allah and … very unfortunately, there is an Islam from the Mullahs … I appeal to all of them to please give the youngsters the right reading of Quran'[6]), he presents a viable and acceptable variant of 'Muslimness' for the Indian national imaginary. For the Indian (Hindu) middle-class denizen, Shah Rukh Khan's sophisticated and erudite demeanour offers a comforting and palatable departure from the dominant images of ghettoised Muslims, insular and illiterate. Jyotika Virdi points out that though Khan 'never underplayed his Muslim identity', he was 'also embracing other religions', thus underlining 'the principle and the national definition of secularism in India:

[2] Shah Rukh Khan, 2007c.
[3] Shah Rukh Khan, 2007a.
[4] Shah Rukh Khan, 2007b.
[5] Shah Rukh Khan, 2007a.
[6] Shah Rukh Khan, 2008.

that we embrace anything' (Agha 2022). As he celebrates Hindu festivals, underlining his familiarity with the majority religion, and attempts to clarify the true meaning of *jihad*, the inherent threat of his Islamic affiliation is assuaged, and subsumed by his Indian secularist and pacifist ethos.

> I have read the holy Quran ... Nowhere in the Quran does it say that *jihad* will lead to *jannat* (paradise).[7]

> One needs to understand the meaning of *jihad* ... (it) means overcoming your own frailities, your own streak of violence ... *jihad* is not about killing other people. *Jihad* is about killing the badness in you.[8]

As the liberal, stylish 'Global Indian', Shah Rukh Khan offers a stark contrast to the much-maligned stereotype of the 'barbarian' Muslim and underlines the distinctiveness of the Indian Muslim. In interviews, the actor often emphasises his secular credentials – 'I would like to believe that I am an educated liberal Muslim, who has a Hindu wife and two kids'[9] – presenting himself as the very epitome of a suave, cosmopolitan and urbane *Indian* Muslim [emphasis own]. Interestingly, his choice of on-screen characters, whether Hindu or Muslim, also seem to align with this narrative. Eram Agha notes how 'Just as Khan's Hindu roles have almost exclusively been coded as Savarna, his Muslim characters usually appear to be Ashraf' (2022), thus subscribing to upper-caste credentials and consequently, distancing from any low-brow stereotypes.

In the public professing of his faith, Khan presents a rather palatable and acceptable variant of not only 'Muslimness', but also of religious faith and belief for the 'modern', 'global' Indian denizen – 'My religion is sacred to me. I don't wear it on my sleeves. I am not a fanatic, but yes I am God-fearing. And I believe your deeds define you. You get your brownie points and your whiplashes

---

[7] Ibid.

[8] Shah Rukh Khan, 2007b.

[9] Shah Rukh Khan, 2008.

here during your stay on earth' (Sheikh 2006, 231). However, this rather sanitised version of religion is disconcertingly at odds with the public and social discourse of contemporary India. As the country reiterates its role as an emergent global power, it is also confronted at home with caste politics, ethno-religious strife, gender and class inequities. While the pro-Hindu Right political outfit, BJP has emerged as one of the major national parties, in the aftermath of the 1990s divisive rhetoric, the fissures underlying the facade of India's secularism have become even more apparent with the current debates over religious conversions, Love Jihad and cow vigilantism.[10] It is in this context that Shah Rukh Khan's star text warrants a closer reading, particularly his depiction of Muslim characters – Kabir Khan in *Chak De! India*, Rizvan Khan in *My Name is Khan*, Raees Alam in *Raees* and the religiously ambiguous protagonist of *Pathaan*.

From *gaddar* (traitor) to *Bharat ki shaan* (the pride of India)

Chak De! India (dir. Shimit Amin, 2007) was by Bollywood standards, a *hatke* (different) film. With no song and dance sequences, or romantic interludes, or even a lead heroine, the film was a marked departure from Shah Rukh Khan's familiar Raj and Rahul prototypes. Instead, it narrated the tale of the Indian women's hockey team's journey, from the perennial underdog to world champion, under the guidance of their coach, Kabir Khan (Shah Rukh Khan). However, the film was noteworthy for another reason – it was the first time that the actor was essaying the role of a Muslim protagonist; his earlier role as the Afghan, Amjad Ali Khan in *Hey Ram* (dir. Kamal Haasan, 2000) was only

10 Right-wing outfits like RSS and VHP vehemently oppose religious conversions of Hindus and have been vocal in demanding more stringent anti-conversion laws. Accusing Muslim men of surreptitiously converting Hindu women by alluring them in romantic relationships, they perceive Muslims as a threat to the Hindu community. In recent years, cow vigilantism has also been on the rise, with 'cow protection' groups often engaging in violence against those suspected of cow smuggling or beef consumption.

a cameo. Moreover, Shah Rukh Khan's portrayal of hockey coach, Kabir Khan, a liberal urbane Muslim, presented a stark contrast to popular Hindi cinema's formulaic Muslim stereotypes and reiterated the actor's own liberal politics.

Discussing Muslim representation in Bollywood films, Kalyani Chadha and Anandam P. Kavoori describe the community's cinematic depiction as 'exoticized, marginalized, and demonized' (2008, 131–145). Similar to Hindi cinema's other stereotypes (the dissolute and drunk Christian, the Bengali, South Indian, and Parsi comic caricatures with their accented speech), the Muslim character also functioned primarily to reiterate and reaffirm the hegemonic value of the Hindu, North Indian (and) upper-caste male protagonist's primacy in the narrative world. As Manisha Sethi notes, 'Traditionally, mainstream Bollywood has reserved normalcy for the Hindu hero while encoding minorities with signs of cultural exaggeration' (Sethi 2002). Consequently, unlike his (upper-caste) Hindu counterpart, the Muslim protagonist was rarely accommodated within the cinematic space (with the exception of peripheral characters like the hero's loyal friend or the elderly servant) – signalling, in a sense, the nation's own rather ambiguous and problematic accommodation of its Muslim citizen-subjects. Presented either as remnants of an antiquated culture in the popular 1950s and 1960s Muslim Social films (Bhaskar and Allen 2009), or vilified as 'figures of violence, betrayal, inhumanity, bestiality, irrationality, deracination and irresponsibility' (Rai 2003) in post-2000 narratives, the Muslim in Hindi films has been traditionally (and still is) designated as the perennial 'Outsider'. This 'Othering' conforms to what Charles Ramirez Berg terms as the 'mediated stereotype' – 'an agreed-upon vision and a shared sign of the Other in precise and material form', which 'operates by gathering a specific set of negative traits and assembling them into a particular image' (2002, 38–39). Moreover, 'explicit codes' of their attire and religiosity make the Muslim characters 'emerge as stereotypes represented by well-defined signs of speech, appearance, dress, social and religious practice' (Kazmi 1994, 239). In the aftermath of the 1999 Kargil conflict with Pakistan, increasing sectarian violence and communal strife, and the spectre of global Islamic terrorism in a post-9/11 world, accommodating the Muslim character in the Hindi film narrative became even more problematic and implausible. We need to place Shah Rukh Khan's portrayal of *Chak De! India*'s Kabir Khan in this context.

Unlike the formulaic Muslim stereotypes in Hindi cinema, there was nothing in Kabir Khan's demeanour or appearance that marked him as explicitly Muslim. Apart from his habit of saying *aadab*, the Muslim term of greeting, and his evoking of a Muslim prayer at a crucial moment in the film's narrative, there is little that betrays his religious identity. But in spite of the lack of 'explicit codes' and reiteration of a liberal cosmopolitanism, Kabir Khan's tenuous claims to (Indian) citizenship are underlined, thus implying the Muslim subject's problematic accommodation within the national imaginary. The film begins with the final of the Men's Hockey World Cup, with the host nation, India, trailing arch rival Pakistan by a goal in a game that has at stake more than just sporting laurels. The Indian team is awarded a penalty shoot-out and an opportunity to level the score. In the crucial penalty kick, Kabir Khan (Shah Rukh Khan), the Indian captain and Asia's best centre forward fails to deliver and India loses to Pakistan. With a Muslim last name, Khan falls an easy prey to media frenzy and a nation desperate for a scapegoat. As angry fans burn effigies and 24x7 news channels hold court on whether the player is to be blamed for his team's debacle, the Indian Hockey Association decides to sack him from the captaincy. The graffiti on his house proclaims him a *gaddar* (traitor), neighbourhood kids clamber to look at the Muslim traitor who betrayed the nation, and onlookers snigger, '*Aise logon ko Partition ke waqt hi Pakistan chale jaana tha*' ('Such people should have left for Pakistan at the time of Partition'). The ignominy and shame forces Khan to forsake familiar surroundings and his favourite sport.

As Kabir Khan's fall from grace illustrates, the Indian Muslim is perilously vulnerable to accusations of being a *deshdrohi* (traitor). In the film, Khan's failure to deliver comes to haunt him again and again. The selectors ridicule him and even his players bring it up. Senior player Bindiya Naik, disgruntled with Khan's control, reminds the team of his ignominious past – '*Pakistan ka captain tha, India ke uniform mein... World Cup mein desh ko bech diya*' ('He was Pakistan's captain in the Indian uniform … he sold the country's honour at the World Cup'). As Khan himself rues, '*Afsoz is baat ka hai ke main apne mulk se haar gaya, jisko mera khoon pasina, dil jaan deke bhi yakeen nahin hota ke main uske team se khela tha aur zindagi bhar uske team se khelta rahoonga*' ('What I regret is that I lost to my country, and in spite of all my blood, sweat, and toil, I cannot convince it that I played for its team and all through my life I will play only for its team'). His avowed and emphatic patriotism 'betrays his own intense, unrequited longing for unequivocal, unconditional acceptance as an Indian in the body politic that treats him not only as alien but as an apostate' (Chakraborty 2012, 853). Thus, Kabir Khan's failure is not merely confined to the arena of sports, but rather embodies his failure to convincingly assert his loyalty and subscription to the Indian nation-state, and consequently, underlines the dilemma of the Indian Muslim. As Saisuresh Sivaswamy points out, the Indian Muslim 'has to constantly fight two demons: One from the past, of Partition and his/her perspective on Pakistan … and another ghost from the present, when Muslims are usually accused of engineering terrorist plots in India' (Sivaswamy 2007).

Though the film attempts to underline the contentious issues of Muslim citizenship, it also positions Khan as a liberal Muslim and, thus, consequently, invests him with the ability to articulate the anxieties and hopes of the national imaginary. Kabir Khan is never shown as offering *namaz*, or speaking in chaste Urdu; rather, he is always shown dressed in western attire and he never makes any reference to his religious beliefs. Thus, devoid of any explicit markings of his religious identity, the Muslim protagonist now becomes eligible to represent the nation. It is Khan who chides the girls for their regional and linguistic differences and extorts them to perform as a national team. In his first interaction with the team, he drives home the point – not only is he the boss, but they have to conform to his nationalist rhetoric. As each girl rattles off the name of her state, he asks them to leave; they will be allowed to play only when they realise they are playing for their country and not their state. In a country still divided by regional, linguistic, caste and religious fissures, Khan seems to transcend the barriers more effectively than the hegemonic Hindu, Hindi-speaking North Indian protagonist.

However, in spite of his lack of explicit codes, *Chak De! India* still emphatically underlines Kabir Khan's religious identity. After a humiliating defeat at the hands of defending champion Australia, Khan is shown reciting a Muslim prayer – '*Nasrum Min Allahe wa fathun qareeb*' ('Allah, bring me strength and bring victory closer') – possibly one of the rare moments in the film when his 'Muslimness' is emphasised. However, instead of contradicting his liberal persona, the scene only reaffirms his claims to Indian citizenship and his secular credentials. Khan's recourse to religion is not construed as a sign of his religiosity but rather his fervent desire for the team's victory, for the nation's triumph. Consequently, in the aftermath of the team's victory in the Championship's final, Khan is hailed as the '*sachcha Hindustani*' ('true Indian'), '*India ki jaan, Bharat ki shaan*' ('the spirit of India, the pride of India').

'My name is Khan. And I am not a terrorist.'

Co-produced by Shah Rukh Khan's Red Chillies Entertainment and Karan Johar's Dharma Productions, distributed worldwide by Fox Searchlight Pictures and starring Bollywood's favourite celluloid couple (Khan and actress Kajol), *My Name is Khan* (dir. Karan Johar) was one of 2010's most eagerly awaited releases. Johar's films tended to eulogise familial and romantic relationships; his blockbuster *Kabhi Khushi Kabhie Gham* (dir. Karan Johar, 2001) was promoted with the tagline, 'It's all about loving your parents'. *My Name Is Khan* was no different, however, unlike Johar's previous ventures, the film highlighted a pertinent political issue – Islamophobia and discrimination against Muslims in post-9/11 America. Though the focus still remained firmly on the family and romantic relationship of its protagonists, the film examined the 'question of belonging ... that plagues the Muslim American and Muslim Indian' (Gill 2015, 123). It also promised to present Shah Rukh Khan in a rather different avatar.

In the film, the actor plays Rizvan Khan, a man with Asperger's Syndrome, a far cry from his usual suave, cosmopolitan, urbane avatar. As the awkward, shy, hesitant Rizvan, who hates physical touch and is reluctant to make eye contact, *My Name is Khan*'s protagonist was an antithesis of Khan's usual screen archetype – 'It was a role without any crutches of stardom. There was no star gaze .... There was no flamboyant walk' (Bamzai 2010). Consequently, as Jaspreet Gill points out, by marking the Muslim male body as 'special' (Asperger's Syndrome), it gives Rizvan 'the license to state what would normally remain unspoken; thus, actively working against a meta-narrative of the Muslim terrorist that pervades the global media' (2015, 124). For Khan, who often craved 'something different' from his stereotypical and formulaic romantic roles, *My Name is Khan* provided the opportunity to showcase his acting prowess. However, it also marked Khan's return to the Muslim protagonist, albeit in a different setting than the critically acclaimed *Chak De! India*.

Contrary to *Chak De! India*'s Kabir Khan, who embodied the problematic accommodation of the Muslim subject within the national imaginary, *My Name is Khan*'s Rizvan Khan speaks to the travails of Muslim citizenship in a post-9/11 America. It was no surprise that the film also resonated with a global Muslim audience, specifically Arab-Americans (Kapoor 2020). Unlike Kabir Khan, Rizvan is not concerned with questions confronting the national imaginary; instead, his notion of community and citizenship are now articulated in the diasporic realm. Originally from Mumbai, Rizvan moves to San Francisco after his mother's death, where he meets Mandira (Kajol), a single mother with a young son. Despite the objections of his brother to their inter-religious nuptials, Rizvan and Mandira get married and settle down to blissful domesticity in the fictional California town of Banville. In its Hindu–Muslim coupling, *My Name is Khan* presents one of the rare instances of inter-faith conjugality in popular Hindi cinema.[11] However, unlike the reality of contemporary India, where the transgressions of inter-religious and inter-caste unions are often met with violence and brutality, Mandira and Rizvan, by virtue of their international/global locale, seem to transcend the issues that beset the nation. The couple have a secular wedding ceremony, where references to their individual religions are almost negated, and their marital life seems to present a utopian ideal. As Rizvan offers *namaz* and Mandira prays to her Hindu deities, their peaceful cohabitation not only reiterates post-liberalisation India's secular ambitions, but also, Shah Rukh Khan's own assertion of his secular and cosmopolitan familial life, where Hindu idols and the Quran are accorded equal respect.

In a talk show on Muslim subjectivity in contemporary India, Khan mentions how the decision to downplay Rizvan's 'Muslimness' was a conscious one – 'Can we play him like we play a hero? We don't need to play the religious part of him as the hero. Let it be absolutely *normal*, because I am a Muslim, and I don't wear it any other way'[12] [emphasis own]. Yet, Rizvan Khan's identity as a Muslim, particularly in a post-9/11 world, is central to the film's narrative, and emblematic of the (Indian) Muslim's global citizenship. As Rizvan greets everyone with a *salaam alaikum* (peace be unto you), offers *namaz* in public, recites verses from the Quran, emphasises the compassionate ethos of Islam, and reiterates, '*Musalman hona buri baat nahin*

[11] Though Hindi films have occasionally portrayed inter-faith unions, these have tended to be usually Hindu–Christian, with invariably the Hindu man paired with the Christian woman – underlining not only Hindu masculinity's prowess to rehabilitate the (fallen/Westernised) Christian woman, but also the spiritual and cultural fragility of the Hindu woman, which deems her as inaccessible for the non-Hindu man (particularly the Muslim). Consequently, Hindu–Muslim romances have also tended to pair the Hindu man with the Muslim woman, where the latter is usually co-opted into the Hindu cultural realm.

[12] Shah Rukh Khan, 2010. 'Being Muslim in Today's India'.

hain' (being Muslim is not a bad thing), his identity as a Muslim is emphatically foregrounded. While millennial India necessitated the camouflaging of the Muslim's religious ethos under the cloak of nationalism, the (Indian) Muslim, in the diasporic realm, confronted by the spectre of post-9/11 racial profiling and discrimination, is prompted to reaffirm their distinctiveness.

As Rizvan and Mandira's idyllic world is disrupted with their son's death in a schoolyard skirmish, and Mandira blames her husband and his religion ('I should have never married a Muslim'), the Muslim protagonist's tenuous sense of belonging is further exacerbated. Taking his wife's angry outburst at face value – 'Why don't you go tell the President of United States, "Mr. President, my name is Khan, and I am not a terrorist"?' – Rizvan embarks on a journey that transforms him into 'a Forrest Gumpian folk hero … (who) attempts to make America see the errors of stereotyping Islam' (Bamzai 2010). As the film's narrative progresses, and Rizvan's quest takes him across America, his repeated assertion, 'My name is Khan, and I am not a terrorist', embodies not only a post-9/11 world, but also, the vulnerability of the Indian Muslim's global subjectivity. His allegiance and loyalty to his new homeland is only validated with his acts of 'patriotism' – reporting Muslim extremists to the FBI and rescuing the inhabitants of a hurricane-hit Georgia town. In his on-screen narrative of vilification, victimhood and eventual redemption, Khan underlines the binary rhetoric of the 'good Muslim' and 'bad Muslim'. As Mahmood Mamdani argues, the divisive politics prevalent in the post-9/11 milieu not only explicitly linked Islam with terrorism, but also, 'turned religious experience into a political category, differentiating between "good Muslims" from "bad Muslims", rather than terrorists from civilians' (2002, 366).

The contentious citizenship of the Indian Muslim, both in the national and the global sphere, is underlined not only in Shah Rukh Khan's on-screen renditions, Kabir Khan and Rizvan Khan, but also in the actor's own star text. While the controversy over his IPL remarks reiterates the Indian Muslim's problematic inclusion within the national imaginary, his repeated detentions at American airports (August 2009, April 2012, August 2016), due to a match with a namesake on the U.S. terror watchlist, are often perceived in the context of post-9/11 Islamophobia. The opening sequence in *My Name is Khan* is reminiscent of Khan's own experience – as airport officials question Rizvan, viewers are reminded of both Rizvan and his off-screen counterpart's vulnerability as Muslims. In an article titled "Being a Khan" for *Outlook Turning Points* magazine, Khan mentioned how he gave his children 'pan-Indian and pan-religious' names (Aryan and Suhana) so that they might not encounter discrimination and Islamophobia (Khan 2013).[13] Khan's response in the media, following the IPL controversy, further underlines the fragility of the Indian Muslim's citizenship. In exclusive interviews to select media outlets, the actor repeatedly emphasises his allegiance to the nation, making frequent references to his father, who had participated in the country's freedom struggle.

> I pay my taxes, I try to be okay law-wise and then, suddenly you are subjected to questioning of this form, and I get very emotional about the things that people say, because my parents gave me nothing else … I'm not saying I'm the most patriotic, but … I'm a good Indian.[14]

In his interviews, Khan also emerges as the voice of the secular, cosmopolitan India, as he questions the undue importance accorded to regional and ethno-religious identities, pointing out the incongruity of such rhetoric with the narrative of the modern, emergent global India.

> All this (religion, regionalism) is a subset of your country identity, of your national identity. When did subsets become more important than the set itself? And that is something that is unacceptable.[15]

13 Though the choice of 'pan-Indian and pan-religious' names for his children does reiterate Khan's secular credentials, he may not have been incorrect in anticipating a hostile Islamophobic reaction. Bollywood actors Saif Ali Khan and Kareena Kapoor Khan faced severe backlash and trolling when they chose 'Muslim' names for their sons, Taimur (b. 2016) and Jehangir (b. 2021).

14 Shah Rukh Khan, 2010a.

15 Ibid.

> If we are going to talk about regionalism every second, if you're going to talk about religion every two minutes, if you're going to talk about Khans and Kumars and Khannas every 30 seconds ... I think nobody should (then) talk about India shining and India becoming bright.[16]

Shah Rukh Khan's own star text, particularly his cinematic portrayals of Muslim subjectivity, reiterates not only the Indian Muslim's tenuous claims to (Indian and global) citizenship but also contemporary India's inherent fissures and contradictions. As Khan responded to the Shiv Sena diatribe with repeated assertions of his secular credentials – 'I'm a bloody good Indian' – and his legacy as the son of a freedom fighter, the controversy exposed his vulnerability as a Muslim, both within the national and the global space. While incidents involving his detention at U.S. airports are often couched within the rhetoric of his religious affiliation, thus underlining the Muslim subject's vulnerability in a post-9/11 world, the questioning of his patriotism, at home, speaks to the nation's inherent fissures. Post-liberalisation's claims of modernity and secularism thus are juxtaposed with its recent history of divisive politics, sectarian violence and communal strife. However, Shah Rukh Khan's rendition of the Indian Muslim would undergo a further resignification in Rahul Dholakia's *Raees*.

'*Baniye ka dimaag aur Miyanbhai ki daring*'

In *Raees* (dir. Rahul Dholakia, 2017), the audience is introduced to a very different avatar of the Bollywood superstar – a kohl-lined, bare-bodied, bloodied Shah Rukh Khan whipping himself with a cluster of blades as he participates in the Muharram *taziya* procession. As Sivaswamy remarks, 'Raees Alam is the most "Muslim" role Khan has essayed so far ... (he) inhabits the world of mohallas, Moharram and maatham, something that Shah Rukh Khan the actor maybe did long ago, but never ever on screen' (Sivaswamy 2017). The film elicited some controversy since it was the third consecutive Muslim character that the actor portrayed

---

[16] Ibid.

after *Ae Dil Hai Mushkil* (dir. Karan Johar, 2016) and *Dear Zindagi* (dir. Gauri Shinde, 2016). However, in *ADHM*, he had a cameo while in *Dear Zindagi*, the focus was on the protagonist, Kaira (Alia Bhatt) with Khan in the supporting role as her therapist, Dr Jehangir Khan. Moreover, as Hasan Suroor underlines, these characters were 'only nominally Muslim' where there was 'no hint of parading his faith' (Suroor 2017). In contrast, the actor seemed to have forsaken any such pretence at essaying the archetypal Moderate Muslim in *Raees*.

As a 'gangster film', the genre conventions of *Raees* were far removed from the archetypal SRK yuppie NRI romance. However, as Lalitha Gopalan has pointed out, gangster films predominantly revolve around issues of power, authority and dominance, and consequently, function as 'a site of writing the nation' (2002, 107). Omar Ahmed, in his discussion of *Raees*, also underlines the crucial significance of the film's genre, allowing it 'to tap into the wider social and political anxieties of contemporary Indian society' (2019, 114) and employing the inherent thematic violence 'as a perfect foil for subversive political messages' (2019, 120). It also allows Khan to portray the liminal figure of the gangster as the protagonist, 'taking up a position that occupies both the nation and the community, a dual position rarely granted to Muslim characters' (Ahmed 2019, 121).

Essaying the role of the 1980s Gujarati mafia kingpin and bootlegger Abdul Latif, Shah Rukh Khan's portrayal of the 'unabashedly Muslim' (Agarwal 2017) Raees not only marked a departure from his formulaic role as the romantic 'Global Indian', but also, from his previous renditions of the Indian Muslim. In contrast to both Kabir (*Chak De! India*) and Rizvan (*My Name is Khan*), Raees is 'very much a product of the ghetto' (Agarwal 2017), thus embodying the marginalisation of the urban disenfranchised Indian Muslim. The ghettoisation of the Muslims in Indian cities underlines not only their significant 'economic deprivation', but also, their 'sense of physical insecurity' and 'increasing socio-spatial segregation' (Gayer and Jaffrelot 2012, 2). Subsequently, the 'ghetto Muslim' is marked as overtly religious, thus further reiterating his inherent extremism as well as his lack of education. In *Raees*, however, we see a more acceptable variant of the *miyanbhai* (a colloquial term for the Muslim), whose religious subscription is superseded by his business etiquette, the practicality of the *baniya* (trader). A devout and orthodox Muslim, Raees's work ethic is shaped by his mother's constant iteration – '*Koi dhandha chota nahi hota, aur dhande se bada koi dharam nahi hota*' ('no business is small and no religion is bigger than the business you do'). As the tagline of the film, '*Baniye ka dimaag aur miyanbhai ki daring*' ('The brains of the trader and the daring of the Muslim') celebrates both his business acumen (*baniya*) and his bravado (*miyanbhai*), Raees 'allows the otherness of the "Miabhai" to be embraced via the familiarity of the "Baniya"' (Gupta 2017).

Raees might be an orthodox devout Muslim but he displays no traces of religious fundamentalism. As an elected political representative, he initiates a low-cost housing project, *apni duniya* (our world), for his constituents, and distributes food to both Hindu and Muslim residents during communal riots, reiterating his motto that humanity trumps religion – '*sab hamare log hain*' ('they are all our people'). As a cinematic incarnate of the Indian Muslim, particularly the ghettoised lower-class *miyanbhai*, the film's implicit message is clear – Raees Alam might be devout, but his religiosity should not be equated with extremism or fundamentalism. It is only when he unwittingly smuggles RDX in the guise of gold, which is later used in serial bombings across North India (a reference to the 1993 Mumbai bomb blasts), that he is doomed to an ignominious end. By agreeing to the Mumbai-based don, Musa (a reference to Abdul Latif's own association with Dawood Ibrahim), Raees falls prey to the anti-national Muslim, the antagonist in the narrative of the nation, and consequently, reaffirms the image of the ghettoised Muslim who can never be a true Indian. As he woefully rues in the film, '*mohalla bachate bachate shehar jala diya*' ('while trying to save the neighbourhood, I burnt down the city'), it is a clear message that the Indian Muslim needs to think beyond his *quam* (community) or else he will inevitably succumb to the taint of a *deshdrohi* (traitor). What makes such a tragic denouement inevitable is Raees's pronounced Muslimness – his attire, his *tabeez* (religious amulet) and kohl-lined eyes all not only explicitly mark him as the Muslim 'Other', but also deems him impossible to be perceived as an (authentic) Indian citizen. In his on-screen role as Raees Alam, Shah Rukh Khan displays the 'explicit codes' that were absent in his previous portrayals of the Indian Muslim (Kabir and Rizvan). Just as the chaste Urdu, *sherwani* (traditional Muslim attire) and strict observance of religious norms (*namaz* and Haj) defined the 1950s' and 1960s' Muslim protagonist as antiquated and archaic, incapable of embodying the modernistic ambitions of Nehruvian India, similarly Raees's overt (Muslim) appearance makes him untenable for millennial India.

Raees holds particular relevance, not only in terms of enumerating the subjectivity and citizenship of the Indian Muslim, and his role in the national imaginary, but as Trisha Gupta asserts, 'it is absolutely important for the optics of this film that this protagonist is a Muslim in Gujarat where the Hindutva project is on its way to political and social hegemony' (2017). With Gujarat being a stronghold of the Bharatiya Janata Party (BJP), a right-wing political party with Hindu-nationalist ideologies (Banerjee 2005), since 1995, the state laid the foundation for the political dynamics on the national front. Since BJP assumed power at the Centre in 2014, debates over 'Love Jihad', beef ban and cow vigilantism have become prominent, bringing into question the issue of minority citizenship. With the rise of Hindutva politics and increasing divisiveness, the Indian Muslim now inhabits a place in the margins (Waikar 2018), often ostracised and discriminated against. Though *Raees* seems to evoke the 1980s and 1990s, the period that Latif was active in Gujarat, its relevance in the current political and social environment cannot be disregarded. As Amit Agarwal mentions, 'There is an almost daring foregrounding of Muslim identity … making a passionate case for seeing the community as a victim of rather than the perpetrator of terrorism' (2017). For Arnesh Ghose, 'Relevant, stylish and politically charged, *Raees* is SRK's most important film till date' (2017), underlining the significance of the film in the current scenario. Raees's state-sanctioned encounter by the police at the end of the film explicitly reiterates not only the untenability of accommodating the minority subject, who is so explicitly coded as the 'Other' and thus, incongruous with the majority, but also 'resonates as a symbolic gesture of the Hindutva extermination of the Muslim' (Ahmed 2019, 125).

Though Raees Alam might seem a departure from Khan's usual oeuvre as well as his previous portrayals of the Indian Muslim, the protagonist, similar to Kabir Khan (*Chak De! India*) and Rizvan Khan (*My Name is Khan*), embodies the travails and tribulations of the Muslim minority citizenship. However, *Pathaan* further complicates this on-screen rendition of the Indian Muslim, where Indianness and Muslimness are deigned compatible only when inhabiting separate, discrete spaces. Consequently, it also situates the Indian Muslim's subjectivity in the context of the nation's embrace of an increasingly polarising and divisive right-wing rhetoric.

'Desh ka sawaal hai'

The fourth installment in Yash Raj Films' Spy Universe, *Pathaan* was one of the most highly anticipated releases of 2023. With its slick action sequences and A-list star cast, it promised Hindi film audiences the ultimate theatrical experience. It also heralded the return of Shah Rukh Khan to the big screen after a hiatus of four years. After three decades as one of Hindi film industry's most successful and popular stars, both at home and abroad, Khan's cinematic trajectory was at a crossroads. Deemed too old to reprise his 1990s' archetypal romantic hero, his recent experimentative forays – *Fan* (dir. Maneesh Sharma, 2016), *Jab Harry Met Sejal* (dir. Imtiaz Ali, 2017), *Zero* (dir. Aanand L. Rai, 2018) – had been commercial disappointments, prompting questions about his stardom and longevity. *Pathaan*, where Khan played an action hero, a marked departure from his quintessential romantic roles, was expected to reinstate his former glory and superstardom. Despite the right-wing rhetoric and calls to boycott the film, the response to *Pathaan* was phenomenal. The film was hailed as an ode to Indian nationalism, a unifying narrative during a time of divisiveness and hate. *Pathaan* was not only the most successful film in Khan's decades-long filmography, which was later surpassed by his subsequent release, *Jawan* (dir. Atlee Kumar, 2023), but also, emerged as the highest-grossing Hindi film ever. The film's blockbuster success came at a time when Khan was emerging from both a professional and a personal low. In October 2021, his son, Aryan Khan was arrested by the Narcotics Control Bureau (NCB) on drug-related charges following a raid at a cruise ship party. He was later released on bail after spending almost a month in jail, with the case being finally dismissed in May 2022. The lack of evidence and the inordinate delay by even a celebrity of Shah Rukh Khan's stature to secure bail for his son was seen by many as a deliberate ploy to frame Aryan Khan and exert pressure on his superstar father to be a more vocal advocate of majoritarian politics. As Ira Bhaskar points out, Khan is 'a Muslim celebrity whose embodiment of India's secular, multicultural social and cultural identity represents a perspective that openly challenges the majoritarian vision of the government in power' (2023, 138). Thus, *Pathaan*'s release became a means for his fans to show their emphatic support for their celluloid icon. As Shah Rukh Khan fans trooped in hordes to watch the film, reserved entire auditoriums, and danced with gay abandon in the theatres, the film's success was an exuberant reaffirmation of Khan's cinematic aura and fame. However, for many the film was also an unabashed celebration of India's secular ethos and cultural diversity, tenets that seem to be increasingly under threat in the current divisive climate of Hindutva extremism.

Pathaan opens with a vengeful Pakistani army general determined to exact revenge on the Indian state for the abrogation of Article 370, revoking the special status granted to Jammu & Kashmir – a narrative that seems congruent with the country's anti-Pakistan stance and right-wing Hindutva rhetoric. However, contrary to the hyperbolic nationalism omnipresent in recent films like *Sooryavanshi* (dir. Rohit Shetty, 2021) and *The Kashmir Files* (dir. Vivek Agnihotri, 2022), '*Pathan* is patriotic without being jingoistic or hateful' (Ramani 2023), 'devoid of divisiveness and Islamophobia' (Lakshmi 2023) and a marked departure from 'the kind of toxic nationalism' espoused in these 'majoritarian and homogeneous notions of the nation' (Bhaskar 2023). Unlike other contemporary narratives, *Pathaan*'s patriotic tone is not defined by an unabashed vilification of Pakistan. As Prathyush Parasuraman remarks, the film clearly enunciates that 'to love India is *not* to hate Pakistan, but to want to keep India safe from any enemy' (Parasuraman 2023a). If General Qadir (Manish Wadhwa) epitomises the fundamentalist, fringe elements in Pakistan insistent on jeopardising any attempts at brokering peace, ISI agent Rubina (Deepika Padukone) represents the sane voices persevering to improve the bilateral relations between the two nations. *Pathaan* makes another significant intervention in its delineation of patriotism – for Pathaan (Shah Rukh Khan), the nation is a mother unlike Jim (John Abraham), for whom the nation is a lover. This maternal versus romantic binary is apparent in the divergent perspectives of the protagonist (Pathaan) and the antagonist (Jim). Feeling betrayed by his lover-nation, Jim embarks on a destructive trajectory, from an elite special operative to a dreaded mercenary, devoid of any semblance of humanity. In contrast, Pathaan, despite his many trials and tribulations, remains steadfast in his loyalty and allegiance to his mother-nation. As Parsuraman comments, 'It is one of the most of the most fascinating, provocative ways to think of nationalism … while lover can betray, a mother never betrays' (Parasuraman 2023a).

In *Pathaan*, Khan plays a RAW agent, motivated by the same patriotism, loyalty and allegiance to 'Bharat Mata' as his fellow YRF Spy Universe RAW agents, Avinash 'Tiger' Singh Rathore (Salman Khan, *Ek Tha Tiger* and *Tiger Zinda Hai*) and Kabir Dhaliwal (Hrithik Roshan, *War*). Despite the similarities, there is a crucial difference between Pathaan and his compatriots. Unlike Tiger and Kabir, his moniker, 'Pathaan', marks him as a non-Hindu, but neither is he explicitly coded as a Muslim; he is 'a casteless, classless man without a religion or orgin story' (Parasuraman

2023b). When Rubina, a Pakistani spy and Pathaan's love interest in the film asks him whether he is actually a 'Pathaan' (implying he is from Afghanistan), followed by the inevitable question – '*Tum Mussalman ho*?' ('Are you a Muslim?'), he responds rather cryptically – '*Pata nahin main kya hoon, kaun hoon*' ('I don't know what I am, who I am'). He then explains – he is an orphan, was found abandoned in a movie theatre (interestingly, a reference to Shah Rukh Khan's own off-screen narrative – losing his parents early in life followed by his superstardom in Hindi films), and spent his life in state-run orphanages and juvenile homes. As he describes it, '*mere desh ne meri parvarish ki*' ('my country brought me up'), which prompted him to join the Indian army and dedicate his life to the nation, like a dutiful son fulfilling his obligations – '*Ek achche bete ki tarah, mujhe bhi mere ma baap ki sewa karni chahiye*' ('Like a good son, I should also serve my parents'). Pathaan's relationship with his surrogate parent, India, is thus defined by obligation, duty, and a sense of responsibility as expected from the model (minority) citizen. However, it is a relationship that is devoid of any reciprocity. The minority subject can no longer demand anything from the state; instead, he is expected to completely dedicate himself to the nation's service, a mandatory requirement to not only prove his allegiance but also, assert his claims of citizenship. Pathaan's iconic line in the film – '*Ek soldier yeh nahin poochta desh ne uske liye kya kiya, poochta hai woh desh ke liye kya kar sakta hai*' ('A soldier does not ask what his country can do for him, he asks what he can do for his country') – is an attestation to the minority's role in the majoritarian nationalist project. It also consequently mirrors the experience of the Indian Muslim in contemporary India, where the onus of proving their allegiance and loyalty is solely their responsibility, and not contingent upon the state.

The precarious predicament of the Indian Muslim has been further exacerbated by the Indian government's recent attempts to define citizenship, particularly with the implementation of the National Register of Citizens (NRC) and Citizenship Amendment Act (CAA). The CAA, which was passed in December 2019, assures an accelerated pathway to Indian citizenship for religious minorities from Afghanistan, Bangladesh and Pakistan, which includes Hindus, Sikhs, Buddhists, Jains, Parsis and Christians but not Muslims. The inclusion of religion as a qualifying factor for citizenship not only undermines India's secular tenets but also, places the Indian Muslim in a vulnerable position, where their claims to citizenship must be now supplemented by documentation and evidence. In the north-eastern state, Assam, where the NRC has been implemented since 2013–2014, the lack of appropriate papers can often lead to an Indian (Muslim) citizen being designated an illegal (Bangladeshi) immigrant (Hari and Nagpal 2022). While for other Indian religious demographics (not just the majority Hindus but also, religious minorities like Sikhs, Jains, Buddhists, Christians) and the lack of documents does not inevitably threaten their citizenship, but for Indian Muslims, it is imperative that they prove and demonstrate by tangible evidence their Indianness. Consequently, the failure to do so would invariably mean losing their claims to the Indian nation-state, labelling them as stateless vagabonds.

Thus, Pathaan, symbolic of the Indian Muslim, cannot rely on the nation for a sense of belonging, kinship or familial ties. Such a reciprocal relationship becomes possible only when he is adopted by an Afghan village as their own. Stationed in Afghanistan as part of a joint Indo–U.S. operation, Pathaan saved the village from a misdirected drone attack, risking his own life. The indebted villagers nursed the critically injured Indian soldier back to health and as a token of gratitude, welcomed him as one of their own – '*Aaj se, hum tere aur tu hamara, hamara Pathaan*' ('From today, we are yours and you are ours, our Pathaan'). As an elderly Afghan woman ties a 'taveez' (talisman) on Pathaan's arm, he finally has a family he can call his own and is no longer simply a ward of the state. For Pathaan, thus, it was not merely a physical resuscitation but more significantly, a spiritual and religious awakening, and finally finding acceptance and belonging, which had eluded him in his homeland. The relationship with his new (Muslim) family was one of *apnapan* (intimacy) and reciprocity, a stark contrast to the conformity and adherence that was expected of him as the model (minority) citizen. Pathaan's Afghan family, with whom he makes it a point to celebrate Eid every year, consequently also reiterates the dynamics of South Asian kinship that can be imagined beyond the physical and geographical borders of the nation. However, this also results in a crystallisation of Pathaan's 'Muslimness', evident not only by his physical markers (the 'taveez' and the beard) but also, by his greetings (*salaam*, *adab*, *dua*), his emphatic response to Rubina's '*salaam walaikum*' ('peace be unto you') – '*walaikum assalam warahmatullahi wabarakatuhu*' ('may the peace, mercy, and blessings of Allah be with you too'), which elicited cheers from audiences in the theatre (HT Entertainment Desk 2023) – and of course, the references to Pathaan's '*mehman nawazi*' (Afghan hospitality). We know Pathaan as a soldier, an anonymous entity, an automaton who exists only to serve his country, but the nuances and details only emerge when he bequeathed his identity as a Muslim.

Consequently, this also divorces his religious subscription from his national identity. The genesis of Pathaan's religiosity and faith is no longer tethered to India, but must be now situated outside the physical and geographical realm of the nation, in Afghanistan. He may be an Indian by birth, a fact that he has no control over, but his religious identity is one of his own volition – 'Pathaan is a Pathan, not because he was "born" that way, or because his "blood" is Muslim, but because he has chosen to be' (Menon 2023).

Conclusion

The reel avatars of the Indian Muslim, as essayed by Shah Rukh Khan, cannot be perceived in isolation but rather needs to be read both in the context of the sociopolitical milieu and his own star text. A cursory glance at the trajectory of these characters – Kabir, Rizvan, Raees and finally, Pathaan – reveals the inherent ruptures in the nation's accommodation of its minority (Muslim) subject. Comparing *Chak De! India* with *Raees*, Omar Ahmed describes the former as a 'schizophrenic text' that 'suggests that the Indian

Muslim should seek to prove their duty to the nation' (2019, 122). In comparison, Raees, despite his liminality as both a criminal and a Muslim, can still be regarded as 'secular and capitalist' (Ahmed 2019, 122) due to his firm belief that '*Koi dhandha chota nahi hota, aur dhande se bada koi dharam nahi hota*' ('no business is small and no religion is bigger than the business you do'). It is his emphatic subscription to *dhandha* (business), above everything else, that helps him align with post-liberalisation India, where socialist ideals have been discarded in favour of consumerist aspirations. Unlike Kabir Khan, Raees is not encumbered by the burden of his minority citizenship and the demands to prove his loyalty to the nation. However, as his ignoble end illustrates, for the majoritarian state, with its Hindutva doctrine, Raees is a threat that must be vanquished. There exists absolutely no space for a minority subject, who with his proletariat, subaltern presence offers a potent (and secular) alternative to the ineffectual state. In contrast, Kabir Khan in *Chak De! India*, despite his public humiliation and social ostracisation, could still return to his old, familiar milieu and be accepted within the national fold. This was possible not only because Kabir had explicitly demonstrated his loyalty and patriotism by orchestrating the victory of the women's hockey team, but also because he did not pose any tangible threat to the majority. While Raees's appearance and actions were replete with visible markers of his Muslimness, Kabir was devoid of such explicit coding.

There exists a similar distinction between *My Name Is Khan* and *Pathaan* in their delineation of minority citizenship and subjectivity. As Priya Ramani underlines the crucial difference between the two – 'Unlike in *My Name Is Khan*, where SRK has to inform us and his fellow Muslims that "God's path is love's path, not the path of terror and war," in *Pathan*, SRK doesn't spend any time educating us about good Muslims and bad Muslims… Pathan is only interested in our shared humanity and how we must come together to fight those who threaten it' (Ramani 2023). Pathaan does not engage in any pedagogical discourse, educating and informing about both Islam and Muslims; his objective is to save his nation and its people. Where Rizvan was emphatic that he is not a terrorist despite his last name, Pathaan does not even have a last name, thus liberating him from the constant presence of his religious identity. Interestingly, though he is christened as 'Pathaan' much later in his adulthood, there is no mention of his previous name. While both Rubina and Jim are given detailed backstories that explain their motivation, Pathaan's antecedents are ambiguous, practically non-existent. What motivates Pathaan is his love, loyalty and patriotism towards his country; when the nation is at stake ('*desh ka sawaal hai*'), he is willing to sacrifice anything and everything. In contrast, in *My Name Is Khan*, we not only encounter Rizvan's mother, brother and sister-in-law but are also, familiarised with his childhood milieu, the Mumbai chawl and his mentor. *Pathaan* allows no such familiarity and intimate connections. The only way the Muslim minority subject can now be included within the nationalist project is by divorcing his religious identity from his national identity. Consequently, by making his Indianness and Muslimness discrete and separate from each other, it makes him more palatable and the (Indian) Muslim can be finally not only accommodated but also, celebrated. Devoid of his Muslimness, Pathaan embodies a refreshing and distinct brand of patriotism, that is not only devoid of hyperbolic jingoism and majoritarian rhetoric but also, unmistakably intertwined with Shah Rukh Khan's own star text as a liberal, secular Indian Muslim. In doing so, it also engages in an 'unfettered affirmation of SRK's Muslim identity' and thus, 'makes no apology for everything that is Muslim – and cool about SRK' (Prabhala 2023). As Mukul Kesavan summarises, 'It's a mistake to think that Shah Rukh Khan has used patriotism to buy himself a hit. Rather, he has fashioned a non-majoritarian patriotism that lets him be himself (not Raj, nor Vikas) and allowed his audience to identify with him.' (Kesavan 2023).

However, it is also rather telling that in 2023, Shah Rukh Khan's on-screen avatar could no longer afford to be both an Indian *and* a Muslim. Interestingly, Khan also no longer gives interviews where he shares his personal opinions and beliefs, whether it is about his Islamic faith or the state of the nation. In some way, it mirrors the predicament of Pathaan, where to assert himself as a patriotic Indian, his Muslimness must be exorcised from his Indianness, thus ensuring that there is no conflict between his patriotism and his faith. The emphasis on this separateness further reiterates the vulnerability and precariousness of the minority (Muslim) citizen-subject in an India dominated by majoritarian rhetoric and politics.

References

Agarwal, Amit. 2017. "The Message in the Bottle: Shah Rukh Khan's 'Raees' Is Deeply political." *Scroll.in*, 4 February 2017. scroll.in/reel/828487/the-message-in-the-bottle-shah-rukh-khans-raees-is-deeply-political. Accessed on 24 March 2025.

Agha, Eram. 2022. "Tightrope Act: Shah Rukh Khan's Silent rebellion." *The Caravan*, New Delhi, 31 December 2022. https://caravanmagazine.in/film/shah-rukh-khan-silent-rebellion. Accessed on 24 March 2025.

Ahmed, Omar. 2019. "'Chariot of Fire': Genre Slippages, Iconographic Agitation and Ideological Subversion in SRK's Raees." *Studies in South Asian Film & Media* 9, no. 2: 113–28.

Bamzai, Kaveree. 2010. "His Name Is Khan." *India Today*, 1 March 2010, 46–51.

Banerjee, Sumanta. 2005. "Civilising the BJP." *Economic and Political Weekly* 40, no. 29: 3116–119.

Berg, Charles Ramirez. 2002. *Latino Images in Film: Stereotypes, Subversion and Resistance.* Austin, Texas: University of Texas Press.

Bhaskar, Ira. 2023. "On *Pathaan*: Betrayal, Commitment and Belonging." *BioScope* 14, no. 2: 137–42.

Bhaskar, Ira, and Richard Allen. 2009. *Islamicate Cultures of Bombay Cinema.* New Delhi: Tulika Books.

Bhattacharjee, Subhadeep. 2010. "Shiv Sena Threatens Shah Rukh Khan over IPL." *Oneindia Entertainment*, 29 January 2010. entertainment.oneindia.in/bollywood/news/2010/shiv-sena-slams-shahrukh-290110.html. Accessed on 24 March 2025.

Chadha, Kalyani, and Anandam P. Kavoori. 2008. "Exoticized, Marginalized, Demonized: The Muslim 'Other' in Indian Cinema." In *Global Bollywood*, edited by Aswin Punathambekar and Anandam P. Kavoori, 131–45. New York: NYU Press.

Chakraborty, Mridula Nath. 2012. "Nationalist Transactions: *Chak De! India* and the Down-and-out Sports Coach." *Continuum* 26, no. 6: 845–58.

Chopra, Anupama. 2007. *King of Bollywood: Shah Rukh Khan and the Seductive World of Indian Cinema*. New York, NY: Warner Books.

Dudrah, R., E. Mader, and B. Fuchs, eds. 2015. *SRK and Global Bollywood*. New Delhi: Oxford University Press.

Dwyer, Rachel. 2015. "Innocent Abroad: SRK, Karan Johar, and the Indian Diasporic Romance." In *SRK and Global Bollywood*, edited by Dudrah et al., 49–69. New Delhi: Oxford University Press.

Dyer, Richard. 1998. *Stars*. London: British Film Institute.

Express News Service. 2015. "There's Extreme Intolerance in India: Shah Rukh Khan on 50th birthday." *The Indian Express*, New Delhi, 3 November 2015.

Gayer, Laurent, and Christophe Jaffrelot. 2012. "Introduction: Muslims of the Indian City. From Centrality to Marginality." In *Muslims in Indian Cities: Trajectories of Marginalisation*, edited by Laurent Gayer and Christophe Jaffrelot, 1–22. London: C. Hurst & Co.

Ghose, Arnesh. 2017. "#Review: Relevant, Stylish and Politically Charged, *Raees* is SRK's Most Important Film Till Date." *Man's World*, Mumbai. mansworldindia.com/cinema/review-relevant-stylish-politically-charged-raees-srks-important-film-till-date/. Accessed on 24 March 2025.

Gill, Jaspreet. "*My Name Is Khan*: Reinventing the Muslim Hero on the Global Stage." In *SRK and Global Bollywood*, edited by Rajinder Dudrah, Elke Mader and Bernhard Fuchs, 122–137. New Delhi: Oxford University Press.

Gopalan, Lalitha. 2002. *Cinema of Interruptions: Action Genres in Contemporary Indian Cinema*. London: BFI.

Gupta, Trisha. 2017. "Miya-Baniya Bhai Bhai?" *Mumbai Mirror*, 5 February 2017. mumbaimirror.indiatimes.com/opinion/columnists/trisha-gupta/miya-baniya-bhai-bhai/articleshow/56978783.cms. Accessed on 24 March 2025.

HT Correspondent. 2015. "Venom against SRK for Intolerance Comment Spills Over: Who Said What." *The Hindustan Times*, New Delhi, 5 November 2015.

HT Entertainment Desk. 2023. "Pathaan's 'epic' Reply in 'Salaam Alaikum' Scene Gets Cheers and Whistles from Fans. Here's What it Means." *The Hindustan Times*, New Delhi, 30 January 2023.

Hari, Amrita, and Sugandha Nagpal. 2022. "The National Register of Citizens (NRC) in India and the Potential for Statelessness *In Situ*: A Cautionary Tale from Assam." *Contemporary South Asia* 30, no. 2: 194–201.

Hasan, Mushirul. 1996. "The Myth of Unity: Colonial and National Narratives." In *Making India Hindu: Religion, Community, and the Politics of Democracy in India*, edited by David Ludden, 185–210. New Delhi: Oxford University Press.

Kapoor, Priya. 2020. "Shah Rukh Khan: Journey from Charisma to Celebrity." In *Stardom in Contemporary Hindi Cinema*, edited by Aysha Iqbal Viswamohan and Claire M. Wilkinson-Weber, 31–44. Singapore: Springer.

Kazmi, Fareed. 1994. "Muslim Socials and the Female Protagonist: Seeing a Dominant Discourse at Work." In *Forging Identities*, edited by Zoya Hasan, 226–43. New Delhi: Kali For Women.

Kesavan, Mukul. 2023. "Mr. India: In Pathaan, Shah Rukh Khan is an Indian Everyman." *The Telegraph*, Kolkata, 12 February 2023.

Khan, Shah Rukh. 2007a. "I Don't Give Messages, I Try to Entertain People." Interview by Saisuresh Sivaswamy and Savera R. Someshwar. *Rediff.com*, Mumbai, 14 February 2007. specials.rediff.com/movies/2007/feb/14slid1.htm. Accessed on 24 March 2025.

———. 2007b. "Jihad Is about Killing the Badness in You." Interview with Saisuresh Sivaswamy and Savera R. Someshwar. *Rediff.com*, Mumbai, 19 February 2007. specials.rediff.com/movies/2007/feb/19slide2.htm. Accessed on 24 March 2025.

———. 2007c. "Films Are for Entertainment, Messages Are for the Post Office." Interview with Namrata Joshi. *Outlook*, New Delhi, 22 October 2007. outlookindia.com/article.aspx?235838. Accessed on 24 March 2025.

———. 2008. "Interview: SRK on Mumbai Siege and Terror." Interview with Rajdeep Sardesai. *CNN-IBN*, New Delhi, 7 December 2008. ibnlive.in.com/news/islam-does-not-preach-terror-shah-rukh-khan/79834-3.html. Accessed on 24 March 2025.

———. 2010a. "I am a Bloody Good Indian: SRK to NDTV." Interview with Barkha Dutt. *NDTV*, New Delhi, 8 February 2010. ndtv.com/article/india/i-am-a-bloody-good-indian-srk-to-ndtv-15986. Accessed on 24 March 2025.

———. 2010b. "Being Muslim in Today's India." *We The People*, NDTV, New Delhi, 8 March.

———. 2013. "Being a Khan." *Outlook Turning Points*, New Delhi, 21 January 2013.

Khan, Shahnaz. 2009. "Reading Fanaa: Confrontational Views, Comforting Identifications and Undeniable Pleasures." *South Asian Popular Culture* 7, no. 2: 127–39.

Lakshmi, Rama. 2023. "Pathaan Is Shah Rukh Khan's Love Letter to his Fans. And RSVP for boycott gang." *The Print*, 28 January 2023. https://theprint.in/opinion/newsmaker-of-the-week/pathaan-is-shah-rukh-khans-love-letter-to-his-fans-and-rsvp-for-boycott-gang/1339012/ Accessed on 24 March 2025.

Mamdani, Mahmood. 2002. "Good Muslim, Bad Muslim: A Political Perspective on Culture and Terrorism." *American Anthropologist* 104, no. 3: 766–75.

Mazumdar, Ranjani. 2000. "From Subjectification to Schizophrenia: The 'Angry Young Man' and the 'Psychotic' Hero of Bombay Cinema." In *Making Meaning in Indian Cinema*, edited by Ravi S. Vasudevan, 238–66. New Delhi: Oxford University Press.

Mazzarella, William. 2003. *Shoveling Smoke: Advertising and Globalization in Contemporary India*. Durham, North Carolina: Duke University Press.

Menon, Madhavi. 2023. "How 'Pathaan' Gives Secular Credentials of Bollywood a New Boost of Life." *Frontline*, Chennai, 14 January 2023.

Parasuraman, Prathyush. 2023a. "Pathaan on Prime Video: Shah Rukh Khan In Air, In Water, On Land, On Ice, And In Our Hearts." *Filmcompanion.com*. 21 March 2023. https://www.filmcompanion.in/reviews/bollywood-review/pathaan-review-shah-rukh-in-air-in-water-on-land-on-ice-and-in-our-hearts. Accessed on 24 March 2025.

———. 2023b. "Shah Rukh Khan: The New Action Hero on the Block." *Frontline*, Chennai, 26 January 2023. https://frontline.thehindu.com/columns/counter-culture-shah-rukh-khan-the-new-action-hero-on-the-block/article66397284.ece. Accessed on 24 March 2025.

Prabhala, Anupama. 2023. "The Ground Beneath SRK's Feet: The Flight of the Family in *Pathaan*." *BioScope* 14, no. 2: 143–49.

Rai, Amit. 2003. "Patriotism and the Muslim Citizen in Hindi Films." *Harvard Asia Quarterly*, 7, no. 3: 4–15.

Raina, Badri. 2010. "Constructing Shah Rukh Khan." *Outlook*, New Delhi, 3 February 2010.

Ramani, Priya. 2023. "Pathan: Hot Agent & Hot ISI Agent Create Liquid." Priya Ramani's Substack. 25 January 2023. https://priyaramani.substack.com/p/pathan-reclaiming-jai-hind?r=74ux3&utm_medium=ios&utm_campaign=post. Accessed on 24 March 2025.

Sanghvi, Vir. 2023. "Pathaan Is not Just Any Other Hindi Movie. It's a Battle for India." *The Print*, 26 January 2023. https://theprint.in/opinion/sharp-edge/pathaan-is-not-just-any-other-hindi-movie-its-a-battle-for-india/1335177/ Accessed on 24 March 2025.

Sethi, Manisha. 2002. "Cine Patriotism." *SAMAR: South Asian Magazine for Action and Reflection*, 115. http://samarmagazine.org/archive/articles/115.

Shiekh, Mushtaq. 2006. *Still Reading Khan*. New Delhi: Om Books International.

Sivaswamy, Saisuresh. 2007. "SRK and the M word." *Rediff.com*, Mumbai, 13 August 2007. rediff.com/movies/2007/aug/13sai.htm. Accessed on 24 March 2025.

———. 2017. "Review: Raees and fall of the Don." *Rediff.com*, Mumbai, 25 January 2017. rediff.com/movies/report/review-raees-and-fall-of-the-don/20170124.htm. Accessed on 24 March 2025.

Srinivas, Lakshmi. 2005. "Communicating Globalization in Bombay Cinema: Everyday life, Imagination and the Persistence of the Local." *International Journal of Comparative American Studies* 3, no. 3: 319–44.

Suroor, Hasan. 2017. "SRK's New 'Muslim' Roles: His Playing a Muslim in Three Successive Films Triggers another Silly Edition of India's Culture Wars." *The Times of India*, 8 February 2017. https://timesofindia.indiatimes.com/blogs/toi-edit-page/srks-new-muslim-roles-his-playing-a-muslim-in-three-successive-films-triggers-another-silly-edition-of-indias-culture-wars/ Accessed on 24 March 2025.

Uberoi, Patricia. 2006. *Freedom and Destiny: Gender, Family, and Popular Culture in India*. New Delhi; New York, NY: Oxford University Press.

Varma, Pavan K. 1998. *The Great Indian Middle Class*. New Delhi; New York: Viking.

Waikar, Prashant. "Reading Islamophobia in Hindutva: An Analysis of Narendra Modi's Political Discourse." *Islamophobia Studies Journal* 4, no. 2: 161–80.

THIRTEEN

'Religious Mentality' and the Coming of a Nation: The Birla Mandir in New Delhi

ANNE HARTIG

A few months into India's independence/partition, Ghanshyam Das Birla (1894–1983), a driving force and financial backbone of the Indian nationalist movement, agreed to give an interview to Margaret Bourke-White (1904–1971).[1] The American photojournalist, who covered this significant period of modern history for *Life* magazine, was clearly thrilled to speak to one of India's most affluent and influential businessmen. Ghanshyam Das (also known as GD) and his family not only held strong ties with Mohandas Gandhi (1869–1948) and other leading figures but were also involved in a large and varied number of enterprises and philanthropic endeavours.[2] The most visible was (and continues to be) the patronage of impressive temples dedicated to different deities throughout the country.[3] Among other things, such as his friendship with Gandhi, GD also briefly spoke with Bourke-White about the family's patronage of temples, emphasising: 'Frankly

1 Much has been written about Ghanshyam Das Birla and his family. For a general overview see Kudaisya (2006). The interview between GD and the American journalist can be found in Bourke-White's *Halfway to Freedom* (1950).

2 The family promoted the development of education. For instance, they supported the foundation of the Banaras Hindu University (BHU) and, on Gandhi's request, Aligarh Muslim University. They also established institutions, such as planetariums, museums and hospitals in different parts of India, and were involved with mass media, such as newspapers (*Hindustan Times*) and publishing (Gita Press).

3 Birla temples share the same fate as most other modern temples, attracting a lot of popular but little scholarly attention.

speaking . . . we build temples but we don't believe in temples' (qtd. in Bourke-White 1950). He explained that the temples were built 'to spread a kind of religious mentality' (qtd. in Bourke-White 1950). How can we understand the patronage of temples if not in terms of piety? What does 'religious mentality' serve as a proxy for? I argue in this chapter that the temple-building project undertaken by the Birla family was contributing to the political project of nation-building. Being the first massive temple patronised by the family, my focus is on the Lakshminarayan/Birla Mandir in Delhi. Inaugurated on 18 March 1939, it is not only the first of many impressive Birla temples but also an important example of the (Hindu) temple in the modern period. Addressing modern desires, it outlines the departure of the temple from historical temple architecture. I intend to annotate the contours of this temple-building project in the course of this chapter, arguing that the temple stood as a crucial site for the articulation of a discourse on national identity that was bound with religious identity.

The nineteenth-century concept of the nation-state, according to which the people of the nation are conscious of and share a common identity and culture (ethnicity and language), became a defining political and social force leading to the foundation of various modern states in Europe and elsewhere.[4] This idea also found cache among some sections of the Indian populace. Primarily upper-caste (Hindu) elites and political leaders perceived the fragmentation and diversity of the Indian people as a central problem – if *united* they would have the power to reclaim 'their' land and establish an independent modern Indian state, not unlike the European model.[5] However, due to the ethnic, racial and linguistic diversity, they struggled to identify a common bond that could encompass this diversity, or, in other words, generate a sense of community among the people. It is against

[4] Important publications on the development of nationalism in India include Jaffrelot (1999), Bapu (2013), Bhatt (2001), Chatterjee (1999), Gould (2004), Hansen (1999), Rajagopal (2001) and Markovits (1985). Jones (2006), Van der Veer (1994), and Zavos (2000) focus particularly on the role of religion and religious organisations within this context.

[5] See Bapu (2013), Jaffrelot (1999) and Markovits (1985).

this backdrop that religious belief and affiliation were established as a distinctive and central marker of belonging.[6] Concomitantly, the very idea or definition of religious adherence was expanded. For instance, marginalised groups, such as the Untouchables (Dalits), were gradually absorbed into the larger Hindu fold; other religious beliefs of the continent, such as Buddhists, Sikhs and Jains were also enfolded in this new definition.[7] If religious identity and its functions were changing, religious architecture had to reflect these new movements. In this vein, the chapter focuses on the Lakshminarayan/Birla Mandir, pointing to its central role in this shift.[8] It outlines the circumstances leading to the temple's construction, charting the rise of the (Hindu) nationalist movement, which (re-)defined 'Hindu' and coupled it to 'India'. Accordingly, it reads the Lakshminarayan/Birla Mandir in this context of the coming of a new nation, as well as the reconfiguration of a capital city.

In 1911, the colonial government decided to shift the imperial capital to Delhi, trying to escape violent demonstrations of nationalist sentiments of Calcutta, giving new importance to Delhi.[9] However, in Delhi, too, emotions were running high.[10] According to Jones, the increase in religious controversy and communal riots prompted organisations, such as the Bharat Dharma Mahamandal, the Sanatan Dharma Sabha and the Hindu Mahasabha, to set up quarters in the city (Jones 1986). Delhi's population was nearly equally divided between the Hindus and Muslims, the former

---

6 See Jaffrelot (1999), Van der Veer (1994) and Zavos (2000).

7 For instance, in reaction to the Khilafat movement, Vinayak Damodar Savarkar established a framework closely associated with that of the (ethnic/racial) nation. He claimed that Sikhs, Jains, Buddhists and others in India-originated religious groups share the same racial and cultural roots and must thus be considered one nation (Savarkar 1969).

8 For more details, see Hartig (2017).

9 The making of New Delhi has constantly attracted scholarly attention. Nilsson (1973), Irving (1981) and Metcalf (1989) are foundational publications in this regard. Later important studies include Hosagrahar (2005), Legg (2007) and Guerrieri (2018).

10 See, for example, Gupta (1981), Jones (1986) and Hosagrahar (2005).

exceeding slightly.[11]The significance of building a temple in Delhi has to be understood in this complex constellation. For the agents of Hindu nationalism, who claimed that the Indian subcontinent is essentially marked by Hindu culture and history, Delhi was a sore point – although commonly associated with Yudhishthira's splendid capital Indraprastha, described in the Mahabharata, Delhi played no particularly important role in Hindu imagination and sacred geography, which reflected also in its lack of a major *tirtha* (sacred place, site, temple, etc.).[12] This absence stood out in great relief against the abundance of Islamic architecture. On the eve of the construction of the new imperial capital, the Archaeological Survey of India (ASI) prepared the *List of Muhammadan and Hindu Monuments* (1916–1922).[13] This document listed around two hundred mosques only within the walled city against a total of less than one hundred temples in and around Delhi. These pre-modern temples were seldom situated on main roads, and had altogether low visibility in the urban-scape.[14] Further, their design blended with that of the surrounding buildings, having greater resemblance with Mughal buildings than with historical temples. Some temples, such as the Ladliji Mandir and the Citragupta Mandir (Figure 13.1), closely resembled diwans of Mughal emperors. Also the Shivalayas (Figure 13.2) scattered over the city, featured architectural elements and designs, such as slender tapered columns, lobed arches and a bulbous dome, that immediately recalled the small pavilions of Mughal palaces and gardens. Delhi's Muslim-dominated architecture-scape contrasted the Hindu nationalists' narrative of India as Hindu Rashtra (Hindu nation). If the construction of temples generally takes place at religiously significant sites, the construction of a massive Hindu

[11] See Gupta (1981) and Blake (2002).

[12] Compare with Jones (1986), Taneja (2008), Rajagopalan (2010) and Talbot (2016).

[13] See Sanderson (1916–1922). The report was particularly critical as it was meant to be used to plan the construction of New Delhi and to avoid the demolition of any structure of historical or religious value.

[14] This section draws from Asher (2000, 2003), as well as from my own research.

temple in Delhi was clearly politically motivated, intended to transform Delhi into a Hindu capital.[15] Supplanting this material and living past the Lakshminarayan/Birla Mandir draws upon a mythical origin – installed at the gate of the temple's park, is a plaque, showing Yudhishthira laying the foundation of Delhi.

Figure 13.1 View of the Citragupta Mandir in Paharganj, Delhi (Source: A. Hartig)

But the extant Islamic architecture was nonetheless instructive for Hindu nationalists. They scrutinised Islam and Christianity for means of generating and fostering a sense of community, and noted the pivotal role played by mosques and churches.[16] Balakrishna Shivram Moonje (1872–1948), a Brahmin from Nagpur, who later became the president of the Hindu Mahasabha and founding member of the Hindu nationalist, paramilitary organisation Rashtriya Swayamsevak Sangh (RSS), for

Figure 13.2 A Small Shivalaya in Katra Neel, Old Delhi (Source: A. Hartig)

[15] Compare with Jones (1986), Rajagopalan (2010), Taneja (2008) and Talbot (2016).

[16] Compare with Davis (2015).

instance, identified the mosque as a place where Muslims could strengthen their sense of community.[17] Moonje was not the only one at the time imagining the Hindu temple doing the same for Hindus. In his influential book *Hindu Sangathan: Saviour of the Dying Race* (1926), the leading Arya Samajist Swami Shraddhananda (1856–1926) argued on similar lines.[18] According to Shraddhananda, the reluctance among Hindus to *unite* derived from the lack of a common meeting place. Like Moonje, he compared the situation of the Hindus to that of the Muslims and their places of worship – specifically the seventeenth-century Jama Masjid (which was said to be the largest mosque in Asia at the time of its construction) and the Fatehpuri Masjid, both in Delhi, stressing that these mosques were built to accommodate several thousands of Muslims. Delhi's temples however could accommodate but a fraction of these numbers. As the photograph, taken inside the Yogmaya Mandir (Figure 13.3), exemplifies, there was just about enough space for around a dozen devotees in the city's historic temples. It is in this complex context that several agents of Hindu nationalism reviewed the possibilities of constructing a massive Hindu temple and large congregational space in the imperial capital city.

Figure 13.3 Aarti inside the small *garbhagraha* (sanctum) of the pre-modern Yogmaya Mandir in Mehrauli, Delhi (Source: A. Hartig)

17 See Jaffrelot (1999).

18 Compare with Jaffrelot (1999).

Finally, the Benares Hindu University's founder and member of the Imperial Legislative Council, the nationalist, Madan Mohan Malaviya (1861–1946) persuaded the British government to permit the construction of the Lakshminarayan/Birla Mandir (Chaturvedi 1982).[19] However, the land allotted by the government had its drawbacks. It was situated at the fringes of New Delhi, not in its centre, reflecting the colonial administration's hierarchies.[20] In the past, only royal/elite figures would have had the resources to carry out such an ambitious project. In the nineteenth and twentieth centuries, increasingly, temple construction costs were borne by those who had gained from colonialism – indigenous trading and banking communities.[21] In the case of the Lakshminarayan/Birla Mandir (Figure 13.4), it was the affluent Birla family who almost single-handedly sponsored the construction of this pet-project of Hindu nationalists.

Figure 13.4 View of Delhi's Lakshminarayan/Birla Mandir, from Mandir Marg (earlier Reading Road) (Source: A. Hartig)

19 On 26 March 1933, Malviya and Maharaja of Dholpur, Udaybhanu Singh, laid the temple's foundation stone.
20 New Delhi was organised according to the then existing sociopolitical hierarchy, with the Viceroy's House raised centrally on the top of a hill.
21 For more details on temple patronage in the nineteenth century, see Bayly (1973), Hardy (2007) and Michell (2015).

Considering what was at stake with the construction of this temple, its patrons must have pondered extensively how to present themselves in stone. Eventually, they commissioned Sris Chandra Chatterjee (1873–1966), a forward-looking architect and urban planner responsive to nationalist ideology.[22] While some of his contemporaries tried to induce a sense of community among India's diverse population through religion and language, Chatterjee identified architecture as central means in this direction. The Calcutta-based architect, who was also a devoted follower of Gandhi and supporter of the Congress Party, was keen to create a new unique/national architectural idiom and identity for an independent and modern India. The Lakshminarayan/Birla Mandir and other buildings, such as the Arya Dharm Sangha Dharamshala (1935) in Sarnath and the headquarters of the Hindu Mahasabha (1939), a stone's throw from the temple in Delhi, were part of a much larger vision – he hoped that his designs would eventually be followed across the Indian subcontinent as a part of a vision of 'Indian national architecture', but this never materialised (Chatterjee 1942; 1949).

In keeping with the nationalist spirit of his time, Chatterjee took great pride in the art and culture of ancient India, understanding it as an essential part of Indian identity. Consequently, the vast vocabulary of pre-modern Indian art and architecture served as his inspiration. Chatterjee mentioned, for instance, that he intended the Lakshminarayan/Birla Mandir to feature a figure of Surya driving seven horses, sun-windows and four large carved wheels like those at the thirteenth-century Sun Temple at Konark.[23] Aiming for an '[a]ll-India Hindu style of architecture', Chatterjee did not echo the style of a particular previous architectural era but attempted to combine, as he said, 'all Classical styles of ancient Indian architecture' (Chatterjee 1942). He extracted forms and

[22] To date, the most comprehensive study on the architect is Gupta (1991).
[23] However, these important motifs were eventually 'omitted in the course of construction without any knowledge or consent of the architect' (Chatterjee 1942).

motifs, such as the *chaitya* arch/window, from their original context and synthesised them into what he refers to as 'neo-Indian style' (Chatterjee 1942). In his effort to create an architecture suitable for modern India, Chatterjee not only experimented with design but also with different materials and techniques. Instead of building the Lakshminarayan/Birla Mandir of stone – as his forbearers would have done, Chatterjee utilised a large variety of materials, including, for instance, concrete, plaster, manufactured stone, marble and glass. The colouring was also distinct – painted in unmistakably Hindu colours, yellow and dark red.

The Lakshminarayan/Birla Mandir was laid out as per the historical *pancayatana* (quincunx) layout, followed, for instance, by the sixth-century Dashavatar Mandir in Deogarh and the eleventh-century Kandariya Mahadeva Mandir in Khajuraho. However, the popular historical layout was adapted to the times. For instance, aiming to create a temple where Hindus from across sectarian boundaries would meet, shrines dedicated to Shiva and Devi were added on either side of the temple's central shrine dedicated to Lakshmi and Narayan. This arrangement entailed an unusually spacious *mahamandapa* (pillared hall in front of the sanctum). A gallery, running overhead around the hall (Figure 13.5) provided additional space for large congregations – exactly what the agents of Hindu nationalism, such as Moonje and Shraddhananda, had been aiming for. That the creation of congregational space was a decisive concern in designing the temple is also illustrated in the adjoining park.[24] In addition to an artificial mountainous landscape, which is dotted with colourful cement animals, addressing modern desires for leisure and entertainment, this park has extensive lawns and a stage (Figure 13.6) that, to date, accommodate large gatherings numbering in thousands. Additionally, the temple's 'Gita Bhavan' was built to accommodate smaller regular gatherings. It is likely

24 The park has been discussed in great detail in Jain (2017b). As leisure became a more integral part in modern life it has become a necessity for temples to provide some form of leisure and entertainment. Compare with Srinivas (2006).

that the idea to build this hall, which houses a larger-than-life *murti* (icon) of Krishna, was inspired by Shraddhananda (Davis 2015). The influential Arya Samajist, who aspired to unify the Hindu nation by promoting the Bhagavad Gita as their bible/ national text, urged the construction of temples that could hold large congregations, and an additional hall where the scriptures could be recited daily.[25]

Figure 13.5 Photograph of a large gathering, during the 1930s, at the Lakshminarayan/Birla Mandir (Source: All India Arya [Hindu] Dharma Seva Sangha)

[25] Compare with Davis (2015).

Figure 13.6 Stage and lawn at the temple's adjoining park, named 'Indraprastha Dharma Vatika' (Source: A. Hartig)

Gatherings, large or small, may be powerful means to generate a sense of community but they are temporary, that is, their effect is short-lived. To ensure something permanent, the ideological framework on which the temple was built found expression in diverse didactic plaques, marking a critical departure from the pre-modern temple.[26] There are images of various deities (Figure 13.7) with elongated faces and limbs, demonstrating an affinity with the Bengal School.[27] There are also plaques with images of artistically lower quality of popular (Hindu) men and women,

[26] A detailed study of these images would be incredibly helpful for an in-depth understanding of the role and meaning of the Lakshminarayan/Birla Mandir, as well as other modern (Birla) temples. Aggravating the situation is that the authorities do not permit photography inside the temple. Additionally, the temple's gallery is no longer accessible for the public, making it impossible to undertake a comprehensive study of the programme.

[27] The Bengal School was an artistic movement countering the academic style promoted by the British. In search for forms of expression of a national identity, artists turned to the frescoes at Ajanta and Bagh and miniature paintings. Fascinated by the idea of Pan-Asia and Pan-Asianism, East Asian painting techniques and styles became important sources of inspiration.

for instance, the seventeenth-century poet Tukaram (Figure 13.8) and Shabari, a devoted female follower of Ram.[28] Born out of Hindu ideals and morality, these images were meant to encourage onlookers to emulate the pious path. However, there are also more complex compositions, conveying the Hindu nationalist agenda. At the entrance to the Gita Bhavan, for instance, is a plaque (Figure 13.9) that attests to the significance of the Bhagavad Gita.[29] Here, the Bhagavad Gita is shown as a boat navigating its Gita-abiding passengers, including leading figures of the nationalist movement, such as Madan Mohan Malviya, Bal Gangadhar Tilak (1856–1920) and Gandhi, through a crocodile-infested stormy sea that, according to the accompanying inscription, represents 'the painful ocean of worldly life which is full of the crocodiles of lust, anger, greed and infatuation'. Nationalist Hindu leaders are borne by the power of the Holy Scripture, cementing the idea of a unitary and pan-Indian 'Hinduism' guided, like the Abrahamic religions, by a religion of the book.[30] Further, there are painted images of Chandragupta, Ashoka, Shivaji, Guru Nanak and other historical figures, several of which are kept, like masterpieces in a museum, behind glass and framed with heavy wooden frames.[31] This exhibition of historical figures extends into the park. It evokes India's long Hindu heritage by establishing a line of achievements of 'Arya (Hindu)' heroes. Conspicuous by their absence are Islamic and Christian figures. Instead of inserting Mughal emperors, such as Akbar and Shah Jahan, the Rajasthani ruler Suraj Mal, the Mewari king Pratap Singh I, and even Prithviraj Chauhan have been included in this chronology of brave men, that narrates the

---

[28] Generally, these images were accompanied by short explanatory excerpts in Sanskrit, Hindi and/or English.

[29] On the role and significance of the Bhagavad Gita as crucial in the thinking and discourse of the time, see Davis (2015).

[30] Compare with Davis (2015). Furthermore, the temple features a 'Ved Mandir'. Instead of housing a *murti*, this small north-facing shrine contains a copy of the Vedas wrapped in cloth, attesting the primacy of scriptures.

[31] I will discuss the influence of the museum on the modern temple elsewhere.

nation, while also acknowledging the patron's roots in the Mewar region.[32] As such the exhibition seems inspired by resistance against Muslim and British invasion, implying what Vinayak Damodar Savarkar (1883–1966) proclaimed in the instrumental treatise *Hindutva: Who is a Hindu?* – 'Hindu' and India are synonymous. Moreover, there are a few images visualising other popular themes of the Hindu nationalist framework, such as the notion of 'Greater India' (Akhand Bharat: Undivided India).[33] For instance, one of the door jambs at the park's gates has been enhanced with an image showing an ancient Candi Mandir, built by Maharaj Kirtivarma in Java (Figure 13.10). Other door jambs are decorated showing temples in China and Myanmar. Further, the temple's park contains a model of an 'Old Hindu Temple' built in Java by the same king. These references clearly signal Hindu/India as a religion/culture/nation dominating South and Southeast Asia.

Figure 13.7 Image of goddess Saraswati inside the Lakshminarayan/ Birla Mandir (Source: A. Hartig)

Figure 13.8 A plaque at the Lakshminarayan/Birla Mandir, New Delhi, showing the Maharastrian poet Tukaram (Source: A. Hartig)

32 Prithviraj Chauhan occupies a precarious position in this heroic assembly. After all, it was his defeat that gave way to Muhammad Ghori and other outsiders occupying large parts of India (Talbot 2016).

33 For more details on this concept, see Bayly (2004).

Figure 13.9 A plaque from the Lakshminarayan/Birla Mandir in Bhopal similar to the one at the Lakshminarayan/Birla Mandir in Delhi, showing the Bhagavad Gita as a boat (Source: A. Hartig)

Figure 13.10 Carved door jamb at the Lakshminarayan/Birla Mandir, showing an ancient temple, that, according to an inscription, was built by Maharaj Kirtivarma in Java (Source: A. Hartig)

Apart from these images there are numerous plaques inscribed with slokas, maxims and quotes from the scriptures. The Sanskrit quotes from scriptures are often followed by translation in Hindi, and, sometimes, in English, making the scriptures accessible to literates. One of the issues addressed in these plaques is that of entry. Several of the plaques, especially those near an entrance, stress that 'Harijans' (a patronising term coined and popularised by Gandhi for Untouchables) are allowed to enter. Having been introduced to the idea of putting an end to untouchability by Lajpat Rai (1865–1928), a leading Arya Samajist and, like Gandhi, beneficiary of the Birla family, Ghanshyam Das publicly rejected the concept and supported Gandhi and his campaigns.[34] Thus, entry to Untouchables became a leitmotif of all Birla temples.[35]

[34] As a representative of Gandhi's All India Harijan Sevak Sangh, GD even campaigned in Kerala for the Temple Entry movement in 1936 (Kudaisya 2006).

[35] Today, Birla Mandirs are celebrated for being open to all people. See, for instance, Hutchinson (1947). However, many of those actually affected

This inclusivity and liberality however came with reservations, prejudice and policing.[36] A plaque near the temple's entrance, for instance, emphasises that the temple is open to *all* Hindus (including Harijans), on the condition of 'cleanliness'. Further, it insists that sick people and beggars are not allowed to enter, or even approach the temple. Other plaques champion the idea of a Hindu *community*, affirming 'Sanatanists, Aryasamajists, Buddhists, Jains, Sikhs, etc.' as 'Aryadharami Hindus' (Figure 13.11). That this idea too leans on Savarkar's Hindutva is substantiated in another plaque that mentions that with 'exception of all foreigners … and distinguished and famous Indian gentlemen, no local Muslim and Christian Gentlemen should enter the temple Gardens … without the permission of temple Authorities'.[37] Apart from addressing once again the issue of Muslim and Christian presence, this inscription hints at the founders' desire to demonstrate the presence and rising power of Hindus not only to the Indian subcontinent but to the world at large. Old photographs capture well how in its early days, the Lakshminarayan/Birla Mandir with its three towering *shikharas* (superstructure built over the sanctum) was all the more visible, with the barren landscape now working towards accentuating the temple's imposing profile, symbolising a powerful Hindu presence in India's modern capital (Figure 13.12). That the massive temple on Reading Road (today Mandir Marg) aroused great public interest was obvious since its inauguration, during which, according to *The Times of India*, nearly 50,000 people gathered.[38]

were rather critical. They regard the impressive temples as a political gesture that does not address the root causes of poverty. The workers at the Birla mills, for instance, threw doubt on why the Birla family did not have the same resources to improve their deplorable living and working conditions (Bourke-White 1950).

36 Compare also with Jain (2017a).

37 The temple authorities assured Jain that this regulation has never been enforced (Jain 2017a). That Muslims and Christians were not welcomed also shows that, according to another inscription, during fairs and festivals only Hindus were permitted to do business.

38 The temple was inaugurated by Gandhi on 18 March 1939.

Figure 13.11 Plaque at the Lakshminarayan/Birla Mandir evoking the concept of 'Hindu'[39] (Source: A. Hartig)

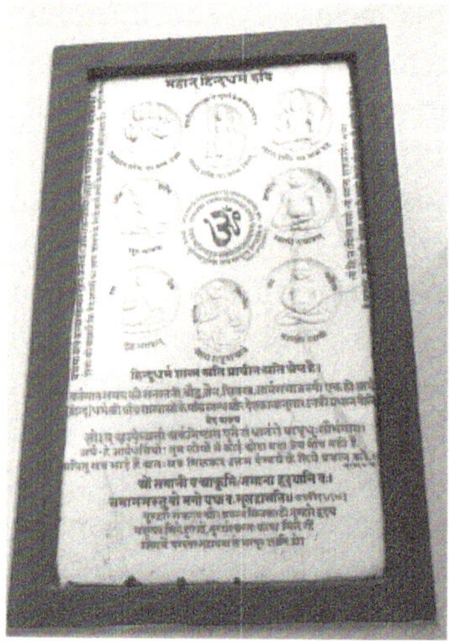

Figure 13.12 View of the Lakshminarayan/Birla Mandir and the adjoining park, shortly after its inauguration in 1939 (Source: All India Arya [Hindu] Dharma Seva Sangha)

The construction of the Lakshminarayan/Birla Mandir was positioned as a step towards (re)claiming Delhi and Hindu India, as witnessed by publications of the period. The English weekly *The Hindu Outlook*, a mouthpiece of the Hindu Mahasabha, wrote: 'It is said that such a big and beautiful Temple was [sic.] never built at Delhi since the days of the last Hindu Emperor - Prithvi Raj Chauhan" (qtd. in Jones 1986). If nineteenth-century and early twentieth-century colonial narratives of Delhi sketched Delhi as a city of mosques, tombs and forts, Krishna Gopal's guidebook *Delhi in Two Days*, published in the late 1930s, portrayed Delhi as a Hindu city, built on the ruins of Yudhishthara's Indraprastha.[40] For Gopal, the Lakshminarayan/Birla Mandir added 'an unrivalled gem to the glories of the Imperial Capital, which no discriminating visitor can afford to ignore' (Gopal circa 1939). Thus, the cover

[39] An identical plaque can be found at the Hindu Mahasabha's headquarter.
[40] Yet another idea that finds reference at the Lakshminarayan/Birla Mandir.

of his publication features an illustration of the city's landmarks that show the Lakshminarayan/Birla Mandir towering over the silhouette of the Jama Masjid and the Council Chamber (Parliament House), symbolically indicating Hindu/Indian supremacy over the Muslim and British structures.

Being an impressive temple, the Lakshminarayan/Birla Mandir has been attracting several hundred people daily, including national and international tourists. Accordingly, the temple must be understood as a medium that, like, for instance, pictures and other visual media, has considerable impact on the discourse of religion, identity, history and nation. The analysis of the Lakshminarayan/ Birla Mandir's architectural and visual programme reveals how its 'religious message' mixed with Hindu nationalist ideology. Further, it suggests that the temple was planned to serve as a unifying matrix that not only brings together Hindus/Indians but also defines and propagates Hindu/Indian history, Hindu/Indian culture, Hindu/Indian art and Hindu/Indian architecture, thereby, imbuing national identity with certain *sacredness.* In other words, the construction of the temple and its message seem to be more political than GD led us to believe. As outlined in the chapter, it is in the context of the colonial period that upper-caste (Hindu) elites and political leaders identified religious belief as a means to generate feelings of social cohesion, essential to take collective political decisions forward. Further, they understood that this required a substantial amount of homogeneity, which was yet to be ensured. Rooted within the wide matrix of social interests, the temple turned into a major political playground, including references to the framework of nationalist ideologies. Its politics of entry make it very clear who 'belongs' to the nation and who doesn't. It does so even as it opens its doors to groups who were refused entry to temples.

References

All India Arya (Hindu) Dharma Seva Sangha. 19--. *A Glimpse of the Lakshminarayan Temple, New Delhi*. Delhi: Imperial Fine Art Press.

Asher, C. 2000. "Mapping Hindu–Muslim Identities through the Architecture of Shahjahanabad and Jaipur." In *Beyond Turk and Hindu: Rethinking Religious Identities in Islamicate South Asia*, edited by D. Gilmartin and B. Lawrence, 121–48. Gainsville: University Press of Florida.

———. 2003. "Hidden Gold: Jain Temples of Delhi and Jaipur and their Urban Context." In *Jainism and Early Buddhism: Essays in Honor of Padmanabh S. Jaini*, edited by Olle Qvarnström, 359–77. Fermont, CA: Asian Humanities Press.

Bapu, P. 2013. *Hindu Mahasabha in Colonial North India, 1915–1930: Constructing Nation and History*. London: Routledge.

Bayly, C. 1973. "Patrons and Politics in Northern India." *Modern Asian Studies* 7, no. 3: 349–88.

Bayly, S. 2004. "'Greater India': French and Indian Visions of Colonialism in the Indic Mode." *Modern Asian Studies* 38, no. 3: 703–44.

Bhatt, C. 2001. *Hindu Nationalism: Origins, Ideologies and Modern Myths*. Oxford: Berg.

Blake, S. P. 2002. *Shahjahanabad: The Sovereign City in Mughal India, 1639–1739*. Cambridge: Cambridge University Press.

Bourke-White, M. 1950. *Halfway to Freedom: In the Words and Pictures of Margret Bourke-White*. Bombay: Asia Publishing House.

Chatterjee, P., ed. 1999. *The Partha Chatterjee Omnibus: Comprising Nationalist Thought and the Colonial World, The Nation and its Fragments, and A Possible India*. New Delhi: Oxford University Press.

Chatterjee, S. C. 1942. *Magadha: Architecture and Culture*. Calcutta: University of Calcutta.

———. 1949. *India and New Order: An Essay on Human Planning*. Calcutta: Calcutta University Press.

Chaturvedi, S. 1982. *Nāgar Śailī ke Naye Hindu Mandir*. Delhi: Prabhat Prakashan.

Davis, R. 2015. *The Bhagavad Gita: A Biography*. Princeton, New Jersey: Princeton University Press.

Gopal, K. circa 1939. *Delhi in Two Days: A Complete, Upto-date and Illustrated Guide, of Old and New Delhi with History and Map*. Delhi: Model Press.

Gould, W. 2004. *Hindu Nationalism and the Language of Politics in Late Colonial India*. Cambridge University Press.

Guerrieri, P. 2018. *Negotiating Cultures: Delhi's Architecture and Planning from 1912 to 1962*. Oxford: Oxford University Press.

Gupta, N. 1981. *Delhi between two Empires 1803–1931: Society, Government and Urban Growth*. Delhi: Oxford University Press.

Gupta, S. 1991. "Sris Chandra Chatterjee: The Quest for a National Architecture." *The Indian Economic and Social History Review* 28, no. 2: 187–201.

Hansen, T. 1999. *The Saffron Wave: Democracy and Hindu Nationalism in Modern India.* Princeton: Princeton University Press.

Hardy, A. 2007. *The Temple Architecture of India.* Chichester: Wiley.

Hartig, A. 2017. "Shifting Sites of the 'Sacred': Contestations Around the Regional, the National and the Global in Contemporary Hindu Temple Architecture in Delhi." Unpublished PhD Thesis: School of Arts and Aesthetics, Jawaharlal Nehru University, New Delhi.

Hosagrahar, J. 2005. *Indigenous Modernities: Negotiating Architecture and Urbanism.* London: Routledge.

Hutchinson, P. 1947. "Religion Around the World." *LIFE* 22, no. 10: 106–18.

Irving, R. 1981. *Indian Summer: Lutyens, Baker and Imperial Delhi.* New Haven, CT: Yale University Press.

Jaffrelot, C. 1999. *The Hindu Nationalist Movement and Indian Politics, 1925 to the 1990s: Strategies of Identity-Building, Implantation and Mobilisation.* New Delhi: Penguin Books.

Jain, K. 2017a. "Gods in the Time of Automobility." *Current Anthropology* 58, S15: S13–26.

———. 2017b. "Tales from the Concrete Cave: Delhi's Birla Temple and the Genealogies of Urban Nature in India." In *Places of Nature in Ecologies of Urbanism*, edited by Anne Rademacher and K. Sivaramakrishnan, 108–36. Hong Kong: Hong Kong University Press.

Jones, K. 1986. "Organized Hinduism in Delhi and New Delhi." In *Delhi Through the Ages: Essays in Urban History, Culture and Society*, edited by R.E. Frykenberg, 332–50. Delhi: Oxford University Press.

———. 2006. *Socio-religious Reform Movements in British India.* Cambridge: Cambridge University Press.

Kudaisya, M. 2006. *The Life and Times of G.D. Birla.* New Delhi: Oxford University Press.

Legg, S. 2007. *Spaces of Colonialism: Delhi's Urban Governmentalities.* Oxford: Blackwell.

Markovits, C. 1985. *Indian Business and Nationalists Politics 1931–39: The Indigenous Capitalist Class and the Rise of the Congress Party.* Cambridge: Cambridge University Press.

Metcalf, T. 1989. *An Imperial Vision: Indian Architecture and Britain's Raj.* London: Faber and Faber.

Michell, G. 2015. *Late Temple Architecture of India 15th to 19th Centuries: Continuities, Revivals, Appropriations, and Innovations.* New Delhi: Oxford University Press.

Nilsson, S. 1973. *The New Capitals of India, Pakistan and Bangladesh.* Lund: Studentlitteratur.

Rajagopal, A. 2001. *Politics after Television: Hindu Nationalism and the Reshaping of the Public India.* Cambridge: Cambridge University Press.

Rajagopalan, M. 2010. "Postsecular Urbanism: Situating Delhi within the Rhetorical Landscape of Hindutva." In *The Fundamentalist City? Religiosity and the Remaking of Urban Space*, edited by N. AlSayyad and M. Massoumi, 257–82. London: Routledge.

Sanderson, G. 1916–1922. *List of Muhammadan and Hindu Monuments.* Calcutta: Superintendent Government Printing.

Savarkar, V. 1969. *Hindutva: Who is a Hindu?* Bombay: Veer Savarkar Prakashan.

Shraddhananda, S. 1926. *Hindu Sangathan: Saviour of the Dying Race.*

Srinivas, T. 2006. "Divine Enterprise: Hindu Priests and Ritual Change in Neighborhood Hindu Temples in Bangalore." *South Asia: Journal of South Asian Studies* 29, no. 3: 321–43.

Talbot, C. 2016. *The Last Hindu Emperor: Prithviraj Chauhan and the Indian Past, 1200–2000.* Cambridge: Cambridge University Press.

Taneja, A. 2008. "History and Heritage Woven in the New Urban Fabric: The Changing Landscapes of Delhi's 'First City': Or, Who Can Tell the Histories of Lado Sarai?". In *Patterns of Middle Class Consumption in India and China*, edited by Christopher Jaffrelot and Peter van der Veer, 157–69. New Delhi: SAGE Publications.

The Times of India. 1939. "Mr. Gandhi Opens Temple.' *The Times of India*, Delhi, 21 March 1939.

Van der Veer, P. 1994. *Religious Nationalism: Hindus and Muslims in India.* Berkeley: University of California Press.

Zavos, J. 2000. *The Emergence of Hindu Nationalism in India.* New Delhi: Oxford University Press.

FOURTEEN

Guru-led Faith Movements in India: The Case of The Art of Living Foundation

HIMANI KAPOOR

One of the important transformations to emerge on the global scene of religion, especially Hinduism, over the last few decades has been the rise of faith-based organisations led by gurus. Many of these groups cut across national and cultural boundaries, predominantly promoting meditation and particular forms of yoga. Since yoga is often considered to be easily adaptable to different cultures, many guru-led organisations take pride in increasing their geographical footprint and adding different ethnicities, races and social groups to their organisation. Does it mean that such organisations are potential avenues to proliferate a certain kind of cosmopolitanism in religion that cuts across all borders and boundaries while still being sustained by faith? Or do these groups represent yet another means of advancing what has been termed 'soft Hindutva' (Nanda 2009)?

This chapter analyses one such guru-led organisation, namely The Art of Living Foundation (AOLF), in its potential for promoting religious cosmopolitanism. The idea of religious cosmopolitanism here, refers to the set of ethos by which 'cultural and religious differences are neither hierarchically organised nor dissolved, but accepted for what they are and indeed positively affirmed' (Beck 2010). In other words, religious cosmopolitanism pertains to the set of principles where cultural or religious differences are not eliminated, but accepted as they are and even embraced.

The reasons for choosing AOLF for this study are, first, that AOLF along with its leader Sri Sri Ravi Shankar (hereafter Sri Sri), has attracted wide public attention and media coverage, and has a strong international following and, second, and more importantly, that the organisation proposes the motto of *Vasudhaeva Kutumbakam* or 'one world family' as its ideal. Apart from having a living guru, the organisation takes pride in addressing issues related to peace-keeping and conflict resolution. For these reasons, other yoga gurus and their groups having a significant following in India and abroad, do not fit neatly into this study. While it may be possible to comment on the idea of cultural nationalism and guru-led organisations, for which gurus like Swami Ramdev and Chinmayananda Saraswati, are apt examples, Sri Sri is distinct for his intermittent engagement with secular ideals as well as identity politics. The chapter looks into the different ways in which the AOLF negotiates the cosmopolitan ideals of 'one world family' with cultural nationalism in India.

Before setting up the AOLF in 1981, its founder-leader was earlier associated with another widely known faith-based organisation by the name of Transcendental Meditation (TM). As a part of TM, Sri Sri had travelled extensively around the world as a teacher. In terms of its international footprint, the AOLF has had a significant following after the establishment of its international centres in 1989, in USA and Germany. Today, the organisation is known to have a huge number of followers, and according to the official webpage of AOLF, it now has a following of about 350 million people worldwide spread across 155 countries.

Irrespective of the transnational outreach, and a strong emphasis on a cosmopolitan outlook, it has often been termed as a Hindu religious organisation at heart. For instance, Alexis Avdeeff in his paper, "Internationalisation of a contemporary Hindu Movement" (2010), associates it with 'internationalized Hinduism'. On the other hand, Stephen Jacobs in his perceptive study of the organisation, *The Art of Living Foundation: Spirituality and Wellbeing in the Global Context* (2015) has called it both secular and religious at the same time. Rather than categorising the AOLF as a New Religious Movement (NRM), or a Hindu-Inspired Meditation Movement (HIMM),[1] Jacobs categorises the

[1] The term HIMM or Hindu-Inspired Meditation Movements has been suggested by Lola Williamson in her work *Transcendent in America: Hindu-*

AOLF as a Hindu-Derived Meditation Network, which capitalises upon the modern-day preoccupation with well-being and health.

The first section of this chapter briefly discusses the history of the AOLF in national and international contexts. Thereafter, it contrasts the promotional material published by the organisation in the form of pamphlets and videos, in India and abroad, to throw light on the differences in its outlook at both these sites. The final section takes into consideration the articles published in the monthly magazine, *Rishimukh*, in the context of its deployment of Hindu nationalism and archaic primordialism.

What is The Art of Living Foundation?

The AOLF represents itself as 'a non-governmental organisation, involved in humanitarian projects with a special focus on stress elimination'. Although there are a number of areas that the organisation works with, for instance as an NGO and also a retail outlet for consumer goods and health-related products, primarily, the organisation is engaged in teaching yoga and breathing rhythms, by way of offering short-term courses, which can be taken in lieu of a certain fee. Here, trained volunteers demonstrate and teach a variety of yogic exercises, meditation, and the yogic techniques that are unique to The Art of Living Foundation, like the Sudarshan Kriya (a form of rhythmic breathing exercise). Depending upon the age, interest and ability of the participant, there are a variety of courses offered, wherein there may be different individual as well as group activities on offer, mostly directed at physical and mental well-being.

Most of the promotional material and advertisements published for promoting the AOLF courses, by and large highlight the various national and international social service initiatives under its wing. In the monthly magazine *Rishimukh*, two sections are routinely dedicated to the various social work tasks taken up by

---

Inspired Meditation Movements as New Religion (2010) where she studies three popular guru-led faith movements established in USA: Transcendental Meditation, the Self-Realization Fellowship and Siddha Yoga.

the organisation. Some of these include peace-keeping missions in places like Kashmir, Sri Lanka, Iraq, Costa Rica and Kosovo among others. Other humanitarian projects include disaster relief, rural development, prisoner rehabilitation and charitable schools.

In India, the organisation was set up initially with a rural school by the name of Ved Vignan Maha Vidya Peeth in 1981. By the next decade, the organisation had significantly grown to have international centres in various countries with a growing network of followers from different parts of the world. Interestingly, the same decade also marked the emergence of a new middle-class following the liberalisation of the Indian economy in 1991. This class had a higher disposable income in addition to being more upwardly mobile. Much of the AOLF's following in India belongs to this upwardly mobile middle-class with a high disposable income (Jacobs 2015, 157).

Having been awarded the Padma Vibhushan Award by the government of India in 2016 (the second-highest civilian award conferred by the Indian State), Sri Sri is also a well-known public figure, who frequently travels to various places in India and abroad, to spread AOLF's teachings and other humanitarian efforts. The initiatives taken by the organisation towards peace-keeping in certain conflict-stricken parts of the world have been emphasised in its various publications. Sri Sri's biography indicates that his peace-keeping negotiations have also been instrumental in spreading the values of non-violence around the world. It also states that as a child he had questioned caste-based discrimination, purposely flouting the norms of purity by going on a bicycle ride with the caretaker of his family's paddy field, who was considered untouchable (Narasimhan 2018). For his followers, he is the epitome of joy and love.

Cosmopolitan v/s Religious Community Orientation: AOLF's Promotional Pamphlet and Videos

In one of the promotional pamphlets published by the AOLF research centre in Germany, the scientific research associated with yogic breathing and Sudarshan Kriya is shared. The main health benefits highlighted in the document include reduced stress levels, improved immunity and enhanced brain function. Interestingly, the underlying philosophy of breath control, known as *pranayama*, is not mentioned in these promotional materials. The *pranayama* is simply described as a 'science of health promotion', a sort of time-tested practice of exercise and 'restoring optimal health'. The pamphlet goes on to say that these exercises taught at AOLF 'continue to be independently investigated by modern medical science'.

The short description of the AOLF at the end of the pamphlet also declares that the Foundation's International Research and Health Promotion Center (IRHPC) welcomes scholarly research on its programmes from all 'interested parties'. The front page of this pamphlet shows two people doing *pranayama* on one side and the depiction of a chemical experiment on the other. The bar and pie diagrams are eye-catching and interestingly, do not say anything about the philosophical idea of the *self*, or for that matter the principles of yoga. While Vedic primordialism does play a part in the validation of the health benefits associated with the *Sudarshan Kriya*, it is however the supposed verifiability of the research that is strongly emphasised. Added to this is the openness to be 'independently investigated by modern medical science at universities, hospitals and other research institutions'. This adds to the credibility that its potential audiences may associate with the organisation. In this context, Joanne Punzo Waghorne, in the essay "Engineering an Artful Practice: On Jaggi Vasudev's Isha Yoga and Sri Sri Ravi Shankar's Art of Living" offers the observation that a 'new kind of proof texting', is at play, wherein instead of isolated quotations from sacred texts, data from the emergent fields of neurosciences and cognitive studies is invoked, which appeals to the legitimacy of science interestingly mirrored by the rise of serious interest in cognitive science within the academic study of religion. The brand of yoga therefore which gets promoted is curiously divested of its traditional trappings. The reference to Vedic testimony here garners further authenticity.

In the same vein, the promotional video 'Meditation Then and Now',[2] published by the AOLF, United States, is meant for its 'Youth Empowerment and Skills Workshop' (YES Plus), for young adults. The animated video begins with the image of a meditator, perhaps a sage, and a voice in the background informs us that some of the world's first scientists discovered secrets about the body, mind and consciousness by keeping their mind really still.

The video goes on to suggest that meditation is universal, '...just like you don't need to be Italian to eat pasta'. The video later enumerates certain benefits of meditation like getting good grades, growing smarter, stronger, faster, etc. It ends with the animated representation of Sri Sri, with an invitation to 'dive deeper'. Here again, the assertion, repeated time and again, is that the Indian sages who discovered the benefits of meditation were indeed scientists, though not in the typical way. Much like the pamphlet discussed earlier, the promotional video appeals to the modern day where validation from Western science is enough to garner authenticity.

Counter to such representations, the promotional video[3] of the same Yes Plus programme in Bangalore does not deal with such scientific aspects or health benefits associated with the programme. The video features the personal experiences of young adults from different countries. While one participant from Denmark talks about 'being alive once again', another from the USA shares how he got more 'clarity' in his life. The participant from India, on the other hand, talks about having been able to overcome depression and highlights the strong community orientation of the AOLF; he observes, that even though participants 'live seven oceans away ... yet the people are one'. The video ends with glimpses of

---

[2] See: artofliving.org, 'Meditation then and Now', available at: https://www.artofliving.org/yes-course-18-30-yrs#distance=10&sSearch=&st=&lat=&lng=&ctype=52613,253133&acol=0&c=&cc=&d1=&d2=. Accessed on 27 February 2025).

[3] YES Plus Course – Art of Living International Center, Bangalore, available at https://www.youtube.com/watch?v=p4tTNv5pkhg on. Accessed 27 February 2025).

Sri Sri talking about youth being 'global citizens'. More than the health-related aspects of the AOLF courses, the promotional video meant for the Indian audiences revolves around this transnational aspect of the organisation; the idea of being able to connect with a 'global' community.

This contrast is not to suggest that scientific 'proof texting', that is the take-off point to woo a Western audience, is simply divested for advances made to the Indian counterpart. What can, however, be more certainly suggested is that while the pressure to assert authenticity is more for a Western audience, for an Indian public, the presentation of arguments in favour of the health-related benefits of yoga takes a backseat when compared to the offer of a 'cosmopolitan rootedness'. Jacobs suggests that 'export' of 'philosophical ideas and yoga to the West not only provided a certain prestige to the cultural heritage of India, but also in the process transformed them' (Jacobs 2015, 208–09).

The rationalisation of rituals and their re-dubbing as secular and scientific practices[4] further adds to this prestige element, and therefore, for the Hindu followers in India, such 'scientific' aspects further strengthen their faith in the organisation which is additionally rooted in their own tradition. Jacobs associates the Indian middle-class's need for being grounded in the ancient Vedic traditions, yet being commensurate with modernity, to 'rooted cosmopolitanism', a term he borrows from Kwame Antony Appiah's 'Cosmopolitan Patriots' (Appiah 1997, 617–39).

Yoga along with certain routine rituals followed at the AOLF centres put together an amalgamation which appeals to the members who are convinced that the practices are scientifically relevant and rational, apart from being globally accepted. One therefore sees different modes of persuasion actively used for its prospective audiences at the international and the national levels. At a local level, however, identification with Hindu roots plays a greater role.

---

[4] See: Art of Living, 'Significance of Navratri Yagnas'. Available at https://www.artofliving.org/navratri/significance-yagnas. Accessed on 23 September 2025.

AOLF and the Hindu Imagination: Reading *Rishimukh*

The cosmopolitan dimension of Sri Sri's message gets far diluted on the Indian terrain. This has been voiced by some of the scholars who studied the organisation closely. For instance, Alexis Avdeeff (2010, 8–13) argues that even though a universal nature of the message propagated by Sri Sri has enabled the organisation to have a large community of transnational followers, nevertheless, 'this inclusivist spirituality with universalistic aims' takes an 'identity turn' in India through Sri Sri's political discourse, who, 'seems to be inclined to vigorously defend Hindu interests'. Avdeeff in his study takes into account the various occasions where the founder–leader has voiced majoritarian Hindu interests, for instance, his objections to proselytism of Christian missions in South India, his strong indictment of the State Government of Karnataka for allocating more money to churches and mosques than Hindu temples, and the supposed purpose of some of the tribal programmes (like Sri Sri Tribal Welfare) to contain religious conversions to Christianity (ibid.). A section of the followers of the AOLF is captured by the appeal to the archaic sense of belongingness to a primordial Hindu community. This is often reinforced through overt proclamations of Hindu cultural supremacy. Some of Sri Sri's lectures, while advocating for the equality of all religions, implicitly assert the overarching superiority of Vedic knowledge, positioning it as a comprehensive framework that surpasses other, more modern, religio-cultural traditions. By implication, Islam and Christianity, the other two competing religions in India, are considered relatively modern and, therefore, less authentic and reputable. For instance, the following is a short analysis of one of Sri Sri's talks published in the June 2016 edition of *Rishimukh*.

This talk is in the context of the bombings in the Brussels Airport in March 2016. Although the date and venue of the talk are not mentioned in the issue, the picture accompanying the excerpt shows him sitting in front of an audience with a microphone in his hand, wearing a white robe, bordered by saffron and green colours, symbolising the Indian flag. He repudiates terrorism and questions the assumptions of Islamic universalism suggesting that such youth involved in the bombings need to be 'educated' about the different traditions and religions of the world. In this process, he debunks religious indoctrination at madrassas. He suggests that teaching yoga will be the solution to the problem (of religious extremism), and that seminaries and madrassas need to be 'de-radicalised'. He further mentions a meeting with a professor who told him that the values of non-violence and truth were dear to Prophet Mohammad who said that 'Hind' was in his heart. He further suggests that these values are the 'principles of Hind', and concludes, saying that the Vedas, which he calls the 'first book of wisdom', were written in India, and it is this knowledge which must reach out to people.[5]

Even though Sri Sri's repudiation of religious indoctrination is in the context of a certain incident involving Islamist terrorism, he distinctly places the Hindu Vedic doctrine above and beyond the Islamic worldview. Thus, in order to refute the claims to Universalism of Islamic theology, he nonetheless exchanges it for another kind of religious universalism, touting the Vedas as the mainspring of human wisdom. It is therefore not surprising to find a similar tone of Vedic universalism in another piece published in the magazine a few months later. The December 2016 issue of *Rishimukh* celebrates the graduation of 41 scholars of the 'heritage school' called the Veda Agama Samskrutha Maha Patashala, dedicated to Agamic Studies. The article reports that the school teaches students from all over the country to 'conduct temple rituals, puja, *abhishekas* and other rituals'. The 'syllabus' includes the 'study of the Veda, Agama, Sanskrit Language, astrology, yoga, music, sculpture and religious epics' (*Rishimukh* 2016).

It is interesting to note that the curriculum of the school does not mention anything in its training which may help employ its pupils outside the Hindu temple. The rising number of schools training for priesthood has been highlighted by Meera Nanda, who argues that such schools are now being associated with social

5 "Multicultural education: The only way to deal with terrorism: Excerpts from talks by HH Ravi Shankar" Rishimukh, Jun. 2016, pp 8–11.

welfare and progressive development, and hence, enjoy sanction by the state as well as funds from corporates. Here, the emphasis is on rote learning, correct memorisation and the correct reproduction of the sound of Sanskrit verses with no room for critical thinking (Nanda 2009). It is noteworthy that both agamic schools and madrassas primarily provide religious education to their students, with minimal emphasis on secular subjects or standard primary and secondary education. However, the articles in *Rishimukh* treat them as fundamentally different, essentially due to the religions they represent. The inherent contradiction between the indictment of one religious pedagogy and an enthusiastic promotion of another goes curiously unchecked in the talk given by the founder–leader too. It is interesting, however, that these contradictory arguments continue to be a part of the AOLF portfolio. Avdeeff (2010, 13) aptly calls the organisation an

> Incarnation of two seemingly contradictory logics, The Art of Living Foundation appears as a transnational movement participating fully to the process of religious globalisation, but also as a major actor in the enduring phenomenon that is the Hindu revitalisation in contemporary India, providing thereby its contribution 'to the global picture of the politicisation of religion'.

Amanda Huffer's discussion about neo-Vedantic Hinduism brings in a different perspective to the issue. In her paper "Backdoor Hinduism: A Recoding in the Language of Spirituality", Huffer argues that beneath the spiritualism, lies a re-coding of neo-Vedantic Hinduism. She adds that the rhetoric of guru discourses and their universalism continues to adapt to the changing times. Citing the 'lingering effects of the discomfort with cultural difference' (Huffer 2011), she highlights that Indian gurus have been unable to propagate a religion truly pluralistic in spirit, but this inability may have some of its roots in the reticence of the Western audiences to accept something culturally different. This 'recoding' of the language of guru-philosophies is what she terms as 'backdoor' Hinduism. Therefore, as far as their transnational audience is concerned, the popular ritualism of the organisations signifies a shift in the multiculturalist public's validation of difference, while its generalised rhetoric provides a blanket of security for those still uncomfortable with the influx of 'foreign' religions (ibid.). AOLF's endorsement of a Hindu worldview, and its founder's endorsement of Hindu universalism, can also be looked at as a way to balance its disparate domestic and international avatars. Thus, a strategic syncretism is visible in the AOLF philosophy as it brings together ideas from opposing worldviews. It envisages the world as one family, adopts the concerns of social unrest in the world and upholds values of non-violence and equality, while also engaging in a particular kind of populist cultural nationalism and Vedic primordialism, and tacitly supporting Hindu hegemony.

Primordial Nationalism: A Closer Look at 'Bharath Gyan'

This section examines the *Rishimukh* issues published from January 2016 to December 2017, to have a deeper understanding of the organisation's day-to-day trappings within India. The magazine is available in Hindi and in English, including various other regional languages. It carries regular sections, on yoga, meditation, health, psychology, nutrition, latest news about Sri Sri's visits in India and abroad, a section on social service initiatives by the name of *seva*, a regular feature on religious tourism called 'Spiritual Sojourn' covering mostly a south Indian Hindu temple, news about the organisation covered in national and regional newspapers, excerpts from Sri Sri's talks, and a special section about the knowledge of India, by the name of 'Bharath Gyan'.

'Bharath Gyan' is a regular feature in *Rishimukh*, and the contributors, D.K. Hari and Hema Hari, have authored a book series by the same title. The idea of these books, as the name suggests is to share knowledge or *gyan* about India. The AOLF India webpage describes it as a 'research organisation that endeavours to bring forth knowledge from the ancient times'. The vision statement discloses that the idea behind setting up the organisation is 'to offer credible evidences that establish India as a land rich in science and knowledge along with culture and spirituality'.[6]

The founder duo, who had earlier been multinational corporation professionals and software engineers reportedly quit their careers to write about Indian history and culture. A bulk of the literature collaborated by them is not only published as regular features in *Rishimukh* but also as separate book editions running in various volumes. The titles of some of the books published include *Historical Rama, Historical Krishna, Understanding Shiva, Ayodhya – War and Peace*, etc. The 'historical evidence' of their work they suggest is established by 'modern methods of tracking time and history'. The 'modern methods' which are not aptly dwelled upon or explained are put to use to assign exact dates according to the Western calendar to events like the birth of Lord Rama, Lord Krishna, date of the Kurukshetra war, etc. One of the articles, published in December 2017 suggests that the work of 'Bharat Gyan' is to establish the 'historicity of personages such as Rama, Krishna and many other legendary figures of ancient India'. The article goes on to suggest that this also establishes that the descendants of these religious figures 'would also have been historical' (*Rishimukh*, December 2017).

Likewise, according to the article published in the November 2016 issue, the Bhagavad Gita can be precisely dated. The article thereby says that since Gita Jayanti is celebrated on a particular day of the lunar calendar, the year 2016 marks the Gita's 5083rd year (*Rishimukh*, November 2016).[7]

However contrived this amalgamation of myth and history may be, the larger question arises when documented history is

---

[6] See: 'Bharath Gyan'. Available at https://www.artofliving.org/in-en/bharathgyan. Accessed on 27 February 2025.

[7] This particular admixture of myth and history one may argue is not uncommon to the Indian scenario. The Gita Jayanti Samaroh is a week-long state sanctioned festival organised by the Kurukshetra development Board, Haryana. One of the monographs published by the Kurukshetra Development board does talk about Krishna as a historical administrator, dedicated to his country.

downplayed in favour of mythic tradition. On the exact dating of Bhagavad Gita, for instance, such narratives do not take into account the significance of the oral tradition and transmission processes like the *smriti* tradition that account for different versions and renditions of the same text.

In this context, historian Peter Heehs' paper, "Myth, History, and Theory" (1994, 1–19) throws light on the contestation between myth and history. He identifies that this conflation of myth (mythos) with scientific history (logos) is not restricted to the Indian scenario or the third-world societies; he cites various examples of this amalgamation in countries like the USA and Greece. While myth and history can easily coexist, each having the legitimacy of its own, the conflict, he suggests arises when the methods of logos are used in order to legitimise mythos. He says, 'From the point of view of logos, problems involving conflict between logos and mythos could be avoided if each kept to its proper sphere. Conflict arises when proponents of a mythical view use logos methods or institutions to force acceptance of their claims on others' (ibid.).

The 'Bharath Gyan' series therefore exemplifies the above-mentioned conflict between mythos and logos. For instance, one article (*Rishimukh* 2017) suggests that there is an 'inseparable link' between Lord Rama and Ayodhya that goes back to more than seven millennia. The 'Babar–Ayodhya link' on the other hand is 'just 500 odd years old' (ibid., 40). It further establishes that the Sikh community 'of the Sodi and Vedi clan are descendants of Luva and Kusha, the twin sons of Rama respectively' thereby making the Sikh community a 'joint stakeholder of Ayodhya, Rama and the temple at Rama Janmabhoomi' (*Rishimukh* 2017). Two years before the Indian Supreme Court ruled in favour of building the Ram temple on the then-disputed territory of the Ram Janmabhoomi, the articles published in 'Bharath Gyan' contributed to the sentiment that favoured the Hindu temple at the location.

The above arguments aim not only to systematically validate the Hindu claim over the Ram Janmabhoomi site but also to acknowledge the Sikh community as a legitimate stakeholder in the dispute. The Bichitra Natak, a part of Dasam Granth, does include references to the ancestry of the Sikh Gurus, linking them to Luv and Kusha (Pattnaik 2023). However, the article published in 'Bharath Gyan', attempts to create a shared historical stage without providing substantial evidence to support its claims. The underlying assumption behind such arguments, as has been stated above, is that India has primarily been a homogeneous Hindu culture, until its occupation by the Muslim invaders. The usage of the word 'Hindu' in non-Islamic sources is known from the fifteenth century, even then, the recognition of a religious identity does not automatically establish a religious community. Therefore, the notion of a Hindu community does not have as long an ancestry as is often presumed (ibid.). Even in the normative texts of Brahmanism, the Dharmasastras, it is conceded that there were a variety of communities, determined by location, occupation and caste, none of which were necessarily bound together by a common religious identity (Thapar 1989). What may be called the 'Hindu community' or a 'Hindu way of Life' even now is fraught with its own contradictions as it takes for granted the existence of the diversity within. Historically speaking, therefore, the claim supporting a pan-Indian adherence to a 'Hindu way of life' would be a highly problematic argument to make; something that one finds repeatedly in the 'Bharath Gyan' articles.

Heehs (1994, 10) points out that 'when tradition is invented in the twentieth century, it tends to use the discourse of science, our prevailing cultural "myth"'. In a similar vein, Chetan Bhatt in his study, *Hindu Nationalism: Origins, Ideologies and Modern Myth* (2001), calls an invention of tradition of this kind as primordial nationalism. Tracing the history of Hindu nationalism through the nineteenth century, Bhatt identifies a kind of cultural primordialism that played a major part in not only the Hindu nationalist thought but also the resurgence of cultural nationalism in the light of the existing debates about minorities, secular citizenship, ethics and modernity. *Rishimukh*'s deployment of cultural myths comes very close to the primordialism he describes as a characteristic of the postcolonial Hindu nationalism.

Conclusion

Before coming to a conclusion about the various kinds of publics attracted to the organisation, one may want to differentiate between the ideas of religious universalism and religious cosmopolitanism, or what Ulrich Beck, in his work, *A God of One's Own: Religion's Capacity for Peace and Potential for Violence* (2001), has called a 'cosmopolitan religiosity'. Here, Beck makes clear demarcations between these two categories. Religious universalism, he says, is noticeable for its structural intolerance, and is characterised by demonising unbelievers. It also opens up new abysses between religions and creates potential for violence. Religious cosmopolitanism, on the other hand, may be distinguished from such templates by its recognition of religious otherness as a guiding maximin thought, action and social existence (Beck 2010, 70–71).

Different types of transnational communities within faith-based organisations can thus be distinguished based on the overarching philosophies they promote. While subtle assertions of Hindu hegemony align more with religious universalism than cosmopolitan religiosity, the AOLF cannot be strictly categorised as absolutist in its ideological foundation. The organisation does not mandate adherence to specific rules, and its participants come from diverse religious backgrounds. Jacobs, in his study of the AOLF across the UK, Germany and India, observes that the organisation prioritises yogic techniques over doctrinal teachings. One interviewee noted, 'The beauty of AOL is that there is no indoctrination. There are no rules' (Jacobs 2015, 87). Similar sentiments were echoed in other interviews cited by Jacobs. Many AOLF followers, particularly in the West, do not associate the organisation with Hinduism. Interestingly, a German follower I interviewed as part of a broader study made a similar argument about AOLF being essentially non-Hindu. The 48-year-old entrepreneur stated, 'Gurudev accepts all kinds of religion and wisdom and teaches diversity and multi-religion education.' She even suggested that one can 'practice pranayamas without honoring God Shiva, but believing in Jesus Christ, for example' (interview dated 28 April 2019, Berlin, email extract). Therefore, it is challenging to classify AOLF strictly as an example of either religious universalism or religious cosmopolitanism. Elements such as rationality, modernity, transnational community orientation and Vedic primordialism all contribute to solidifying the AOLF community within India and globally.

To understand these diverse segments of its audience, a deeper comparative ethnographic study of the organisation, considering both Indian and Western audiences, is necessary. Nevertheless, it is clear that for his Indian following, Sri Sri and The Art of Living Foundation display an ideological inclination towards reviving a Hindu historical community. This community is rooted in the primordiality of a uniform Hindu (Vedic) culture and relies on archaic and mythological archetypes as a means of cultural nationalism. For the Western counterparts of the organisation, these contours may not be as evident, as the organisation does maintain a relatively different portfolio for its international centres, as apparent in their distinct ways of promotion within and outside India. This is also augmented by the fact that the guru maintains a relatively low profile at his international centres. This dual approach allows The Art of Living Foundation to cater to a broader audience while preserving its core ideological tenets. The varying interpretations and receptions of its teachings highlight the complexity and adaptability of the organisation's global outreach.

REFERENCES

Appiah, Kwame Anthony. 1997. "Cosmopolitan Patriots." *Critical Inquiry* 23, no. 3: 617–39.

Avdeeff, Alexis. 2010. "Internationalisation of a Contemporary Hindu Movement: Between Universalist Ambition and Nationalist Orientations: The case of The Art of Living Foundation (Vyaktivikas Kendra) and Its Transnational Community." Paper presented at 21st European Conference on Modern South Asian Studies (ECMSAS), Bonn, Germany, July.

Basu, Manisha. 2016. *The Rhetoric of Hindu India: Language and Urban Nationalism*. Delhi: Cambridge University Press.

Beck, Ulrich. 2010. *A God of One's Own: Religion's Capacity for Peace and Potential for Violence*. Cambridge: Polity Press.

Bhatt, Chetan. 2001. *Hindu Nationalism Origins, Ideologies and Modern Myth*. New York: Berg.

Heehs, Peter. 1994. "Myth, History, and Theory." *History and Theory* 33, no. 1:1–19.

Huffer, Amanda J. 2011. "Backdoor Hinduism: A Recoding in the Language of Spirituality." *Nidan: International Journal for the Study of Hinduism* 23: 53–72.

Jacobs, Stephen. 2015. *The Art of Living Foundation: Spirituality and Wellbeing in the Global Context* (Routledge New Religions). New York: Taylor and Francis.

Jaffrelot, Christophe. 1993. "Hindu Nationalism: Strategic Syncretism in Ideology Building." *Economic and Political Weekly* 28, nos. 12/13: 517–24.

Joshua, Anita. 2019. "Sri Sri's past views raise eyebrows." *The Telegraph*, New Delhi, 9 March 2019.

Nanda, Meera. 2009. *The God Market: How Globalization is Making India More Hindu*. Noida: Random House India.

Narasimhan, Bhanumathi. 2018. *Gurudev: On the Plateau of the Peak: The Life of Sri Sri Ravi Shankar*. Chennai: Westland Publications.

Pattnaik, Devdutt. 2023. "The Changing History of Luv-Kush." *The Times of India*, 1 December 2023. https://timesofindia.indiatimes.com/india/the-changing-history-of-luv-kush/articleshow/105661157.cms?from=mdr

Rishimukh. December 2016. "41 Vedic Scholars Graduate from the Art of Living Heritage School."

Thapar, Romila. 1989. "Imagined Religious Communities? Ancient History and the Modern Search for a Hindu Identity." *Modern Asian Studies* 23, no. 2: 209–31.

Vijay, Hema. 2013. "History Matters." *The Hindu*, Chennai, 31 December 2013. http://www.thehindu.com/features/friday-review/history-and-culture/history-matters/article5522782.ece Accessed on 24 March 2025.

Waghorne, Joanne Punzo. 2014. "Engineering an Artful Practice: On Jaggi Vasudev's Isha Yoga and Sri Sri Ravi Shankar's Art of Living." In *Gurus of Modern Yoga*, edited by Mark Singleton and Ellen Goldberg. New York: Oxford University Press.

Williamson, Lola. 2010. *Transcendent in America: Hindu-Inspired Meditation Movements in America*. New York: New York University Press.

Index